Muhammad Ali: The Glory Years

Muhammad Ali:
The Glory Years

Felix Dennis & Don Atyeo

With additional material by Mark Collings

miramax books

Printed in Singapore.

For information address:
Hyperion, 77 West 66th Street, New York, New York 10023-6298.

ISBN: 1-4013-5193-X

First Edition

10 9 8 7 6 5 4 3 2 1

Editor: Teresa Maughan
Technical Editor: Mark Collings
Picture Research: Teresa Maughan
Image manipulation and enhancement: Ian McKinnell
Cover and book design: Jimmy Egerton

Foreword © José Torres by arrangement with the author

Cover photography © 2001 Sonia Katchian

CONTENTS

"I don't believe all the stuff I say."

Muhammad Ali

To write a biography of Muhammad Ali is to grapple with the futility of statistics, to learn that cameras mimic reality rather than reflect it, and to confront a bewildering catalogue of contradictions. Ironically, more words have been written about this man, more praise heaped upon his shoulders and more abuse smeared across his character than any living athlete.

Ask a cab driver in Kuala Lumpur, a farmer's wife in Cornwall, a judge in Cape Town, an antique dealer in Hong Kong, a dentist in Jerusalem…ask them, "Who is the all-time greatest Heavyweight Champion of the World?" They may not know the name of the President of the United States or who was the first man to land on the moon, but still, after all these years, there is no hesitation in identifying the Heavyweight Champion of the World. It is Muhammad Ali—The People's Champion.

In writing this book we spoke extensively with Muhammad Ali in his prime. We tracked and trailed him across the globe, from Kentucky to Kinshasa and back, enjoying access unheard of in current times. We spent weeks with his family in Ali's hometown of Louisville, and months with Ali himself in Zaire as he prepared for one of the greatest sporting upsets of all time. We hung around him for days, wincing at his poetry, debating his philosophies, admiring his ring craft. In addition we talked to his opponents, interrogated his friends and enemies, interviewed his trainers and teachers from the very beginnings of his career.

Yet, for all of this, Ali remains elusive. None of the usual metaphors relating to "missing pieces in a jigsaw" can apply. All the facts that a writer might require are there for the taking. Ali himself is the most hospitable and approachable of gods, and we have approached him. The doctrines of his religion are available for study, and we have studied them. His moral convictions and skill as a boxer are recorded in videotapes, books, and magazines, and we have watched and read perhaps a great deal too many of them.

But in the final analysis it is the reader who must make his own value judgements. It is as if the limelight in which Ali still basks serves only to shield his true character, both from the world at large and, we suspect, from Muhammad Ali himself.

"I don't believe all the stuff I say," Ali once told a group of onlookers at a sparring session. "I say it only to make people angry—then I go to the bank laughing." A few hours later that same day, driving his limousine packed with newsmen down a country road, this man, who doesn't believe all the stuff he says, delivered a short speech: "We ain't nothin' on this earth. We don't own nothin'. We just borrow it for a while. Listen to this—death is the tax the soul has to pay for having a name

and form. Heavy." Only Muhammad Ali could have made such a statement to a group of cynical journalists with any hope of convincing them of his sincerity.

Bundini Brown, his long-time corner man and wise fool, once said: "I know seven Muhammads, but only three stay around with him all the time. He's a little boy…he's a fighter… and he's a prophet."

Perhaps it is the interplay of these three characters that produced the contradictions one finds throughout Ali's personal and private life. It was always hard to accept his role as champion and messiah to black people in the face of his frighteningly chauvinistic dismissal of women. Harder still to swallow the voluble rhetoric expressed in his attitude towards white people when one remembers that Ali's trainer for decades was Angelo Dundee. One would march to a press conference prepared to hurl these loaded, nagging suspicions in a hypocrite's face. And then walk away, bemused and confounded, probably roaring with laughter, as Ali would defuse all criticism with a line of doggerel, a sly wink, and a contagious charming smile. A master of saying nothing in the most quotable way or compressing the most complicated of philosophies into a short anecdote, Ali never sought to answer these contradictions. Rather he flaunted them, almost as proof that he was only human. Muhammad Ali is still loved almost as much for his faults, for his outrageous egotism and undying love affair with his own talent, as for his boxing abilities.

This book is primarily a record of Muhammad Ali in his prime: the story of Sonny Liston and astounding upsets, extraordinary belief and cruel exile, Frazier, Foreman, and Rumbles in the Jungle—in short, the glory years. It is not simply a book about boxing, although there is blood and blurred leather splashed liberally enough within it. It is a book about a man who honestly could not pass a simple Army intelligence test and yet who dreamed of one day becoming a "black Kissinger": a man who declines to show the original manuscripts of his poetry for fear of ridicule at his third-grade handwriting and yet who has undisputedly raised the consciousness of black people across the earth: a man who is in love, like every good American, with sleek fast cars and chandeliers in the living room, and yet who once sacrificed his career to demonstrate his conviction and allegiance to the will of Allah.

"I can drown a drink of water,
I can kill a dead tree,
Don't mess with Muhammad Ali!"

Felix Dennis, Don Atyeo *London, May 2002*

OPPOSITE AND FOLLOWING: Cassius Clay in 1960. He has only just turned pro, yet he cons *Life* magazine photographer Flip Schulke into taking his picture by convincing him that he does all his training underwater. The next morning, Cassius and trainer Angelo Dundee stage an underwater "training session" in the hotel pool. *Life*, completely fooled, runs five pages on the upstart boxer. Cassius, of course, has never thrown a punch underwater in his life; in fact, he has never even learned to swim. He does, however, learn the power of press manipulation.

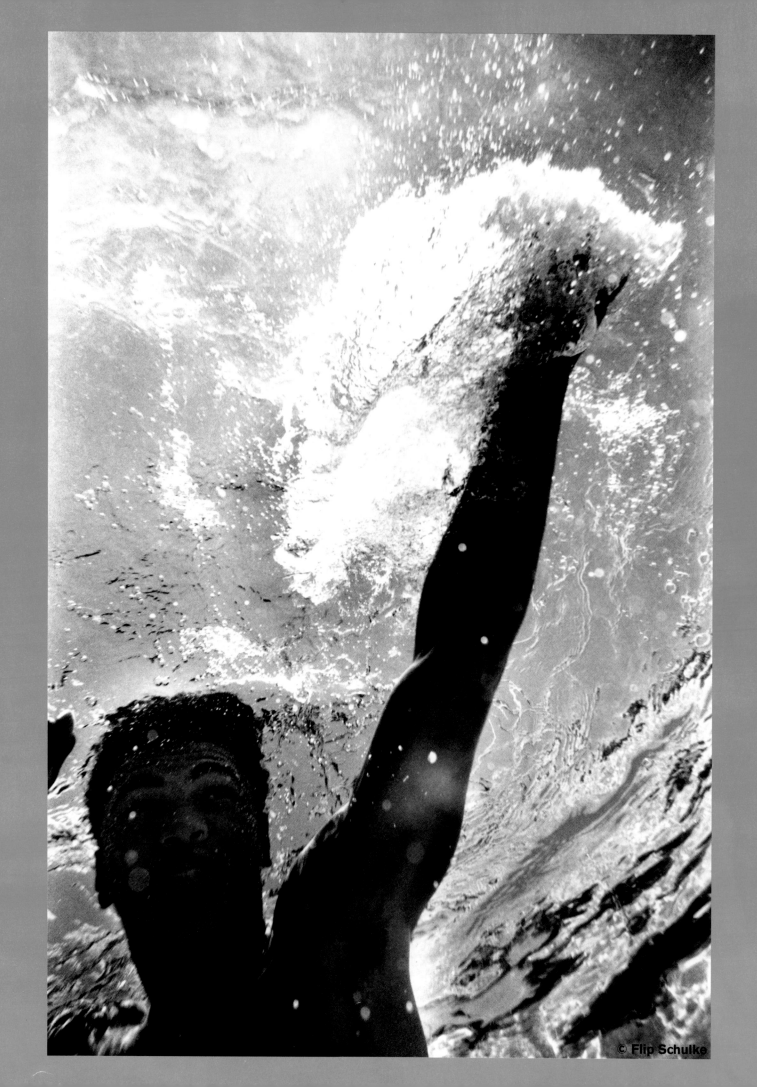

© Flip Schulke

On Muhammad Ali

José Torres

On October 28th, 1974, two days before the Muhammad Ali vs. George Foreman fight in Kinshasa, Zaire, I went to the Bowery section of Manhattan to discuss the possible result of that match with the area's most prominent frequenters: the unemployed, homeless, alcoholic, so-called "bums." As I spoke with a few of them—tape recorder in hand—I was astounded by their analysis of the fight. They were making more sense than some media "boxing experts."

After spending over four hours talking freely with them, I went home to discover that of the 40 interviews I'd conducted, 32 made real sense. Most interesting, 16 picked Ali to win, the other 16 chose Foreman. I remember writing of my disappointment in realizing that 50 percent of the "bums" I'd interviewed were going to be as correct in their choice of the winner as the genuine experts boxing had to offer.

The consensus? "Ali's too smart for George." And: "George's too strong for Ali."

I was also very concerned with their response because I had written in the New York Post that "my heart is with Ali; my money with Foreman." But should I let these cast-asides from the Bowery who selected Ali sway me? Of course, I wouldn't. Instead, I allowed history to humble my bleeding ego.

To delve deeper into this topic I need, of course, the help of Muhammad Ali.

To begin with, the media and many fans saw Ali's pre-fight diatribes as part of his natural conduct. His "wild threats" and "out-of-control" poses were perceived by many as premeditated ego trips designed by Ali himself to amuse crowds so that he could salivate with their attention. I remember some skeptics whispering that such behavior was the idea of a Caucasian public relations maverick, hired by boxing promoter Don King to increase his profit. Others felt it was a panicked Ali trying to comfort himself…hiding from fear.

Baloney! What Muhammad Ali really did with his berating and tongue-lashing of his rivals was to educate many a fan—and some media "experts"—about the power of the mind. He exposed these particulars over and over again to show us what really separated a winner from a loser at the highest level of professional boxing. He didn't talk about it. He showed us!

His pre-fight behavior was Ali's smart dispensation of psychological punches long before throwing a physical one. He always contended that his bouts started not at the sound of the first bell, but the moment he planted his signature on a fight contract.

Interestingly, during his pre-fight antics, Ali forced the boxing community to speculate about his misunderstood but entertaining style. Unfortunately, only a very few ever bothered to discern it. I have never seen or heard one single boxing expert explain correctly why Ali insisted on "going crazy" before each fight. Meanwhile, "The Greatest" always laughed at their speculations. For he knew, as a genuinely true ring artist, that a KO punch is the one the recipient fails to predict or see coming. So that, in order to burden his opponent's ability to observe, anticipate, or "feel" a swift punch coming his way, Ali strove to sway his rival's concentration and relaxation with his "out-of-control behavior" before they squared off. Every time an opponent of Ali walked into the ring enraged or intimidated, "The Greatest" had done his job. He'd already, magically, clogged his rival's "radar," affecting in the process his ability to see every coming punch. A hysterical or scared fighter could never engage the seemingly excited but totally relaxed Ali in a ring with any expectation of success. "The Greatest" simply

OPPOSITE: Ali takes a breather from a rigorous training session at his camp in Zaire, Africa, 1974.

invited those truly interested in the "Art of Self-Defense" to watch not the bullet, missile, or bomb that everyone saw striking the opposition, but to understand the unseen devices that prepared and propelled the ammunition to hit the bull's eye more often than not.

These clandestine triggers are better known as character (will, desire, determination) and intelligence (timing and accuracy). When a boxer has these psychological and emotional elements in working order, his/her punches become faultless missiles of victory. He/she is ready to join a champ's reign in any battlefield.

Such effervescence is clearly conveyed to us all by every champion, but none has done it more prominently and deliberately than the artistic genius of Muhammad Ali. Lamentably, only a very few have bothered to search seriously throughout the hidden arsenal of every boxing champion.

Ali went as far as to limit his physical weaponry in order to strengthen and highlight his psychological and emotional ones. No one ever saw him punching below the jaw, or hardly witnessed Ali blocking punches with his arms and elbows like every other good champion. He punched in rallies like an amateur rather than in sets of combinations like every other good champion. He didn't slip punches, or bend under them. Instead, he pulled back his torso to evade impacts—like someone in the middle of a train track trying to avoid being hit by an oncoming train, not by moving to one or the other side of the track, but by running backwards. Ali also carried his guard low, his jaw forever exposed—a definite no-no in boxing. No fighter can ever get away with such horrific faults.

Except, of course, Muhammad Ali. In fact, dozens of his imitators—some with great talent—wound up with short, awful careers never knowing that they all lacked Ali's emotional and psychological supremacy in the ring.

Around 20 years before the new millennium arrived, the world found out that Ali was in poor health, suffering from Parkinson's syndrome. This is an illness that attacks the body's "motor system." He has difficulty walking, speaking, and most of his body joints tremble involuntarily. Yet, his intellect remains normal. Most people, including some doctors, have speculated that he owes his present condition to his past profession. My father was a Parkinsonian for 27 years and he'd never boxed. If he had, people would have blamed boxing for his condition.

These days, "The Greatest" despises pity but welcomes respect and consideration, his legendary dignity always with him. He's probably the most recognizable face on the planet, and those who once upon a time wished to see him defeated in the ring, have changed their minds.

To Cus D'Amato—the late quintessential boxing manager—Muhammad Ali meant perfect boxing.

"He was a paradox," Cus once told me. "His physical performances in the ring were absolutely wrong but very much entertaining. Yet, his brain was always in perfect working condition.

"He showed us all," Cus continued, a broad smile written across his face, "that all victories come from here," hitting his forehead with his index finger. Then he raised a pair of fists, saying:

"Not from here."

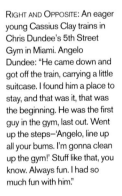

RIGHT AND OPPOSITE: An eager young Cassius Clay trains in Chris Dundee's 5th Street Gym in Miami. Angelo Dundee: "He came down and got off the train, carrying a little suitcase. I found him a place to stay, and that was it, that was the beginning. He was the first guy in the gym, last out. Went up the steps—'Angelo, line up all your bums. I'm gonna clean up the gym!' Stuff like that, you know. Always fun. I had so much fun with him."

Fifteen minutes of fame

Victor Bockris

Muhammad Ali has been one of the biggest influences on my life, and yet in many ways he remains a mystery to me. I first met him in November 1972, at a turning point in my career. I had been writing and publishing poetry for two years and in the process I had become far more interested in the way poets spoke rather than wrote about their lives. In an interview with Patti Smith in August 1972, I asked her, "Who would you most like to give a poetry reading with?" "Muhammad Ali," she replied.

A couple of months later I read that some radical Oxford University students wanted Muhammad Ali to be their next professor of poetry. W.H. Auden had held the largely honorary post until his death. Ali was quoted as responding: "Oxford University, that's a big university, wants me to be a professor of poetry and some kind of social something. They say I won't have to go there but once or twice a year for a lecture. And the salary they pay won't pay my telephone bills, but I'd said I'd come over for the prestige. Very few boxers can be professor of poetry at Oxford University."

I knew I had found my man. Ali had become a counterculture hero in the 1960s. After having his license suspended by the World Boxing Association and his passport confiscated by the Justice Department in 1967 for refusing to fight in Vietnam, he had earned his living performing.

When I phoned Ali at his training camp, I was really surprised when he answered the phone. I blurted out that I was a poet and wanted to interview him about his poetry. He immediately warmed to the request, believing, as I later came to see, that because I had a strong British accent I was somehow connected with the Oxford University proposal.

As I drove down Highway 61 to Deer Lake, Pennsylvania, I thought, "What would Ali be like, he'd been through so much?" When I arrived at the half-built training camp, no one was around. I walked tentatively into a courtyard unsure what to expect when suddenly Ali's famous face, as perfect as it had looked in a million photographs, thrust out from a doorway to what had to be the gym calling, "Over here!"

Ali is the only famous person I have ever met who greeted me on our first meeting stark naked. As soon as I reminded him that I wanted to interview him, he dressed in a pair of black trousers, a black shirt, and a pair of heavy work boots. We sat down at a table, and I asked Ali how he had started writing poetry.

For the next 90 minutes Ali delivered himself of a brilliant rap. First he regaled me with his early work—the juvenilia, if you will—of:

*Moore will
hit the floor
in round four*

and…
*this is no
jive, Cooper will
fall in five.*

Ali offered another poem: "People say to me, 'What's going to happen next time you meet Joe Frazier? What's going to be the outcome of the fight?' And here's the fight in poetic rhyme:"

*Ali comes out to meet Frazier, but Frazier starts to retreat
If Frazier goes back an inch further, he'll wind up in a*

ABOVE: Poet and author Victor Bockris with Ali at Fighter's Heaven, Ali's Deer Lake training camp.

OPPOSITE: The Man Who Would Be King. "I'm young, I'm handsome, I'm fast, I can't possibly be beat."

ringside seat.
Ali swings with a left, Ali swings with a right.
Look at this kid carry the fight.
Frazier keeps backin', but there's not enough room.
It's a matter of time till Ali lowers the boom.
Now Ali lands with a right, what a beautiful swing,
And the punch lifts Frazier clean out of the ring.
Joe Frazier's still rising, but the referee wears a frown,
For he can't start counting till Frazier comes down.
Now Joe Frazier disappears from view, the crowd is gettin'
frantic,
But our radar stations have picked him up. He is somewhere
over the Atlantic.
Who would have thought, when they came to the fight,
That they would have witnessed the launchin' of a colored
satellite?

Then Ali segued into his political works like:
clean out my cell
and take my tail
on the trail
for the jail
without bail
Because it's better in jail
watchin' television fed
than in Vietnam somewhere dead.

From there, he explained, he had recently moved into a more personal vein with a longer heroic form. He read two of the best, the mature *Truth* and his masterpiece *Freedom*, with its now poignant stanzas:

Better with cries and pleas
Or in the clutch of some disease
Wastin' slowly by degrees.

Better than of heart attack.
Or some dose of drug I lack
Let me die by being black.

After which he exhaled, "Bad!" When I protested that as a matter of fact I thought it was rather good, he shot me a hard look to see if I was putting him on, then gently explained that "in our language, bad means good." He told me he used his poetry to draw fans to his fights, and that he had taken boxing to a much larger audience with his charm and style. Then he moved on to his prose work. During his time away from boxing, he had, like many of the counterculture figures of the era, lectured at college campuses for large fees. His peers on the circuit were Allen Ginsberg, Andy Warhol, and Timothy Leary. All of them were under FBI surveillance. The FBI files on Ali provide, if nothing else, a useful itinerary.

From this time he had perfected six lectures, each dealing with standard moral issues from his point of view. "My lectures are not built for no one people," he told me, giving me an example of the kind of material he had used back in the 1960s. "Everybody can listen to them and find a place. It's not just something for blacks or for whites.

This is my lecture, 'The Purpose of Life.' I say everything was put here to accomplish a purpose by God. Trees have a purpose. The moon has a purpose. Cats, dogs, rats have a purpose. Buses have a purpose. The rain has a purpose. Everything has a purpose, and most surely God's highest form of life, Man, has a purpose too. 'What is your purpose? Why were you born? What are you here to accomplish?' And the moment the person answers this question, he's on the first step to the real path to wisdom. But before thinking about his life purpose and not being conscious of his purpose, he remained disconcerted because the very secret of life is the desire to accomplish something, and the absence of this desire makes life useless."

Another example was his diamond-in-the-rough "The Art of Personality" lecture, which formed the basis of his philosophy. Ali had a seductive habit of working his interlocutor into his raps, which most celebrities don't bother to do. The version I received started out, "I attract people! Now here you are, a poet. You come to me. I mean, I attract poets. Boxers don't attract poets," and went on to describe how he had identified and put together all the different segments of American society, from the poor man on the corner to the rich divorcée, and attracted each of them to him by developing a Barnum-and-Bailey type personality. Of course this personality was a mask. Away from the spotlight and the microphone, I found Muhammad Ali to be a quiet, shy, restless guy.

Our first encounter stretched into an eight-hour marathon. It left me with two lasting images. The first one came from the only question he asked me during that first visit. He was pulling on a pair of practice gloves as we walked into the gym after watching the 1971 Ellis fight on video when he casually asked, "Does it look like it hurts?" "No," I answered, "because we see too much violence on TV, we think it's all acting." A man of few words when he wasn't performing, Ali simply turned to his right and slammed the heavy punch bag hanging from the ceiling. He hit it with such force that it swung upwards in a 45-degree angle from the floor. When I heard his glove smack the bag, I felt my ribs shatter into confetti.

OPPOSITE: Ali training for the "Rumble in the Jungle," Zaire, Africa, 1974.

I done wrestled with an alligator,
I done tussled with a whale.
Handcuffed lightning,
And threw thunder in jail.
I can run through a hurricane
And not get wet.
Only last week,
I murdered a rock,
I injured a stone,
Hospitalized a brick.
I'm so mean I make medicine sick.

BELOW: "I don't believe all the stuff I say." Cassius, the "publicists' dream", in full flow in Miami Beach, 1960.

The second image was of how alone he appeared to be in his camp, with no security of any kind. I got the strong impression that in between training for his fights (he fought six times in 1972), he was bored.

I had no idea that Ali had made a habit of collecting writers since 1962, but before I left he told me that he had been looking for a "white longhair" to take his messages to other white longhairs in the colleges across the country, since he didn't have time to deliver his lectures now that he was boxing again. The door would always be open at Deer Lake, he told me, and I should call him when I wanted to come up.

I was in London in March 1973, when Ken Norton upset Ali's campaign to regain his throne. Even Ali's greatest supporters in the sports world, like the journalist Howard Cosell, counted him out: "Losing to Norton was the end of the road, at least as far as I could see. So many of Ali's fights had incredible symbolism, and here it was again. Ken Norton, a former Marine, in the ring against the draft-dodger in San Diego, a conservative Naval town. Richard Nixon had just been re-elected with a huge mandate. Construction workers were marching through the streets supporting the war in Vietnam, which showed no signs of winding down. After that loss it seemed as though Ali would never get his title back again."

I felt my heart sink, but my allegiance to Ali as a hero became ten times stronger when I saw the iconic photograph taken immediately after the fight. His naked torso looked as unblemished as an ancient Greek statue. His arms hung at his sides, the gloves spent now and useless. It was the angle of the head that seemed more poignant: the photo could have been of a rock star in the midst of a tragic song. Ali had always said that he was "pretty"— his appeal had been based on the vulnerability of beauty and youth from the beginning. Now Ali appeared even more beautiful in defeat. This image showed me he had raised his status as a hero in the counterculture by maintaining his dignity, his spirit, at a time when we felt we too were fighting for survival.

Cosell's gloomy forecast had not been based only on Ali's loss to Norton. In January 1973, Joe Frazier had lost the heavyweight crown to a new contender, the 22-year-old George Foreman, whose hero was Sonny Liston and who was mowing down opponents from Frazier to Norton. When Ali narrowly managed to win his rematch with Norton in September, it just made the stakes ever higher and our lives more exciting. Ali became our Ulysses. Now we could all live with our hearts in our mouths. Every member of Ali's own entourage did not rate his chances of beating Foreman.

But in 1974 Ali beat Joe Frazier in their second epic contest at Madison Square Garden in New York. This was the time when Nixon was resisting the Senate's subpoena of his tapes. "My phone is tapped now," Ali told me, "Elijah Muhammad's phone is tapped. It ain't stopped. They still snoop on us. So Watergate, it don't surprise me." Soon Ali found himself next in line for Foreman and the title. It was Ali, more than anybody else, that the public wanted to see Foreman fight. We had to know once and for all, did Ali still have it, or was the dream really over? 1974 became the pivotal year between the sixties and seventies. With Nixon out of the White House that August and President Ford's brief to heal a shattered nation, Ali's quest took upon itself a multitude of significances.

Between the autumn of 1973 and the spring of 1974 I returned to Fighter's Heaven four times. Things were changing around Ali by then, and becoming very tense. Up in Deer Lake there were always crowds of people. There were men in well-tailored suits with guns under their arms. The Muslims were more in evidence. In my most recent interview with Ali, done in the living room of his house, surrounded by 20 people while hundreds more pressed up against the windows outside, his answers had lost their humour and playfulness.

I asked him what he thought about people who constantly complained that their lives were not rewarding enough. He replied: "…Nobody is his own enemy except his own self, and by such thinking one becomes his own worst enemy. Great men such as our leader Elijah Muhammad, great men such as Columbus, such as Napoleon, never liked to say, 'I cannot!' When a man says, 'I cannot' he has made a suggestion to himself. He has weakened his power of accomplishing that which otherwise could have been accomplished."

Although I was still impressed by the manner in which Ali was able to produce 5,000 words in 45 minutes as if he were reading them out of a book, there was no eye contact, no human connection. The words might as well have been recited by his brother Rahman, who stood behind him punctuating Ali's sentences with "Yes! Tell them, brother!" For the first time I felt uncomfortable about being young, white, and well dressed.

So it was with some trepidation that I visited Fighter's Heaven in the summer of 1974. I was led to a naked Ali sitting on a couch in the gym with people flanking him on both sides and behind. I was introduced as the man who had done the *Penthouse* piece; he shook hands and thanked me in a whispery voice for printing his words just as he had spoken them. But then somebody pulled him away. It reminded me of another occasion when I had been sitting in Ali's cabin, tape-recording one of his lectures to a group of listeners. An aide had burst in and announced, "The King of Africa is on the phone!" Pausing momentarily, Ali looked up and said, "Tell the King of Africa to call back on Tuesday. Tell him Muhammad Ali's too busy to talk to him today!"

OPPOSITE: Angelo Dundee, Wali "Blood" Muhammad, Bundini Brown and Ali, at an exhibition match before leaving for Zaire in 1974.

BELOW: Ali during training.

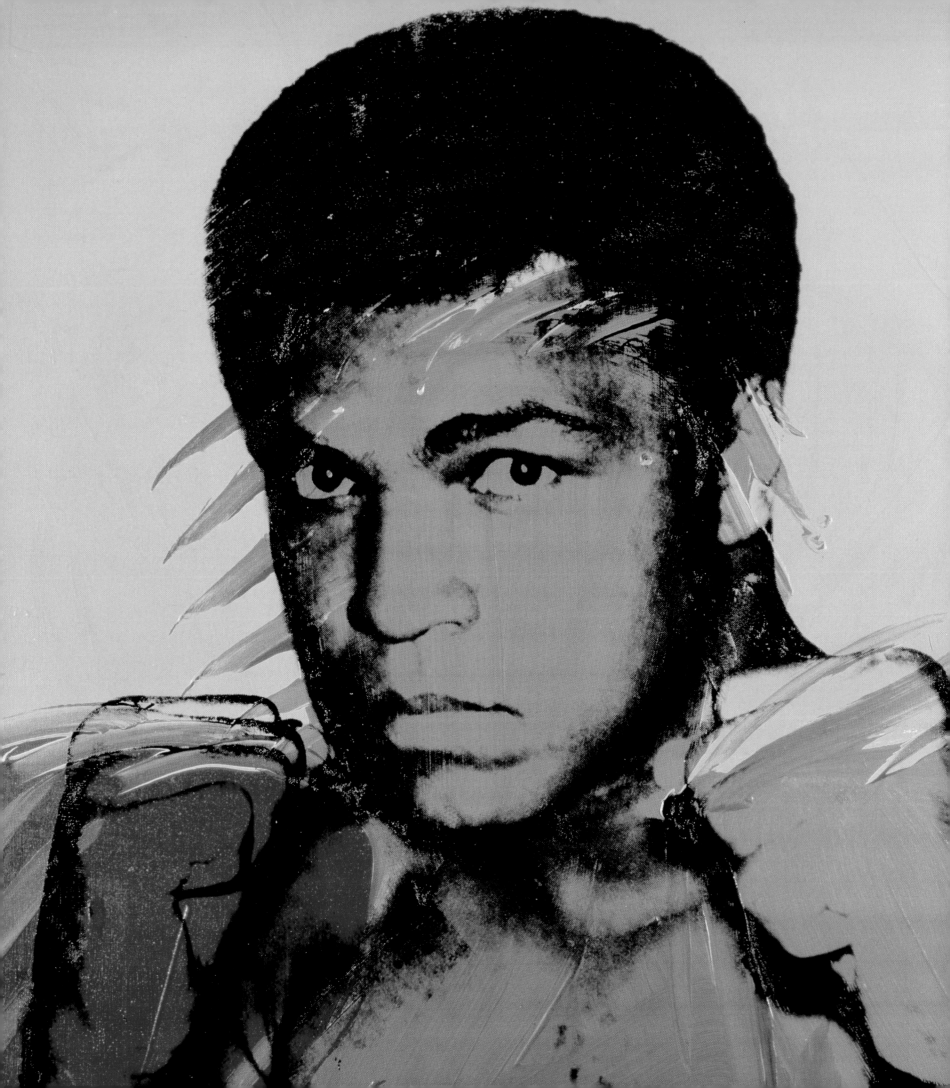

It was funny but also sad, because I could see that Ali had, as it were, left the ground. And maybe, like David Bowie's Major Tom, he was losing contact with Ground Control. Ali was an extraordinary man in that he had got all of us playing his game, but I began to wonder who was writing the script these days. They kept him so befuddled with travel, photo sessions, interviews, and meetings with public dignitaries that he hardly had the time to check in with his accountants and find out where his money went. Hell, he hardly had time to stand to get measured for a new suit.

Like a great rock star, though, Ali performed best under the greatest pressure. As he approached the Foreman fight, he told me one day that I could come up and interview him. He was beginning to focus on building the fighter who could perform in the biggest event of his life. Everything he had ever said about fighting for the persecuted and downtrodden was going into that performance. Ali held the dreams of millions in his gloves as he stepped into the ring at 4am on October 30, 1974.

Avidly I listened to David Frost's live commentary on the fight on the tinny radio in my New York apartment. I was thrilled when he erupted, "*Ali has knocked Foreman down! Ali has done it!...And the fight is over!* [With awe]. What a great champion! Oh, what a great, great man! There's pandemonium here…"

On August 15, 1977, the day before Elvis Presley died, I went back to Fighter's Heaven for the first time since Ali had regained his heavyweight crown. But this time I was riding down with Andy Warhol and his entourage. Warhol was embarking on a series of portraits and prints of the ten greatest living athletes, and Muhammad Ali was his first assignment. He was taking me along as a buffer, in case Ali gave him a hard time.

It was a difficult assignment from the moment we arrived, on schedule at 10am. Ali did not emerge from his cabin until 10:45, and then virtually ignored Warhol. He was jet-lagged, having just returned from Sweden at the end of a two-week publicity tour. Once seated in front of the backdrop where Andy was to take Polaroids of him, Ali continued to direct his monologue at me. He seemed reluctant even to look at Andy, who in frustration kept snapping useless profiles of the boxer talking.

Finally Ali addressed the subject at hand. "How much are these paintings gonna sell for?" he asked.

"Twenty-five thousand dollars," answered Warhol's business manager, the sleek Fred Hughes. "Can you turn yourself a little towards the camera, champ?"

"Who in the world could they get to pay $25,000 for a picture?" Ali asked incredulously. (He took up painting shortly thereafter.)

Ali launched into a rap about God, concluding, "Man is more attractive than anything else! Look at me! White people gonna pay $25,000 for my picture! This is a little Negro from Kentucky couldn't buy a $1,500 motorcycle a few years ago and now they pay $25,000 for my picture!"

Warhol thought it was his picture they were paying for. "Could you just, uh, stop talking?" he requested in a querulous voice. The gym fell silent, sensing a power shift. No one had ever asked Muhammad Ali to shut up before.

"I'm sorry," Ali chuckled. "I should be doing your job. You paying me." And he obligingly assumed a series of classic poses,

which Andy was quick to capture. "I wish you could take more pictures in five weeks when I get more trim. A little more prettier." Ali pinched the tire of flesh round his belly.

"Just three more," Andy urged, moving in. "Could you put your fists close to your face?"

"How about this?" Ali brought his fists up below his chin.

"That's great! Closer to your face…"

"Do I look fearless?" Ali growled.

"Very fearless," Andy assured him. "That's fantastic!" This archetypal boxer's pose was the one used for the portrait.

We followed Ali to his cabin where he read us a new poem about flying on the Concorde, and I optimistically switched on my tape recorder. Once you had shown interest in his poems, he was always easier to interview. But it turned out Ali had a much more informed notion about who Andy Warhol was than I had credited him with, and he was determined to make use of the meeting to deliver an important message to him. Almost as soon as Ali had finished the poem, I noticed with concern that he was fishing in one of three open briefcases at his side, while his eyes were fixed on Andy's face. When his big hand came up clutching a thick stack of index cards held together by a rubber band, I knew we were in for a lecture. Over the next 45 minutes, Ali segued back and forth between two lectures whose titles, "The Real Cause of Man's Distress" and "Friendship", might just as well have been plucked from the contents page of *The Philosophy of Andy Warhol*. Ali addressed them straight at Andy.

"You're a man of wisdom and you travel a lot, so you can pass on some of the things I say. We live in a world where black is usually played down; it's not your fault. They made Jesus Christ like you, a white man, they made the Lord something like you, they made all the angels in Heaven like you, Miss America, Tarzan— king of the jungle is white, they made angel food cake white. You been brainwashed to think you're wiser and better than everybody; it ain't your fault. I'm just a boxer, and a boxer is the last person to have wisdom, they're usually brutes. I'm matching my brain with yours and showing you I'm not going to get on you, but I'm gonna make you feel like a kindergarten child."

FOLLOWING: Ali expounds on life to his ever-growing entourage at his Deer Lake training camp.

BELOW: Andy Warhol manages to cajole a pose out of an uncooperative Ali. "Could you just stop talking?" the artist finally quavers. To everyone's amazement, "The Lip" obliges. OPPOSITE: The finished portrait, "by far the best painting I have ever had done of myself".

I had sat through maybe ten of Ali's lectures. Nothing critical he said had ever been aimed at anyone personally, but this, I could see, was going to be different. I blanched internally, realizing that Muhammad Ali was going to lecture Andy Warhol on the very same moral crisis in our society that many people had been blaming on Warhol for the previous 15 years. I didn't know how Andy would react, but I didn't think it would be well. But there was nothing I could do to stop Ali once he launched his attack.

"You got rape is high in New York, right? The whole country. Prostitution. Homosexuality. They marchin' and you shocked to see so many. The gay people, all the news and murder and killing. They rob. Everything just go wild. Ain't no religion seem to have no power. The church is the Pope, the everything, don't mean nothing. They talk on Sunday the same song, they sing their message. All hell starts back. And everything's failing. The governments are crooked, the people don't know who to trust. And everything's gone wild—racism, religious groups bombin' each other. The Muslims now fighting over in Egypt and Libya, Bangladesh and Pakistan. The whole world is fighting. Everybody's in trouble, right?…" Ali continued his tirade, his voice rising with every sentence: "…and the magazine stands are so filthy you can't even walk by with your children. [Screaming] RIGHT? WALK DOWN THE STREET AND LOOK AT IT, YOU GOT CHILDREN! WOMEN ARE SCREWING WOMEN! MEN ARE SUCKING EACH OTHER'S BLOOD…"

When I first started interviewing Ali, I sometimes felt as if I was seeing another orator on the level of Martin Luther King in the making. But four years and nine fights later, Ali was not only missing his points, he was rushing his text, losing its rhythm, and at times rendering it meaningless. Not unlike Elvis Presley in his last days on stage, Ali no longer knew which way was up or down. He seemed to believe that if he repeated the same thing over and over again, Warhol would come to agree with him and he would want to help Ali get on the lecture circuit and deliver these rants to millions of people. But by now, Ali had pushed all the wrong buttons in Andy.

At the outset of his career as a filmmaker, Warhol made a series of films called *Screen Tests*. His idea was that if he trained his stony gaze fixedly on a subject's face while they talked at length about their most personal problems, the person would break apart mentally on camera, creating a spectacle, or at least a revealing portrait. Now he turned that look and technique, an artistic equivalent of "rope-a-dope", against Ali. Just as Foreman was rendered tired and confused after punching away at Ali's body, so now was Ali rendered tired and unfocused by pounding away verbally at an unresponsive Warhol.

"I'm getting tired of talking," Ali finally admitted, for perhaps the first time in his life. Warhol remained immobile and silent, and Ali carried on: "I'm all right, boss, I'm the first heavyweight champion that was his own boss. Ain't got nobody to tell me when to work, when to train. I don't have to train today. I don't have to run. I didn't run. I can do anything. I can leave town today. I'm free. Herbert Muhammad is the boss, and he never even seen me train, he don't come to bother me. I'm totally free. I'm the first black world man they ever had."

Between a series of similar assertions, the champion's feeling of desperation began to emerge: "By fighting two more fights I can do all this preaching. I can get this ministry started…but if I say retire and then go to call a press conference to tell you all that I want to be an Islamic evangelist, then they won't print it, they're gonna hide it, they won't let it out. But they gotta do it if I'm in the ring, just knock 'em out and grab the mike: 'Isamaleka' means peace on earth to all my brothers of the world. All my Muslim brothers all colors of the world. Isamaleka. Two billion are watching. 'Hello,' I call out to the Pakistanis and Indians, Morocco, Africa, I tell you, I know them. So what I'm saying they rejoice. How can I get that if I don't fight? I talk to the world when I fight, I mean the world is there. So if I fight two more fights, three more fights, I talk to the world three times and I might have 45 press conferences and you all take pictures of my mosque. If I don't fight, you wouldn't be here."

Warhol did not utter a word until we were out of earshot of Ali. "His problem is he's in show business. It's hard to get out. I mean, it's like he could be threatened. But I'm surprised fighters don't take drugs, because it's just like being a rock star. You get out there and you're entertaining 30,000 people. I mean, you're a different person. I think that's why Ali's so different. But what I can't figure out is, is he intelligent? I know he's clever, but is he intelligent?"

Six weeks later, Ali was about to fight Earnie Shavers, a match in which he knew he was going to be badly hurt. The businessman who had commissioned the athletes series, Richard Wiseman, delivered a copy of Warhol's portrait to Ali in Madison Square Garden the day before the fight. Ali gazed at it for several minutes, then he said, "It is by far the best painting I have ever had of myself."

"It's a strong picture," Wiseman responded.

"I can also see a softness and compassion," Ali replied. "As a matter of fact I can see many moods." The eyes and mouth are both ambivalent. If you took away the fists and did not know that it was Muhammad Ali, it could be a painting of someone who was very sad, on the verge of tears…a child about to cry.

Once Ali had proved that he still had it as a boxer, rather than designing a creative program for himself which would have assured him of a lifelong career, he remained in harness—whether by his own volition, or because of outside pressure which he found impossible to resist—fighting a bunch of increasingly poor-looking fights for immediate financial gain.

Like Elvis Presley, he was cocooned in a world of private jets, limousines, hotel suites, and entourages, and supplied with an endless parade of beautiful women. But, like Elvis, he was not free. In both cases the hero ended up alone, destroyed by his own work. At least Ali survived.

The Louisville Lip

"I'm running down Broadway and all of a sudden there's a truck coming at me. I run at the truck and I wave my arms, and then I take off and I'm flying. I dream that all the time."

Muhammad Ali

OPPOSITE: September 11th, 1954. Twelve-year-old Cassius Clay Jr. poses for the camera before entering the ring against Ronnie O'Keefe for his first fight as a flyweight. The bout is captured for posterity by the local TV network's weekly amateur boxing program. From the very beginning, fighter and medium are locked in step.

It is hardly surprising that the traditional account of Cassius Clay's introduction to boxing, milked and distorted as it has been by an entire generation of sportswriters and thumbnail biographers, should read suspiciously like a sub-plot in a third-rate novel. We can take our pick from a variety of equally unreliable permutations, but the skeleton of that bizarre chain of events seems sound enough.

One late September evening in the fall of 1954, two young boys aged ten and twelve stood crying on the pavement outside their junior high school in Louisville, Kentucky. The boys, who were friends, had good reason to be crying. They were looking for a cop to report a robbery. A kindly passer-by directed them to the Columbia Gym in South 4th Street located in the basement of a four-story white stone building that served as a local community center.

There they found Joe Martin, an off-duty Louisville patrolman, supervising his regular amateur boxing class. Martin was seated at his desk, watching over a score or so of enthusiastic youngsters working out on speed bags, sparring in a makeshift ring, and shadow boxing in scattered groups. Through their tears the two friends explained to Martin that somebody had stolen the eldest boy's brand-new, red-and-white Schwinn $60 bicycle, a present from his father only a few days previously. Martin took down the details and promised to do what he could.

"If I catch the guy who stole my bike," sobbed the eldest boy angrily, "I'll whip him good!" He sounded as though he meant it. Martin was silent for a moment. Finally he asked, "Do either of you boys know how to box?" The boys admitted that they did not.

"Then why don't you come down here to learn?" suggested the patrolman, always eager for new recruits to the club. "You'd be better able to defend yourselves. We'll teach you here."

Cassius Clay never did recover that bicycle, but he took Joe Martin's advice and began regularly attending classes at the gym. His progress from the very beginning was remarkable. On November 12, 1954, just six weeks after joining the Columbia Gym, Cassius boxed in his first public amateur bout. Weighing 89 pounds and standing scarcely 4ft tall, he faced a local youngster, Ronnie O'Keefe, in a three-minute, three-round match, and won a split decision. Prophetically, his ring debut was featured on a Louisville television program, *Tomorrow's Champions*. Clay's career had begun as it would continue.

The city of Louisville, Kentucky, named in honour of the French king Louis XVI, stands in a flood plain on the left bank of the Ohio River. Founded some 200 years ago by a handful of settlers, its population now stands at more than a quarter of a million inhabitants, the principal commercial and industrial capital of the state. Often referred to as the "Gateway of the South", the locals joke that Louisville grew rich by marketing vice. In an overwhelmingly "dry" state, it is an alcoholic oasis boasting several whisky distilleries within its city limits. Tobacco is the second-largest industry, with every major American cigarette manufacturer owning a considerable stake in the district. Horseracing is also a profitable concern in the city that hosts the famous Kentucky Derby. The rambling white, wooden mansions that have survived progress and the bourbon and tobacco factories, ooze Southern graciousness. But for the most part, Louisville is depressingly similar to any other middle-sized industrial metropolis, its downtown streets filled with bars and fast-food chains and its newsstands crammed with gun magazines. Over the two weeks that we visited Louisville in late 1974, eight muggings ended in brutal murders.

ABOVE: The new Olympic light-heavyweight gold medallist Cassius and brother Rudy return to their childhood home, the white clapboard house at 3302 Grand Avenue, Louisville, in 1960.

OPPOSITE: The earliest surviving photograph of Cassius (left), aged four, with his two-year-old brother, Rudolph, taken in 1946. According to his father, Cassius Clay Sr., young Cassius was a good boy. "Both them boys, him and his brother, were good boys growing up. They didn't give us any trouble."

Cassius Marcellus Clay II was born in Louisville General Hospital at 6.35pm on January 17th 1942, the first child of Cassius Marcellus Clay Senior and Odessa Grady Clay. At birth he weighed a decidedly average six pounds and seven ounces. His younger brother, Rudolph Arnet, followed a couple of years later.

Clay's early home life was uneventful enough. Shortly after Rudy's arrival, the family moved into a white clapboard house at 3302 Grand Avenue in the West End of Louisville, a predominantly black and fairly tough neighbourhood. The house was small with only four rooms on the single floor and a large elm tree in the back yard. Here, Cassius and Rudy grew up together, through childhood and adolescence into their late teens. Today the (now pink) clapboard house still stands.

Clay's father was a self-employed sign-painter by trade, with a somewhat erratic income, but while the Clay family was never wildly prosperous it was never desperately poor. Cassius was a strong and healthy baby, though somewhat precocious. His mother recalled: "He started talking at the age of ten months, and once he started he always had something to say." One afternoon as Mrs. Clay coddled him in her arms he lashed out and smacked her hard in the mouth, loosening a tooth, which later had to be removed.

"When Cassius Junior was a baby," Mrs. Clay told us, "he just dragged himself up in the crib before he could crawl. He started jumping up and down shouting 'Gee-gee, gee-gee.' Those were his first words. From then on we all called him Gee-Gee."

"I knew what I was doing," Cassius told the *Saturday Evening Post.* "Gee-Gee stood for Golden Gloves." Ali's friend and resident "witch doctor" Drew "Bundini" Brown claimed that Gee-Gee quite plainly stood for Gift-of-God.

Cassius grew rapidly; by the age of three his mother had to pay for him on bus journeys. "The drivers would always insist he must be five," she remembered. His father recalled that Cassius "was a large, good-looking baby with a real big head. I used to look at him and say, 'That's gonna be nothing but another Joe Louis'. " The Clays' eldest son was always extremely protective towards his younger brother. "If I had to punish Rudolph," Mrs. Clay told the author George Sullivan, "Cassius would run and hit me and say 'Don't you whup my baby!' Then he'd put his arms around Rudolph and walk him away and say to him, 'She better leave you alone, Rudy.' Cassius always wanted to play with children that were older, and he always wanted to be the boss too." In another interview, Mrs. Clay admitted that she had difficulty controlling her eldest boy. "He was a wild boy, sometimes," she confessed. "In fact, Gee-Gee should have been a baseball player. He was always running around throwing rocks in the street. He told me that's where he learned to bob and weave the way he does—ducking rocks."

Odessa Clay was a doting mother and wife, dedicated to the welfare and comfort of her family but obsessed with the rigors of conventional morality and decency. She insisted on strict table manners at meals. Neither of the brothers was allowed outside the house barefoot, and cursing in the home was forbidden. (Even in adulthood, Ali's language is surprisingly restrained. During the hundreds of hours of transcribed interviews that we have researched he appears to have sworn only once or twice, and then under extreme provocation.) Every Sunday Mrs. Clay escorted Rudy and Cassius to the local Baptist church. Even when money was tight she would resist the temptation to purchase groceries from the corner store on credit. Certainly she was the stabilizing influence in the Clay household, as Muhammad Ali confirmed in an interview with José Torres for the latter's book *Sting like a Bee…*

"My mother is just another sweet little fat, homey mother. She loves clothes. She doesn't meddle. She doesn't bother nobody. She has a light skin, a heavy-set lady, and she is just as sweet as she can be. She don't smoke. She don't drink. She's just a real picture of a good mother."

What disruption there was at 3302 Grand Avenue came from another quarter, for the marriage between Mr. and Mrs. Clay solidly endorsed the old proverb that "opposites attract." Muhammad Ali's father was once described—somewhat harshly—by one American journalist as a "frustrated Titian." He was a sign painter and graphic artist from necessity and not by inclination. Sign writing merely served to earn a daily crust: his real passion and talents were reserved for moonlit landscape scenes and portrait painting in oil. When times were hard, Mr. Clay was prone to drink. When drunk he sometimes beat his wife and railed against the white establishment which had conspired to prevent him from becoming a famous painter. The Louisville Police Department's records show that Cassius Clay Sr. was arrested twice for disorderly conduct, twice for assault and battery, once for ignoring parking tickets, once for disposing of mortgaged property, and four times for reckless driving. Mrs. Clay was forced to call the police on three separate occasions when her husband's drinking bouts turned dangerously sour.

Clay Sr. was scornful of biographers and journalists who liked to suggest that his own brushes with the law and authority contributed to his eldest son's attitudes and prejudices at the time. "Heck, it's easy

OPPOSITE: Cassius' first trainer and mentor, Louisville policeman Joe Martin, admires the ring which his protégé won as Golden Gloves champion of 1959. With Martin's encouragement, boxing becomes young Cassius' world. Hunt Helm in the *Louisville Courier-Journal*: "At Central High School in those days, Clay was known as the kid who drank water with garlic, who drank milk with raw eggs, who wouldn't smoke, who wouldn't drink even carbonated soda pop, who ran and shadow-boxed as often as he walked, who was very shy, especially around girls (his first kiss made him faint)."

to get into a little scrape," he said, "but let them show where I've ever spent even one night in a jail…they can't do it." Indeed, they couldn't. The elder Clay was also proud of his independence. He maintained that he was "never out of work for one day in my life and never worked for nobody but me."

Muhammad Ali's relationship with his father during his childhood and adolescence is difficult to fathom. From the age of 12, the main focus of the boy's life was undoubtedly boxing. This in turn made it inevitable that his trainers, Joe Martin and Fred Stoner, should come to exert a rival influence as "father figures." Ali himself, while talking to José Torres, hinted obliquely at this:

"My father is a hep-cat. He is a hep fella, 57 years old, crazy about the girls. He outlooks me. He'll go around the block four times if he sees a nice girl. He likes nice heavy-set ladies weighing around 195 pounds…calls 'em stallions. My daddy is a playboy. He is always wearing white shoes and pink pants and blue shirts and says he'll never get old. He's just like another of the fellas. He's just a brother, more brother than daddy and we have a lot of fun. Another thing about my father…that's why I talk so much—'cause he out-talks me!"

Ali's observation that Clay Sr. was "just like another of the fellas…more brother than daddy" is perhaps closer to a truth than a casual, flattering remark.

The Clay family have many stories and anecdotes centering on Cassius' prodigious appetite. One Christmas, for example, Mrs. Clay purchased a large turkey for the traditional family dinner. Young Cassius was convinced that this single bird would prove insufficient for the occasion and insisted on buying a duck with his own pocket money. Later, he devoured the entire duck himself before turning to his portion of turkey.

Joe Martin, too, recalls his protégé's insatiable appetite. On boxing tours as a young amateur, "he would eat enough food for three or four other boys. His meal money—ten dollars a day—was never enough."

Ali's father was also fond of reminiscing that he "went without good shoes to provide the right diet for my boy." Without wishing to take away any credit from the senior Clay, this claim would seem to

be stretching a point. Mr Clay's involvement with his son's career prior to the Olympic Games of 1960 could hardly be described as anything but indifferent. He never appears to have witnessed any one of the scores of amateur tournaments in which Cassius competed, except those featured on WAVE, the local television channel, apparently limiting himself to post-fight lectures about his son's relationship with Joe Martin. "You have to watch out for those cops, son," he would say over and over again. Nobody disputed that there was little love lost between Cassius Clay Sr. and Joe Martin. Much later, this animosity towards the patrolman proved to be a decisive factor at a crucial point in Cassius' career.

All of this aside, photographs of young Clay between 1954 and 1960 reveal a magnificently developing physique, though whether this is a testament to the farsighted sacrifice of his father, or to the baking prowess—"he just loves cakes and pies"—of his mother, is anyone's guess.

Muhammad Ali's ancestral origins are an unusual mixture. His father was once heard to remark that the family has "white blood in its veins", a conjecture which was unlikely to endear him to Ali's Islamic brethren. Nevertheless, it is almost certain that the Clays of Louisville can trace back their antecedents to the freed slaves of their namesake, an extraordinary 19th century Republican politician, General Cassius Marcellus Clay, "The Lion of Whitehall". He was born in 1810, the eldest son of Green Clay, an enterprising pioneer and Southern plantation owner with an eccentric penchant for exotic Christian names. On his father's death, young Cassius inherited a substantial fortune, heir to some 2,000 acres of prime Kentucky tobacco estate boasting a work force of more than 40 slaves. Ironically, the new master of Whitehall had by this time come to embrace the radical abolitionist ideology of William Lloyd Garrison and Charles Summer at Yale University. Returning to his new inheritance, Cassius Clay methodically set about liberating those slaves under his own control and campaigning for the abolitionist cause.

This was a bold move for any man, however powerful, in the Kentucky of the 1840s, where abolitionists were considered for the most part a traitorous breed. Clay's zealous behavior earned him mortal enemies among many of his contemporaries and social ostracism from all but a very few. But "The Lion" was well able to take care of himself. Standing 6ft 3in, weighing 215 pounds and an expert with a Bowie knife, he was a dangerous opponent in word and deed.

Clay fought in the Civil War, where he distinguished himself and eventually rose to the rank of general. After unsuccessfully running for the vice-presidency, he was appointed American Ambassador to Russia by Abraham Lincoln where he astounded the Czar's court by wearing a Bowie knife at official functions. His fascination with this weapon led him to author a gory handbook, *The Technique of Bowie Knife Fighting*. "Go for the jugular, but if thwarted…shift and drive the hilt with great force in a line with the navel. This produces great shock and invariably puts an end to the encounter."

General Clay ended his life as he had lived it, a curious figure of social outrage and bloody violence. At the age of 84 he married Dora Richardson, the 15-year-old sister of one of his tobacco tenants, single-handedly fending off a five-man vigilante group intent on liberating his adolescent bride in the process. Nine years later, in 1903, Cassius Marcellus Clay fought his last battle and died as he would

BELOW: The Clay Clan, from front left: Aunts Louise Clay, Eva Wadell and Coretta Clay, Cassius' grandmother Edith Clay, cousin Gillie Plunket. Back row: Aunt Mary Turner, brother Rudy, Cassius Sr., Cassius and mother Odessa.

ABOVE: Local Hero—the new AAU and Golden Gloves champion receives Kentucky's "Amateur Athlete of 1959" award from local dignitaries Bill Moore and Paul Fischer.

OPPOSITE: Joe Martin checks Clay's 170lbs at the official weigh-in before the 1959 National Golden Gloves. National Golden Gloves coach Chuck Bodak: "When Cassius first came in, he looked like a young colt, very spindly legged and wiry…but even then there was an aura about him. People would stop and look and not know what they were looking at, but they were looking at him. And each year after that, the improvement was obvious. The more he matured, the sharper he got. I mean, you'd've had to be blind not to see how good this kid was."

have wished, with a knife in his right hand. Attacked in his home by three men, the 93-year-old "Lion of Whitehall" succeeded in dispatching two of his opponents (one with his beloved Bowie), before succumbing to his injuries.

As was common in those days, many of General Clay's freed slaves borrowed the name of their former master. One of them was Muhammad Ali's great-great-grandfather.

Odessa Clay's family history is less well documented and a good deal less dramatic than that of her husband. Her light skin (and even her eldest son's own facial features) seems to indicate a mixed parentage at some point along the line. Writing in the *London Daily Express*, Desmond Hackett elaborates:

"The story goes that back in 1870 a splendid fellow by the name of O'Grady out of County Clare followed the old familiar trek from Auld Ireland to the new country over the water and married a colored girl. His son in turn married a colored girl. One of their daughters was Odessa O'Grady." Mrs. Clay continued to sign her name "Odessa Grady Clay" throughout her life.

This, then, is Muhammad Ali's extraordinary ancestral heritage. Part Irish, born of black working-class parents, the great grandson of a black slave, and christened after a mad-dog abolitionist. Small wonder that this genetic chemistry laid the foundations for the self-styled "savior of boxing" and a man who thought he was managed by 'The Son of God'.

Between the ages of 12 and 18, Clay fought 108 amateur bouts, winning an even 100. Throughout this period he trained with Joe Martin and intermittently with a black coach across town from the Columbia gym, Fred Stoner. Unlike the bluff, hardboiled Martin, who famously used his ever-present chromium-plated .38 to shoot two would-be thieves on his front steps, Stoner was a spare, nervous little man who persevered with his job as boxing coach at the dilapidated Grace-Hope Community Center for the majority of his career.

It seems there was little love lost between Ali's two old trainers; perhaps the one thing upon which they both agreed was that at that time boxing was a declining sport.

It is not easy to assess the individual professional influence of Stoner or Martin upon Clay. We interviewed both men and found each adamant in his claim to have been solely responsible for coaching the youth to championship status. "I taught him everything he knows," sums up the implication of both trainers. The truth almost certainly lay somewhere in between.

Ali himself was at the time meager with praise or gratitude towards his amateur trainers. "Taught myself 98 per cent of what I do," he told the *Saturday Evening Post*, "I just luck through on natural ability." When pressed on the point he would plump for Fred Stoner. Just before his "Fight of the Century" with Joe Frazier, Ali told a journalist, "Lyin' on my bed last night I thought of Fred Stoner. Trained me when I was 12. Had some good fighters but white managers always took 'em away. I want him to be in my corner, share some of the glory."

In 1956 Cassius won his first novice Golden Gloves title at the tender age of 14. He began appearing regularly on the *Tomorrow's Champions* program and Martin, who was instrumental in choosing which competitors would appear on certain weeks, selected opponents carefully for Clay. "I knew how to match him," he told us. "I was careful. I didn't put him in with no one I knew could beat him."

Joe never managed to cure Clay's habit of holding his gloves low, almost casually, at his sides. But he did encourage him to keep his elbows in and snap his punches. "That's why Clay cuts fighters the way he does," Martin says. "I taught him that. I teach all my boys to snap the punches."

Cassius seemed set to fight for his first national Golden Gloves championship by the spring of 1957, having established himself as a major contender in the amateur light-heavyweight division. But a pre-fight physical examination revealed that the boy had apparently developed a heart murmur. Joe Martin insisted that he rest for four months without training. It must have been an anxious time for young Cassius but the symptoms vanished as mysteriously as they had appeared. The malady never recurred again during his fighting years.

Martin was a strict disciplinarian with all his pupils, and clashes with the headstrong teenage Clay were inevitable. "I made him toe the line," he remembered. "He was always bragging that he was the best fighter in the gym and that someday he was going to be champion. Maybe he was, but I wasn't about to take any of his lip. I told him, 'You'll do what I say. When I say it's raining outside, I don't want you looking out no windows.' One time I threw him out and told him I would let him back when he remembered who the boss was." It was presumably during this period of exile that Cassius temporarily transferred his allegiance to Stoner's gym across town.

Clay won the Louisville Golden Gloves Light-Heavyweight competition in 1958 and advanced to the quarter-finals of the Tournament of Champions in Chicago. Here he suffered his first major defeat at the hands of Tony Madigan, an opponent he would face twice again. "Cassius was hurt in the stomach," Martin recalls, "and I signalled the referee to stop it. I didn't want the kid to get hurt unnecessarily."

A year later, Cassius avenged his loss against Madigan, an experienced Australian and the British Empire amateur champion, to win the Chicago Golden Gloves Light-Heavyweight Championship. This was his first major title win, a hard-fought and narrow victory. A month after that success, Cassius collected the National Amateur Athletic Union Light-Heavyweight Championship in Toledo, scoring a unanimous decision over Johnny Powell. A sports editor for Associated Press described Clay in that bout as looking like "a youthful Joe Louis".

Clay was still a high school student at this time, though little of his attention was given to scholastic work. At 13, while attending DuValle Junior High School, Clay had scored his first actual knockout. It wasn't official. "This boy had a T-square in his hand," Cassius remembered, "and he said he was going to whip me. It was in a mechanical-drawing class. I hit him two left hooks and knocked him unconscious."

From DuValle, Clay duly progressed to Central High. His performance here was well below average, his best subjects art and mechanical drawing. "I was the baddest cat at Central High," he recalled. "Didn't bring no lunch to school. Didn't do no homework. Passed all my tests, though. Used to tell 'em, 'Give me the answer or I'll hit you!' They give me the answer all right." In class Cassius often sat with his feet on the desk and doodled. One of his recurrent sketches was the back of a boxing robe inscribed "Cassius Clay, World Heavyweight Champion." "During lunch hours and times like that, I'd imagine I could hear my name over the loudspeaker announced as the Champion of the World." The high school principal, Atwood Wilson, was an

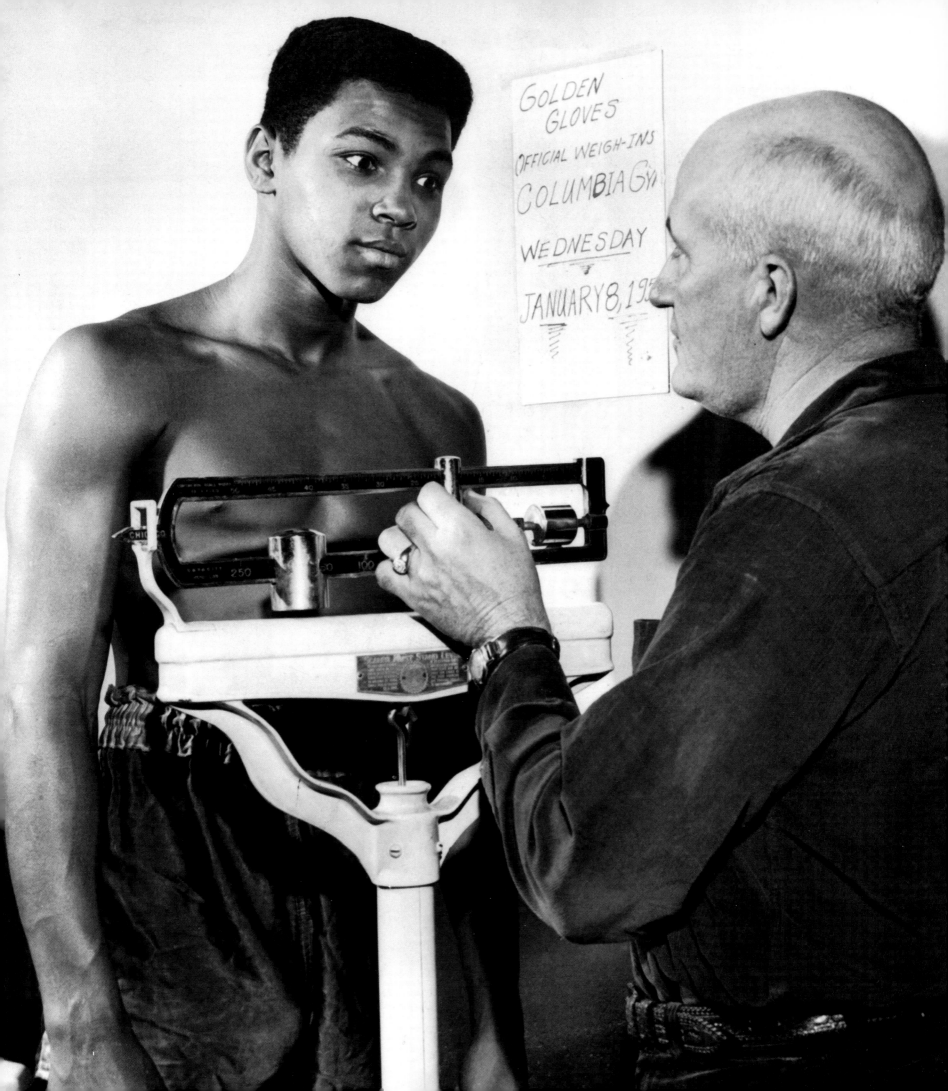

ABOVE: Rome, September 3, 1960. Clay throws a hard right at Australian champion Tony Madigan during the light-heavyweight semi-final. It is a close-run thing, with Cassius scraping a narrow points win against his more experienced opponent.

OPPOSITE:
The 'Louisville Lip', 1963.

understanding man. "Cassius changed a great deal after he came to school," remembered Wilson. "At first he was always in skirmishes around the building. But he continually improved in schoolwork and attendance. He was only an average student, but we planned his program to help him in his career. He took courses like income tax and accounting. We didn't want him to make financial mistakes like some other fighters."

Despite Mr Wilson's encouragement, Clay's grades remained consistently low. In particular he had trouble reading and writing. Even to this day Ali is embarrassed to display the originals of his many poems for fear of ridicule over the erratic spelling and handwriting. Although he denies it, close friends confirm that it would take Muhammad weeks to plow through an ordinary length book.

Competing in the finals of the Pan American Games trials in September 1959, Clay conceded his last amateur defeat, losing on a split decision to Amos Johnson in Madison, Wisconsin. Johnson, an experienced marine from Stockton, California, confused Cassius with his awkward southpaw style. The defeat broke Clay's winning streak of 36 consecutive wins.

Clay then stood 6ft tall and weighed around 170 pounds. Physically he had developed well and his ever-increasing ring craft had convinced Joe Martin that he had a potential world-class fighter under his wing. But Clay had already begun to display a certain arrogance, even at 17 years old, badmouthing his opponents and boasting that he would one day be Heavyweight Champion. This bragging was for the most part good-humored, although Cassius was undoubtedly serious. Martin found it hard to take at times. The patrolman wasn't used to this kind of behavior and when Cassius started hinting to local

newspapers that he could predict which round an opponent would fall, Martin stepped in: "I told him to cut that stuff out. I told him 'Anyone can talk big, let's see you hit big.' I might as well have been talking to a brick wall." The local press had already latched onto Clay's running mouth. Cassius thrived on their attention and admitted it openly. "Man, I love to see my name in print," he told one reporter. "I love to see my name where everyone can read it. Someday I'm gonna see it in bright, bright lights."

In February 1960 Clay breezed to his sixth Kentucky Golden Gloves title. A month later he travelled to Chicago to win the Tournament of Champions, temporarily fighting as a heavyweight so that Rudy could compete as a light-heavyweight without having to face his elder brother. Rudolph Clay had emerged as a fine amateur boxer, but without the flair and grace of Cassius. For a time he contemplated a serious professional career, but the overbearing shadow of his brother led him to abandon these ambitions early on.

Cassius' speed as a heavyweight continually confounded his opponents. After Chicago, he travelled on to the National Golden Gloves finals in Madison Square Garden, New York, where close to 15,000 fans watched him knock out Gary Jawish of Washington, DC. Jawish held a 40-pound advantage over Clay and outboxed him in the first and second rounds, but Cassius opened up in the third and floored his heavier opponent with a pair of beautiful rights. Clay had had to "load-up" with water before the weigh-in to make the weight.

Clay successfully defended his 178-pound National AAU title in April of 1960, scoring a second round TKO over Jeff Davis of Mobile. He was named the tournament's outstanding boxer and gained the right to participate in the Olympic trials, which were held in San Francisco later that year. Despite having his Olympic nomination in the bag, Cassius entered the Eastern Regional Olympic try-outs held in Louisville in late April. He won all three of his matches by TKOs. (Unhappily, his brother Rudy was eliminated in the competition.)

Cassius was reluctant to travel to San Francisco that May. Long flights had come to terrify him. On at least two previous occasions he and Martin had been involved in mid-air dramas that had badly frightened the young amateur. Joe Martin recalls, "Once we were on a flight going into Chicago and we went through a terrific thunder and lightning storm. It tossed the plane all around and Clay was half scared to death. He hated to fly." Eventually, a special committee of regional Olympic officials visited the boy in Louisville and succeeded in persuading him. His desire for recognition was already stronger then his aversion to flying.

The Cow Palace in San Francisco echoed to boos and jeers of boxing fans as Clay climbed into the ring for his second Olympic elimination fight. Local newspapers had made hay with Clay's "bragging and boasting in a clean, pure, decent amateur tournament." Cassius won the elimination, but Joe Martin warned him that he would remove him personally from the competition unless he "buttoned his lip." Clay sullenly complied.

The final fight of the Olympic trials was perhaps Clay's toughest so far. His opponent was Army Champion Allen Hudson, a tall, slim black fighter with a strong left punch. Hudson caught Clay in the first round with a long left hook and knocked him to the canvas. Clay recovered quickly, but it was not until the third round that he landed an unexpected right cross to the point of Hudson's chin as the pair

ABOVE: Cassius, complete with box camera, interviewed before his departure for the Rome Olympics.

OPPOSITE: Rudy (left) slams a medicine ball into his brother's stomach during training, January 1960.

BELOW: Eight amateur champions pose after the Louisville Tournament of Champions on February 18, 1959. Back row: Cassius Clay, Jimmy Ellis, coach Joe Martin, Johnny Hampton, and Donnie Hall. Front row: Fred Stokes, Joe Martin Jr., Bill Laskey, and Herschel Rice. Jimmy Ellis would become a recurring feature of Muhammad Ali's subsequent career, both as a sparring partner and as an opponent.

came out of a clinch. Knowing that his future career hung in the balance, the Louisville kid hammered home his advantage in a flurry of blurred leather. Hudson's knees were giving out on him as the referee stopped the fight and declared Clay the winner. The Army Champion's protests that he was fit to continue fell on deaf ears. Cassius Marcellus Clay II was the light-heavyweight representative of the US Olympic Boxing team.

After winning against Hudson, Clay refused point-blank to fly home. He threw away his return flight ticket and borrowed the money to take a train from San Francisco back to Louisville.

Cassius, aged 18½, stood 6ft 1in and weighed 180 pounds. He did little except box, train to box, and travel to box. From time to time he took part-time jobs—babysitting, working with his brother at a local roller-skating rink and light maintenance duties at Nazareth College in Louisville. (One afternoon he fell asleep in the library of the college when he was supposed to be dusting. A nun discovered him and today a plaque memorializes the spot, reading "Here slept Cassius Clay.")

In June of 1960 Cassius graduated from Central High. He ranked 376th in a class of 391 and was awarded a diploma inscribed "Certificate of Attendance," given principally because of his athletic achievements. Only one disciplinary action was recorded against him: he had hit a teacher with a snowball.

Clay's timidity at the prospect of flying emerged again in July as his departure for the Rome Olympics drew near. Joe Martin recalls, "I took him over to Louisville Central Park, sat him on a bench and had a long talk with him. I told him this was his one big chance for money and for fame and he'd better take it." To his trainer's relief, Clay nervously agreed to fly with the rest of the US team. Martin himself would be unable to accompany Cassius, his brother having fallen seriously ill in Louisville. For the very first time, Clay would be fighting without Joe Martin or Fred Stoner in his corner. The patrolman fretted over this and remained openly apprehensive about Clay's predilection for shooting his mouth off. He exhorted his protégé to "behave yourself and be a credit to America."

Clay hit Rome like a tornado. His exuberance was overwhelming. Like visiting royalty, he showboated and shadow boxed for crowds on the Via Venito. He made friends with Bing Crosby; he signed autographs for tourists and well-wishers. Roaming from one national area to the next, Clay shook more hands than a presidential candidate. Wielding an ancient box camera he snapped hundreds of photographs of other athletes: Russians, Chinese, Italians, Ethiopians—virtually anybody who stepped within camera range. Once when he was talking with an American reporter, a group of Indians walked by. "Excuse me," breathed Cassius excitedly, "I just gotta get some shots of those cats with beards!" He even found time to yell rudely at Floyd Patterson, then the World Heavyweight Champion who was visiting Rome on a pilgrimage to the Vatican. "Hey Floyd," he shouted, "I seen you! Someday I'm gonna whup you! Don't you forget, I am the greatest!" Patterson stopped to wish Clay luck and found himself suddenly escorted by the young amateur on a guided tour of the Olympic Village. Floyd was impressed with Clay. "The only unusual thing about him was this overenthusiasm," he remembers, "but other than that he was a very likeable guy."

Many of Clay's teammates in the village found his behavior incredible. "You would have thought he was running for mayor," said one. Petros Spanakos, the US bantamweight entrant, recalls a typical Clay anecdote: "Cassius received a five dollar postal order from Joe Martin in Louisville. He confided in me that he had something like a check. I told him how to endorse it and cash it. Immediately he snatched it away from my hand and waved it before all the other boxers saying, 'Man, I got me a $5,000 bonus from my coach.' He received such cusses in reply that he reduced the figure to $500. Of course, he asked me not to reveal his appetite for blowing things up."

Clay undoubtedly had the time of his life in Rome. Without "mother hen" Martin to cramp his style and drone on about his responsibilities, Cassius revelled in the unfamiliar pleasures of international notoriety. Many felt that he was working harder at being a hero than a boxer. Interviewed and photographed continually by the world's press, his American coaches began to worry lest his training schedule should suffer. Although he rose at six for a two-mile run, he rested before breakfast and slept until lunch. Through the afternoon he usually worked out in the gym; but after dinner at 6pm it was party time with a vengeance, dancing with admiring Italian girls, introducing himself to other residents in the village, and bragging to anyone who would listen that he would soon be an Olympic champion. Nat Fleischer, of *The Ring* magazine, found Clay one afternoon blowing furiously on a battered harmonica to the delight of a crowd of onlookers. Fleischer did his best to remind Clay of the class of opponents he could expect to fight and urged him to resume serious training. Apparently, he succeeded.

Clay understandably aroused a certain amount of resentment from teammates and other competitors, but his boyish charm and sharp wits disarmed all but his harshest critics. "Everyone is so friendly," he told a US journalist. "The weather is great and I love it. This Rome is great!"

Nineteen countries were represented in the 1960 Olympic light-heavyweight boxing division. Many of their contestants were vastly more experienced than the cocky Clay, even though, by amateur standards, the Louisville kid was virtually a veteran boxer. Communist countries in particular were able to enter fighters with ten to 20 years of experience under their belts and still keep within the Olympic regulations simply because at that time there were no "professional" boxers behind the Iron Curtain.

Clay's opening bout against Belgium's Yvon Becaus presented few problems. The lanky Becaus seemed totally unable to cope with Clay's furious combination punching. In the second round Clay landed a pair of left hooks followed by a hard right. The referee immediately stepped in to save Becaus further punishment.

For his second fight, Clay drew the Russian Gennady Schatkov. Schatkov's wide experience made him a much harder opponent than Becaus, but Clay doggedly pursued the Russian, outjabbing him for an undisputed victory.

Clay's excellent performance against Schatkov had clearly boosted his confidence for the semi-final where he faced his old rival Tony Madigan, the Australian champion he had beaten the previous year in the National Golden Gloves competition in Chicago. Madigan was

a tough customer, one of the few to have outpointed Clay in the latter's almost unblemished amateur career. Both fighters were anxious to take the deciding "best of three."

It was a memorable fight, with Clay forced to box all three rounds on the retreat as the aggressive Australian hunted relentlessly for an opening. What he lacked in finesse, Madigan more than made up in brute persistence, one of that breed of boxers prepared to absorb unlimited punishment for the chance to land his speciality punch—a right hook to the jaw or solar plexus. Clay needed all his fancy footwork and agility to stave off his antagonist, slipping a rapier-like left jab again and again into Madigan's face, clocking up precious points to earn him a close but deserved victory.

Almost a fortnight later, on September 5th, 16,000 screaming fans crowded the Palazzo dello Sport for the Olympic light-heavyweight finals. Clay found himself matched against the Polish champion, Zbigniew "Ziggy" Pietrzykowski—"Someone with 15 letters in his name," as Cassius described him in a postcard home.

Ziggy was a southpaw and for Clay that meant trouble. Two of his rare defeats back in the States had come from southpaw opponents. The fight began slowly, Pietrzykowski cautious of Clay's burgeoning reputation, and Clay experiencing his usual trouble adapting to the awkward stances of a left-hander. By the middle of the second round the American appeared to have solved the problem and throughout the third and final round he began butchering the Pole almost at will. Ziggy had fought over 230 bouts in his career, but he had never been hit as fast and as frequently as this. At the final bell,

OPPOSITE: Cassius, after winning the 1960 Golden Gloves heavyweight title in New York's Madison Square Garden.

Pietrzykowski lay draped helplessly over the ropes, blood streaming down his face from cuts around the eyes, nose and mouth. Clay, by comparison, appeared barely touched, "looking as if he had completed a few training press-ups," as one ringside journalist wrote. It was a proud moment for Cassius Clay as he stepped onto the podium. He was now the finest light-heavyweight amateur boxer in the world and the winner of an Olympic Gold Medal to add to his already sizeable collection of cups, plaques, and trophies displayed in the front room of 3302 Grand Avenue.

That night Clay slept with the medal still wrapped around his neck. "First time I ever slept on my back," he laughed later. "Had to or I would've cut my chest!" He was still wearing it next day when a Russian reporter approached him and asked how it felt to win a gold for a country where he couldn't expect to eat at the same table as a white man in many states. Joe Martin would have blushed with pride at Clay's patriotic rejoinder. "You tell your readers we got qualified people workin' on that," he snapped, "and I ain't too worried about the outcome. The USA is still the best country in the world!"

Clay flew back to the best country in the world in triumph, first to New York, where he was met at Idlewild Airport by Joe Martin. Martin had good news to add to his congratulations. The millionaire vice-president of Reynolds Tobacco Company, who already knew Clay and had offered the youth a summer job on his Louisville estate some months back, had confirmed that he was prepared to sponsor Cassius' professional career. Reynolds arranged for the young champion to stay in his private tower suite at the Waldorf-Astoria Hotel and for the next four days Clay was pampered with VIP treatment. Martin took him to see the sights: the Empire State Building, Radio City Music Hall, and the Statue of Liberty. In Harlem, Clay met his boyhood idol, former champion Sugar Ray Robinson. He combed Greenwich Village "lookin' for beatniks. You know where them cats hang out, man?" and paraded in Times Square wearing his Olympic blazer, the gold medal dangling casually on a chain around his neck. In a penny arcade he had three copies of a phony newspaper printed up with the headline "Cassius Signs For Patterson". "Back home," he said, "they'll think they're real. They won't know the difference."

BELOW: Arm raised by brother Rudy, the new Olympic Light-Heavyweight Champion shows off his medal to his old schoolmates at Central High. Later, in his heavily doctored autobiography *The Greatest*, Muhammad Ali would claim that he threw his Olympic medal in the river after his eyes were opened to the plight of the black man in America. Although the medal did disappear, the river incident was a fabrication. In all probability, Ali simply mislaid it.

As Clay strolled through Times Square on his way to Jack Dempsey's restaurant to sample cheesecake, a passer-by stopped to slap him on the back. "Aren't you Cassius Clay?" he asked. "Yeah, man," Clay grinned. "That's me. How'd you know who I was?"

"I saw you on TV," said the stranger. "So did lots of people. They all know who you are."

Clay shuffled his feet and stared down at the ground, feigning modesty. "Really?" he said. "You really know who I am? That's wonderful." To Cassius, being recognised in New York by an anonymous stranger was worth half a dozen gold medals.

The benevolent Mr. Reynolds offered to pay for presents for Cassius' family—a $250 gold watch for his mother and $100 watches for his father and brother. At the Waldorf, Clay wolfed down five steaks a day at $8.50 a steak. Clay took to the good life like a fish to water. It all seemed like a dream, a dream he had always known would come true. While he was in New York he spoke to journalist Dick Schaap about his immediate future:

"I dream about what it's going to be like. I'll have a $100,000 home and a beautiful wife. And I'll own two Cadillacs and then I'll own a pretty Cassius Clay Hotel in Louisville and if business is good I'll branch out to New York and California."

There were other ambitions Cassius discussed with Schaap. How he wanted to be a credit to his race. How sometimes he felt he ought to quit boasting and "let my fists do the talking, like Joe Louis." How other times he longed to be like his hero Sugar Ray Robinson: "He walks down the street and everybody goes, 'oooh and aaah', and he's got a big flashy car and he owns a lot of buildings and all that stuff."

Perhaps even more interestingly Clay confided to Schaap a dream to gladden the heart of any Freudian analyst:

"I'm running down Broadway, that's the main street in Louisville, and all of a sudden there's a truck coming at me. I run at the truck and I wave my arms, and than I take off and I'm flying…go right up over the truck, and all the people are standing around and cheering and waving at me. And I wave back and I keep on flying. I dream that all the time."

Clay's homecoming to Louisville with Joe Martin was a spectacular occasion. Crowds gathered at Stanifold Field Airport cheering and waving as Mrs. Clay rushed forward to kiss her son stepping down from the plane. Rudy thumped his brother on the back. Even Clay's father had turned out—the first time that he had publicly displayed any interest in his eldest son's boxing career.

Twenty-five police cars escorted Cassius' victory parade through the town to his old Central High School where a reception had been hurriedly prepared. Cheerleaders sang his praises and a sign hanging over the entrance to the school read "Welcome Home Cassius Clay!" The governor sent his greeting. The mayor spoke of "this swell kid." There was pandemonium as Clay entered the school's auditorium. He seemed subdued, almost over-awed. When they called on him to speak he rose and said softly, "I want you all to know that I appreciate this. Thank you very much." Uncharacteristically, but perhaps understandably, Clay was at a loss for words. For once there were no pearls of wit and wisdom. His family were proud of him. Joe and Fred were proud of him. His town was proud of him. Even his school was proud. For a brief, exhilarating moment in his life, Cassius Marcellus Clay II had nothing to prove.

Lame Ducks and Other Pigeons

"I think the boy needs a good spanking, Archie."

Bill Faversham

"So do I, but who's going to give it to him?"

Archie Moore

OPPOSITE: Cassius Clay, professional boxer, soon after his arrival at Chris Dundee's Miami Beach gym in 1960. Angelo Dundee: "When he first came, he was 189 pounds, and then he grew. His stature got bigger and bigger because he was a young kid growing up. He got taller, his body widened out—and he never lifted a weight in his whole life, never did a push-up, never did a pull-up."

Cassius had barely unpacked his suitcase in Louisville before the offers began flooding in. Having reluctantly accepted Joe Martin's advice to resist the temptations of immediate pro status earlier that summer, Clay could now look forward to following in the footsteps of Floyd Patterson, then reigning world heavyweight champion. Floyd, too, had distinguished himself in an Olympic Games as the 1952 middleweight gold medallist, and had used that victory as a springboard to incredibly swift professional success. In fact, to become the youngest ever world heavyweight champion—a feat Cassius fully intended to emulate and surpass. Now that his amateur dues had been paid, Cassius was hungry for prestige, for money, for recognition, and for big-time fights.

Several universities and colleges offered Clay scholarships, but these he rejected out of hand. Famous boxing personalities began to vie for possible management deals. Archie Moore cabled Clay: "If you desire to have an excellent manager call me collect." Cassius was ecstatic and bewildered. Three former world champions, among others, were hammering on his door. Initially he leaned towards Sugar Ray Robinson, and for a while it seemed possible that the old master and his young fan might enter into partnership. But Joe Martin had other plans in mind.

Accompanied by his family's lawyer, Alberta Jones, Clay paid a visit to Martin's house in South Louisville for business discussions. Martin outlined the proposal he had negotiated with William Reynolds. The deal offered a guaranteed income for Cassius over the next ten years in addition to a $10,000 bonus on signature of contract. The terms of the contract also specified that Joe Martin would act as Clay's manager and trainer, exercising sole discretion in the selection of opponents. Reynolds' intentions, Martin explained, were to provide the financial stability necessary for Clay to set about the business of mastering his profession at the pace best suited to his abilities. The millionaire's concern was primarily to prevent Louisville's sporting pride and joy from being rushed into earning his keep at the risk of a damaging early defeat.

This was a comparatively generous offer, and Martin pressed heavily for the boy to accept. But Mr Clay Sr., suspicious and possibly jealous of the patrolman, appeared unhappy that his son should be managed by a cop. To him, all cops spelled trouble and Martin was no exception. He declined to sanction any agreement involving Martin and urged his son to remember the sacrifices of his parents: "Son, I went without shoes for long hard days to provide you good food and good clothes. Now you should listen to me."

Joe Martin reacted cynically to these entreaties. "All of a sudden you'd think the old man did all the work," he said. "The old man never did care about what the kid was doing until Clay got all of that publicity. He's something, he is. He's got all the brains God gives a goose—about half-a-teaspoon full."

This long suppressed confrontation between father and coach wasn't all that worried Cassius. Although impressed with the financial arrangements of the Reynolds' proposal, he remained dubious on another score. Had Martin the necessary experience and contacts to guide him through the jungle of professional boxing? This consideration, combined with Clay Sr.'s more partisan objections, finally tipped the scale. Blood had proved thicker than old loyalties and Clay felt justified in severing his connections with Martin and consequently rejecting William Reynolds' sponsorship. Later, Cassius told José Torres: "He (Martin) is an amateur man. I needed a professional man. He did a lot for me, other people did much for me, but I did most for me."

ABOVE: Cassius Clay signs his first professional contract on October 26, 1960, with the Louisville Sponsoring Group. Standing, from left: Mr. and Mrs. Clay, Bill Faversham, W. L. Lyons Brown, James Ross Todd, and George W. Newton IV. Seated: Pat Calhoun (left), Cassius, and Vertner D. Smith.

OPPOSITE: Cassius Clay's first fight as a professional in 1960. His opponent is Tunney Hunsaker, a police chief and part time boxer from West Virginia. Hunsaker's waistline tells the story.

At this point, the Clays were approached by another wealthy Louisvillian, Bill Faversham Junior, who was vice-president of Brown and Forman Distillers, a family-owned liquor corporation based in Louisville. A burly, grey-haired man in his late fifties, and a life-long fight fan, Faversham had been watching Clay's meteoric rise through the amateur ranks with some interest. In Faversham's own words: "It was his speed, this amazing speed which impressed me. I was having a dinner party in my house, playing bridge in the TV room with an old friend, Pat Calhoun. We watched Cassius win the Olympic tryouts on television and Pat said to me. 'What do you think about this boy, Bill?' I said, 'Let's wait and see how he does in the Olympics.' So after Clay had won the Olympic medal I approached my friend and boss, Wise Brown, Chairman of the Board of Brown and Forman, and I asked Wise if he would be interested in forming a little group for Cassius Clay when he came back from Europe. Well, Wise said he thought this was a great idea, so that's how it all started."

Faversham invited the Clay family and their attorney to dinner at his home. His proposal was to form a syndicate of 11 men to be known as The Louisville Sponsoring Group. Most of its members were to be either related to, or in some way associated with, the Brown family. Five or six of them should be millionaires; all of them would be wealthy men. Earnings from Clay's fights, advertising endorsements or other extracurricular activities were to be equally divided between Clay and the Group. Clay would receive a bonus of $10,000 on signing, a $4,800 no-strings guarantee for the first two years and an advance of $6,000 against future earnings over the following four years. A minimum of 15 per cent of Clay's earnings would be automatically paid into a pension fund for the boxer, not to be touched until he reached 35 years of age or had quit boxing permanently.

In addition, the Group undertook to absorb all training, travelling, and fight expenses, including his trainer's salary. Faversham was to act as "Manager-of-the-Record" and would be mainly responsible for selecting Clay's opponents.

This was an offer Clay could hardly refuse and he accepted without haggling. The formal contract signing ceremony took place on October 26, 1960 just three days prior to his premier professional fight. Without

knowing it Clay had committed himself to becoming one of the world's first "corporation athletes". It was a wise decision—the Group served him faithfully and flexibly over the next six years, though Clay's metamorphosis into Muhammad Ali created considerable strain between the two parties.

Although Ali has been quoted as claiming that his former managers "invested in me, buying and selling stock in me, getting on trains for the big fights like they were going to some kind of slave festival to watch their slaves perform…" those words were spoken in anger when his back was against a wall of white racism and all his experiences —real or romanticized—became ammunition in a battle for survival. Ali's real feelings towards the former members of The Louisville Sponsoring Group are probably better expressed in his reaction on hearing that Bill Faversham had suffered a dangerous heart attack; waking the Group's lawyer in the middle of the night, he insisted on them both driving several hundred miles to Faversham's bedside in an intensive care unit. Whatever his faults, Muhammad Ali rarely forgot an old friend in trouble.

With his $10,000 bonus Clay purchased a cherry-pink second-hand Cadillac for his parents. Automobiles have always fascinated him. By 1975 he owned two Rolls Royces, a Volkswagen, a station wagon, a Jeep, a nine-passenger Chevrolet van, a Mercedes 3000, a Ford Falcon, a Blue Bird mobile home, and a huge Greyhound bus with a shower, a kitchen and room enough to throw a party for 20 people. The Cadillac was a modest enough beginning.

Louisville boxing promoter Bill King handled Clay's debut as a professional, matching him to fight Tunney Hunsaker on October 29, 1960. Hunsaker was a part-time boxer, a police chief from Fayetville in West Virginia with a 17 to 8 record and little else to recommend him. Nevertheless, Cassius trained diligently under the guidance of Fred Stoner, sparring with Rudy and rising every morning at 5am to run a couple of miles in Chickasaw Park. King billed Clay as the conquering hero, "The Olympic Champion turning pro in his first fight", and Louisville's Freedom Hall was packed with 6,000 home supporters on the night.

Cassius ducked into the ring wearing his Olympic shorts with the letters USA emblazoned up the side. He looked fit, though still a little insubstantial for a heavyweight. Hunsaker was an older man with rolls of fat around his midriff, every inch a "pigeon"—boxing's derogatory terminology for fighters prepared to meet promising youngsters whose managers consider they need experience with easy meat before graduating to the hard stuff. This match had been arranged prior to Clay's contract with the Group and though Faversham wasn't too happy about it, there was little he could do to prevent it. At least King had guaranteed Clay the princely sum of $2,000; it wasn't a figure to be sneezed at so early in his career.

The fight proved to be an uninspired event. It started slow and stayed slow, running the entire six rounds without producing any of the spectacular jabbing and accuracy that earned Clay his Olympic victory. Local newspapers expressed disappointment that Clay had been unable to knock out his opponent. First-fight knockouts are almost a convention in championship boxing history; the record books show that Marciano, Joe Louis, and Floyd Patterson, to name but three, all baptized their professional careers with knockouts. True, Clay outpointed the plodding Hunsaker without difficulty, but it was hardly an auspicious beginning.

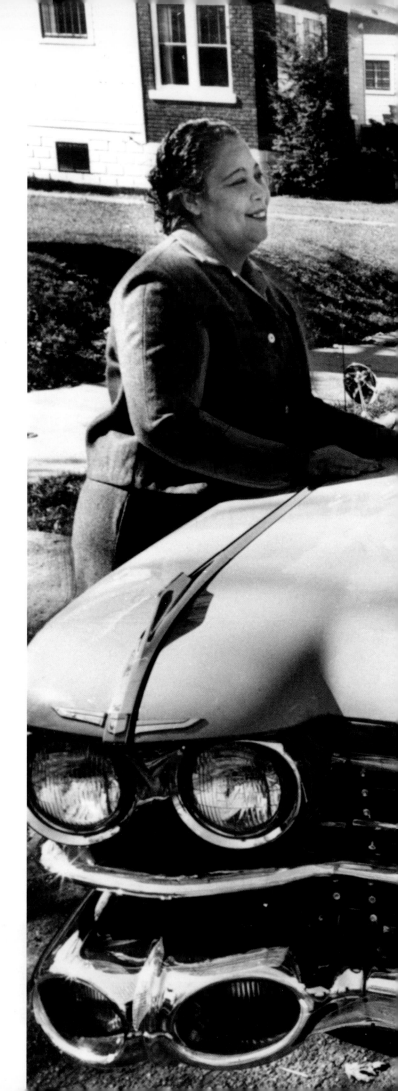

OPPOSITE: Cassius delivers a cherry-pink Cadillac convertible to his mother, purchased with his $10,000 bonus check from the Louisville Group. It is the beginning of his lifelong love affair with the American auto industry.

Following his protégé's bout with the Virginian sheriff, Faversham decided on a change of scenery and a fresh training program, dispatching Cassius to the West Coast boxing camp of Archie Moore, known affectionately in boxing circles as "Archie's Salt Mine". Moore's camp was located in the Mount Woodson area of San Diego, a secluded, spartan environment where novice fighters chopped wood, cooked their own meals, swam in the private pools, and strengthened their legs running several miles a day across Californian hillsides. A master boxer and legendary craftsman, Moore had trained and encouraged many champions in his time. Faversham's hope was that "the old professor" would establish a rapport with Clay. With 25 years of professional experience behind him, Moore should be able to teach his egotistical young dog a new trick or two.

Moore was impressed with Clay but astounded by his arrogance. He sparred with him for several "eyeball-to-eyeball sessions", concentrating on body punching and close-quarters technique, but the youth seemed reluctant to consider direct advice. Moore remembers: "I saw an utterly astounding potential in that young man. I wanted to make an all-round fighter out of him. He was green but he told me he had no use for learning in-fighting. He thought he would never have to do any in-fighting because he was gonna be so swift and always out of range etc. It was useless arguing with him, though he'd listen hard enough if I taught him something he thought was useful to his style of fighting. Finally, I told him, 'Well, son, if you're going to do all the teaching, why don't you go home for the Christmas holidays?'"

Clay had been at the Salt Mines only three weeks before the old professor telephoned Faversham to suggest that perhaps it would be best if the kid returned home. Cassius had already telephoned Faversham to complain that Moore was trying to change his natural style. "I think the boy needs a good spanking, Archie," exploded the manager. "So do I," replied Moore, "but who's going to give it to him?"

Clay's behavior had irritated others at Moore's ranch, too. Dick Sadler (former manager of George Foreman) was Archie's personal trainer and told the following story:

"I rode with Clay from the West Coast down to Texas where Archie had this fight. We went by train and it was a pretty wild ride. First the kid would be standing shouting out of the carriage, 'I am the greatest, I am the greatest!' He'd shout this at the passing cars and sheep and fields and stuff. Well, after a while he started singing this number by Chubby Checker about the twist. He didn't know the words, just kept on and on singing, 'Come on baby, let's do the twist, come on baby, let's do the twist!' And it got to me. It was driving me crazy to tell you the truth. So I said, 'Jesus, son, you done twisted all across California and Arizona.' By the time we got to New Mexico I told him, 'Look, sing the charleston or the boogaloo or any damned thing, but get off the twist, man!' Seven hundred miles of twisting, twisting and, 'I am the greatest'. It drove me crazy!"

While Clay played prima donna up on the East Coast, Faversham had been getting down to business. His primary concern was to locate a trainer with the discipline to check Clay's adolescent excesses, and the understanding to nurture the boy's obvious talent. Archie Foster, one of the members of the Group, informed Faversham that his colleague, Lester Malitz, a television-boxing producer, had suggested they contact Angelo Dundee.

Dundee, a small, round-faced Italian American in his late thirties operating from Miami, Florida, was already acknowledged as one of the most competent trainers and managers in the busi-

ABOVE: Cassius relaxes in his hotel room before a bout.

OPPOSITE: Cassius, still proudly sporting his Olympic sweatshirt, trains in Bruner's Headline Gym three weeks before his first professional fight against Tunney Hunsaker. Angelo Dundee: "Training him was a whole different ballgame from most fighters. You didn't have to push. It was jet propulsion. Just touch him and he took off."

ness—a highly skilled corner man and a patient, dedicated coach. Future world champions Willie Pastrano and Luis Rodriguez were both managed by Dundee.

Faversham flew out to Miami with Worth Bingham, publisher of the *Louisville Courier* and fellow member of the syndicate. They explained the Group's interest in Dundee as a prospective trainer and asked for his reactions. Angelo's response was immediate. He told Faversham and Bingham that he would be happy to work with Clay. Although he felt that the kid had a long way to go in many respects, he was confident he could handle him. He concurred that Clay was certainly champion material. Faversham and Bingham were impressed by the straightforward, reliable trainer-manager and promised they would be back in touch shortly.

Cassius and Angelo Dundee were already familiar with each other. Dundee tells the story:

"I first met Cassius in 1957 when he was an amateur. I went to Louisville with one of my fighters, Willie Pastrano, who was fighting Johnny Holmes at Freedom Hall. Willie and I were staying at the Sheridan Hotel, lying around our rooms watching TV, when I get a call from the lobby of the hotel. It went something like this: 'My name is Cassius Marcellus Clay Junior. I am the Golden Gloves champion of Louisville, Kentucky. I won the Pan American Games a month ago and I'm gonna win the Olympics and I wanna talk to you.'

"So I put my hand over the phone and I said to Willie who was lying on the bed, 'Willie, there's some kind of nut downstairs wants to talk to us.' Willie says, 'Well, TV's lousy so have him come up.' Anyway, up he came. He was a big, kind of good-looking kid and he had his brother Rudy with him. Straight off he starts, 'I know you, Willie Pastrano, I know you. I seen you fight.' Then he turns to me. 'I know you, Angelo Dundee. I seen you working with Luis Rodriguez. You're a cut man, you worked with Carmen Basilio. I seen you on TV.' He goes on like this telling me all the fighters I worked with and stuff like that. Then he starts asking questions. 'How do you train your fighters? How many miles do they run each day? What do they eat? How long do they abstain from sex before a fight?' Well, I explained how each fighter is an individual and this and that, but he was very inquisitive. He was

hungry to acquire information, any information about boxing. He stayed talking to Willie and me for about three or four hours.

"Whenever I came to Louisville from then on, he would look me up. I was friendly with the promoter there, Bill King, and I got to take a lot of fighters there. Cassius would always be there. Waiting to spar and see fights and stuff. I got to meet his mother and father and he took me over to his house. A really warm kid, I used to get him passes to the fights and sometimes he would help out before a fight.

"He was always trying to get to box with professional fighters but I would never let him. I didn't like the idea of an amateur working with pros. But he finally caught me off guard one day when we were training for a fight in Louisville. I let him box with Willie Pastrano. I shouldn't have done, but I did. So, I let him box with Willie that day and he really made Willie look like nothing! The speed and the quickness. He looked like he'd won a decision over Willie in a two-round spar! I told Willie, 'Well, it looks like you had better take it easy, looks like you're stale.' But actually it was how good the kid was.

"Then there was the time he got back from the Olympics. I was down in Louisville and he got hold of me and said, 'Angelo, how come you haven't approached me yet for management?' So I told him, 'It's this simple. If you wanna be a fighter, I got a gymnasium down in Miami Beach on 5th Street. Come down and see me.' 'My God, Angelo,' he says, 'you're something else. Here I got all these guys offering me money and Cadillacs and all you can offer me is to come down to Miami Beach!' 'Certainly,' I said, 'because I'm a fight manager. That's my business. Boxing is my business, that's all I do. I got no liquor store, I got no bar, I got no grocery store. Boxing is all I do and I'd be happy to work with you.'

"Next thing I know they've sent Cassius up to the Salt Mine. But it couldn't work. I know that. Archie Moore was still fighting then, the Light-Heavyweight Champion. Now there's gotta be friction. There's only room for one star in a camp like that. So they sent Clay back to Louisville.

"Just after that, travelling from Louisville back to Miami with Dick Sadler, he was with Archie then, Dick paid me the finest compliment of any fight man. He says, 'How do you get along with the kid?', meaning Cassius. I told him, 'Beautiful, we get along fine together.' 'You really do?' he asked. 'Yeah, Dick, I get on great with him.' He looked at me and said, 'Well, Angelo, you deserve a purple heart with nine clusters!' I knew what Dick meant, but the whole thing with Cassius is to be able to understand him. I understood him."

Shortly after the Miami visit, in early December, Faversham called Dundee. "Okay, you got the job," he said. "When do you want me to send the kid?" Angelo suggested that Clay should join him after Christmas and make a fresh start in the New Year. Faversham agreed that would probably be best. Five minutes later he was back on the phone to Miami. "Listen, Angelo, this kid wants to come now. He wants to fight. He says Christmas has nothing to do with it. Every day will be Christmas when he fights. That's what he tells me. Can I send him down?"

Clay had his way. Dundee met Cassius a few days later off the train and drove him to his new temporary home in downtown Miami. It was not exactly the Hilton. "I picked up the kid and drove him down to the hotel. I didn't want him to be alone so I put him in with another fighter from the gym. Unbeknownst to me, there was only one bed

OPPOSITE: Chris Dundee's 5th Street Gym, which Cassius Clay treats as a second home, and to which Muhammad Ali will return again and again. Here Ali relaxes during training for his 1971 fight against Joe Frazier.

FOLLOWING PAGES: Man and machine. Louisville boyhood friend, Bob Thurman: "They bought him a new Cadillac, 'cause he'd won the Olympics, and he asked me to put a new stereo in there. He'd turn that stereo right up and you'd hear it from one end of the street to the other. But, jeez, I enjoyed it. I'd never seen one before."

BELOW: Besides Cassius' love affair with automobiles, there is his love affair with mirrors.

in the room so they both had to share this big old double bed. Years later Cassius tells me, 'You didn't really like me, did you Angelo? You put me in a stinking hotel with no air conditioning and with a guy that smelled. Remember that guy? He was from the islands, a Caribbean fighter. He smelled bad, he had body odor.' But Cassius didn't tell me about it at the time. He didn't care about anything. He could put up with any situation because he wanted to be a fighter so bad."

Dundee's 5th Street Gym was not exactly the Hilton either, a sweat-stained, battered room decorated with boxing posters and filled with all the usual equipment: a boxing ring that had seen better days, two heavy bags, two suspended speed bags, a full-length mirror or two. It was a place that Cassius Clay would come to know intimately over the years.

Angelo Dundee remembers: "He'd be the first guy into the gym and the last to leave. Sometimes he'd run the five miles from his hotel to 5th Street. I never had any trouble coaxing Cassius to that gym. Be a problem sometimes to get him out, though!"

In Angelo, Cassius had been fortunate acquiring a trainer with the instinct to appreciate his potential talent and the flair to contrive its development. Dundee understood the necessity to manipulate and humor Clay's capricious ego, rather than confront it with the specter of greater experience. Cassius could not be "told" or "instructed" about boxing. The normal relationship between boxer and trainer had to be discarded—Archie Moore's experience had shown that. Clay's talents and willpower were vast, but his precocious self-confidence rendered him stubborn to direct criticism. Instead, Dundee began to employ subtler tactics: flattery, cajoling, white lies, and encouragement.

"I knew he was championship quality from the beginning," insists Dundee. "But every fighter is different. You couldn't tell Cassius, 'I want you to do this. I want you to do that, throw a left jab, move your head.' That was the wrong way, he wouldn't respond. So, instead, I'd walk over to his corner and I'd say, 'Hey, you're looking great today, you're really jabbing beautiful. That's a beautiful uppercut; you're throwing it off your left foot and bending the knee just fine. Gives you more impact. Hey, that side to side movement is tremendous.' Now Cassius wouldn't have been doing any

of that stuff but he was hip. The next rounds he'd go right out there and do it. That way he'd take the credit, he's the innovator. See what I mean?"

Dundee has always been modest with his success about Clay, but his modesty has method: "I never messed with his natural stuff. You can't improve what a fighter has naturally, you know. You leave it alone, add a little here, smooth out a few wrinkles there. But you don't tamper with it. Cassius' natural ability was phenomenal. I never messed with it.

"I'm not his boss: we're a team. We work together and I know how to work with him. This is because of my upbringing, coming from a small town in South Philadelphia and having humble parents. You don't see me at press conferences with Muhammad Ali. There's only room for one star. You don't see me hogging any cameras and shooting off. He is the star. He is the man."

Clay's second professional fight was booked for December 27, 1960, barely a couple of weeks after he had joined the 5th Street Gym. Angelo's brother, Chris Dundee, who promoted many of Clay's early fights, matched him against Herb Siler at the Miami auditorium in a preliminary bout for the main event of the evening, Willie Pastrano vs. Jesse Bowdry. The fight lasted four rounds before Clay scored a TKO with a right to Siler's body and a left hook to the jaw. Once again, it was a sluggish, uninspired affair.

In the New Year, Cassius boxed three matches in 11 weeks, all of them in Miami. On his 19th birthday, January 17th, he stopped local boy Tony Esperti in three, cutting Esperti's left eye with several stiff jabs. Three weeks later, in Miami's new Convention Hall, he floored Jim Robinson with a flurry of lefts and rights after only two minutes of the first round.

Encouraged by the boy's progress, Faversham and Dundee fixed Clay's first main event for February 21st against Donnie Fleeman, a Texan with an impressive record of 51 fights, 45 wins, 20 of them KO. Fleeman himself claimed never to have been knocked off his feet. This was Clay's first big-time pro bout and he quickly began babbling to the local newspapers. "I plan to be heavyweight champion someday," he confessed. "If I can't beat this fellow, I ought to change my plans. He ain't even ranked."

Fleeman might not have been ranked, but his experience and durability seemed to provide him with a sizeable advantage. In the event, Cassius literally ran rings around him, bloodying his nose, cutting him over both eyes and forcing the referee to step in during the seventh round.

Clay was still growing physically. He now stood 6ft 2in, weighed around 190 pounds and boasted an extraordinary reach of 78½ in. He trained continually at 5th Street, pushing himself harder than any of his gym mates and badgering Dundee for practice spars with the more experienced fighters. Dundee recalls: "Every day he came in. 'I wanna box. I wanna box.' He'd want to box anybody in the damn gym. Any shape, any size, anybody. I'd tell him, 'Take it easy today. Work out on the floor. What's your hurry?' Oh no. 'I wanna spar. I wanna spar. Let me fight him, Angelo.' At first the pros would give him a little bit of a hard time because he was giving away a lot of weight, but eventually he got to the point where he could handle anything in the gym."

Harold Conrad, the New York boxing promoter, also remembers Clay's predilection for challenging his elders: "I was promoter for the fight between Ingemar Johansson and Floyd Patterson in March of

ABOVE: Against Hawaiian Kolo "Duke" Sabedong in Las Vegas. It isn't the prospect of the fight that bothers Cassius, but the plane ride there and back.

OPPOSITE: Angelo Dundee raises his protégé's arm after Lamar Clark's exit during the second round of their fight in Louisville. Dundee: "We went home to Louisville for Lamar Clark, a real beauty. Clark was knocking everybody out, but Muhammad ended it in the second round." The bout marks the first of Clay's controversial predictions. "I said he would fall in two and he did," Cassius tells reporters, adding earnestly, "I'll continue this approach to prove I'm great."

1961. We needed a sparring partner for a public workout by Johansson in Miami. Clay was eager, so we used him and he made a monkey out of Johansson. He kept yelling out, 'Six months and I can whip this guy…maybe I can whip him now!' Fact is, I think he could have licked him then."

In April, Faversham arranged for Cassius to fight back in Louisville with Lamar Clark, a tough and experienced farmer from Cedar City, Utah. Clark possessed one speciality—he knocked people out. He had knocked out his last 45 opponents and expressed the opinion that this uppity Olympic wonder kid would prove no exception. Clay had other ideas. Gathering his coterie of local journalists, Cassius gave them the word. "This Clark will fall in two," he promised.

Five thousand four hundred people came to the Fairground Coliseum that night, and the sports editor of the *Louisville Times* conjectured that "many of them have come to see Clay get knocked out of his white trunks." But the editor was to be disappointed and the ladies could spare their blushes. Clay hammered his opponent, broke his nose and battered him to the canvas three times before knocking him out in the second round.

Journalists crammed into Clay's dressing room after the fight. His successful prediction had excited their interest and they pressed him for an explanation. "I just had the feeling he must fall," Cassius answered mysteriously. "I said he would fall in two and he did. I'll continue this approach to prove I'm great."

Following the Clark victory, Dundee allowed Cassius to rest up for a few weeks. He finally made it back to Miami in late May bloated with home cooking, 15 pounds overweight. His next match was a month away, against Kolo "Duke" Sabedong in Las Vegas. Cassius

pleaded with Dundee to take the train to Vegas, but Angelo was less than enthralled with the prospect of the three-day train ride and insisted they fly. A reporter asked Clay if he felt nervous at facing Sabedong who stood 6ft 6in and weighed 226 pounds. "I'm not afraid to fight," he wailed. "I'm afraid of the flight!"

While in Las Vegas, Clay was to meet a man whose style and outrageous buffoonery significantly influenced his future. Invited by a local radio program to discuss the Sabedong fight, Cassius trotted along to the studios and fed his usual lines. The interviewer thanked him and turned to ask similar questions of his next guest, "Gorgeous George", a handsome wrestler with a big match in the offing. By contrast with Clay's smart-aleck but generally polite behavior, George launched into a tour-de-force of verbal ferocity. He pounded on the table, knocked over microphones, stamped his feet, shrieked at the top of his voice:

"I'm gonna kill him [his opponent]! Why they shouldn't even bother to hold the match! It's a waste of time! He's a dead man! If that sucker messes up the pretty waves in my hair, I'm gonna tear the limbs from his body! I'll pull his arm out of its socket and beat him over the head with it! If that sucker beats me I'll get the next plane to Russia, no, no, I'll crawl across the ring on my hands and knees to him! But I cannot be defeated. I am the world's greatest wrestler!"

Cassius was stunned by this tremendous performance. His admiration increased when he discovered that 15,000 wrestling fans had sold out yet another "Gorgeous" match and he resolved to exploit this tailor-made angle in his own career. Predictions and quick wits were obviously not enough in the big leagues. It was time for his mouth to turn fully professional.

Clay outpointed Sabedong easily, but the bout went the full ten rounds. Cassius had been unable to land any clean punches on his lumbering opponent and blamed it on the plane trip. As if to confirm his suspicions, their plane on the return journey hit rough weather over Chicago. When the turbulence was over Clay turned to his trainer angrily. "Dundee, you tricked me! You talked me into this. Never, never again!" Angelo Dundee laughed about the incident later, but at the time Cassius was serious enough. "He was shaking," Angelo recalled, "shaking like a leaf."

Clay's next three engagements were all in Louisville. On July 22nd in the sweltering heat of a midsummer night banked by the glare of TV cameras he narrowly outpointed his first ranked opponent, Alonzo Johnson. Lathered in sweat, Cassius was derisively booed as the referee announced his decision. Ten marathon rounds in a neon oven had strained the patience of this fickle crowd who, only months previously, had feted their Olympic hero.

On October 7th, Cassius faced the Argentinian Alex Miteff, successfully fulfilling another prediction by dropping him in six, though not before some anxious moments in the second round when Miteff landed a murderous right cross to the jaw. Clay's recovery from this blow dispelled any doubts about his ability to absorb punishment as well as dish it out.

For his last fight of 1961 Clay returned to his hometown on November 29th to fight Willie Besmanoff, a stocky German Jew who, despite a fair record, had been inactive for six months. Prior to the fight Clay abused Besmanoff viciously. "I'm embarrassed to get into the ring with an unrated duck," he sneered during a tele-

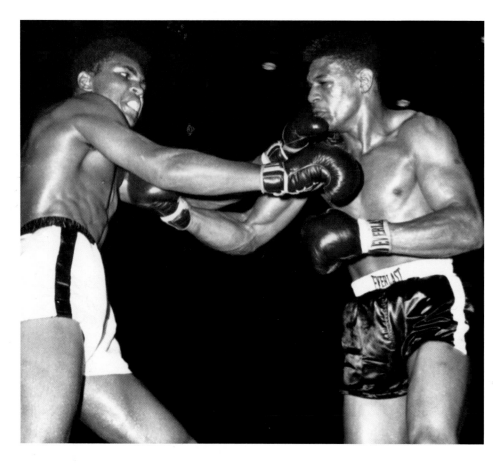

ABOVE: Clay fends off Alonzo Johnson during their televised bout in Louisville on July 22, 1961. Johnson is his first ranked opponent, and it takes all he has to nudge a ten-round points decision. The crowd is not amused.

OPPOSITE: The fourth-round TKO over Don Warner on February 28, 1962, is an altogether more satisfactory bout than Alonzo Johnson. When asked why he had taken him in the fourth when before the fight he'd predicted the fifth, Cassius replies that he'd had to deduct a round because Warner had neglected to shake hands at the weigh-in.

PRECEDING PAGES: The first ever promotional shots of Cassius Clay, taken in the 5th Street Gym in 1960. Cassius would sign them and hand them out to the kids who flocked to the gym to watch him train.

vision interview. "I'm ready for top contenders like Patterson and Sonny Liston." To journalists anxious for another prediction, Clay announced, "Besmanoff must fall in seven."

At the opening bell, Besmanoff rushed from his corner. Enraged by Clay's insults he sought swift vengeance, but in his fury, the German's rusty defenses disintegrated, a wide-open target for Clay's powerful jabbing. Time and time again Besmanoff hurled himself clumsily at the younger man only to cannon into the ropes, raining blows at a shadow. Clay punched crisply and accurately, never faltering in his relentless barrage of Besmanoff's face. "Kill the head and the body dies," was Muhammad Ali's favorite training litany.

By the fifth round it would have been easy for Clay to finish the match, but he had promised those gentlemen of the press round seven and round seven it would be. The crowd was on its feet, booing and cursing. Angelo Dundee shouted from the corner, "Stop playing around!" Clay ignored them, toying with his man, casually jabbing at will, waiting for the minutes to tick away as the doomed German, bleeding from his nose and mouth, groped desperately to come to grips with his tormentor.

Round seven, and Clay moved purposefully away from his stool, where seconds before Dundee had been berating him for his foolish behavior. Striding towards the bloody Besmanoff, Clay hit him with a hard straight right. Besmanoff went down, struggled hopelessly to his feet and stood defenseless as Clay hit him again with two lefts and a short, chopping right to the jaw. They were terrible blows. Besmanoff catapulted onto his back, arms and legs extended in a drunken cross on the canvas. The referee didn't even bother to count him out.

This was an impressive performance and Cassius knew it. "Boxing needs me," he confided to reporters afterwards. "When I lay a man down, he's supposed to stay down! I should be champ before I'm 21…you write that down in your notebooks!" Angelo Dundee concurred. "When he wasn't playing around", he remarked to Faversham, "he looked like a champion."

In early February of 1962, Dundee received an unexpected phone call from the Madison Square Garden promoters in New York. A scheduled heavyweight bout between two top contenders in five days time had been abruptly cancelled. Would Dundee and the Louisville Group be prepared to consider a substitute match at the Garden? Cassius Clay against Sonny Banks? Dundee hesitated momentarily. The offer was a handsome tribute to his pupil's burgeoning media power, especially as Clay had been a professional for only 16 months. But a loss at the Garden, the Mecca of contemporary boxing, could irreparably damage the kid's confidence and seriously retard his future prospects on the East Coast. He discussed the matter with Faversham and they agreed that Clay could almost certainly handle Banks. The exposure and experience were worth the risks. Clay was on his way to the Big Apple.

On the Wednesday before his premiere at the Garden, Cassius attended a monthly luncheon of the New York Boxing Writers' Association at Jack Dempsey's restaurant on Broadway. His performance amongst these veteran scribes proved a considerable success. Decked out in a rented tuxedo, ruffled shirt and string tie, Clay launched into a graphic description of his own genius, his ambition to become the youngest ever world champion and the miserable fate that awaited his unhappy opponent. "The man must fall in the round I call," he lectured amused journalists. "In fact, Banks must fall in four." The flamboyant Clay came like a breath of fresh air to New York's stagnant boxing scene and for the next few days the sports pages were crowded with his wit and arrogance. The antics of "Gaseous Cassius", "The Mighty Mouth", and "The Louisville Lip" dominated the headlines.

Sonny Banks hailed from Detroit, an agile young boxer with a fast left hook that had helped to win him nine of his 12 professional bouts. Clay entered the ring in his spotless white shoes and shiny trunks, pretty as a picture, confidently acknowledging the catcalls of an audience who had come primarily to see "The Lip" get what was coming to him. Using his superior reach and footwork, Cassius played the fool in the early stages of the first round, lowering his hands to his sides, waving his chin derisively at Banks, and generally acting like an imbecile. This lack of concentration allowed Banks to catch him with a long left to the side of the jaw. It wasn't exactly a lethal blow, but Clay went down for a mandatory count to the ecstatic roar of the fans. More surprised than hurt, Clay skillfully defended himself until the bell gave him a breather, coming back in command of the fight by the third and finishing Banks in the 26th second of the fourth. His jaw must have been sore, but he couldn't resist gloating to reporters afterwards: "I told you. The man fell in four!"

Though his fighter had won an important match, Dundee was unhappy. Clay's manic bravado had nearly cost them the fight. Anxious to withdraw from an environment that pandered to the boy's sense of self-importance, Angelo rejected several offers from the promoters at Madison Square Garden and hustled Cassius back to Miami. There they were due to meet Don Warner on February 28th at the Miami

ABOVE: February 10, 1962, and Sonny Banks goes down in the predicted fourth. "I told you. The man fell in four!"

OPPOSITE: July 20, 1962, and this time it's Alejandro Lavorante, the man whom the press believed would finally "test Clay's jabbering jaw", who hits the canvas in the predicted fifth.

Auditorium. Warner was a two-handed puncher with a string of knock-outs to his credit, but Clay demolished him easily, effecting yet another prediction of sorts as he hooked his opponent through the ropes in the fourth, blood spraying all over the ring. "How come you took him in the fourth, Cassius?" demanded a sportswriter. "You told us it was going to be the fifth." Clay replied that he had found it necessary to penalize Warner a full round for having neglected to shake hands with him at the weigh-in. Everyone, except Warner, was amused.

Clay's next fight was to be his first showing at Los Angeles on April 23rd. Retired champion turned promoter Joe Louis had guaranteed "The Lip" a purse of $6,000 and the press agents were kept busy working overtime as the Californian media lapped up Clay's eloquent hysteria in an extended round of radio and television appearances. Clay strutted into the ring a clear six-to-one favorite. George Logan was another left hook merchant, but all he would be hooking that night was the ropes. Clay's cha-cha footwork and rapid jabbing synchronized perfectly. With his eyes bleeding profusely from several cuts and gashes, Logan was spared further punishment in the fourth round as the referee awarded Cassius a TKO.

Barely a month after his Los Angeles debut, Clay was back in New York City preparing to meet Billy Daniels, an undefeated local boy with an impressive record showing seven knockout victories. Clay's own star was rising fast. The Ring magazine, "the Bible of boxing", had him rated number eight world heavyweight contender, and 'The Lip's' record spoke for itself, 13 fights, 13 wins, ten by KO or TKO.

Clay vs. Daniels was an unattractive bout, both for the participants and spectators, full of clinches and continual cries of "break" from the referee. Billy Daniels stood more than an inch taller than Clay

and his rangy arms allowed him to score heavily against Cassius' head. "The Lip" seemed unable to find his normal stride and his opponent was ahead on points when the referee finally stepped in at the seventh to award Clay a TKO. Luckily, a cut had appeared over Daniels' left eyebrow, but the victory had been so close that Faversham wisely declined to accept Daniels' challenges for a rematch. "Why should we fight him?" he asked newsmen. "We're not afraid of him, but we haven't anything to gain."

Cassius flew back to the West Coast in July, threatening to dispose of his next opponent, Alejandro Lavorante, in five at their meeting scheduled for Los Angeles on the 20th of that month. Almost 12,000 people packed the Sports Arena to the tune of $70,000 to watch him do it. Clay's share of the gate, $12,500, more than double his last purse in the same city, reflected his growing (anti-)popularity, and the class of competition was reckoned to be somewhat stiffer. Lavorante had been ranked number three world heavyweight contender in his prime, a powerful, lumbering Argentinian whose record showed a knockout over Zora Folley and a narrow defeat by Archie Moore. Boxing writers suggested that Lavorante might well be the man to "test Clay's Jabbering Jaw" and cure him of his habit of carrying both gloves low, "hanging his chin out to dry."

In the first round, Lavorante landed a pair of hard hooks to Clay's body, clearly winding him. Cassius bicycled out of trouble, his face grimacing with pain and contorted in anger. In the second, "The Lip" retaliated with an unusual, sideswiping right to Lavorante's jaw, wobbling his opponent visibly. From that moment Clay proceeded to demonstrate exactly whose chin was the more vulnerable, cutting both Lavorante's eyes and savagely mauling his face with long-range jabs. Having dropped the Argentinian twice in the fourth, Clay's wicked right hand concluded the proceedings in the fifth, right on schedule, leaving the hapless Lavorante sprawled in a neutral corner.

As the referee raised Clay's hand to announce him the winner, Cassius spotted Archie Moore shooting pictures from the apron of the ring. Above the noise of the crowd Clay shrieked hysterically, gesticulating with his bloodstained gloves: "You're next, Archie! You're next, old man!"

For Alejandro Lavorante there would be only one next time. Two months later he sustained serious brain damage during a fight with Johnny Riggens. After lying in a coma for 19 months he died in April of 1964.

In the autumn of 1962, approaching his 50th birthday, Archie Moore was nearing the end of a long and distinguished boxing career. He had been fighting professionally nearly 26 years, the last decade of which as the Light-Heavyweight Champion of the World. The New York Athletic Commission had only recently stripped him of this title, citing as their reason Moore's failure to defend the championship against Harold Johnson, a man he had already thrashed on four previous occasions. Archie Moore, "the old mongoose", held an all-time record for knocking out opponents in his weight—135 of them—an average of five per year for more than a quarter of a century. His punching abilities and ring craft were legendary. He was technically old enough to be Clay's grandfather.

Faversham contracted Cassius to meet Moore on October 23rd 1962. Two weeks prior to the fight Ailene Eaton, the promoter, postponed the match until November 15th claiming insufficient

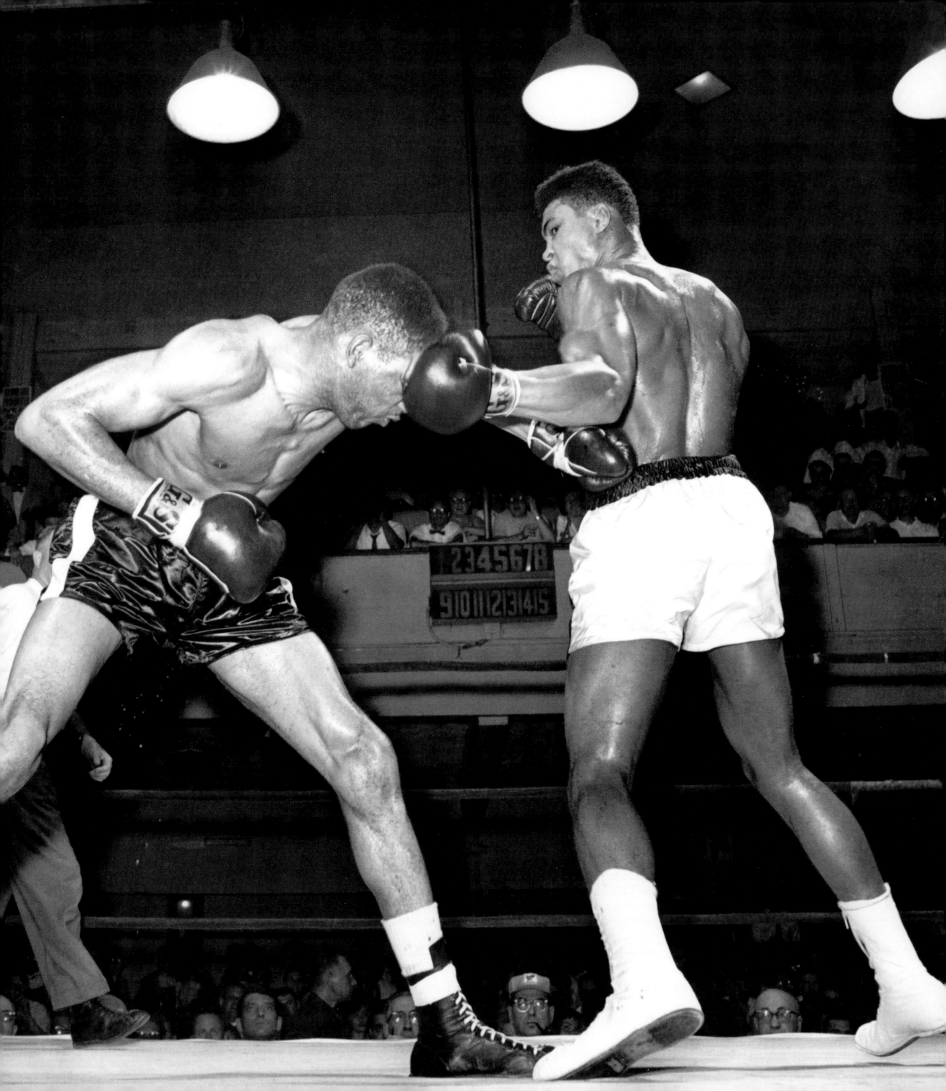

ABOVE: By now, Cassius' mouth is as famous as his fists. Not that he cares. At Idlewild Airport, en route to meet Henry Cooper in London, he delights photographers by whipping out a giant button purportedly sent to him by heavyweight champion Sonny Liston in order to "button his lip". Cassius replies to Liston by holding up eight fingers and predicting he would finish off the champion in the eighth when they meet. The photographers find that even funnier.

OPPOSITE: Cassius Clay in 1962, prior to his fight with Archie Moore.

bookings at the venue in Los Angeles and for the closed-circuit outlets. Doubtless he was hoping that the contestants would improve matters by publicly insulting each other during the interval and Clay, at least, was delighted to oblige. He knew this to be the most important bout of his career to date. If he could defeat Moore convincingly he would be on the home straight for a title fight with Sonny Liston. The poetry and abuse flowed almost faster than journalists could note it down:

> Archie has been living off the fat of the land
> But I'm here to give him his pension plan.
> When you come to the fight don't block aisle or door,
> 'Cause ya all going home after round four!

"I'll annihilate the old man!" Cassius ranted in a television program. "He's old, he's rusty, he's fat and dusty. I'll say it again, I've said it before, Archie Moore must fall in four!"

Moore himself was no newcomer to breast-beating tactics of this kind, but Clay's needling irritated him nonetheless. Archie trained diligently, muttering threats that he had "seen and heard too much" and promising to develop a custom-made 'lip buttoner' punch to "shut that fresh boy's mouth."

Clay was supremely confident of thrashing Moore. The prospect of defeat simply never entered his head. At the Loop Hotel, the press headquarters in Chicago for the Liston vs. Patterson fight, Cassius upstaged both contestants by reciting for journalists a poem he had written in honor of his upcoming bout with Moore:

> It was that night in the Coliseum
> That's when I annihilated him.
> I gave him a lot of sand
> The one they call the old man.
> He was old and I was new
> You could tell by the bombs I threw.
> I had left jabs to fire like pistons
> They were twice as rough as Liston's.
> The people cried, "Stop the fight!"
> Before Clay could put out the light.
> He was trying to remain the great Mr. Moore
> For he knew Clay had predicted four.
> I swept that old man clean out of the ring
> For a good new broom sweeps up anything.
> Some say the greatest was Sugar Ray
> But they haven't seen Cassius Clay!

The fight itself proved to be something of an anti-climax. It was clear from the opening bell that time had taken a heavy toll on Moore's prodigious talents. Even though the veteran had trained himself almost to the point of exhaustion, his paunch hung barely restrained by the elastic support built into his trunks. His hair was graying, his footwork slow and methodical, the lightning reflexes a dull parody of yesteryear.

Clay took the offensive from the outset, jabbing, hooking, and punching with frightening rapidity as the old professor marshalled his defences. Towards the end of the second round Moore caught Clay with a cunning right and the crowd leaped prematurely to its feet, but his younger opponent back-pedalled quickly and the moment was lost. Just before the bell "The Lip" landed a right of his own across

Moore's mouth, ripping back his head and dislocating his mouthpiece. Moore trudged wearily back to his corner, refusing the stool. "If I'd sat down then," he confessed later, "I never would have gotten up."

The third round provided no respite for Moore and all his experience could do little to shelter him from the hail of Clay's punches. "The Lip" was in peak condition, 200 pounds of honed muscle, arms pumping with unerring accuracy at the shuffling target bobbing and weaving in the center of the ring.

The crowd leaned forward excitedly at the signal for the fourth as Clay closed for the kill, mercilessly battering through his opponent's guard. The old professor had slipped one thousand, ten thousand punches in his career, but nothing could have stopped the left-right combination that put him on the canvas. Clay stepped back, raising both hands in the air, dancing towards his own corner in triumphant jubilation. But Archie Moore was a hard man to keep down that night.

Defeat was nothing new to him, but he must have known this to be his last fight in the major leagues. Resolved to salvage some little dignity in his swan song, Moore rolled to his side and staggered to his feet at eight. Seconds later Clay hit him again and the veteran flopped leadenly backwards; turning away from the corpse, Cassius marched towards a neutral corner in time to witness a remarkable display of courage. Slowly, unbelievably, Moore crawled first to his knees and then upright. Clay rushed towards him, seething with frustration at this aging warrior's stubborn refusal to concede the inevitable. He had already drawn back his right glove when referee Tommy Hart slipped in between them, grasping Clay's hand by the wrist and proclaiming him the victor. Archie Moore had finished on his feet.

"I hated to beat him," Clay insisted in his dressing room. "He is an old man and I hated to beat him. But I had to use him as a stepping stone."

Clay's superb performance against Moore convinced Faversham and Dundee that the time was ripe to begin campaigning for a crack at boxing's ultimate prize. Sonny Liston, the "indestructible" new World Heavyweight Champion, still had to fullfil his contractual commitment of a return against former title holder Floyd Patterson, tentatively scheduled for April 1963. Considerable controversy surrounded this match, from both the commercial and the official points of view. Patterson's wretched performance against Liston in September of '62 had dimmed his crowd-pulling potential, while there seemed little doubt that a Clay vs. Liston bout would excite nationwide, possibly worldwide, interest, ensuring a $1,000,000 bonanza in gate receipts and television exploitation. But Patterson naturally resisted any suggestion that he should meet Clay. He argued that he had already shown himself capable of defying historical odds. He was, after all, the only boxer to have regained the heavyweight crown when he knocked out Ingemar Johansson in June of 1960. Why should he jeopardise the opportunity of retrieving the championship a third time by fighting the Louisville Lip?

The World Boxing Association (WBA), one of the more powerful boxing authorities, threatened both Patterson and Liston with withdrawal of recognition if they proceeded with their second fight. The WBA, for reasons best known to itself, had never recognised "return-bout clauses". Clay was momentarily heartened by the

ABOVE: After defeating a dogged Doug Jones in 1963, Clay is joined in his dressing room by his boyhood idol Sugar Ray Robinson and Cleveland Browns football star Jim Brown. Outside the crowd boos long and hard after Cassius scrapes through on a slim points decision.

OPPOSITE: Archie Moore loses his battle against Clay's prediction and finally falls in four. Moore: "I was made for him in that I used a wrap-around defense to cover up. I would leave the top of my head exposed, and that's what he wanted. He had a style, he would hit the top of a man's head. If someone is plunking you on top of the head, you cannot think correctly. And this is what he did. He made me dizzy and he knocked me out."

FOLLOWING PAGES: (Top) Cassius drops ex-football star Charlie Powell in the predicted third round. (Bottom and page 71) The predictions go out of the window when Clay meets Doug Jones who he predicts will fall in six. It is only Cassius' heroic 10th round display that saves him. The 18,000 fans cry fix to a man.

WBA's intransigence. If Liston backed off from the Patterson fight, there was still a slim chance of achieving his ambition to become history's youngest ever Heavyweight Champion.

While the internal machinations of pro boxing's politics ground on, Faversham was concerned to keep Clay active. He booked him to meet ex-football star Charlie Powell in Pittsburgh on January 24th. Clay dropped Powell in two minutes 40 seconds of the third round, exactly as per prediction, in front of 17,000 enthusiastic fans who had braved near-arctic conditions of 20 degrees below to crowd the Civic Arena. Clay's mouth was talking a new lease of life into the fight game. His drawing power across the country staggered even experienced promoters and Faversham's telephone rarely ceased ringing.

Throughout February, Clay entrenched himself in Miami, training daily at the 5th Street Gym for an upcoming fight in March against Doug Jones at Madison Square Garden. His hopes of a stab at the heavyweight championship before his 22nd birthday were receding fast. In the face of almost universal opposition from other international boxing authorities, the WBA had agreed to sanction the Patterson vs. Liston engagement: a bitter blow to Cassius, and worse was still to come. While limbering up for the big match, Liston strained a knee ligament swinging a golf club for the benefit of press photographers.

With the fight postponed, at least until the end of April, Clay watched helplessly from the sidelines as precious months slipped past. Occasionally he would drop by Liston's Miami training headquarters, more to abuse the world champion in public than to watch him working out. "What are you fighting that glass jaw nigger for, you ugly brute?"

he shouted one afternoon as journalists scribbled frantically in their pads. "He don't deserve it. He's just holding up more worthy opponents!"

Cassius arrived in New York in early March. Almost immediately he buckled down to a new propaganda war, granting dozens of television and radio interviews, jawing continually into microphones and flashing his contagious smile before an endless stream of cameras. And the poetry was improving by leaps and vowels—at least it rhymed:

> Jones likes to mix, so I'll let it go six
> If he talks jive, I'll cut it to five.
> And if he talks some more, I'll cut it to four.
> And if he talks about me, I'll cut it to three.
> And if that don't do, I'll cut it to two.
> And if you want some fun, I'll cut it to one.
> And if he don't want to fight, he can stay home that night!

Madison Square Garden's box office found itself besieged with ticket requests and many thousands of fans were turned away disappointed. For the first time in its history, the Garden sold out a full week before the night of a fight. "They're dusting off the seats where the pigeons used to sit," laughed Cassius. "The Garden's too small for me." The record attendance figure was even more impressive in view of a virtual blackout of newspaper coverage resulting from a local strike, a situation that Clay considered almost a personal affront.

In his campaign tour of the metropolis, Clay revelled in the persona of "the man they love to hate", only too aware that the majority of spectators were shelling out up to $12 a seat in the fervent hope of witnessing his crushing defeat.

> People come from all around
> To see Cassius hit the ground.
> Some get mad, some lose their money,
> But Cassius is still sweet as honey.

Sweet as honey, bold as brass, and sharp as a knife. Clay's abrasive tongue assured him of a warm reception in the unlikeliest of environments, even as a surprise entrant in a Greenwich Village poetry contest. Squatting in the Bitter End club, incongruously dressed in a shiny tuxedo and surrounded by the remnants of New York's Beat generation, Clay launched into an interminable monologue, climaxing modestly with his "Ode to a Champion".

> Marcellus vanquished Carthage,
> Cassius laid Julius Caesar low.
> And Clay will flatten Douglas Jones
> With a mighty, measured blow!

At this point the competition abruptly terminated as Clay declared himself the obvious winner, brandishing his arms in a victor's salute. "It's no contest!" he bellowed, "I am the Heavyweight Champion Poet of the World!" Nobody present ventured to disagree with him.

The night before the fight, Bill Faversham visited Clay at the Hotel Americana where he found Cassius busy with his brother Rudy and a new friend, Drew "Bundini" Brown. Clay was scribbling in a pad, repeating his signature on every leaf. He planned to tear off these ready-made autographs at the celebration party the following evening.

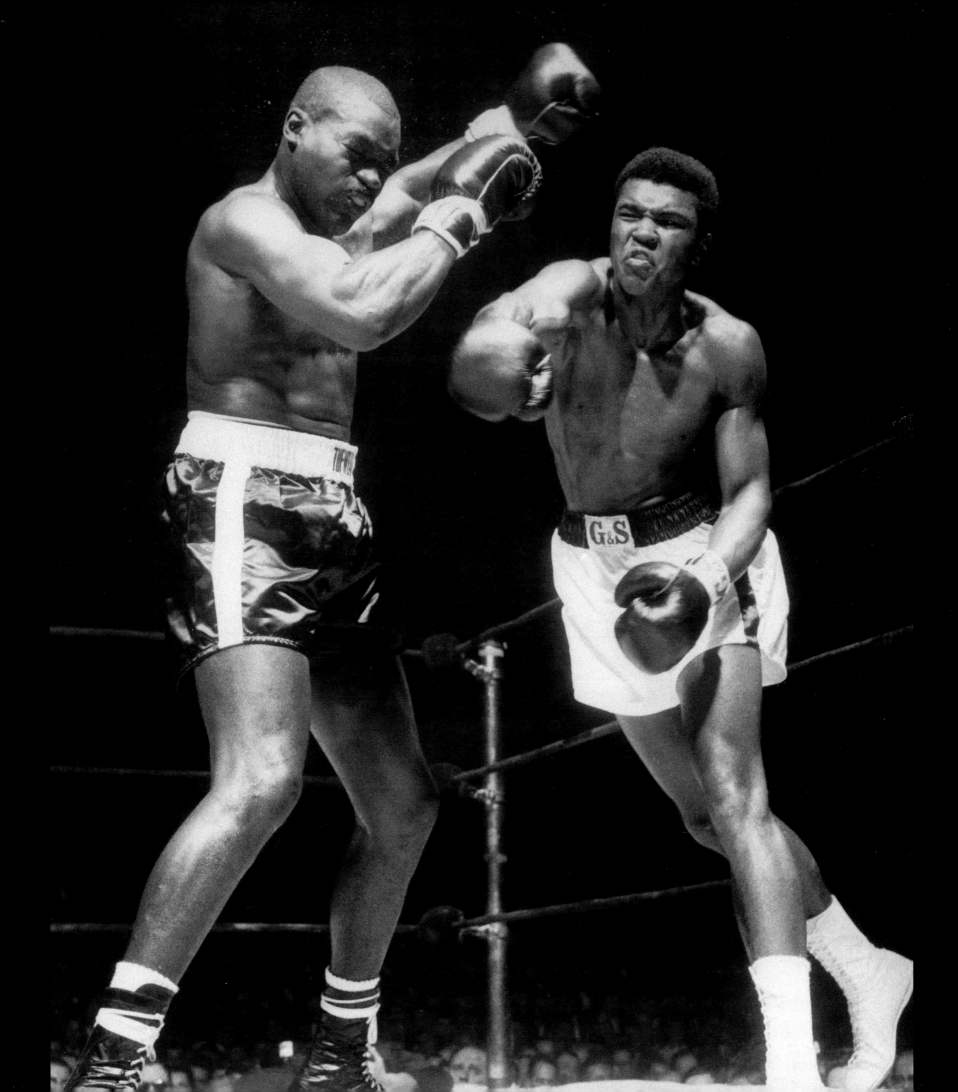

ABOVE: Cassius declares himself Heavyweight Champion Poet of the World at Greenwich Village's Bitter End club after defeating seven opponents.

PRECEDING PAGES: It takes all of Clay's courage to force a controversial last minute victory over Doug Jones in Madison Square Garden. Angelo Dundee: "Something that a lot of people forget that's overshadowed by all the flashiness and the hand speed is the amount of guts that Ali had. Take the Doug Jones fight. I remember it very well. Muhammad died. [Jones] gave him problems. But, you know, he won. There were no three ways about it."

OPPOSITE: Muhammad Ali with the enigmatic Drew "Bundini" Brown—Ali's witch doctor, Ali's worshipper and, as the self-professed author of *Float like a butterfly, sting like a bee*, Ali's poet laureate. "I get sick before a fight," Bundini once told a reporter. "It makes me feel like a pregnant woman. I give the champ all my strength. He throw a punch, I throw a punch. He get hit, it hurts me."

"Cassius told me that he wanted a new Cadillac," Faversham recalls. "He already had one Cadillac but this new model was important to him. Naturally, he couldn't afford it, he was still in debt to us at that point, but I could see he wanted the car badly. Well, this Doug Jones fight was a really important one and I didn't want him worrying about anything. We bought him the Cadillac. It was kind of an expensive way to get him in the right mood but it had to be done."

Bundini Brown remembered the day he met Cassius Clay with vivid clarity. He has told and retold the story scores of times. It was an event that transformed his life:

"It was Bobby Nelson, Sugar Ray Robinson's brother-in-law, who introduced me to the champ. [Bundini claimed to have always called Ali "the champ".] Bob called me at my house, said to come on over, there was somebody he wanted me to meet. Clay was sitting on this couch, sitting like he was already a king. I sat down on the floor and we began talking. I didn't know it but I guess he was testing me. He asked me what kind of a fighter did I think he was. I told him I thought he was a phony. He didn't like that! 'What do you mean I'm a phony?' he says, I told him that nobody in any sport ever called the round on nobody. We were talking loud and things were getting heated. Maybe if we'd gone on that way I wouldn't be with him today. Anyway, he looks at me finally and says, 'I call the round, I just do the best I can and they fall.' I stopped needling him then, I realized what he was saying was the truth."

Bundini was an exuberant, enigmatic man, an imposing figure with a scar running down his right cheek. Many journalists have commented that it would be easy to mistake him for Ali's older brother. Jimmy Dundee has said that "if you put a headdress and

beads on him, you'd have a witch doctor." There are many in the world of professional boxing who felt that Bundini's eccentricities bordered on madness, but others came to know him better.

George Plimpton, the sports writer, has described him aptly as "a strangely gentle man in the midst of all that violence." José Torres wrote, "He looked to me like a man who would shoot you without a minute's notice. But after you spent time with him, you can find softness beneath his hypnotic eyes."

Born in Sandford, Florida, in 1929, Drew Brown shined shoes during the years of the Great Depression and joined the US Navy just after the outbreak of World War II at 13 years old. He was discharged from the Navy after attacking an officer with a meat cleaver. "The officer made it to the deck and jumped overboard," Bundini laughed. "Any man would jump overboard when he is facing sure death."

For the next 12 years Brown served in the merchant marine, travelling around the world, so he claimed, 20 times. It was on one of these trips that a Lebanese girl gave him his nickname Bundini. (He pronounced it "Bo-dini.") To his death he professed ignorance of the name's meaning. Bundini drifted into boxing as he had drifted all his life, wandering by chance into Sugar Ray Robinson's Golden Gloves Barbershop in Harlem. Here he was introduced to Johnny Bratton, a well-known boxer, and over the next few months Brown found himself hanging out with Bratton, assisting in training and providing entertainment in the dressing rooms.

Clay invited Bundini to the hotel the day after they'd met, promising to find him tickets for the fight. Angelo Dundee recalls: "First time I saw Bundini was just before that Doug Jones fight. He come marching into the hotel and straight off he and Cassius begin fooling around, shouting about spacemen and stuff. A real double act. First guy I ever met who could talk nearly as fast as the champ. But I got to like him. The trick is if you try to understand him he'll drive you crazy, so I don't try."

Bundini swiftly established a unique role in Clay's entourage. Ostensibly he was an "assistant trainer", but there was much more to their relationship than the label might suggest. In practice he served as Muhammad Ali's faithful court jester, psychic healer, and companion-in-hysteria. It was Bundini who suggested what is possibly Ali's permanent literary epitaph:

Float like a butterfly,
Sting like a bee.
Your hands can't hit
What your eyes can't see…

Bundini accompanied Clay to the Garden that night in the limousine. Eighteen thousand seven hundred people had been crammed into the arena and thousands more were watching in closed-circuit cinemas scattered across America. This was the biggest non-championship bout held at the Garden for 13 years.

Doug Jones was a tough customer, a 26-year-old Harlemite with a 24-21 record and rated number two world heavyweight contender by the WBA and number three by *The Ring* magazine. He had stolidly endured Clay's provocative media baiting. At one press conference Cassius announced that he was reducing his earlier six-round prediction by two rounds. Jones was so short, he told newsmen, that it would only require four rounds to "flatten him."

OPPOSITE: Clay talks to journalists after defeating Archie Moore. "He is an old man and I hated to beat him," he said. "But I had to use him as a stepping stone."

FOLLOWING PAGES: The Lip, gagged and padlocked, 1964. Angelo Dundee: "There's only one disease in this profession, and that is silence. When the press isn't looking to talk about boxing, we're dead."

BELOW: Cassius arrives at the Doug Jones weigh-in accompanied by Angelo Dundee, who had taped his mouth to avoid antagonizing the New York State Boxing Commission. Angelo Dundee: "I used that as a gimmick… I was always looking for a little extra ink. I was going to the weigh-in and I said, 'Put a tape over your mouth.' He thought about it and says, 'Yeah, okay, we'll do it.' But then, as the weigh-in progressed, he says, 'All the newspapermen are here. I can't do it no more.' And he took the tape off!"

(Jones stood 6ft even to Clay's 6ft 3in.) "I'll let my leather do the talking," was Jones' response, but even he had to laugh when Angelo Dundee marched a bug-eyed Cassius into the weighing-in ceremony with a massive strip of adhesive tape across his mouth. "I knew that the New York State Boxing Commission would take a pretty dim view of any hysterics Cassius might pull," Angelo said. "The tape seemed like a good idea."

Clay came out jabbing and moving fast, his superb footwork a marked contrast to Doug Jones' inelegant shuffle. The Harlemite advanced continually, leaving Cassius content to jab with his left, moving easily around the ring. Thirty seconds of the first round had gone as Cassius prepared to slip off the ropes, flicking out a lazy jab with his left. But Jones had been waiting, had anticipated the jab coming, ducked underneath it and shot out a murderous straight right.

Cassius leaned back, hoping to ride the blow but it careered into his jaw. The crowd was going crazy as Clay lurched backwards into the ropes, arms spread wide to counterbalance his buckling legs. Angelo Dundee shouted from their corner, "Grab him, Cass, hold on!" Jones pummelled grimly, looking for a spectacular first round knockout, but Clay locked him into a clinch. Throughout what remained of that round Cassius held and entangled Jones, jabbing instinctively to ward off his furious attack.

By the second round Clay's head had cleared and he was back on his toes, frustrating his opponent's every punch, relying heavily on his extra height and reach. The left jab was working wonders and in the third he whipped a beautiful combination to

Jones' head and body, though apparently lacking the confidence to follow through. Later, Jones admitted, "That was the only time he hurt me."

In the fourth ("I'll talk no more—Jones falls in four!"), Clay stepped up the pressure, throwing fast lefts and rights and moving on to the offensive. The closing seconds found him hammering at Jones, trapping him against the ropes, recklessly eager to fulfil his prediction. The fans booed derisively at the sound of the bell—Jones was still very much on his feet.

It was a discouraging moment for Cassius; boxing gamblers by now had become accustomed to his accurate predictions and this failure to "call the round" on schedule preyed on his concentration. Over the next few rounds Clay struggled dangerously behind on points as Jones took the initiative and at the end of the eighth Angelo Dundee cautioned his fighter that if he didn't take the last two rounds convincingly he would throw the fight. Looking unusually grim, Clay unleashed a barrage of punches in the ninth and tenth. His feet planted uncharacteristically flat on the floor, Clay stood in the centre of the ring, slugging it out with Jones, piling up precious points as he landed four or five blows to every one from his opponent. It was an impressive finish to an otherwise lackluster performance.

The atmosphere in the Garden tensed as the MC stepped forward to announce the judges' decision. "Judge Artie Aidala and Judge Frank Forbes both score the fight five rounds for Clay, four for Jones, one even." The stadium erupted in a roar of booing and shouts of "Fake! Fix! Fix!" Fortunately, nobody was able to hear the MC continue with the referee's almost unbelievable scoring of eight rounds to Clay, one to Jones and one even. Had they done so there might well have been a riot. As it was, debris and trash showered into the ring. Paper cups, bottles, programs, and cigar butts were hurled by the enraged fans. Angelo hustled Cassius through a gauntlet of abuse and missiles to the relative quiet and safety of their dressing room, the ugly cries of "Fake! Fix!" still ringing in their ears. Cassius had been lucky; he had come very close to conceding his first professional defeat. Several observers scored the fight as a clear win for Jones and the controversy about the judges' decision raged on in boxing magazines for months.

Jones' management clamored loudly for a rematch and similar sentiments were expressed in the boxing press. As far as Angelo Dundee and Bill Faversham were concerned, they could whistle at the moon. Clay had absolutely nothing to gain by climbing into the ring with Douglas Jones again!

But the question remained, who would Cassius Clay fight next? There was no lack of contenders but the Louisville Group was anxious to minimize any risk of injury or defeat before the inevitable confrontation with Liston. After exploring the possibility of bouts with Floyd Patterson and Ingemar Johansson, Faversham eventually signed Cassius to meet Henry Cooper, the grizzled but still well ranked British Empire Heavyweight Champion, in London.

June 18, 1963, the night of the Cooper vs. Clay fight at Wembley Stadium and the anniversary of the Battle of Waterloo. Napoleon himself could hardly have aroused more xenophobia in the minds of the British public and press than Cassius Marcellus Clay II. Clay had called Cooper "a tramp, a bum and a cripple." He had proclaimed himself uncrowned World Heavyweight Champion and insisted that this meeting with the Englishman served only to mark a little time, to fend off boredom before "I demolish that ugly bear Liston."

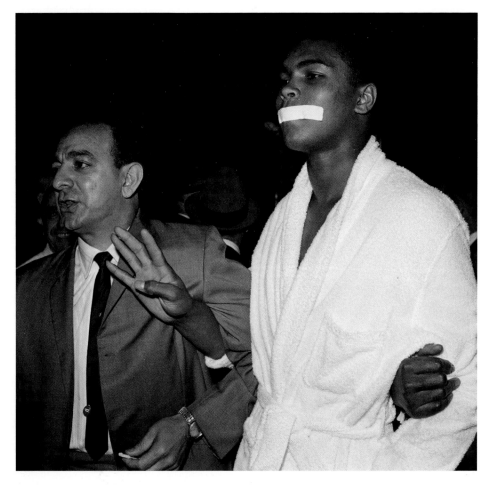

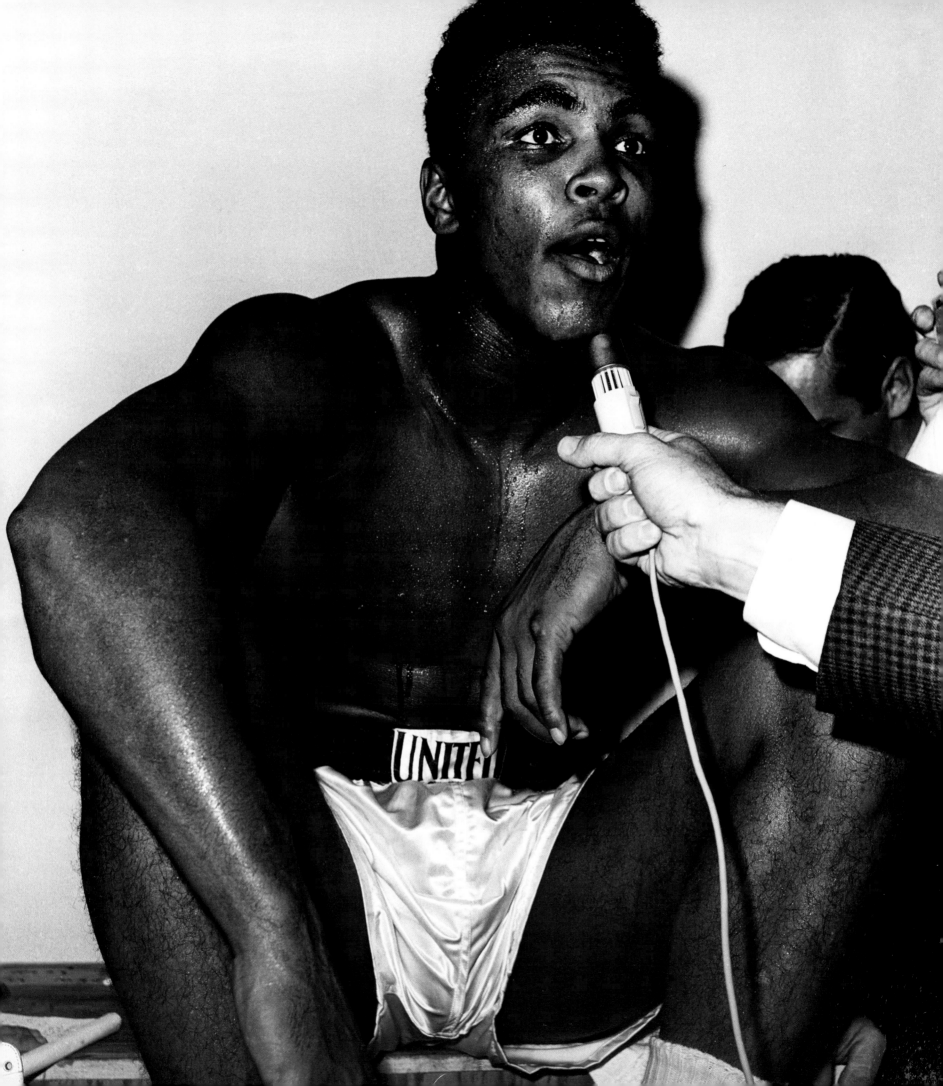

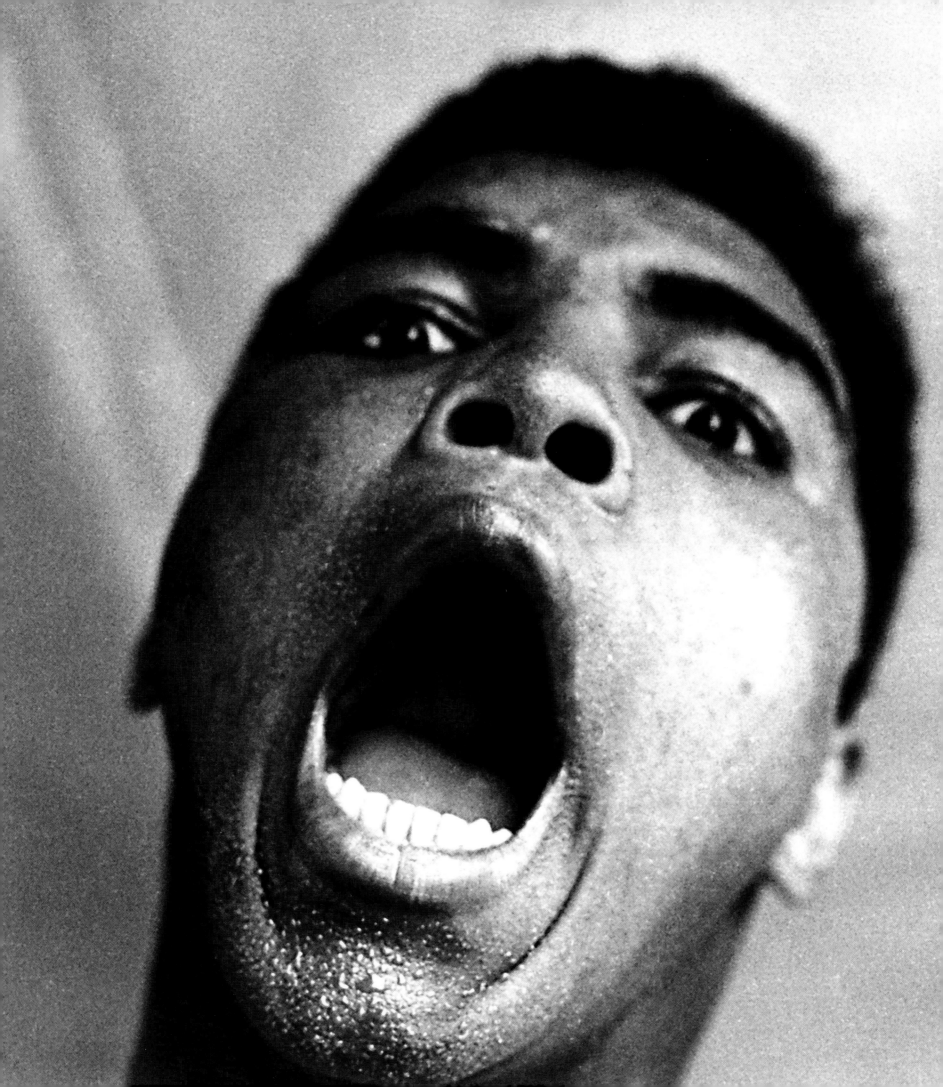

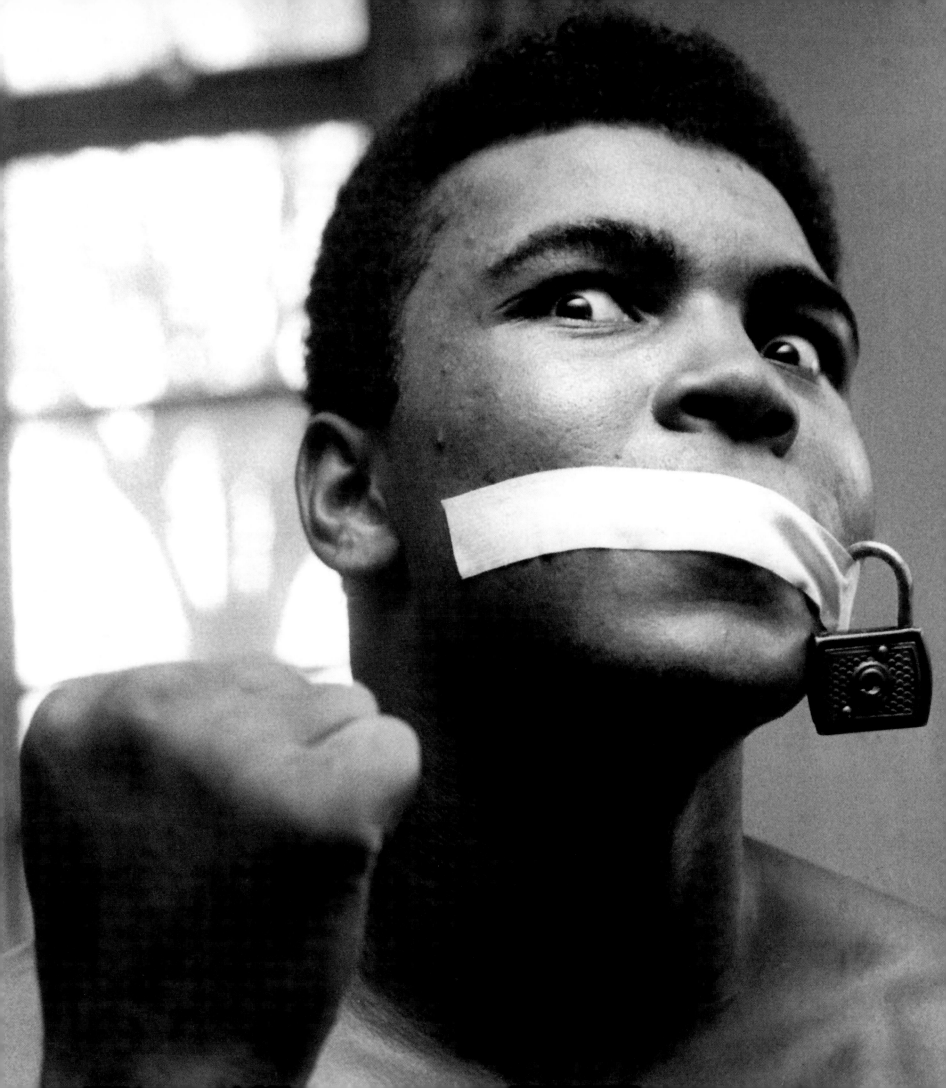

ABOVE: Cassius entertains veteran British champion and national treasure 'Enery Cooper at the weigh-in by predicting Cooper will survive only 'till five.

OPPOSITE: Cassius with Angelo Dundee in pensive mood in the dressing room before his 1963 bout with Charlie Powell.

FOLLOWING PAGES: (Left) June 18, 1963, the moment the boxing world has been waiting for. Henry Cooper unloads his 'ammer and Clay drops to London's Wembley Stadium canvas. Angelo Dundee: "That was a great left hook he caught. If the ropes hadn't been there, the fight would have been over, because he just slid down the ropes." (Right) The bloody end for Henry as referee Tommy Little stops it in the fifth. Cooper: "He always said that punch I hit him with was one of the hardest punches he'd ever took in boxing: 'Cooper hit me so hard he didn't only shake me; he shook my relations in Africa.' If I could have gone to him again, perhaps just landed another one, I could have had him."

Cooper was a much-loved boxer, almost a national institution in Britain. A thorough professional of the old school of British boxing, Clay's rantings and juvenile gimmickry surprised and even disgusted him, but his response was predictably phlegmatic. "Let him carry on," he told the *Daily Mirror*. "I'm on the gate, he's selling tickets and earning me good money. Boxing is a funny business and it doesn't do to shout your mouth off too much. I'm confident I can beat Clay. That's all I want to say."

But Cassius had determined to build himself a needle match. "Can't you get that Cooper to say something?" he sneered in a BBC interview. "Is he that scared?" Weary of this verbal sniping, Cooper had been driven to an unusually savage reply. "Surely, by now," he told Fleet Street, "Clay knows that everybody in Britain, including me, hates his bloody guts." Even the venerable London *Times* assailed "this unsporting American" in their columns by quoting Shakespeare:

> There is no terror, Cassius, in your threats
> For I am arm'd so strong in honesty
> That they pass me by as the idle word
> Which I respect not.
> —(Julius Caesar, Act IV, Scene 3)

Although Cassius repeatedly insisted that Cooper was "not worth training for" and encouraged photographers to accompany him sightseeing at Buckingham Palace, gambling at dog races, and nightclubbing in Soho, Angelo Dundee knew the story. "Clay is as fit as is humanly possible," he said. "He has done miles of roadwork in Hyde Park and has boxed 96 rounds with his brother Rudy and Jimmy Ellis."

Cooper, too, had been hard at work. Acutely conscious of Clay's unorthodox technique, Cooper's manager, Jim Wicks, flew out an old opponent of Clay's, Alonzo Johnson, as a sparring partner for Henry.

"The thing about Alonzo," Cooper recalls in his autobiography, "was that he could imitate Clay's style beautifully. He reckoned he'd had a rough deal in his fight with Clay and was hoping I could get a bit of revenge for him."

Most observers were doubtful of Cooper's chances. Although an experienced fighter with a classic punch often referred to as "the best left hook in the business", he was a slower and older man—almost eight years older than Cassius. Worse still, Henry bled easily. His fragile skin, especially around the eyes, was his own worst enemy.

Clay entered the ring wearing a scarlet robe with the words "Cassius the Greatest" embroidered across the shoulders. He was met by an orchestrated chorus of derision and abuse from the 35,000 fans who had packed the stadium for Wembley's first open-air fight in 28 years. At 207 pounds, Cassius outweighed Cooper by roughly 20 pounds. Without doubt, he looked the fitter and more confident contestant.

The first round brought surprises. Cooper had obviously decided that he must take the fight to Clay, even though the American out-reached him by a massive 4½ in. Usually a slow starter, Henry advanced on his man, forcing the pace, firing lefts and even the occasional right jab and double jab. Cooper's aggressive tactics caught Clay off guard and at the bell he retired to his corner with just the faintest trickle of blood from his right nostril. Considering Cooper's reputation for "bleeding on sight", the irony of this situation was not lost on the thousands of spectators who cheered loudly from the crowded terraces.

Many of Cooper's harder punches, especially the left hook, had only fractionally missed their target and Clay's ability to utilize his height by swaying out of reach of a punch had stood him in good stead. To most boxing trainers, this technique of swaying backwards out of range is dangerous heresy, leaving the head and chin openly exposed for a concealed cross or double jab, besides throwing a boxer off balance and reducing his chances of an effective counter-attack. Only Clay's marvelous speed and pinpoint timing permitted him the luxury of this defense. That Ali's face today is almost totally unmarked is entirely due to this unique practice. Cooper himself remarked later, "I would jab once, then I'd sling in yet another jab, and he'd jerk back from that too. He could judge a punch to the last quarter of an inch. But you've got to give Clay credit. He could play to margins as narrow as that."

In the second round, Cooper intensified his onslaught, rushing at Clay to catch him against the ropes. But Cassius had regained his composure and his left jab began connecting against Cooper's face with monotonous regularity. Cooper swayed and bobbed as he attacked, hoping to fox Clay with a moving target approach, but his rudimentary skill in maneuvering was no match for the American's crisp, accurate punching. Halfway through the round, Clay opened a slight nick above Cooper's rapidly swelling eyes.

Nearing the end of the third round, Clay landed a long left hook to the side of Cooper's head. Cooper moved quickly towards him, hoping to rough him up with a little in-fighting at which Cassius was virtually a novice, but "The Lip" was ready with a vicious chopping right that opened a spurting gash over the Englishman's left eyebrow. It seemed the beginning of the end.

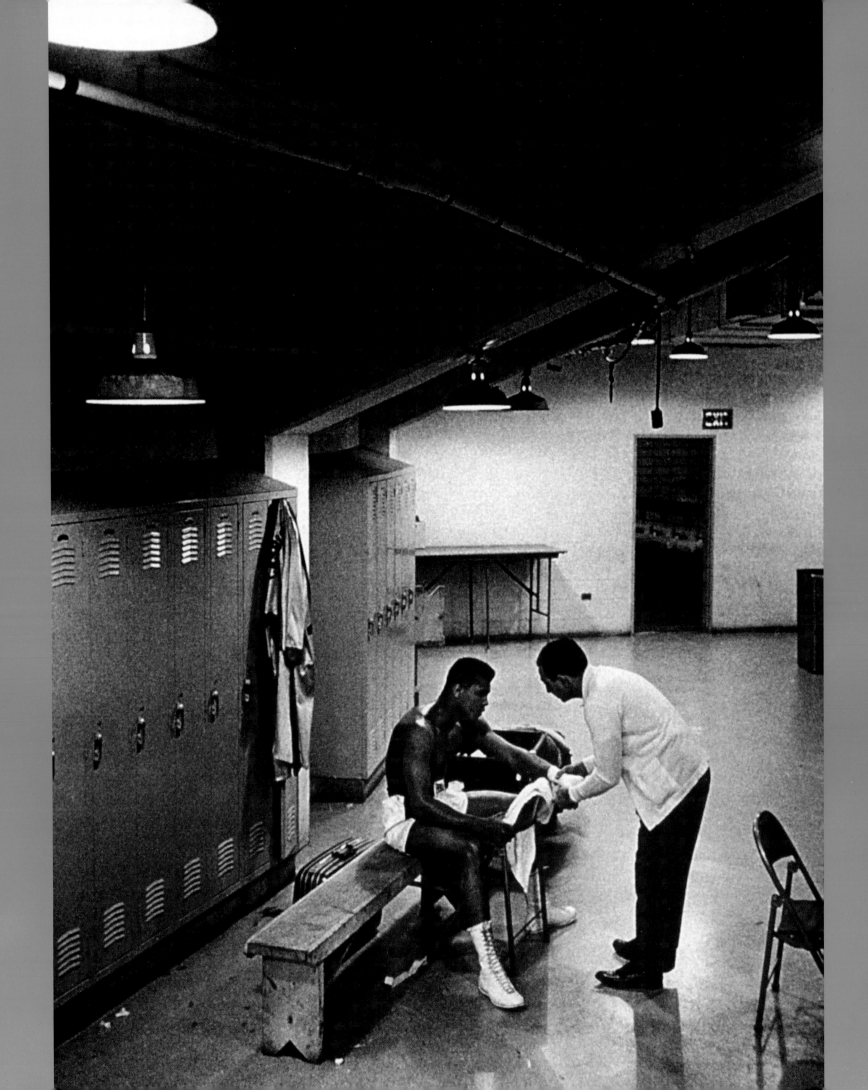

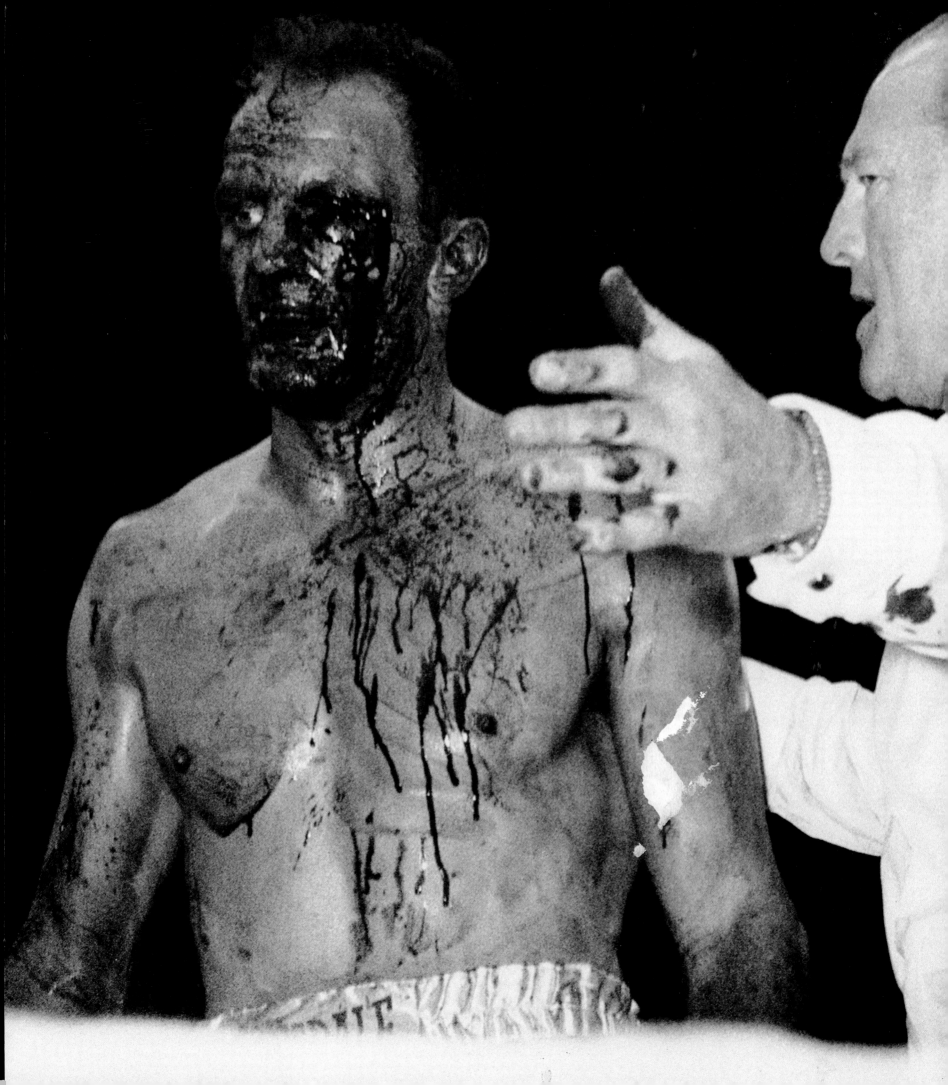

ABOVE: Sonny Liston's manager Jack Nilon finally fixes a date with Cassius: "You can have the fight, kid, and the price will be right."

OPPOSITE: Clay runs alongside Liston's car waving a bear collar. "If I see that bear on the street, I'll beat him before the fight. I'll beat him like I'm his daddy."

BELOW: Cassius announces that his next fight will be for the heavyweight title against Liston.

During the break before round four, Cooper's trainer and expert cut man, Danny Holland, worked feverishly to repair the damage. Holland had his own method of dealing with cuts, pinching the skin around the cut together, using a dry swab to wipe away the blood and applying his own adrenalin and Vaseline mixture to seal the wound. Cooper, ironically, had a swiftly healing skin, but this cut was already one and half inches long and the position looked hopeless. Jim Wicks was still arguing with his fighter to call it a day when the timekeeper appealed for "seconds away". Cooper came out of his corner knowing that it was now or never. Blood trickling down the front of his face and cheek, he hunted for an opening while Clay played games, toying with his opponent, pushing both gloves in his face and coasting the round with just an occasional flurry of punches directed at Cooper's eye. Angelo Dundee bellowed at Clay to stop fooling around. Imminent events were to prove his fears only too justified.

Cooper's face was a waterfall of blood, one eye a bleeding ruin. Many of the spectators were chanting at the referee, "Stop it! Stop it!" In the closing stages of the round, the half-blind Cooper, still advancing, jabbed Clay hard against the ropes, jabbed twice, jabbed three times. Clay leaned back with his shoulder blades hooked over the ropes as Cooper let loose with his fearsome left hook. 'Enery's 'Ammer smacked against the edge of the American's jaw, lifting him visibly with the force of impact. It was the ropes which had trapped Cassius, the ropes that had betrayed him; but now, as his knee buckled and his arms flopped aimlessly to his sides, it was the ropes which partially saved him, cushioning his descent as he slithered to the canvas. "If he had fallen more heavily," Cooper wrote later, "I don't think he would have got up."

The stadium erupted in a turmoil of excitement. Thousands upon thousands of fans climbed on their seats, screaming and cheering, convinced that even if Clay beat the count, Henry would finish him without mercy. Cassius clambered to his feet at five, swaying drunkenly, his arms held low. That he had got up at all seemed a miracle. Cooper moved towards him, his left arm drawn back for the finishing touches as the bell rang for the end of the round. Turning away dejectedly, Henry trudged back to his corner. Victory had seemed so very, very close.

Across the ring, Angelo Dundee dragged Clay to a stool, working desperately to revive his dazed fighter. Suddenly, Angelo attracted the attention of the referee, Tommy Little. Clay's right glove appeared to have split down a seam and Dundee emphasised the point by tearing away a lump of horsehair stuffing. Officials were despatched backstage to locate a new pair, and in the confusion, the interval between rounds was extended by 20 seconds. Every second came as a godsend to the rapidly recovering Clay. Dundee's quick thinking and sharp eyes had probably saved him the match.

When the fifth round finally got under way, Clay wasn't fooling around any more. He crowded his opponent with a stream of fast punches, splattering Cooper's blood across the ring, hammering without pause at that ghastly crimson mask. Photographers around the apron of the ring were splashed with blood. "It was like an abattoir down there," one of them remarked later. The chant of "Stop it! Stop it!" echoed around the stadium. In the front row, Elizabeth Taylor was having what one newspaper described afterwards as "hysterical fits of shrieking and sobbing, begging the referee to intervene." Finally, Jim Wicks had had enough. He called out from the corner, "Stop it ref!" and Tommy Little slipped in between the fighters, raising Clay's blood-soaked glove above his head.

Cooper managed a defiant grin as he turned to the referee. "We didn't do too bad for a bum and a cripple, did we?" he blurted between mouthfuls of blood.

For once, Cassius was gracious enough to retract his abuse. "Cooper's not a bum any more," he admitted magnanimously to reporters the following day. "I underestimated him. He's the toughest fighter I ever met and the first to really drop me. He's a real fighter."

In Clay's dressing room, Jack Nilon was waiting to offer Cassius a chance at the world championship. "I came 3,500 miles to see you tonight," he told Clay. "You fought a great fight and we're ready to take you."

"I'll only fight Liston if the price is right," Clay insisted. "I don't need Liston, he needs me." Nilon's response was immediate. "You can have the fight, kid," he promised, "and the price will be right."

As usual, the "experts" of boxing proved more skeptical than its financial promoters. Peter Wilson, "the world's number one sports writer", as the *Daily Mirror* proclaimed him, put it bluntly enough in his report from the ringside at Wembley: "Any suggestion that Clay—fast though he is, clever at blocking and staying out of range—should be matched with World Champion Sonny Liston in the near future should be laughed out of the rings of the world."

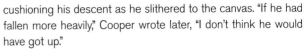

Beauty and The Beast

"You know, fellas, I don't think the kid's all there. I think he's scrambled in the marbles."

Sonny Liston

Sonny Liston's second mechanical demolition of the unfortunate Floyd Patterson in Las Vegas finally cleared the way for serious negotiations between Ali's Louisville Group and the Nilon brothers, Liston's backers. The outcome of the Patterson fight, of course, had never been in any doubt. Few people considered it anything more than a contractual obligation for Sonny and fewer still expected Floyd to improve his performance much beyond the wretched two minutes and six seconds he had survived in September of 1962. In the event, Liston's terrifying glare and punching abilities combined to defeat Patterson in only two minutes and ten seconds of the first round. In the words of one newspaper headline Patterson simply "Froze with Fear and Fell to the Floor."

While Floyd crawled away to nurse bruised kidneys and count his considerable earnings, the world's press began writing about Sonny as "the invincible one", the "Dark Destroyer", and "champion for the next ten years". Opinion about Liston amongst boxing experts was virtually unanimous. "Only old age is likely to take the heavyweight title away from this gorilla of a man," wrote Frank Butler in the *News of the World*. "Sonny Liston has a real problem now," joked American comedian Joe E. Lewis. "He's running out of opponents. After Clay, the only one left for Sonny to fight is Russia."

There is some confusion surrounding the origins of Charles "Sonny" Liston. Journalists and biographers have variously located his hometown as Little Rock or Pine Bluff or Forrest City, all in Arkansas. Similarly, no one can be certain of his birth date. Uncommunicative and surly by nature, Liston especially resented suggestions that at the time of his reign as Heavyweight Champion he

was in fact nearer 40 years of age than the 30 he claimed. Jim Bailey of the *Arkansas Gazette,* in a letter to *The Ring* magazine (August 1965), offered the following information:

"I can't shed any documented light on Liston's age, but we have clearly established that Liston was not born in Pine Bluff, Ark. In fact he has probably never even been to Pine Bluff. [His mother] said Sonny was born on January 18th 1932. She offered no proof except to say it was recorded in their family bible. But it is definite that Liston was born in St Francis County, about 17 miles from the town of Forrest City in eastern Arkansas, 100 miles or so from Pine Bluff.

"There is no record of Liston's birth. This is not unusual in Arkansas for poor Negro families, whose children are delivered by midwives and never properly recorded. His age? Like you, I suspect he is closer to 40 than 30."

Liston was certainly born into a very large family, the son of a cotton sharecropper and youngest but one of 25 children. He disliked his father intensely—"he didn't give a damn about any of us"—and described his mother as "a helpless woman". Raised in a cardboard-walled shack, Sonny received almost no formal education; his father kept him too busy in the fields picking cotton to leave much time for schooling. The extent of the Liston family's poverty can be appreciated by Sonny's claim that he didn't own a pair of shoes until he was ten years old. At 13, the young Liston stole a sack of pecans from a store and sold them for a rail ticket which enabled him to join his mother 400 miles away in the big city of St Louis. Here he rapidly slipped into the life of back-alley gangs and juvenile street crime. In 1950, with a string of minor larceny and assault convictions behind him, he finally collected a five-year jail sentence for his part in the robbery of a place called the Unique Cafe.

OPPOSITE: Cassius the Challenger. "He's too ugly to be the World Champion. The world's champ should be pretty like me."

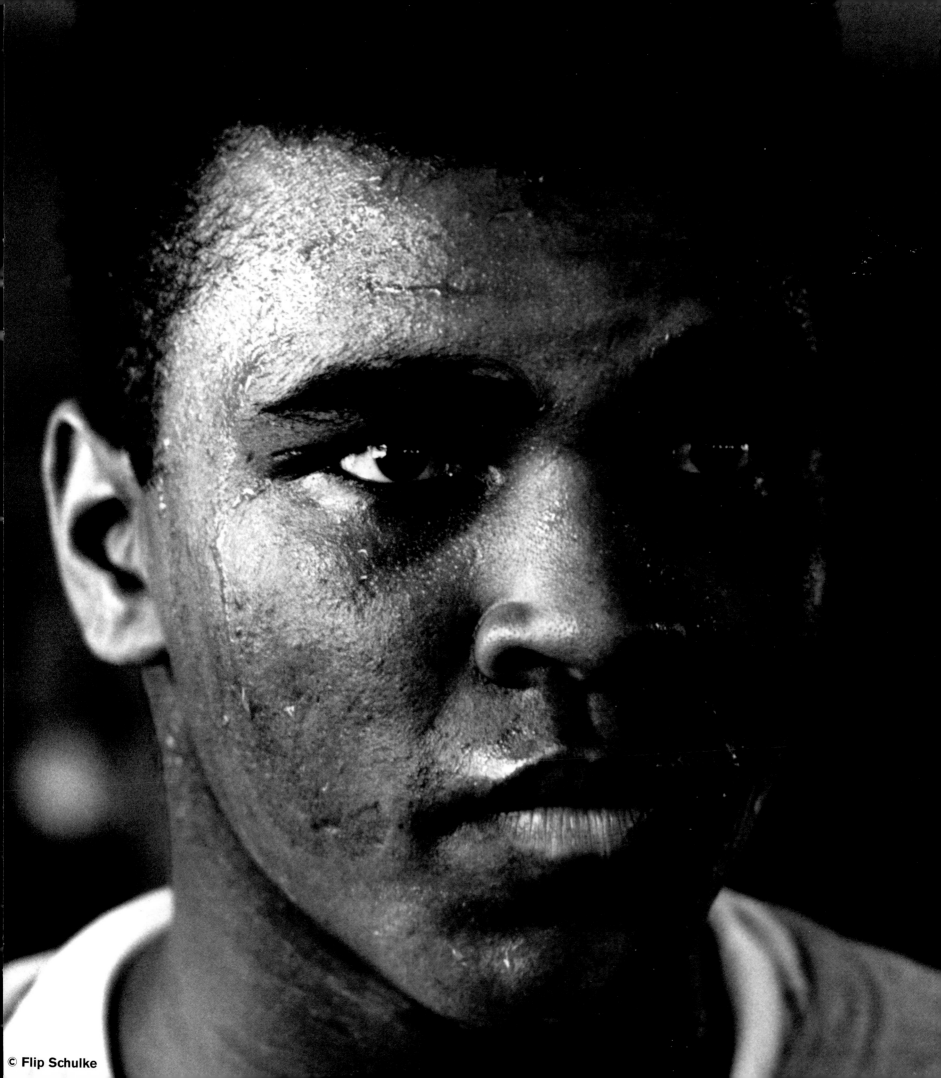

OPPOSITE: Cassius, aided by Angelo Dundee and Bundini, prepares his mental assault on the Champion. He tells the assembled reporters that as a first step he and 30 high school students will picket Liston's training camp. Recalls Ali: "People ask me now, did I think out what I said and did ahead of time or did it just come to me? Some things I thought out, but most of the time, it just came to me. I guess it's like people say; you have to be a little crazy to be a fighter."

While serving his time in the Missouri State Penitentiary, Jefferson City, Sonny was encouraged to take up boxing by a Roman Catholic chaplain, Father Stevens. From his release in 1952 (with only a short break of nine months in 1957 while serving a second sentence for breaking parole), Liston steadily climbed the ranks of professional boxing, often eliminating his opponents in the very early rounds by a knockout. One by one the top ranking heavyweights crashed beneath Liston's bulldozing tactics and massive fists. Cleveland Williams, Mike DeJohn, Willie Besmanoff, Howard King, Zora Folley, Eddie Machen all fell within the distance.

Floyd Patterson, then reigning champion, stalled furiously against meeting Liston, preferring to play out his hand with Ingemar Johansson. But the day of reckoning could not be postponed forever. Floyd bleated publicly that Liston's criminal record weighed against him and there were many who agreed that Sonny's reputation left much to be desired. Liston was "an undesirable contender", ranted one Southern senator; "a detriment to boxing", chorused several newspaper sportswriters. The NAACP (National Association for the Advancement of Colored People) urged a smug, flag-waving Patterson to reject Liston's justified demands for a championship fight. Should he become champion, they argued, "Mr Liston would offer little in the way of an example to the youth of America." Even President Kennedy, whom Floyd met during a sociological mission to the White House, asked anxiously whether Patterson was seriously considering fighting Liston.

Sonny never forgot these pre-championship slurs. The political and cultural ramifications of world sports escaped him entirely, but he understood that certain "big-shots" were apparently conspiring to thwart his one chance in life of making big money. His contempt for organizations like the NAACP came curiously to parallel that of Muhammad Ali, although from different and more personal motives.

Disowned by the leaders and spokesmen of his own race, it is easy to understand Liston's callous dismissal (in an interview shortly after his championship victory) of the "traitors and bums we see on TV every day. All them student protestors and civil rights demonstrators are just a bunch of Communists. They could be run over by a truck for all I care. The NAACP never helped me. Nobody ever helped me. All my life, ever since I was born, I been fighting to earn a crust. Nobody gave a damn if I lived or died."

Liston's ill-concealed bitterness, coupled with his intimidating appearance and sad inability to articulate life's frustrations, earned him an awesome and perhaps unjustified reputation as a dangerous, sullen individual. Even his boxing ability and determination in the ring reinforced a prejudiced public image of Sonny Liston as "the meanest man in boxing". Newspaper commentators describing his fights delighted in the use of morbid adjectives: "murderous punches", "savagery and brutality", "vicious, maiming tactics" were all permutated with monotonous regularity. Where Rocky Marciano was "a classic puncher", Liston was "the heartless monster". Where Joe Louis was a "legendary knockout artist", Sonny Liston was "a ferocious killer" and so on. This media cliché of the simple-minded brute and only partially reformed gangster whose sole purpose in life revolved around inflicting injury or worse to his opponents bedevilled Liston throughout his career. It also offered Cassius Clay a tailor-made opportunity to indulge in his preoccupation with mind games and psychological warfare.

RIGHT: Cassius issues dire threats to a picture of Liston:

If you want to lose your money,
Then bet on Sonny.
He knows I'm great.
He went to school; he's no fool.

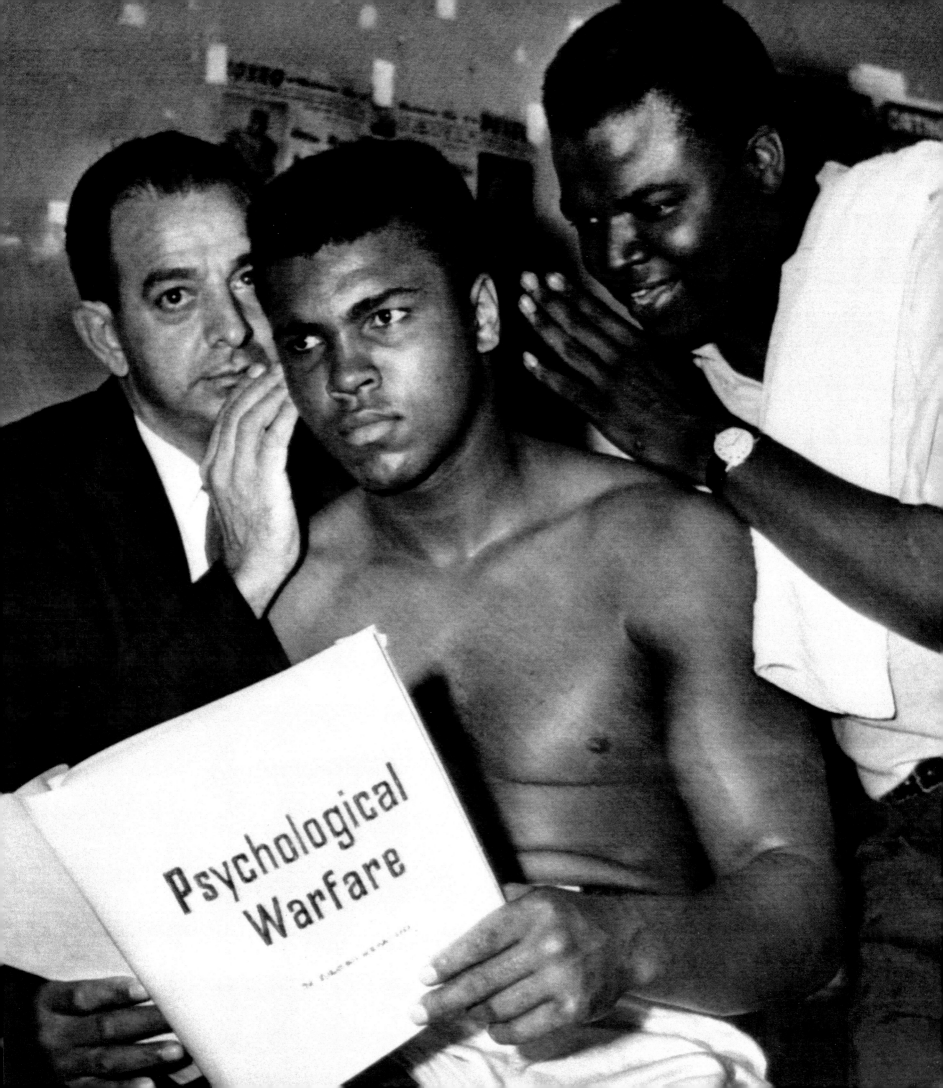

Clay understood perfectly well that Liston was by no means infallible, though there were few enough "experts" who would have agreed with him. Cassius also held a high regard for Sonny's punching power, though he understandably kept this opinion to himself prior to their fight. "Ain't nobody ever heard me say Liston couldn't punch," he told Associated Press years later. "Sonny could've banged a hole in Fort Knox if he wanted. I said he was dumb, I said he was ugly and couldn't dance, but I never said he couldn't punch."

The negotiations that preceded the Liston vs. Clay fight were prolonged and intricate. Both sides argued from positions of strength. Liston was the champion and champions traditionally hold the whip hand in their choice of contender, but Cassius was no ordinary contender. Sonny knew that he stood to make more money meeting Clay than he could hope to earn fighting any three alternative challengers. The potential audience for the fight would undoubtedly break all previous records with closed-circuit and satellite TV beaming it around the globe. Almost before negotiations had begun, international promoters began scrambling for a slice of this multi-million-dollar gate, but in August of 1963 Cassius appeared on television in Louisville to announce that unless Liston's management were prepared to offer better terms they could count him out.

"I worked for this fight," Cassius said bluntly. "I have worked harder than anyone for it. I have talked too much and worked too hard to take a low cut. I built this fight up and I will tear it down. There will be no fight between Liston and me until the money is right. Nobody wants to see Sonny Liston. They all want to see me! I am the talk of the world. I am known as the predictor. I am the prettiest and wittiest boxer in the whole wide world and if I have to take a low cut I would rather not fight. Let me lay it on the line. Liston either meets my price or he can dance elsewhere for peanuts."

This was tough talk and it outraged many of boxing's more conservative commentators, particularly as the majority of them considered the match a farce and Clay's chances of victory negligible. Still, Clay was obviously serious and Bill Faversham backed him to the hilt. "If the money is not right," Faversham warned, "my boy will not fight. He is still young, getting stronger and better. We can wait. Liston won't be there for ever." Later, Faversham recalled that he was secretly relieved over the delay. "I wasn't convinced that Cassius was ready," he confessed to us. "At first it didn't look like Liston's people were prepared to make a realistic offer and to tell you the truth that didn't bother me at all. I felt that Cassius could do with at least another year's experience before he fought Liston."

While the lawyers, managers and promoters haggled furiously over terms, Clay was busy stepping up his campaign of harassment against the champion. Partly, of course, this was to keep the iron hot, raising controversy over the prospect of a fight and consequently upping the ante in the cigar-strewn back rooms where businessmen calculated fractional percentages against potential profits. The advantages of this strategy in the early stages were apparent even to Liston, who obligingly retaliated with all the right noises, threatening to "murder that little faggot" and "shut 'The Lip's' big mouth for good." All this was as it should be. There was nothing new about "needle matches". But

ABOVE: Cassius and entourage (including Howard Bingham far left) stage a 3am invasion of Liston's lawn in his all-white Denver suburb. Liston was not amused: "What you want, black mother?" he hisses through the door before the police arrived.

as the fight drew closer and Clay's vendetta against "that ugly bear" grew wilder and ever more abusive, only a very few close friends of Cassius clung secretly to the belief that the kid was still playing to the gallery. To the majority of observers, Clay's behavior smacked more of fearful hysteria than smart showmanship.

As the leading challenger and officially ranked number one contender for the world title, Clay was fiercely determined to preserve his seniority in the queue. With the Cooper fight behind him he scornfully dismissed any suggestion of a pre-Liston shoot-out against other ranked heavyweights. There simply wasn't any percentage in it. "I don't want to fight no one else," he declared. There are a lot of 'em crawling out of the woodwork trying to steal a little limelight, but I don't see the use tangling with these lower entries. That rabbit Patterson? Johansson? Don't make me laugh. Sure, I can beat 'em all. But why take chances? I could get cut or something and miss out on the big money with the bear."

With no immediate prospects for a bout in sight, Cassius found himself professionally idle for the first time in years. Naturally he kept in shape—Angelo Dundee saw to that—but mostly he would amuse himself in schemes designed to irritate and provoke the world heavyweight champion. In an interview with *Playboy* Cassius recalled that time:

"I had been studying Liston careful, all along, ever since he had come up in the ratings… His fighting style, his strength, his punch. But that was just a part of what I was looking at. Any fighter will study them things about somebody he wants to fight. The big thing for me was to observe how Liston acted out of the ring. I read everything I could where he had been interviewed. I talked with people who had been around him or had talked with him. I would lay in bed and put all of the things together and think about them, and try to get a picture of how his mind worked."

Boxing commentators and sportswriters are obsessed with the physical aspects of the game, "the tales of the tape" as they call them. The measurement of a man's fist, of his reach, of his chest expansion and weight are religiously recorded and exhaustively debated in boxing literature the world over. But to Muhammad Ali, probably the fastest

OPPOSITE: A stony-faced Sonny Liston receives his medical check from Dr. Robbins as the hysterical Clay screams abuse behind him: "I'm ready to rumble now! I can beat you anytime, chump! Somebody's gonna die at ringside tonight! You're scared, chump! You ain't no giant! I'm gonna eat you alive!"

heavyweight of all time, this data has never held any special significance. He has always preferred to concentrate on the behavior patterns of his opponents, rooting for their psychological jugulars much as another boxer might train to meet a southpaw or a right hooker. This isn't to say that Ali neglected to inform himself of his opponent's stylistic characteristics—in fact he has one of the largest private collections of old fight films in existence—but his recognition of the value of psychoanalysis sets him apart.

By dispensing with the traditional attitudes of objective professionalism ingrained in every boxer from his first amateur fight and substituting a violently personal approach, Clay cleverly shifted each psychological confrontation with Sonny Liston onto a territory of his own choosing. Floyd Patterson had lost both his fights with Liston before a single punch had been thrown; the newspaper headline that he "Froze with Fear and Fell to the Floor" had, for once, been literally true. Cassius recognised this and simply extended the principle. He could hardly hope to "freeze" Sonny, but he could bewilder him and wreak havoc on the champion's nerves. Ali's admirers today would claim this strategy to be part and parcel of modern gamesmanship. But in the early 1960s its audacity represented a deliberate avoidance of the spirit, if not the letter, of decent sportsmanship. Ali's clowning and preposterous behavior served a fundamental purpose beyond that of selling tickets. It created tension in unwary opponents, unsure of Ali's real motives, unused to public displays of exhibitionism and uncertain of how to respond.

For all his ranting, it's doubtful whether Ali has ever really "hated" a single one of his adversaries (with the possible exception, on religious grounds, of Patterson and Terrell). But little harm was done if he could trick those facing him in the ring into believing that he hated them. With hindsight one almost feels a kind of pity for the dull-witted Liston as Cassius Clay baited him into the arena of confusion and humiliation.

Liston's return bout with Floyd Patterson in Las Vegas marked Clay's opening shots in this campaign of dirty tricks. Unannounced, and certainly uninvited, Cassius presented himself at Sonny's training camp, an abandoned, windswept racetrack outside the city confines. Jeering at the champion as he sparred in the ring for reporters and photographers, Clay's torrent of abuse startled even his own companions.

"You're a sucker, chump," he shouted. "Look at you, fat, ugly, oh so slow, slow, slow. Why, chump, I betcha you scare yourself to death just starin' in the mirror. You ugly bear! You ain't never fought nobody but tramps and has beens. You call yourself a world champion? You're too old and slow to be champion!"

Visibly shaken but determined to keep his cool, Sonny turned his back and concentrated on demolishing a fresh sparring partner. But Clay would not be denied, taunting him mercilessly and running on all fours screaming "Lookit the bear run! Lookit the bear run!" Eventually, Sonny's patience snapped and, fixing Cassius with his renowned glare, he made as if to leap from the ring. Clay prepared to defend himself and as the tension escalated only the intervention of managers and trainers avoided an unpleasant scene. It all made great copy for the assembled journalists but more importantly it confirmed Clay's suspicions that Sonny Liston would prove easy meat in the war of nerves to come.

Some time after the training camp excursion, Cassius tracked down Sonny to a casino where the champion regularly gambled. Surrounded by his usual entourage of admirers, Clay strolled casually over to the table at which Liston was engrossed shooting craps.

Walking up behind him, Cassius reached forward and snatched away a few chips. Startled, Sonny whirled around. "Man," laughed Cassius, "you sure can shoot dice, that was the fastest I ever seen you move!" Grinning good-humoredly, Sonny turned back to continue playing. A Vegas casino just wasn't the place for temper tantrums. Gambling was a serious business. Reaching out again, Clay seized the champion's dice as they fell from Liston's hands. Controlling his anger, Sonny retrieved the dice and attempted to resume his game. A large crowd had gathered around both men, drawn by the babble of Clay's wise-cracking and smart remarks.

"You're crazy, kid," murmured Liston. "What you tryin' to do?" "Just this," laughed Clay, whipping out a loaded water pistol and squirting its contents at Liston's head. The crowd fell ominously silent. Liston had stopped smiling. He looked hard at Clay with his evil eye and nodded to a vacant corner of the room. "Let's go on over here," he said quietly. "Just you and me."

Recounting his private conversation with Liston later in *Playboy*, Cassius admitted that perhaps he had overplayed his hand. "I ain't gonna lie," he confessed, "this was the first time since I have known Sonny Liston that he scared me. I just felt the power and the meanness of the man I was messing with. Anybody tell me about how he fought cops and beat up tough thugs and all of that, I believe it. I saw that streak in him. He told me, 'Get the hell out of here or I'll wipe you out.' I got the hell out of there…he had really scared me."

But nothing could keep "The Lip" down for long. Seconds after Patterson's crushing defeat, Cassius forced his way through the mass of spectators at the foot of the ring. "This fight was a fake!" he bellowed into the microphones of the world's press. "This fight was a fake and the promoters should apologize for it!" Sonny Liston loomed over the ropes, justifiably incensed at this abuse in his moment of victory. "You!" he growled furiously. "You watch your step. You're next, big mouth!"

These were words to gladden Cassius Clay's heart. Some hours later he gate-crashed Sonny's celebration party to announce for the benefit of incredulous guests: "My brother Rudolph could have beat Floyd Patterson tonight. Who does this Liston think he is? He ain't foolin' me!" Only the imminent approach of a wrathful host curtailed this harangue as friends discreetly hustled Cassius to the nearest exit.

Not content with publicly ridiculing Liston to his face and through the media, Clay occasionally indulged in harassment of a more personal nature. "I had bought this used 30-seater bus," he recalled in *Playboy*, "and we had painted it red, white and blue with THE WORLD'S MOST COLORFUL FIGHTER across the top. Then I had LISTON MUST GO IN EIGHT painted across the side. Anyway, this time me and a few buddies started out for New York [from Los Angeles] and we decided it would be a good time to pay Liston a visit at his new house."

At approximately three o'clock the next morning, headlights blazing and with Cassius pumping on the horn, Clay's bus lurched to a halt outside the Liston residence in Denver, Colorado. "We got the address from the newspapers," Ali remembered. Like a laughing man at a funeral, their arrival shattered the deathly suburban quiet. Lights flickered in upstairs windows. Tired faces peeped from behind closed shutters. "You know how them white people felt about that black man just moved in there anyway," snickered Cassius afterwards, "and we sure wasn't helping it none."

ABOVE: Challenger and Champ deliver their predictions. Cassius says eight: "I predict he will go in eight to prove that I am great; and if he wants to go to heaven, I'll get him in seven." Sonny says two: "My only worry is how I'll get my fist outta his big mouth once I get him in the ring. It's gonna go so far down his throat, it'll take a week for me to pull it out again."

OPPOSITE: "He's ugly, I'm pretty. It's just impossible for him to beat me."

Clay sent one of his companions, the photographer Howard Bingham, on ahead to ring the world champion's doorbell. A disgruntled Liston finally appeared, still rubbing sleep from his eyes and dressed only in a pair of nylon shorty pyjamas. Recognising Bingham, Sonny became instantly suspicious. "What you want, black mother?" he muttered, peeping through the darkness at the illuminated coach parked in front of his drive.

"I was standing right behind Howard," Clay told *Playboy* later, "flinging my cane back and forth in the headlights, hollering loud enough for everybody in a mile to hear me. 'Come on out of there! I'm gonna whip you right now! Come on out of there and protect your home! If you don't come out of that door I'm going to break it down!' Man, he was tore up. He didn't know what to do. He wanted to come out there after me, but he was already in enough trouble with the police and everything. But before he could make up his mind, the police came rushing in with all their sirens going, and they broke it up, telling us we would be arrested for disturbing the peace if we didn't get out of there. So we left. You can bet we laughed all the way to New York."

In another version of the same incident, Clay claimed that he had actually been wrestling with Liston on the lawn when the police arrived. "Liston had to believe that I was crazy," he explained. "That I was capable of doing anything. He couldn't see nothing to me at all but mouth and that's all I wanted him to see!"

By late October of 1963, satisfactory terms between the Louisville Sponsoring Group and Jack Nilon for Sonny Liston had been agreed. Gordon Davidson, the Group's acting attorney, was principally responsible for the fine print and gross percentage of Clay's contractual earnings. By his (privately held) admission, Davidson lacked confidence in his client's ability to deliver the goods against Liston.

"I felt he was going to have a very tough time with Liston," Davidson told us. " When we negotiated the Liston fight we negotiated it on the basis it was going to be Clay's last fight or last big-time fight. I thought that he was going to get demolished, which succeeded in negotiating Cassius more money than any challenger up to that time had ever gotten, 22 per cent of the gross takings. Normally a challenger could only expect 10 per cent or 15 per cent at maximum. I think we cleared something in the order of $1,000,000 or $900,000, plus expenses, money up-front and all the trimmings."

On November 5th, both fighters attended a formal contract signing ceremony in Denver's Brown Palace Hotel. The press were out in force to witness Clay and Liston scrawl their signatures on this historic document and Cassius had no intention of disappointing them. Leaping from his seat he shouted, "Let the annihilation begin! I'm not afraid of this chump! Sonny here is an old man and I'll give him talking lessons and boxing lessons. What he needs most is falling down lessons."

The venue for the fight presented some difficulties. Certain state authorities had made it abundantly plain that Liston would not be granted a licence to box under any circumstances. Their attitude reflected growing concern surrounding newspaper and congressional allegations of Mafia and mob involvement in the upper league of boxing. Liston's previous history of convictions and careless choice of management hardly helped matters. In addition, there had been a revival of campaigns to ban boxing altogether in the United States following the deaths of Alejandro Lavorante, featherweight champion Davey Moore, and welterweight champion Benny "Kid" Paret from injuries sustained in the ring. After con-

sidering offers from promoters in Minneapolis, Chicago, Los Angeles, and Las Vegas, both parties finally settled in December on a surprise choice—Miami. Cassius would be fighting on home territory.

Sonny Liston's arrival at Miami Airport offered a golden opportunity for Clay. "They were making such a big thing of his arriving," he remembers, "you would have thought the Cubans was coming. Well, I wasn't about to miss that!" Liston had hardly stepped off the plane before Cassius was shoving his way through the crowd of journalists and photographers hollering, "Chump! Big ugly bear! I'm going to whip you right now!" Slipping through a police cordon Cassius came face-to-face with the champion.

"Look," warned Liston, "this clowning, it's not so cute no more and I'm not joking!" Clay feigned wild indignation, "Joking? Who's joking?" he raged. "Why, you big chump, I'll whip you right now."

Airport officials bundled Sonny together with his wife and bodyguard into an electric cart. Cassius raced on foot behind them, brandishing his cane and threatening vengeance. In the tunnel leading to the VIP lounge Sonny ordered the driver to stop the cart. Furiously he stalked towards the approaching Clay. "Listen, you little punk," he roared. "I'll punch you in the mouth, this has gone too far!"

Pressmen and airport police raced towards the scene as Cassius threw off his coat. "Come on, chump," he sneered. "I'm ready for you. I'm right here!" Goaded beyond reason Liston threw a wild punch at Clay's bobbing head. "He missed me by a country mile," the challenger gloated later. By this time Liston's management and bodyguards had arrived. Once again the entourage resumed its journey to the lounge. Cassius caught up with them some minutes later, a conga line of panting journalists and furiously clicking photographers behind him. The doors had been securely locked. Banging on the glass with his cane Clay began shouting and gesticulating at the champion inside. "Free! Free! I'll fight you free!" he screamed. Pressing his nose and mouth against the windows for the benefit of photographers on the other side, Cassius hollered the same battlecry over and over again, "Free! Free! You think I'm jiving, punk! I'll fight you free!" Safe at last from this raving maniac Sonny sipped thoughtfully on a Coke. "If they ever let me in the ring with him," he ruminated, "I'm liable to get put away for murder."

Clay's ridiculous but highly effective performance brought uniform condemnation from the press and elsewhere. As the fight drew closer, politicians, sportswriters, and boxing celebrities all expressed their profound doubts as to whether the match should be sanctioned at all.

Rocky Marciano: "Clay is horribly short of experience to be going against a brute like Liston. 'The Lip' should either see a good psychiatrist or a good taxman."

Billy Conn: "Liston will knock him out. Knock him senseless. Liston just needs to hit him. The first shot Liston hits him he's a goner."

Joe Louis: "He [Clay] has got to be joking. I wouldn't give one nickel for his chances."

Jackie Gleason (the comedian): "Clay should last about 18 seconds and that includes the three seconds he brings into the ring with him."

Sol Silverman (the attorney appointed by the governor of California to head a committee investigating boxing): "The proposed Cassius Clay vs. Sonny Liston heavyweight title fight is a dangerous mismatch which could result in grave injury to the young challenger. Such mismatches not only endanger the over-matched boxer, but degrade boxing from a great sport to a sordid racket."

ABOVE: "Man, I'm glad I don't have to pay to see this fight," quips Clay outside the box office. Not many do. A combination of high prices, rumors of Clay's flirtation with the dreaded Black Muslims and the certainty that Cassius will not make it past the first round, combine to keep sales sluggish. On the night there are 8,297 paying ticket holders in an auditorium that seats 15,744. Promoter Bill MacDonald loses $363,000.

OPPOSITE: Before the title bout the contender visits his parents in Louisville and is reassured that, no matter what the rest of America may think, he is still the hometown hero.

On and on droned sportswriters and journalists—"Clay is strutting to his inevitable downfall…" "Stop this suicide fight…" "Clay won't last through the national anthem…" Clay's answer was to turn the screw a little harder. He issued special jackets at his camp with the words "Bear Hunting" emblazoned across the back. Rumors filtered through to Liston that Cassius was planning on picketing his training headquarters at the classy Surfside Community Center. Sure enough, Clay finally showed up in his bus crammed to capacity with screaming teenage girls and other supporters. Plastered all over the bus were signs reading "Big Ugly Bear", "Bear Hunting Season", "Too Pretty to be a Fighter" and "Bear Must Fall in Eight".

"That's the day that Liston lost," Cassius asserted in an interview afterwards. "We heard that he went to pieces. He nearly had a fit. He got so jumpy and under strain that every day different reporters would come telling me, serious, 'Stop angering that man—he will literally kill you!' It was music to my ears. It meant that if he was mad he had lost all sense of reasoning. If he wasn't thinking nothing but killing me, he wasn't thinking fighting. And you got to think to fight."

On the morning of the big day, Clay arrived with his full entourage for the weigh-in at the Cyprus Room in Convention Hall. Flanked by Bundini and Sugar Ray Robinson, Cassius made a dramatic entrance, startling even those seasoned journalists who had come to expect his mouthing off at such occasions as a matter of course. Striding through the crowd, his eyes raking a sea of faces as if in search of his arch enemy, Clay began to shout, "You can tell Sonny Liston I'm here with Sugar Ray! We're coming to rumble! Where is that ugly bear? Round eight, to prove I'm great!"

Security men moved quickly to prevent Bundini and Sugar Ray from accompanying Cassius onto the platform where the scales were located. "You better let me up," warned Bundini. "I'm the only one who can keep him quiet." The guards anxiously waved all three up the steps.

Float like a butterfly, sting like a bee,
Your hands can't hit what your eyes can't see…

Through verse after verse Bundini and Cassius chanted their voodoo challenge, Clay pounding on the stage floor with his cane, his gaze riveted on the door through which Sonny Liston would enter the hall.

Liston's arrival was greeted with respectful, enthusiastic applause from the press. It was also the signal for Clay to go absolutely berserk. Yelling at the top of his voice, his eyes bulging, arms jerking wildly in the air, Cassius had to be restrained by Sugar Ray and Bundini from rushing the champion. Throughout the weigh-in procedure Clay persisted in the manic behavior, even during the routine physical examination, which revealed that his normal pulse rate of 54 beats per minute had risen alarmingly to 120 and even higher.

Dressed only in trunks and robe, Clay's body seemed to be visibly trembling. His voice was shrill and hoarse from shouting. "You're a chump!" he screamed at Liston. "A sucker and a chump! I'm gonna whip you so baaaad! You ugly bear! Chump, chump, chump! It's prophesied for me to win! I cannot be beaten!"

The Miami Boxing Commissioner, Morris Klein, stepped forward to the microphone: "Cassius Clay is fined $2,500 for his behavior on the platform and the money will be withheld from Clay's purse". But there were many present who felt that a fine was hardly the appropriate

solution. "The fight should be called off," seemed to be the general consensus of opinion among the reporters. "This hysterical kid is in no condition to face a killer like Liston."

Dr. Alexander Robbins, the Commission's physician, added weight to this view. "Clay is very nervous and scared to death," he told nodding journalists. "He is burning a lot of energy."

The afternoon papers were emphatic and unanimous: "Clay Scared To Death says Doc", "Hysterical Outburst From Young Challenger", "Temper Tantrums at Weigh-in" they trumpeted. Sonny Liston summed it all up in a snap response as he left the hall. "You know, fellas," he said to a group of newsmen, "I don't think the kid's all there. I think he's scrambled in his marbles."

But there was one "expert" who stood firm for Clay. A man whose efforts had done as much as anyone to put Cassius in the ring in the first place. Joe Martin, the Louisville patrolman, predicted an easy victory for his former pupil: "If I could order a fighter from Sears Roebuck for Clay, I would order one with the boxing style of Sonny Liston. It's made to order for Cassius. I don't believe Liston could ever beat Clay. Clay can run faster backwards than Liston can forwards. It's as simple as that." Needless to say, Martin's opinion went largely unheeded.

Bill Faversham's memories of that official ceremony were still remarkably clear 12 years after the event: "I remember struggling with Angelo [Dundee] to haul Cassius out of there. My shirt was soaked with sweat and my nerves were gone too. Cass had seemed deadly serious and I was pretty worried."

Faversham had much to be worried about. Bill MacDonald, the Miami fight promoter, had already expressed severe dissatisfaction with the sluggish ticket sales. Although the fight had received massive international publicity, the odds were now stacked so heavily in favor of Liston that many fans thought it barely worth purchasing a seat for what promised to be a first round knockout, especially as MacDonald had scaled his prices higher than any fight in boxing history. They ranged from a minimum $20 to an unbelievable $250 per seat. These two factors had both contributed to disappointing gate receipts and on top of all this, the first reports of Clay's association with the Black Muslim sect had begun circulating in the press.

Clay's lunacy, feigned or otherwise, at the weigh-in could hardly have improved the situation and Faversham was concerned that MacDonald might grasp at the first straw of an excuse to protect his half-million-dollar investment by cancelling the fight. His fears were fully justified. Sitting in his hotel restaurant, recovering from the morning's ordeal, Faversham was approached by a boxing writer.

"Hey, Mr. Faversham, have you heard the news?" he asked excitedly. "There's talk that the Commission thinks Cassius is too scared to fight Liston. The fight might be off!" The Louisville Group's manager raced for a telephone and ordered their personal physician, Ferdie Pacheco, to get on over to Clay's motel and run an immediate check on his condition. "We found Cassius lying on the floor, surrounded by neighborhood children, watching TV as calm as you please," Faversham recalls. Dr. Pacheco tested Clay's pulse rate and found it to be absolutely normal. "A case of self-induced hysteria," the doctor diagnosed. A heartily relieved Faversham rang both the promoters and the Miami Boxing authorities with the news. The fight was on.

OPPOSITE: As the two contestants are called into the center of the ring, Clay's eyes lock with Liston's. "Chump," he breathes softly. "Now I've got you, chump." Angelo Dundee: "See, Liston wasn't tall. Liston looked tall. Muhammad was taller. So I gave Muhammad that thing about, when you get in the middle of the ring, stand tall. Look down, because the guy's shorter than you are. He looked down at the guy and said, 'Gotcha, sucker!' And that was it. He really meant it."

RIGHT: An exhilarated Clay at the end of the sixth: "I got back to my stool and under me I could hear the press like they were gone wild. I twisted round and hollered down at the reporters, 'I'm gonna upset the world!'"

FOLLOWING PAGES:
(Left) Cassius gets air before Michael Jordan is even born: The floating Butterfly leaves the Bear flat-footed.
(Right) "I remember thinking something like, 'You old sucker. You try to be so big and bad!' He was gone."

ebruary 25, 1964, the most important night of Cassius Clay's life. The Miami Convention Hall was only half full with close to 8,000 seats unoccupied, but scattered across the continents of America and Europe more than three-quarters of a million fight fans were tuned in via closed circuit or satellite transmission. Out of the 46 sports writers clustered around the ring, 43 had picked Sonny Liston to win by a knockout. The betting odds against Clay stood at 8-1 officially, though it would have been difficult to find a bookie rash enough to accept money on the champion.

Liston appeared to have almost every advantage. He outreached Clay by a clear four inches. His punching power was legendary—"right hand destruction, left hand death," as one of his former managers had put it. True, he was somewhat older then Clay, though by how much was anyone's guess. But heavyweights mature late and Sonny's annihilation of Patterson the previous year had convinced most experts that he was at the peak of his career. Liston had the weight (218 pounds to Clay's 210 pounds); the experience (36 professional fights to Clay's 19) and, most importantly of all, the knockout punch.

There couldn't have been half a dozen spectators in the hall who would have laid a penny for the challenger's chances as he trotted down the aisle from his dressing room at precisely 10pm. Slashed across the shoulders of his thigh-length terrycloth robe were two words—"The Lip." Already aware that, win or lose, this fight would mark the effective end of his name "Cassius Clay", the young Kentuckian preferred to compromise with a pseudonym.

Sonny Liston followed Clay into the ring, hardly acknowledging the deafening roar of applause, the hood of his long gown pulled up over his head, half a dozen rolled towels bolstering his already massive frame. Cassius concentrated on shadow boxing in the opposite corner, relaxed and seemingly oblivious to Liston's intimidating stare. As the two contestants were called into the center of the ring, Clay's eyes finally locked with Liston's. "Chump," he breathed softly. "Now I've got you, chump!"

At the sound of the first-round bell, fans leaned forward expectantly, craning their necks to watch that lethal left hook of Liston's collide with Clay's jaw. Sonny came out almost on the run, a shambling mountain of a man whose face told the whole story. Months of Clay's needling had taken their toll; now he sought sweet revenge. Shuffling forward determinedly, he lashed out with a couple of lefts. Clay moved quickly, circling out of range to his left as he had planned with Angelo Dundee, hands held low, easily outpacing the champion's wild swings.

"Man, he meant to kill me," Cassius acknowledged later. "I ain't kidding! He was jabbing with his left but missing. And I was backpedalling, bobbing, weaving, ducking. He missed me with a right hook that would have hurt me. I just kept running, watching his eyes. Liston's eyes tip you when he's about to throw a heavy punch."

Liston pressed forward relentlessly, maneuvering to force Clay against the ropes or into a corner. Once or twice he caught the kid with blows to the body, but somehow Clay's head always seemed out of range. Towards the end of the round the worm turned. Ramming a straight left jab into the champion's face, Cassius followed it with a flur-

ABOVE: The sixth—" I hit him eight straight punches in a row…" (OPPOSITE:) "…until he doubled up."

PRECEDING PAGES: Liston grimaces as Clay shakes him with a left in the sixth. Angelo Dundee: "I don't know how old Liston was, but then, all of a sudden, all the aches and pains came in. Maybe age caught up with him. I think he thought, 'What am I doing here?'"

ry of lefts and rights. The crowd gasped. Liston snorted in anger and plunged forward to repay this impudence but the young challenger had already back-pedalled away as the bell signalled the close of round one.

"I remember I got back to my corner thinking, 'He was supposed to kill me. Well, I'm still alive! Angelo Dundee was working me over, talking a mile a minute. I just watched Liston; so mad he didn't even sit down. I thought to myself, 'You gonna wish you had rested all you could when you get past this next round! I could hear some radio or television expert all excited…the big news was I hadn't been counted out yet."

The World Champion came out of his corner in the second round throwing leather right, left, and center. Storming Clay into the ropes he began punching to the body, seeking to weaken his opponent at close quarters. This was the moment the experts had all predicted Clay would crack. Nobody disputed "The Lip's" talent in long-range jabbing, but nothing could stand against Liston when he handed out those punishing body blows. Cassius slipped and ducked, weaving his way out of disaster and back into open canvas. He picked at Liston, snapping jabs at the older man's head, moving constantly to his left, stopping only to pile up points with hit and run combinations.

A small cut had opened over Liston's cheekbone, just beneath the left eye. Reaching for that target, Cassius almost threw away his chances as the champion caught him with his hardest punch of the fight, a long arching left to the side of the jaw. "It rocked me back," Clay admitted afterwards. "But either he didn't realize how good I was hit or he was already getting tired, and he didn't press his chance."

Cassius had planned to coast round three, reserving his energy for a counter-attack after Liston had burnt himself out, but the nick under Sonny's eye offered too big a temptation. One good combination was all it needed, a left feint and a short right uppercut smacking into Liston's cheekbone. "I knew it was a deep gash," Clay told *Playboy's* Alex Haley, "the way the blood spurted right out. I saw his face close up when he wiped his glove at that cut and saw the blood. At that moment…he looked like he's going to look 20 years from now."

Round four was quieter, Cassius pacing himself in preparation for the long battle to come and Sonny slowing visibly, unused to the exertions of more than a couple of rounds. A fever of incredulity

began sweeping across the audience. It seemed impossible, unbelievable, that Clay was still on his feet. And for the first time in his career, the mighty Sonny Liston had been cut.

Clay walked back to his corner at the finish of round four shaking his head and screwing up his face. Somehow, caustic or acidic liniment from Liston's wound had found its way into his eyes, temporarily blinding him. "I can't see, Angelo!" he shouted. "I'm blind!" Dundee began swabbing at his face methodically, trying to calm him, urging him to sit down and rest. But the pain was agonizing and Cassius panicked. "I didn't care if it was a heavyweight title fight," he said months later, "I wasn't going out there and getting murdered because I couldn't see."

Holding out his gloves towards Bundini and Dundee, Clay begged them to stop the fight. "Cut them off," he yelled frantically. "Cut off my gloves. Angelo—get me out of here."

"What are you talking about?" his trainer yelled back. "This is the big one, daddy! This is for the title and we aren't going to quit now!"

The bell had already sounded for round five as Angelo shoved Cassius off the stool and slipped through the ropes. "Keep away from him, Cass," he screamed above the babble of confusion, "just keep away from him!" Barney Felix, the referee, waved Clay to box on. "Dammit, Clay, get out here," he commanded. Half blind and utterly confused, Cassius edged cautiously towards the lumbering form of Sonny Liston. "He was lucky," Felix told reporters after the fight. "If Clay hadn't moved in a split second—I mean one second—he'd have been finished. I would have been forced to disqualify him."

Back in Clay's corner, Dundee was under fire from a group of black fans. "This white man has put something in 'The Lip's' eyes!" they shrieked. "It's a conspiracy!" Angelo calmly picked up the sponge he had used on Cassius' face and swabbed his own eyes with it.

Sensing his chance, Liston attacked immediately, scoring with several punishing body shots and hooks to the face. Bundini screamed instructions to his man: "Watch out for that left! Move back, Cass, move back! Grab him, hold him!" Only Clay's astounding footwork and instinctive defense mechanisms saved him from the brunt of the champion's offensive. "Man, in that round, my plans were gone," he recalled. "I was just trying to keep alive, hoping the tears would wash out my eyes." Blinking furiously and with tears streaming down his cheeks, Clay somehow survived the nightmare of round five, staving off Liston's rushes with an almost permanently extended left jab.

Clay's blindness had been Sonny Liston's last real chance to score a knockout. Snorting and blowing, the champion plodded wearily back to his corner at the bell. Slumped on his stool, Liston looked suddenly older, the specter of defeat already branded across his features. In that last round, the "Dark Destroyer" had shot his bolt.

Clay's eyes were clearing as the bell rang for the sixth. This was the moment he had waited for. He had taken everything the bear could hit him with and now…"I knew I was going to make Liston look terrible." Clay beat Sonny Liston without mercy for three solid minutes in round six. "I hit him eight straight punches in a row, until he doubled up. I remember thinking something like, 'Yeah, you old sucker. You try to be so big and bad!' He was gone. He knew he couldn't last."

The hall was in pandemonium as young Cassius jolted and punished his opponent almost at will, hitting him with uppercuts and left-right combinations, splitting his eye wide open with a wicked series of jabs, his left glove drawn like a magnet to Liston's bleeding face.

OPPOSITE: Bundini, Dundee, and the new Heavyweight Champion of the World. "King!" he screams at the stunned audience. "I'm king! I'm the greatest! I've upset the world!" Dundee: "The scenes in the ring were just unbelievable. I got up in the ring and said, 'We can't win! We can't win!' [because] everybody was telling us we couldn't win." Cassius continues his diatribe into his dressing room where he berates the press for its lack of faith: "What are you gonna say now, huh? Never make me no underdog, and never talk about who's gonna stop me. Not a heavyweight in the world fast enough to stop me. Liston's one of the powerfulest in the world, and he looked like a baby." On a hospital stretcher, all Sonny can manage in reply is, "That's not the guy I was supposed to fight. That guy could punch!"

RIGHT: With Liston refusing to leave his stool for the beginning of the seventh, Clay is the first to realise he has won. "I just couldn't believe it when he spat out his mouthpiece. But there it was, lying there!"

"I got back to my stool," remembered Clay, "and under me I could hear the press like they were gone wild. I twisted round and hollered down at the reporters, 'I'm gonna upset the world!'"

Indeed he was, but even Cassius could not have expected how soon. As the warning ten-second buzzer sounded for round seven, he rose from his seat, waiting impatiently for the bell. Gazing across at Liston's corner, he watched in astonishment as a tired, beaten fighter spat out his protective gum shield on to the canvas. "I just couldn't believe it when he spat out his mouthpiece. I just couldn't believe it, but there it was, lying there!" Clay recalled. "And then something told me he just wasn't coming out!"

Leaping in the air, the first to realize that he was already champion, Clay literally danced for joy. "King!" he screamed at a bewildered audience. "I'm king! I'm the greatest!" A swelling roar of cheering and stunned applause filled the hall. Angelo Dundee jumped into the ring, hugging his fighter off the ground. Bundini Brown began crying with happiness. Hundreds of spectators and photographers crushed inside the ropes to congratulate the new World Champion. Cassius jeered at and taunted at the press: "Eat! Eat! Eat your words," he crowed. "I am the king! I am the king!" Talking about those ecstatic first moments later, Cassius said, "It's funny, but all I could think of was that hypocrite press and the lies that they had told."

Inside the dressing room his mother, father, and brother were waiting to greet him. Mrs. Clay was weeping openly. "Mom," laughed her eldest son, "didn't I tell you I was the greatest? I am the Heavyweight Champion of the world!" The following day, a team of specialists examined Liston's left shoulder. Jack Nilon, Sonny's manager, had claimed directly after the fight that he had ordered his fighter to quit following severe pains in his left arm: "He had no feeling in the tips of his fingers," Nilon explained. The doctors confirmed that Liston had suffered "a separation and tear of the muscle fibers with some hemorrhage into the muscle body." In plain language, he had torn the tendon of his left bicep. This muscle damage had swollen the circumference of Sonny's arm by almost four inches. The specialists agreed that such an injury must have caused Liston severe pain and seriously handicapped his punching ability.

Sonny himself was convinced that he had lost solely because of his shoulder condition. "When I threw a left hook in the first round," he told reporters, "the shoulder went out." By the fifth round he had been hard pressed to force a jab, let alone a knockout punch. His face bruised and swollen, eyes shielded by dark glasses and arm in a sling, Liston went on to make it clear that he had not been particularly impressed with Clay. "'The Lip' was as scared as a thief," he said. "He won't be staying champion for too long." Cassius, by comparison, was almost generous when he spoke about Sonny after the fight. "I'm sorry for Liston," he lectured newsmen. "You people put too much load on him. You built him up too big and now he has such a long way to fall."

It was a longer way than even Clay could have envisaged. Although Liston fought again with Muhammad Ali, his brief spell in the big time was already over. On December 30, 1970, Liston was found dead in his home of a drug overdose. Although he was probably well into his forties, he was still fighting, having beaten Chuck Wepner a few months prior to his death. It was ten days before anyone discovered his body.

A.K.A. Cassius Clay

"I have come to destroy the world."

Wallace D. Fard

OPPOSITE: Cassius Clay, championship belt across his shoulder, renounces his "slave name" and adopts his "waiting name"—Cassius X, later to become Muhammad Ali. "I don't have to be what you want me to be," he tells bemused reporters at a press conference following the Liston fight. "I am free to be what I want."

God first appeared in Detroit's Paradise Valley ghetto on July 4, 1930. He came in the guise of a humble silk peddler named Wallace D. Fard or W. D. Fard. Selling his silks door-to-door through Paradise Valley, the mystical Fard collected a small circle of followers who met secretly in squalid tenement basements, transfixed by stories of their glorious heritage lost long ago in "the East." Sometimes Fard would perform miracles: he conjured up in a glass of water the figure of a man praying; on another occasion he dipped a hair from his head in the glass and 10,000 other hairs sprouted from it.

One of this circle of believers was a slight Georgia sharecropper's son named Elijah—or possibly Robert—Poole, who had travelled north to the auto factories of Detroit during the great black exodus of the 1920s. "Poole, then in his middle thirties, was an inconspicuous sort," wrote biographer Peter Goldman in his book, *The Death and Life of Malcolm X*.

"Fragile as an eggshell and pale as beige, but his sleepy eyes and his faltering speech masked a keen native wit and a certain genius for the main chance."

Poole and the silk peddler were drawn together, and one day, according to Scripture, he asked, "Who are you and what is your real name?"

"I am the one the world has been expecting for the past 2,000 years," replied Fard.

"What is your name?" Poole asked once more.

"My name is Mahdi. I am God. I came to guide you into the right path that you may be successful and see the hereafter."

Fard claimed to be the latest—probably the last—in a succession of deities to visit the Earth in human form regularly at 25,000-year intervals. He remained four years in Paradise Valley, nurturing a flock of some 8,000 souls—the Lost-Found Nation of Islam, later to be disparaged by the press as "Black Muslims." As suddenly as he had arrived, Fard vanished to Mecca, say the faithful, where he awaited the end of the world. Before his departure, Mahdi appointed the young disciple his last messenger, exchanged his slave name—Poole—for an "Original Name"—Elijah Muhammad—and entrusted him in an exhaustive series of lectures with the keys to Divine Wisdom. These keys included a secret syllabus of 104 books, which members of the Nation believed had been suppressed by the Government. To the Lost-Found Nation of Islam this is the Gospel.

What Mr. Muhammad learned was the following: the God who created the universe 66 (or 72) trillion years ago was black, and the people he created and placed on earth were blacks. For most of these trillions of years a phenomenally advanced black civilization had flourished upon earth (and also Mars which is apparently inhabited by a race of "skinny" men seven to nine feet in height; under Fard's guidance Elijah was able to tune into these Martians). Allah was the God of this civilization and Mecca its Holy City. Its rulers were black scientists who were capable of raising up mountains and creating animals. They even made the moon by sinking explosives deep into the earth and blowing a third of its mass into orbit. Warfare was unknown on the planet; dissidents merely formed tribes and went their separate ways. A trillion years ago, said Fard, Earth was a black paradise.

As breathtaking as these tales of forgotten grandeur must have been to Elijah Muhammad, living amid the squalor of Paradise Valley, they were overshadowed by one story Fard called Yacub's History. Sixty-six hundred years ago, said Fard, when 70 per cent of the population was satisfied and the rest dissatisfied, an evil genius named Yacub was born. Nicknamed "the big-headed scientist", Yacub persisted

ABOVE: At a 1965 press conference, Ali holds up pictures of his spiritual leaders Wallace Fard and Elijah Muhammad. "The only thing I am afraid of is God and his messengers," he said.

OPPOSITE: Ali addresses a Black Muslim convention in Chicago in 1968. Elijah Muhammad sits behind him. "We go to church, look at pictures of Jesus Christ, and we see a white man. We look at the Last Supper and we see all white people. There are no Chinese at the Last Supper, no Indians, and no Sudanese, all white people. We look at Tarzan in the jungle of hot-ass Africa, and he's white. We look at the angels in heaven, all white angels, no black angels, no Mexican angels. I imagine they died and went to heaven too. When they took the pictures, I heard that all the black angels were in the kitchen preparing milk and honey!"

in preaching against the rulers of Mecca and was finally exiled along with 59,999 of his followers (all figures in Muslim Scripture are extremely precise) to the island of Patmos. Yacub swore revenge on Allah and set about creating a devil race of bleached-out white people. By slaughtering black babies and allowing only the lighter-skinned progeny of his followers to marry, Yacub eventually populated Patmos entirely with blonde, pale-skinned, cold-blue-eyed "devils".

"Mr. Fard taught Mr. Muhammad that this devil race was granted dominion over the world for 6,000 years down to our time," wrote Peter Goldman. "So depraved were the whites that their reign was late getting started; they were run out of the society of black people into the caves of Europe, where they lived on all fours—and where their women kissed and coupled with dogs—while the blacks were wearing silks and building pyramids and tracking stars. Their ascent to power was predestined, but they were too weak and too corrupt to come into it honestly. They achieved it instead by murder, rapine, robbery, sedition and 'tricknology'. Jesus himself was their victim. He was not the white Son of God but a black prophet, a Muslim actually named Isa, and he was stabbed to death, not crucified, by white Roman cops while preaching in front of 'the Jew's store'."

One scientist, Shabazz, foresaw 50,000 years before it happened that the black man was destined for slavery and he led his tribe to the jungles of Africa to toughen them for the coming ordeal. The heat turned their fine hair hard and kinky, but by the time a blue-eyed slave trader named John Hawkins arrived in his ship, *Jesus*, they were prepared. Hawkins and his contemporaries imprisoned the children of the Tribe of Shabazz and carried them in chains from Africa to America where they were brutalized and tricked into accepting the white man's language, culture, and religion. Four hundred years were to elapse before Allah would deliver them and destroy the white devils.

Judgement Day is foretold in *The History of the End of the World*. Twelve months before the End, America will be ravaged by natural disasters—earthquakes, blizzards, hurricanes, and hailstorms. With ten days left, a lone plane will drop leaflets instructing the faithful how they are to save themselves. War will break out in Asia, East and West Germany will resume battle, and two-thirds of the US Army will be destroyed. Tidal waves will drive the remaining population inland to meet their judgement. On the last day the Mother Ship—a man-made planet in the shape of a wheel half a mile across—will release 1,500 "baby wheels," each one carrying three two-ton bombs made of the same explosive which was used to raise mountains in the old days. The bombs will burrow a mile into the earth and the explosions will give off poison gas. The atmosphere will burn for 310 years, taking another 690 years to cool off. Nothing will ever live on the planet again. After this 1,000-year period, the children of the Original People will be led back to witness the destruction and purification.

All this was originally to have happened in 1914. The date was extended to allow Allah and his Last Messenger time to lead the chosen to a land of their own. Muhammad Ali later talked of sometime before the year 2000. Already the Mother Ship was visible in the sky twice a week. It was this wheel which allegedly caused the 1929 stock market crash: a group of wealthy businessmen saw it rising out of the Pacific, panicked, and sold all their shares. Muhammad Ali claims to have seen the wheel many

times—at least once a month—usually on his early morning training runs. Pilot of the Mother Ship will be Wallace D. Fard. "I have come," he told Elijah Muhammad almost 40 years ago in Paradise Valley, "to destroy the world."

With God's abrupt departure, the Nation splintered. Elijah, whose leadership was in dispute, was forced to flee from city to city through the 1930s. During the war he was imprisoned for 3½ years for failing to register with his draft board. On his release he found that the Nation had all but collapsed. Perhaps 400 souls remained to keep the faith, gathering in threadbare storefront mosques sprinkled through half a dozen of the larger cities. The Chicago headquarters was a renovated dog-and-cat hospital. Paradise Valley had no memory of Fard.

In retrospect, reasons for the Nation's decline during that period are not difficult to pinpoint. The dream of black salvation and revenge was certainly enticing. But unless convincingly communicated by an inspired preacher, it sounded suspiciously like gibberish. With Fard in Mecca and Mr. Muhammad in jail, the Nation had no such prophet.

Furthermore, the Message was coated with a strict and, for most people, indigestible Muslim morality. "Cleanliness, no smoking, no drinking. No stealing and love for one another," Muhammad Ali is fond of reciting to his younger fans. "No prostitution, no fornication, no homosexuality and no adultery," he adds for the benefit of their parents. "I've caught myself wishing," said Ali shortly after his Muslim baptism, "I had found Islam about five years from now maybe, with all the temptations I have to resist. But I don't even kiss none, because you get too close, it's almost impossible to stop." If Elijah Muhammad had his way, all girls from the age of 14 on would have worn white ankle-length dresses to avoid arousing "temptation" in their Muslim menfolk. "If we can just control our women we can become an independent nation overnight," said Ali, who in his own home epitomized the Muslims' stringent male chauvinism. "Long dresses represent clean thinking. If you have no good women you can have no good men."

Together with "loose" women, the Nation listed a host of other taboos, which dissuaded potential converts—the eating of pork, for example. For most blacks pork is a staple diet. Elijah Muhammad taught that the swine is a mutant, poisonous creature comprised of one third dog, a third cat, and one third rat. The Nation even frowned on boxing, a situation expediently resolved by Ali's official suspension from the faith for the duration of his career. (This suspension also afforded Ali an excuse to wink occasionally at other Muslim taboos. More than one reporter noticed Ali's predilection for collecting the telephone numbers of the eager young "foxes" who flocked around him.)

The Muslim moral code was a formidable stumbling block on the path to conversion. By the end of the 1940s, the struggling Lost-Found Nation of Islam seemed doomed to remain a fringe religion in a country crammed with holy-rolling soul-savers, all promising to deliver the black man from hell to heaven. Then Elijah Muhammad stumbled upon a trump card—an ace in the form of a Baptist preacher's redheaded son, Malcolm Little.

Little was serving a ten-year burglary sentence in Charlestown State Prison in Massachusetts when he learned that the white man was the Devil. During his short lifetime he had seen his house razed by Ku Klux Klansmen and his father beaten senseless and left to die under the wheels of a trolley car for preaching human dignity. He

ABOVE: *Muhammad Speaks*, organ of the Lost-Found Nation of Islam.

had walked the streets of Harlem as a shoeshine boy, pimp, petty thief and dope peddler. The stiff ten-year prison sentence he had received was more for associating with white girls than for the petty theft with which he had been charged. To Little, Elijah Muhammad's message was blinding. Within five minutes of hearing "the word", he had become the Messenger's disciple. It was a conversion that was to transform both men's lives.

Tutored by Elijah himself, Little devoured the Nation's literature and ransacked the prison library for everything concerning black-white relations. On his release in 1952 he devoted himself to the task of Nation-building. He dropped his "slave name"—Little—and adopted the interim Muslim "X," signifying that he had become "ex-smoker, ex-drinker, ex-Christian, ex-slave." Later he received his "Original Name"—Malik Shabazz. But it was as Malcolm X that Little radically altered the history of race relations in America. Malcolm X preached Mr. Muhammad's message with a burning passion bordering on genius. Coupled with the wildfire, rabble-rousing rhetoric of Yacub's History and the End of the World, he played up demands for "immediate justice". Integration was a sham, he said. Blacks should be given their own territory, either a separate state on the American continent or elsewhere. The whites should also support them for the next 20 to 25 years until they were able to support themselves.

Dr. Martin Luther King considered that the growth of the Nation occurred because "For the first time, the Negro was presented with a choice of religion other than Christianity." But it was more than this. What X was offering was all the trappings of Christianity—spiritual brotherhood, faith and salvation—plus a chance at heaven on earth. Under X, the Nation's membership spiralled. In a few short years the sinister gray suits, pork pie hats, black bow ties, and shorn heads of the Fruit of Islam were a common sight in the ghettos of the North.

Compared with Christianity, the Lost-Found Nation of Islam was still a minor grassroots religion. Many blacks—especially those of New York's Harlem—were unwilling to join such a radical movement without first seeing some sign of its power and authority. As for White America, it remained blissfully ignorant of the Nation of Islam.

Malcolm X killed both birds with one stone in the April of 1957. What has now become ghetto legend began with the beating and arrest of a Muslim named Johnson Hinton by two white cops on a Harlem street corner. Immediately more than 2,000 ominously silent people materialized outside the 28th Precinct station house where Hinton had been taken. The shaken police chiefs called in the crowd's leader, Malcolm X, who demanded that he see Hinton to decide if he needed hospitalization. After a heated exchange, the authorities capitulated. Malcolm X was taken to Hinton, who had had "half his head torn off," according to one eyewitness. The embarrassed police hurriedly escorted their injured prisoner to the hospital. Malcolm X walked out onto the station house steps and stood facing the ranks of deathly quiet Muslims. On a wave of his hands the crowd melted silently into the night.

OPPOSITE: Ali kisses a copy of the Qur'an after it was presented to him in Egypt during a trip to Mecca in June 1964.

Cassius Marcellus Clay first learned that the white man was the Devil shortly before Christmas 1960, on the corner of 2nd Avenue and 9th Street in Miami's black district.

At that time Cassius was floating on cloud nine; the Olympics of a few months ago were still fresh in his mind, the Louisville Group had put money in his pocket, and he was still under the wing of the

great Angelo Dundee. Soon he would have his second professional fight against Herb Siler. Everything was as it should have been in Cassius' world. By chance he stopped on the corner to buy a newspaper from a black vendor. The newspaper was *Muhammad Speaks*, mouthpiece of the Nation, and the vendor a Muslim. Come on over to my mosque and hear about the history of our forefathers, he urged in typical Nation-crusading fashion. "I never had heard no black man talking about no forefathers, except that they were slaves," said Cassius in a *Playboy* interview four years later, "so I went to a meeting. And this minister started teaching, and the things he said really shook me up." Like Malcolm X and 1,000 other brothers before him, Cassius Clay was an instant convert.

Compared with Malcolm X's early life, Clay's childhood had been reasonably free of racial tension. During his teens he had turned a blind eye to the already-simmering race question, preferring to spend his time in the gym. He marched only once at an integrationist rally; somebody poured hot water over him, he remembers. (After joining the Muslims his dislike of the integration movement hardened, in line with Nation policy. "I don't want to get bit by dogs or washed down a sewer by fire hoses," he said. "The Bible says turn the other cheek, but it also says an eye-for-an-eye and a tooth-for-a-tooth. I'm a fighter. I believe in the eye-for-an-eye business.") But racism was difficult to avoid in Louisville, Gateway to the South, situated smack on the Mason-Dixon line. Rahaman Ali: "Louisville had many of the policies that the South had because I remember people had their own places and black people weren't allowed to go into white places…I was born in 1943 and it was about 1950 that I really began to understand about race problems…from 1950 to 1960 there were segregated restaurants, schools, everything…for ten years of my life…my early childhood." Until the 1960s, blacks sat at the back of the bus and the Fountain Ferry Amusement Park was for white children only. The West End, where Cassius was raised, and a suburb called Newburg were the only areas in which a black could buy a house. Downtown department stores had no changing rooms for blacks: "If the clothes didn't fit you had to make them fit…you had to take your chances," remembers one Louisville taxi driver.

Cassius' trainer Fred Stoner had fought for years against racial discrimination in boxing. In 1950 he went so far as to pull his best fighters out of the Golden Gloves in protest. "Everything was segregated," he remembers. "When a rock-and-roll show came, even if it was a black band, the place where they had the show was segregated. The city recreation, the parks, everything…you couldn't go into a park and play tennis, except one little park down by the river in the black part which wasn't worth going into. Down the river a little further was the Shawnee Park, which was all white. You couldn't go to the golf courses to play golf. All those guys who wanted to, they'd have been arrested. I tell you, it was so bad that every time I went to the fights I was looking to be arrested." More than a decade later, Fred Stoner would still get himself into a fury when he remembered past prejudice. Undoubtedly he passed on at least some of this bitterness to Cassius Clay along with the boxing lessons.

The open housing demonstrations forced integration on Louisville, but Cassius was not there to see it. He was, more often than not, down South where segregation still flourished. On many of his inter-minable Southern drives he found himself eating and sleeping in his car because of the hotel and restaurant color bar. One story in partic-

ular he has told on several occasions: after winning the Olympic title he visited Atlanta, Georgia, and failed to find a single restaurant that would serve him. "You're just another 'boy' when you come out of the ring," he commented. When he joined Angelo Dundee he found prejudice in Miami Beach. "The restaurant downstairs wouldn't serve Negroes," remembers Angelo, "and this was in the 1960s. Drew Brown, believe it or not, broke that one up because he went down there and insisted on being fed. He made a scene. Remarkable man, Drew Brown."

Dundee says that Cassius has always liked visiting the black neighborhood of each new city. "Muhammad loves all that stuff. He likes to go: 'Take me where my folks are.' I always remember in this place in Georgia where he went up to a colored feller and asked, 'Where do all the niggers hang out around here?' So the guy says, 'Go down the road there and you make a left and you see a bunch of trees out there and they're hanging there.' Gross joke…"

What Cassius heard at his first Muslim meeting gave him a new perspective on these humiliating experiences, and it is a curious irony that the militant segregation practiced by so many whites helped push Cassius past integration to the equally militant segregationist policies of Elijah Muhammad. (In future years white, hard-line segregationists like Senator Richard Russell would hold up Ali as a laudable example of a man who did not feel "imposed upon or humiliated or insulted by associating with members of his own race." Politics makes for strange bedfellows.) "All my life, I had been seeing the black man getting his head whipped by the white man, and stuck in the

white man's jails, and things like that," Ali told *Playboy*. "And myself, I had to admit that up to then, I had always hated being black, just like other Negroes, hating our kind, instead of loving one another. The more I saw and thought, the more the truth made sense to me."

Before the minister had finished preaching about Yacub, the lost heritage, and the 400-year enslavement, Cassius had seen the light. "Now, I'm the kind that catches on quick. I said to myself, listen there, this man's saying something! I hope don't nobody never hit me in the ring hard as it did when that brother minister said the Chinese are named after China, Russians after Russia, Cubans after Cuba, Italians after Italy, the English after England, and clear on down the line everybody was named for somewhere he could call home, except us. He said, 'What country are we so-called Negroes named for? No country! We are just a lost race.' Well, boom! That really shook me up."

Cassius did not join the Nation immediately; in fact, he told nobody what he had learned. The Muslims were a singularly unattractive proposition for a young Olympic champion with the world at his feet. The taboos surrounding sex, for instance, Cassius regarded with a despairing eye. As a teenager he had never shown much interest in girls, preferring instead to spend his leisure time in the gym. "Oh no," said Mrs. Clay, shaking her head emphatically, "no girlfriends on his mind when he was coming up. No, he was too dedicated to boxing." However, after his Olympic victory girls became unavoidable and Cassius soon discovered that arrival in a city such as New York was a far more spectacular event when accompanied by a coterie of beautiful women. "These are my foxes," he happily boasted to the admirers gawping at his regular sidewalk parades. "Ain't they fine!"

Even more off-putting than the Nation's austere morality was the sinister image that the movement had earned. Malcolm X made news with almost every speech and as the headlines increased, so too did his venom. In April 1962 he made a remark that drove whites into a frenzy. Enraged at the exoneration of a Los Angeles policeman accused of shooting a Muslim, Malcolm X told his followers that God had answered their prayers in France. "He dropped an airplane out of the sky with over 120 white people on it because the Muslims believe in an eye-for-an-eye and a tooth-for-a-tooth," he said referring to a crash that killed most of Atlanta's white cultural elite. "We call on our God, and he gets rid of 120 of them at one whop." Membership in the "Black Muslims" for a man whose livelihood depended on the willingness of people to pay money to see him perform, seemed to be a certain short cut to financial suicide.

But Cassius persevered with the meetings. "Whatever I'm for, I always have believed in talking it up, and the first thing you know, I was in Muslim meetings calling out just like the rest, 'Right, brother! Tell it, brother! Keep it coming.'" In 1961 after half a dozen meetings, Cassius returned to Louisville and told his brother what he had discovered. "When I finished high school," recalls Rahaman, "I went down to Miami with him and I listened and I liked what I heard and I accepted." By the end of 1962 Cassius was developing some rather strong thoughts on topics rarely seen in boxing magazines. "You are only free if you're number one," he told one interviewer. "Otherwise you're a slave. My granddaddy was a slave. They say Lincoln freed the slaves. But look around you. They're still slaves, 'cause they got to make it to the office by 9am. And don't let nobody tell you no different." In August the next year he was photographed at a Malcolm X rally in Upper Manhattan.

ABOVE: In January 1972, Ali returns to Mecca where he kisses the Holy Black Stone to which Muslims face when praying.

RIGHT: "Take me where my folks are." The newest recruit to the Nation of Islam may have been white America's nightmare, but on Harlem streets in 1965 he is simply The Greatest.

The press took little notice of Clay's extracurricular activities. They were more interested in his poetry, predictions, and the Tale of his Tape. No other boxer since Jack Johnson had shown signs of social militancy. It was unthinkable that Clay, with everything to gain from a sympathetic following, would join an organization dedicated to the secession of blacks from the American Dream, just when he had attained that dream.

The rumors began when Cassius returned to Dundee's 5th Street Gym to begin training for the upcoming Liston title fight. He was accompanied by a black man whom he introduced as "Sam". Sam was Captain Sam Saxon, leader of the Miami mosque. When Malcolm X arrived at the Miami camp on Cassius' invitation—a present to X and his wife Betty for their sixth wedding anniversary—the rumors gained a solid foundation.

Malcolm X first met Cassius and Rudy in 1962 while dining in a luncheonette next door to the Detroit mosque. Cassius characteristically walked over to X and pumped his hand saying, "I'm Cassius Clay." "He acted as though I was supposed to know who he was," wrote X in his autobiography. "So I acted as though I did. Up to that moment, though, I had never even heard of him. Ours were two entirely different worlds. In fact, Elijah Muhammad instructed us Muslims against all forms of sport." After lunch all three went next door to hear Elijah Muhammad speak. Cassius and Rudy led the applause and Malcolm was impressed by their sincerity, "since a Muslim rally was about the world's last place to seek fight fans."

From that point Cassius appeared regularly at Malcolm X rallies and the two became friends. "Some contagious quality about him made him one of the very few people I ever invited to my home," wrote Malcolm. "Not only was Cassius receptive to advice, he solicited it. Primarily, I impressed upon him to what a great extent a public figure's success depends upon how alert and knowledgeable he is to the true natures and to the true motives of all the people who flock around him. I warned him about the 'foxes', his expression for the aggressive, cute young females who flocked after him: I told Cassius that instead of 'foxes', they really were wolves." Several of Cassius' friends have described Malcolm X's advice as "brainwashing." Whatever the extent of this advice, there is no doubt that Malcolm X was instrumental in steering Cassius towards the Nation.

Cassius' Miami invitation came at a crucial point in Malcolm X's career. At that time he had been officially suspended from the movement, ostensibly for his most infamous "hate speech". In December 1963 he had told an audience in New York's Manhattan Center that the Kennedy assassination was a case of "the chickens coming home to roost". "Being an old farm boy myself," he had added with a grin, "chickens coming home to roost never did make me sad; they've always made me glad." Next day the speech was splashed in the *New York Times*, and such was the reaction from a country in mourning that Elijah Muhammad, "because of the climate," ordered Malcolm silent for 90 days. (Actually there is ample evidence to suggest that the "chickens" speech was used merely as an excuse by jealous members of the Muslim hierarchy to depose their famous colleague.)

ABOVE: Back to his roots—the reborn Muhammad Ali rides in triumph through the streets of Accra, Ghana, during a month-long tour of Africa in May, 1964. "They will all want to see the new champion of the world who believes the same way they do," he says before he leaves. He is right. Fellow Muslim Osman Karriem: "We were driving down a road in Ghana…and five minutes after we started driving, there was like a beating of drums. Then people started showing up on the roads—'Ali! Ali!' I'd never seen anything like it before. I was sitting there with this kid, and people were coming out of nowhere, lining the road, calling 'Ali! Ali!' He didn't say anything. It's like he was hypnotized. Do you have any idea what it must have been like for him to see thousands of people materialize out of nowhere and know they were there just for him?"

OPPOSITE: Ali reading *Muhammad Speaks*.

After this unprecedented public rebuke by his leader, Malcolm X knew he was locked on an irreversible slide from grace. "I was in a state of emotional shock. I don't know what I might have done if I had stayed in New York during that crucial time…" The invitation was a godsend, especially as, according to Peter Goldman, X saw much more in Cassius than a celebrated recruit; he saw in him a means of reinstating himself at the forefront of the Nation. In desperation he rang the Chicago headquarters offering to deliver Cassius and the title to the Nation on Savior's Day, the day after the fight. His price was reinstatement. Chicago was still unconvinced that Cassius could beat Liston and rejected the offer. Indeed, writes Goldman, Chicago was disturbed at the publicity given Malcolm X on his arrival at the camp. The last thing they wanted was for the Nation to be linked with a loser.

If the invitation was a lifeline for Malcolm X, for harassed promoter Bill MacDonald, already fretting over sluggish ticket sales, it was the straw to break the camel's back. With a month still to go before the fight, the press began hinting at the possibility of Clay's joining the Muslims. The Press Association reported that he had flown to New York to speak on behalf of the "Black Muslims." Cassius admitted "talking to the Muslims", but added that he had also spoken to Jewish and Catholic groups. A Miami paper followed with a detailed account of Clay's sympathetic statements on the Muslims. When the story appeared, MacDonald, already annoyed at indirectly aiding what he labelled a "hate group," threatened to call off the fight unless Cassius "publicly renounced the Black Muslims and denied his affiliation with them…" "If that's your condition," said Clay, "I won't fight." In desperation MacDonald turned to Harold Conrad who was stage-managing the match. "The story broke about two weeks before the fight and there was hell to pay," recalls Conrad. "The local promoter—MacDonald—who'd put up the money came to me and said, 'Jesus, I ain't gonna promote this fight… How can I promote this fight in the South with a *Muslim*?' It shook me. I'd heard some rumblings about his brother being a member, but *Cassius*…I thought I'd blown the fight. I said, 'How do you know he's a Muslim?' He says, 'Malcolm X! He's all over the goddamn place with him!' I said, 'If I get Malcolm X outta town will

that cool you off?' and he says, 'Yeah, just get him away from me.' So I went to Malcolm and I said, 'Listen, if you don't get outta town your boy's gonna blow the title shot, the promoter's gonna blow the fight and we're all gonna blow the money. The smart thing is to get out and come back for the fight.' He saw my point and said, 'You're right.' He left town and came back the day of the fight." A truce was also hammered out with Cassius: if he would keep silent about the Muslims, the fight would go on.

Malcolm X flew home to Long Island. When he returned he brought with him pictures of Floyd Patterson and Sonny Liston in their fight camps surrounded by "white spiritual advisers." "This fight is the truth," he told Cassius. "It's the Cross and the Crescent fighting in the ring for the first time. It's a modern Crusades—a Christian and Muslim facing each other with television to beam it off Telstar for the whole world to see what happens." The fight is destiny, he drummed into his pupil. "Do you think Allah has brought about all this intending for you to leave the ring as anything but the champion?" At the weigh-in histrionics Cassius shouted, "It is prophesied that I should win! I cannot be beaten!"

During his ice cream victory party held in Malcolm X's Hampton House motel room, Cassius received a telephone call from Muslim headquarters in Chicago. After receiving the congratulations, he was offered full membership in the Nation of Islam. At the next day's press conference Cassius moved from the sports pages to the front pages. "Everything with common sense wants to be with his own," he told the incredulous reporters in a barely audible voice. "Bluebirds with bluebirds, redbirds with redbirds, pigeons with pigeons, eagles with eagles, tigers with tigers, monkeys with monkeys. As small as an ant's brain is, red ants want to be with red ants, black ants with black ants. I believe in the religion of Islam, which means I believe there is no God but Allah and Muhammad is his Apostle. This is the same religion that is believed in by over 700 million dark-skinned peoples throughout Africa and Asia. I don't have to be what you want me to be. I am free to be what I want." He had won, he said, because Allah had been in the ring with him and because he prayed five times a day. He had even prayed in the shower before the fight. "All I want is peace," he said as he left.

Cassius Marcellus Clay adopted his "waiting name" and became Cassius X. It was hard for him to abandon his famous signature, but he was consoled by his "Original Name"—Muhammad Ali (literally, "Praiseworthy One"). "He was a great warrior of 1,400 years ago," said Ali proudly of his new namesake, "and he helped translate the Bible into English." Rudolph Arnet Clay became Rahaman Ali—"the One who Loves".

Ali returned to New York accompanied by Malcolm X. The two men toured the United Nations together and were photographed with various African delegates. Ali rented a two-room suite in Harlem's Hotel Theresa where Malcolm had an office. The friendship, however, was not to last. Less than two weeks after delivering the Nation its most famous convert, Malcolm X ended his career as Elijah Muhammad's chief disciple and prophet. The split came when Malcolm realized his enemies in the Nation had closed ranks against him and decided his 90-day suspension was to be a lifetime exile. Together with a dozen dissident members of the Nation he formed his own Islamic movement—Muslim Mosque, Inc. Immediately there were bitter

Muhammad Speaks

REGRETS OF THE DOUBTERS

See Page 12 & 13

MUSLIM FARM REPORT Part I

See Progress Section

OPPOSITE: The new recruit in Nation of Islam "uniform". "I like my life. Integration is wrong. The black man that's trying to integrate, he's getting beat up and bombed and shot. But the black man that says he don't want to integrate, he gets called a 'hate teacher'. Chubby Checker is catching hell with a white woman. And I'm catching hell for not wanting a white woman."

BELOW: Mecca, 1972. Ali prays inside the Holy Mosque during a New Year's pilgrimage with manager Herbert Muhammad (right).

recriminations: Elijah Muhammad denounced his former disciple as a hypocrite; Malcolm's brother Philbert X, a Muslim minister in Lansing, Michigan, called him insane.

Malcolm X felt it his duty to advise Ali to remain with Elijah Muhammad. When Ali did so he was disappointed, but a fragile relationship was maintained between the two. This last vestige of friendship was swept away on Malcolm X's return from a pilgrimage to Mecca. (While touring Ghana, Malcolm had happened to meet Ali, who was conducting his own pilgrimage. X was pleased at the brief reunion, but for once Ali was stuck for words.) Mecca radically altered Malcolm X's stand on matters of color. He found in the East that his fellow Muslims had no color consciousness. All races were the same in Allah's eyes, he was repeatedly told. The revelation set him at loggerheads with his past. "For 12 long years," he wrote in a letter to the *New York Times* on his return, "I lived in the narrow-minded confines of the 'strait-jacket' world created by my strong belief that Elijah Muhammad was a messenger direct from God Himself and my faith in what I now see to be a pseudo-religious philosophy that he preaches."

As Malcolm X mellowed, the vitriolic attacks in *Muhammad Speaks* escalated. "The Bible accurately describes you as 'a dog returning to his own vomit'," ran a line from one article. Another warned: "The die is set, and Malcolm shall not escape, especially after such evil, foolish talk about his benefactor. Such a man as Malcolm is worthy of death, and would have met with death if it had not been for Muhammad's confidence in Allah for a victory over his enemies." "I'm a dead man," he told his closest friends.

On February 21st, a warm, wintry Sunday afternoon, Malcolm X strode onto the stage of New York's Audubon Ballroom and gave the Muslim greeting "Asalaikum Salaam" to his followers. Suddenly a scuffle erupted in the crowd. "What are you doing in my pockets, man?" someone shouted. "Get your hand out of my pocket." Malcolm's bodyguards moved towards the disturbance. "Hold it. Hold it brothers," he called from the stage. "Let's be cool." In that instant a man lunged from the front of the audience and blew a seven-inch circle of buckshot pellets from a sawn-off double-barrel shotgun dead center into Malcolm's chest. X toppled backwards and the man fired his second barrel. The two men who had been arguing rushed down the aisles and emptied their pistols into the prone body.

One of the murderers was captured by the crowd. But for the arrival of the police he would have been beaten to death. The others escaped but were arrested soon after. Two of the suspects were members of the Nation of Islam. One of them, Thomas 15X Johnson, a Muslim "enforcer," had once acted as a bodyguard for Muhammad Ali. The third suspect, Talmadge Hayer, had been seen on several occasions in a Nation mosque. At their trial all three refused to reveal who had ordered the killing. In his summary before the jury the prosecutor remarked pointedly that the very brazenness of the act suggested the answer: "…whoever did it chose to do it in the presence of between 200 and 400 people in broad daylight in a public room…Is it abusing our common sense to suggest that it was done deliberately in the presence of these people as an object lesson to Malcolm's followers that this is what can happen and what will happen?"

Malcolm X's friends and admirers had no doubts as to those responsible for the slaying. The night he died, Elijah Muhammad's Harlem Mosque No. 7—Malcolm X's former ministry—was gutted by fire.

Six days later was God's birthday—the opening of the Nation's annual Savior's Day convention in the Chicago Coliseum. Peter Goldman records: "…they put Muhammad Ali down front to lead the cheering when two dozen of the Fruit marched to the stage in a moving square and parted to reveal the Messenger of Allah. 'We did not want to kill Malcolm and we did not try to,' Mr Muhammad said, his voice faint and breathless. 'It was his foolishness, ignorance and his preaching that brought him to his death.' He gasped on, Ali jumping in yelling 'Yes sir!' or 'Sweet words, Apostle!' and the crowd answering with cheers…" Muhammad Ali had made his choice; for good or ill he had decided to remain a company man.

A decade later, as can be evinced by his version of the darkest chapter in the Nation's short history, Muhammad Ali was still a company man. "Malcolm X had to be punished," he told a British audience in late 1974. "In this punishment he came to my house in Florida and told me he couldn't stand it, couldn't wait, he had to start another movement, he wasn't going to be put out like this, he's not going to

OPPOSITE: The new Muhammad Ali at a Muslim convention.

leave Elijah but he was going to fight from another angle. But he got worse and worse…outright tried to overthrow him, tried to take over his following. When you talk against a man who is so loved, the man himself don't have to put the word out to get you, the people themselves are going to get you. The love for that man will get you killed."

What effects Elijah Muhammad and his Nation of Islam have had on Ali's ring career are incalculable. Malcolm X firmly implanted in Ali's mind the belief that he was invincible which must have been of enormous psychological advantage to a young fighter facing the awesome Sonny Liston. Ali became a fanatic and fanaticism greatly increased his resolve. By the time he learned that he was not invincible, Ali had matured enough to take the lesson in his stride. Conversely, the thought of having to face a dreaded "Black Muslim" must have been at the very least a slightly daunting proposition for many of Ali's opponents, especially the ones he christened "Uncle Toms." In the latter part of his career the Nation provided Ali with an added incentive to fight. Unlike so many others who reach the top only to lose their impetus, Ali has had "his people" to represent. There is some truth in Ali's boast that when he lost, nations mourned.

Despite rumors to the contrary, by the 1970s Muslim membership appeared to have left Ali's finances relatively undiminished. When the Nation, in the form of Elijah's son Herbert, replaced the Louisville Group as Ali's manager, it did so with minimal disruption and considerable shrewdness. Angelo Dundee: "I have a great working relationship with Herbert, I handle everything boxing-wise. We talk real good, we get along great." And would Muhammad someday be reduced to

BELOW: Ali waves a copy of *Muhammad Speaks* during an appearance in Baltimore, Maryland, in May 1964.

opening casino doors or shining shoes in Madison Square Garden like other champions before him? "Not Muhammad. Muhammad won't end up that way. He's putting his money away. It's being taken care of by Herbert and Herbert is a very intelligent man. He was wealthy before he became Muhammad's manager and he knows what it's all about."

As much as the Nation was good for Ali, so too was Ali a godsend for Elijah Muhammad. Even as late as the early 1960s the Harris Poll was finding "massive negative feeling" towards the movement, with a mere four per cent of blacks in favor of Elijah Muhammad's separate state policy. Until Ali, the Nation's star recruit was a gifted but obscure college mathematician. Ali's baptism lent popular and spectacular success to the movement's image. As Malcolm X said, "He upset the odds." Since then Ali faithfully continued this role of "front man," humanizing what is essentially a dour and sometimes brutal religion. Harold Conrad: "He's a big moving force…a spokesman. He talks to the kids, goes on Johnny Carson, gets new members in. They're proud of this guy. He's the bait. Let's face it, how many denominations can have a guy selling like this guy, you know? If the old African missionaries ever had a guy like that they'd have made a lot of money." Just like the Nation of Islam has.

When Elijah Muhammad died in a Chicago cardiac unit in early 1975 he bequeathed an empire, which the newspapers described as "the richest black organization of all time in total assets." The legacy included: 50 mosques headed by the $4 million Chicago headquarters; a bank with assets over $10 million; a restaurant chain; a supermarket network; clothing stores, bakeries, dry-cleaning establishments and a host of other small businesses; a fish importing firm; a private land and air freight transport system; a $1 million printing plant publishing the country's highest-circulation black newspaper; thousands of acres of land in three states; Elijah's private jet; and a fez studded with $150,000 worth of gems. The total was estimated at around $70 million. It may have been much more. "Our leader," said Ali shortly afterwards on his way to look over two Chicago skyscrapers he was considering purchasing, "…now he's got $187 million in buildings."

Seven thousand mourners turned out for Elijah Muhammad's funeral. They included representatives of President Ford and Chicago's Mayor Richard Daley. The funeral removed any doubts that this formerly destitute and despised fringe religion was now a successful and established part of America's religious, social and economic structure. Much of the credit for this meteoric rise must go to Muhammad Ali.

Back in 1964 these glittering achievements were probably undreamed of by the Messenger himself. When Ali took the step after beating Liston, he was walking into total darkness. "A racist Black Muslim heavyweight champion is a bitter pill for racist white America to swallow," wrote Eldrige Cleaver at the time in his book *Soul On Ice*. "Swallow it or throw the whole bit up, and hope that in the convulsions of your guts America, you can vomit out the poisons of hate which have led you to a dead end in this valley of the shadow of death." It was to take another three years before "white America" finally decided.

The Championship Years

"When I looked at a lot of them questions they had on them Army tests, I just didn't know the answers. I didn't even know how to start about finding the answers."

Muhammad Ali

At 10:30pm on May 25, 1965—a full 15 months after Cassius Clay had overturned the boxing world in a Miami Beach convention center—Muhammad Ali finally made his ring debut. Not since Joe Louis' defeat of Jim Braddock in 1937 had a champion taken so long to stage his first heavyweight title defence. But blame for the delay could hardly have been laid at Ali's door—the whole 15 months had been an ugly saga of bitter hostility, ill-humored haggling, and plain bad luck. The eventual setting for the rematch—a high school skating rink in a backwater town—was stark testimony to the trouble which had dogged the fight from the outset.

Liston's year and a quarter had passed routinely. As his shoulder healed and he adjusted to life without a crown ("I feel like when the President got shot"), he returned to the gym vowing revenge. Most fight fans predicted that he would achieve it.

Life for the new champion, on the other hand, was far from routine. Cassius' "bluebirds" speech had provoked a public outcry of unanimous condemnation. Joe Louis: "Clay will earn the public's hatred because of his connections with the Black Muslims. The things they preach are just the opposite of what we believe. The Heavyweight Champion should be the champion of all people."

Harry Markson, Madison Square Garden's boxing director: "Clay's antics have been deplorable. You don't use the Heavyweight Championship of the world to spout religious diatribe. I think responsible promoters will hesitate to touch this kid."

Dr. Martin Luther King: "When Cassius joined the Black Muslims and started calling himself Cassius X, he became a champion of racial segregation and that is what we are fighting against."

Joe Martin: "Clay can't get out of the Muslims—he's the one who put them on the front page—they'd kill him."

The Governor of Maine: "He should be held in utter contempt by every patriotic American."

Even Ali's father joined the chorus: "He was conned," he said, charging that the Muslims had been brainwashing his son since the Olympics. "I'm not changing no name. If he wants to do it, fine. But not me. He's so confused he doesn't know where he's at." Floyd Patterson spearheaded the assault by emerging from retirement and swearing to "win back the title for America." "I am proud to be an American and proud of my people, and no one group of people could make me change my views," he ranted. "Therefore, I challenge you not only for myself, but for all people who think and feel like I do."

Ali shrugged off the mud slinging. "Joe Louis was a sucker," he snorted. "Look what happened to him." Floyd's challenge he simply accepted. "I'll play with him for ten rounds. He has been talking about my religion. I will just pow him. Then after I beat him, I'll convert him." But the controversy was losing Ali money. Lawyer Gordon Davidson had persuaded Madison Avenue that Cassius' wholesome heroics would sell products. "We had all kinds of commercials lined up," remembers Davidson, "and it blew all these out the window. His endorsements became worthless."

The Nation of Islam was not the only cross Ali had to bear; there was also the US Army. Together with thousands of his contemporaries, Ali was in line for the draft. He had registered on April 18, 1960, two months before his 18th birthday, with Local Board No. 47 in Louisville. "I was a Christian at the time," he recalls. "I knew nothing about Islam. I was Cassius Clay. I wasn't Muhammad Ali…if you had drafted me that day I would have went." On March 9, 1962, he was classified 1-A—perfect cannon fodder—and induction seemed a certainty. A month before the Liston bout he was ordered to report to the Army Induction

OPPOSITE: The devout new Heavyweight Champion prays in his corner before a fight.

ABOVE: Cassius Clay gets his first taste of the military in January 1964, when he appears for pre-induction tests at the Miami Draft Board. Here a smiling Lt. Reno Diono tells him what to do. The smiles do not last long. When Ali is re-classified as eligible for service after failing the first time around, he wails: "I don't understand how I got so smart so quick."

OPPOSITE: In the 5th Street Gym, his old "Cassius Clay" fight posters still on the wall. "I don't have a mark on my face, and I upset Sonny Liston, and I just turned 22 years old. I must be the greatest!"

BELOW: A rare poster from the Ali vs. Liston fight that was postponed for six months due to Ali's hospitalization after suffering from an acute hernia.

Center in Coral Gables, Florida. The physical examinations were a pushover; the intelligence test floored him. Cassius had excelled at drawing in school, but mathematics had never been his strong point. Suddenly he was confronted with such questions as:

> **A man works from six in the morning to three in the afternoon with one hour for lunch. How many hours did he work?**
> **a)7 b)8 c)9 d)10**

and

> **A vendor was selling apples for $10 a basket. How much would you pay for a dozen baskets if one third of the apples have been removed from each of the baskets?**
> **a)$10 b)$30 c)$40 d)$80**

"When I looked at a lot of them questions they had on them Army tests, I just didn't know the answers," said Cassius later. "I didn't even know how to start about finding the answers." At the end of the test he had left many questions unanswered. The Army declared his results "inconclusive." Two months later the Army tested him again in Louisville. This time it made up its mind; Ali had scored 16 percentile. The pass mark was 30 percentile. He was classified I-Y—"not qualified for induction into the Army under applicable standards".

Public reaction was immediate and furious. Senators and congressmen received stacks of irate letters demanding to know if a Heavyweight Champion was smart enough to recite poetry and earn a fortune, why wasn't he intelligent enough to carry a gun? The Army insisted Ali was not faking, its psychologists agreeing that he had put forward his "best efforts." Rep. William Bray of Indiana announced that the Army results matched those obtained by Cassius in high school. Bantamweight Petros Spanakos spoke up for his former Olympic teammate. "Cassius has trouble writing letters or anything," he wrote to the *New York Herald Tribune*. "I spelled out, corrected and finally wrote his letters home. This is why I know Cassius Clay honestly failed."

Ali himself was blasé about the uproar. "The truth don't hurt nobody," he told *Playboy*. "The fact is I never was too bright in school. I just barely graduated. I had a D-minus average. I ain't ashamed of it, though, I mean, how much do school principals make a month?" "But was it embarrassing to be declared mentally unfit?" pressed *Playboy*. "I have said I am the greatest. Ain't nobody ever heard me say I am the smartest!"

Given Ali's obvious and sometimes devastating wit and intelligence, it is difficult to accept that at one time his mental agility was rated sub-Army standard. Even in 1964 he was more than a match for many reporters who delighted in throwing him loaded questions. But against this boundless natural ability must be balanced Cassius' formal education. By his own admission school slid over him like water off a duck's back. Later, despite an enthusiastic self-education program, he continued to have difficulty reading, stumbling over multi-syllabic words, and spending long periods on a single page.

Ali ducked much of the storm by moving to the heart of Harlem and surrounding himself with "his people." Here in the Hotel Theresa, a grimy 12-story building fronting Seventh Avenue and 125th Street, the Ali legend took root. He rented a modest two-room suite in the old hotel, which despite its seedy appearance, boasted among its past guests Fidel Castro, Joe Louis, and an interminable string of black show-biz greats. Ali slept late and ate breakfast next door at the Chock Full o'Nuts fast food counter. A Cadillac with a tiny pair of white boxing gloves dangling from the rear vision mirror was the sole touch of flamboyance. Each day The Champ would hold court on the Theresa's front steps, laughing and joking with an ever-present crowd of admirers.

But his persecutors would not be ignored. Less than a month after the title had changed hands, Ed Lassman, a Miami Beach delicatessen operator who doubled as the president of the World Boxing Association, announced his plan to strip Ali of his title. His reasons were twofold. First, there was a clause in the original Clay vs. Liston contract giving Liston's management the right, for $50,000, to promote a return bout. This, charged Lassman, violated a WBA by-law forbidding rematch clauses in fight contracts. Lassman's second reason had far less to do with boxing than with bigotry. "Clay is a detriment to the boxing world," he declared. "Clay's general conduct is provoking world-wide criticism and is setting a very poor example for the youth of the world. The conduct of the champion before and after winning the title has caused my office to be deluged with letters of torrid criticism from all over the world."

In retrospect, it is easy to condemn Louis, Patterson, and many other Ali critics as hysterical hypocrites, prepared to accept as champion a man who numbered known gangsters amongst his friends, but unwilling to stomach the outspoken disciple of an unpopular religion. However, the conversion of Cassius Clay must be viewed in relation to a series of contemporaneous events which shattered the complacency of America, the blooming of an explosive era which became known to historians as the Days of Rage. Bloody civil rights marches shook the South from Selma to Montgomery; Harlem burned and a sea of black faces chanted "Malcolm X, Malcolm X"; Watts ignited and looters were gunned down in the street; Malcolm X died in a hail of bullets and Harlem teetered on the brink of open warfare. The Long Hot Summer had arrived, and in such a climate it was inevitable, even understandable, that many people should turn on Ali.

Lassman and his subsequent actions are more difficult to exonerate. Professional boxing has traditionally been ill served by its various self-styled world-governing bodies. The jealous bickering amongst these groups of old men who fancy themselves as sporting czars has torpedoed more than one potentially spectacular match. The WBA and the equally dubious New York Athletic Commission had irritably carved up control of boxing between themselves by the time of Ali's reign. *The Ring* magazine was particularly scathing in its estimation of Ed Lassman and his "jocular" organization's petty and limited view of its responsibilities. "The WBA once again has turned its major attention to finding fights in distant places in which some of its officials might officiate, for a fee," it reported in June 1965. The Ali witch hunt, the WBA's masterpiece of irrationality, was accurately headlined by another sports magazine as "Boxing's Silliest Hour".

Although Ed Lassman was replaced as WBA president in late 1965 by a more far-sighted administrator who decided to once again recognise Ali as the title-holder, the WBA, the NYAC, and their scores of minor officials in local commissions across the country continued to blight boxing, boxers and Muhammad Ali for years to come.

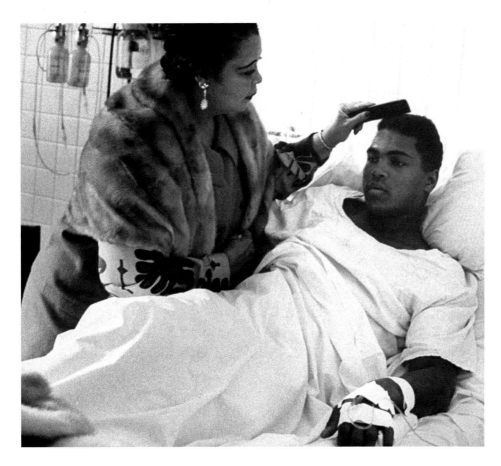

ABOVE: Ali's mother visits him in hospital after his hernia operation. Liston is less than sympathetic. "It could have been worse," he says when he hears the news of Ali's ailment. "It could have been me."

OPPOSITE: Ali and his new bride Sonji, honeymooning in Miami. The independent Sonji soon falls foul of the austere Nation of Islam: "I wanted to be his wife and best friend. I wasn't doing it for the money. It bothers me when people say that. Another thing that bothers me is when they say I taught him everything he knew about sex. Let me tell you, I didn't teach him nothing about sex. He knew what to do when I met him. It's just that I may have made him want to do it." Later, Ali says that the whole time he was married to Sonji he never went with another woman. If so, it was the last time in his career. After Thomas Hauser's oral biography of Ali was published, it was revealed that Ali had had a voracious sexual appetite.

At first, Lassman's plan backfired. Despite Ali's unpopularity, the public was unwilling to see him robbed of his title outside the ring. Many people grudgingly agreed with him when he said he had won the title "fair and clean". The Illinois Athletic Commission voted unanimously to reject the WBA recommendation if it were passed. The New York Athletic Commission announced it would continue to recognize Ali come what may. Although a poll of WBA board members found that Ali would certainly be deposed if the issue came to a vote, Lassman backed down. "It just fizzled out," laughed Ali. "It ain't a court in America that would take a man's job, or his title, because of his religious convictions."

On May 14th, Ali, all but ignored by the press, flew off on the first leg of a promised tour of Africa and the Middle East. "They will all want to see the new champion of the world who believes the way they do," he said. In his retinue was Elijah Muhammad's son, Herbert, a partnership which was to have a powerful impact on Ali's later career.

Ali played to mixed receptions in Africa. In Ghana he received a hero's welcome, met Nkrumah ("Well, I looked at Prime Minister Nkrumah, and it come to me that he looked just like so many Negroes in America—except there he was, the head of a country") and boxed an exhibition with Rahaman before a huge audience in Accra Stadium. He called Ghana his "home." American Embassy officials were astonished by Ali's impact. Events, however, did not work out so smoothly in Nigeria. For reasons best known to himself, Ali walked out of a soccer match and left the country without fighting a scheduled exhibition. Later he blamed his departure on an itinerary mix-up. In

the United Arab Republic, Ali regained some of his aplomb, riding a camel, which he "tamed just like Liston", and visiting the pyramids. "I met Nasser," he recalls. "He embraced me on the steps of the capital; it brought tears to my eyes. I thought, 'Here I am, this little boy from Louisville, standing with one of the great leaders of the world!'" Ali's tour was just five weeks old when he announced a change in plans and returned to the US. His homecoming must have seemed like stepping out of a spotlight into a cupboard.

On August 14, 1964, the *Los Angeles Sentinel* reported that Ali was introducing a Chicago model named Sonji Roy to his friends as "my wife." He had quietly married the 24-year-old Sonji in her hometown of Gary, Indiana, and as a honeymoon the couple drove to Miami where Ali began training for the Liston rematch. Sonji claimed she was a Muslim, but within months the gossip columns were rumoring imminent divorce.

While Ali trained the WBA regrouped for a second assault. The moment the date and site were fixed for the return bout, warned Lassman, Ali would be suspended. Faversham decided to defy the ban and in September scheduled the fight for Boston in two months time. By nightfall of the day the contracts were signed, Ali, Liston, and all others associated with the match had been suspended. Both the Liston and Ali camps obviously considered 30 per cent of all gate receipts and ancillary rights worth risking the WBA's wrath.

On Friday the 13th, four days before the fight, Ali was discussing tactics with Bundini after dinner when he became violently ill. He began vomiting and his stomach, as Bundini put it, swelled "to the size of a football". Ali was rushed in agony to the City Hospital where he underwent an emergency operation for an acute hernia. Doctors said later that if he had entered the ring with the condition, he might well have died. Liston did not waste words on sympathy. "Shit," he commented when he heard the news, "I worked hard for this fight." He did however see one bright side: "It could have been worse. It could have been me."

Ali's hospitalization set the fight date back six months. By late February he had recovered enough to spar before a Muslim convention in the New York Coliseum. Shortly after, he was back in full training showing no sign of his malaise. In comparison, Liston looked deflated and weary. Prior to the original date he had worked himself to a physical peak with long hours in the gymnasium and on the road. The enforced layoff had wrecked his carefully timed program. He still promised to "tear that kid apart", but as the months passed, more and more critics began questioning his age and ability to peak again.

The delay also afforded veterans' and "patriotic" pressure groups the opportunity to wreck the Boston promotion. The attorney general of Massachusetts finally ruled against the match and promoter Sam Silverman pulled out, shouldering an estimated $50,000 loss. The search for a new site presented few problems. By this time promoters had realized the enormous potential of closed circuit television. Live gates had almost become an irrelevancy in the backers' eyes, a situation emphasized by the first Clay vs. Liston match. Even the largest box office receipts paled beside the revenues which could be extracted from networks around the world. In later years heavyweight title bouts would be seriously proposed for matchbox auditoriums, cruising ocean liners and even cities in darkest Africa. The ultimate choice of venue for the Ali vs. Liston rematch was almost as bizarre—Lewiston, Maine.

ABOVE: Ali, resplendent in Nigerian costume, rides a camel during his sightseeing tour of Cairo.

OPPOSITE: The Phantom Punch. Top left: Ali clips Liston with a near invisible punch to the jaw. Top right: Liston goes down on to hands and knees and finally rolls (Bottom Left) on to his back. Bottom right: referee Jersey Joe Walcott forces the triumphant Ali to a neutral corner as Liston tries to struggle to his feet, but the fight is already minutes over.

FOLLOWING PAGES: The disbelieving crowd cries fix as Ali moves towards the fallen Liston. Only a very few at ringside have seen the punch; most believe the mob-connected Liston has taken a dive. Angelo Dundee: "He got hit with a punch like I teach my fighters today. Pop, slide, bang! Liston didn't see the punch. Liston threw a jab. Got nailed side of the head. Down. And he rolled over. There was no doubt about it – he got knocked down. I walked across the ring and say, 'Tough luck, son.' He looked right through me. He walked right by me. He didn't see me. He was still out of it." Years later, a broke Liston remarked that if had thrown the fight, why wasn't he rich?

The majority of Americans were unfamiliar with Lewiston, and several of the less-travelled boxing writers professed ignorance of Maine. Just how backwoods Lewiston was could be judged by the fate of Ali's "secret plan." Ali had hoped to whip a red bullfighter's *muleta* out of his trunks on the bell and wave it at Liston like a matador, but he forgot about it until the actual day of the fight. He ordered Lewiston to be scoured for a *muleta*; not a square foot of red rag could be found in that ghost town.

On May 25th, the live gate—around 2,000 of them, the smallest audience in living memory to witness a heavyweight title bout (the official attendance was 4,280)—filed into St. Dominic's Arena past a motley collection of sullen citizens who looked, as one British magazine reported, "for all the world like a lynching mob in a film". Rumors had circulated before the fight that Ali had been marked as the target in a plot to revenge the assassination of Malcolm X. Three hundred local police, state troopers, civil defense workers, and firemen were on hand to frisk the men and turn out the ladies' handbags. Ali was undisturbed by the rumors. "I fear only Allah and His Messenger," he told reporters. (In later years he would add thunderstorms and jet flights to the list.) The only other sensation to emanate from the curiously muted pre-fight publicity campaign was a report that a leading mobster had backed Liston to the tune of $30,000.

Inside the skating rink the two combatants glowered at each other once again, this time over the head of former World Heavyweight Champion Jersey Joe Walcott who was refereeing the rematch. One minute later, it was all over.

Hardly had the opening bell finished ringing than Ali was darting across the ring to stun Liston with a jarring right cross. It was the first of just three punches that Ali was to land that night. For most of this extraordinary match Ali was content to play a human *muleta*, gliding smoothly out of the path of each Liston charge like a matador before his bull. At one point he stood flat-footed with his arms limp by his sides, offering himself as a target; the bewildered Liston hesitated to accept the invitation. From the outset Sonny looked an old, old man.

Ali's second punch came some 30 seconds before the end when he landed another solid right to the side of Liston's head. Ali's trainer Chicky Ferrara, who had been placed in the opposing corner by Dundee to guard against a repetition of the eye burning which had blinded Clay in Miami, said the shot shivered Liston. "He blinked three times, like he was trying to clear his head, and I looked at Willy Reddish. I could see Reddish looked sick because he knew his fighter was in trouble."

Many fans did not see Ali's third blow. Most—even those at the ringside—did not believe the devastation it caused. Flashing his right hand over Liston's left arm he struck Sonny's jaw with what the boxing press labelled a "phantom punch." The combined speed and accuracy of the blow generated enough power to lift Liston's left foot, upon which most of his weight was placed, off the canvas. Liston sank onto his knees, his elbow, and finally rolled over onto his back like some beached whale. Cries of "Fake! Fake!" rose from the crowd, enraging Ali, who stood over Liston with bulging eyes screaming, "Get up you yellow bum! Get up and fight!" Referee Jersey Joe Walcott tried in vain to force Ali to a neutral corner so as to begin the count. "I was afraid he was going to kick Liston in the head," said Jersey Joe afterwards. "Clay was like a wild man."

As Walcott struggled with Ali, the official timekeeper, a retired local printer, was counting Liston out. He counted to ten and shouted "Out", but amidst the uproar his call went unnoticed. He began counting again. By this time Liston was lumbering into battle again behind Walcott's back. Nat Fleischer (publisher of *The Ring* magazine), shouted to Walcott, "It's over! He's out!" The referee turned, reached out for Ali's hand, and declared him the winner by a knockout. The timekeeper said the fight had lasted exactly one minute. It went into the record book as 1:42. Depending on which figures one accepts it was either the fastest or the second fastest knockout in heavyweight title history.

As Ali stood with his arms raised, the skating rink erupted in a howl of disbelief and derision. Few present, besides the participants, could believe that Liston, who had often won fights by using his head as a battering ram, could have been eclipsed by a punch that New York columnist Jimmy Cannon swore "wouldn't have dented a grape". The popular consensus of opinion held that Sonny had ended his career by taking the easy route to a $480,657 pay check. Canadian Heavyweight Champion George Chuvalo, who had planned his own match with Liston if the Bear had won, spoke for the majority when he burst through the ropes, grabbed Ali's arm and shouted, "Fix! Fix!"

Besides providing *The Ring* magazine with yards of controversial copy for months to come, the fight was also significant in that it was the first time Ali took matters completely into his own hands. In Miami he had followed Dundee's floor plan to the letter—"You have got to jab Liston. He'll be stalking and jabbing, and you have to get off first with your jab." But in Lewiston, Ali's matador strategy was all his own. "I was sick when I saw what Clay was doing," said Dundee later. "Liston was doing just what we had expected him to do and doing it better than he had in Miami Beach. Jabbing and stalking." Ali did not throw a jab for the whole 60 seconds. His counter-strategy had come to him in a dream, he had told a reporter at his Massachusetts training camp three weeks before the fight. "I have had this dream for several weeks," he had said. "It's awful real. What happens at the bell is I rush across the ring and tag Liston with a good right hand. That's a psychological trick old Archie Moore taught me, and it lets the Bear know right now who is in charge. I don't see in the dream if it knocks him out, but he never recovers and I go on to win an early knockout."

On watching the replay, Ali christened his knockout blow the "secret anchor punch." "It's a chop," he said, "so fast you can't see it. It's got a twist to it." He claimed the punch had been taught to him by aging film comedian Stepin Fetchit—Hollywood's classic Pullman attendant—who in turn had learned it from the first-ever black Heavyweight Champion, Jack Johnson.

Ali's minute-victory consolidated his position as champion and exposed the WBA to more ridicule. Yet Lewiston left a sour taste in many mouths. Bills outlawing boxing were drafted in several states including New York. The California legislature considered a resolution calling on the State Attorney General to investigate if closed-circuit televiewers had been duped. An incensed promoter in San Antonio apologised to his closed-circuit patrons for the "shameful spectacle," and donated his proceeds to a boys' club. Boxing greats Jack Dempsey and Gene Tunney proclaimed the bout a deathblow to the sport.

"Boxing wants no more of Liston," decreed *The Ring* magazine after sifting through a deluge of telegrams and letters demanding that something should be done about such a scandalous "fix."

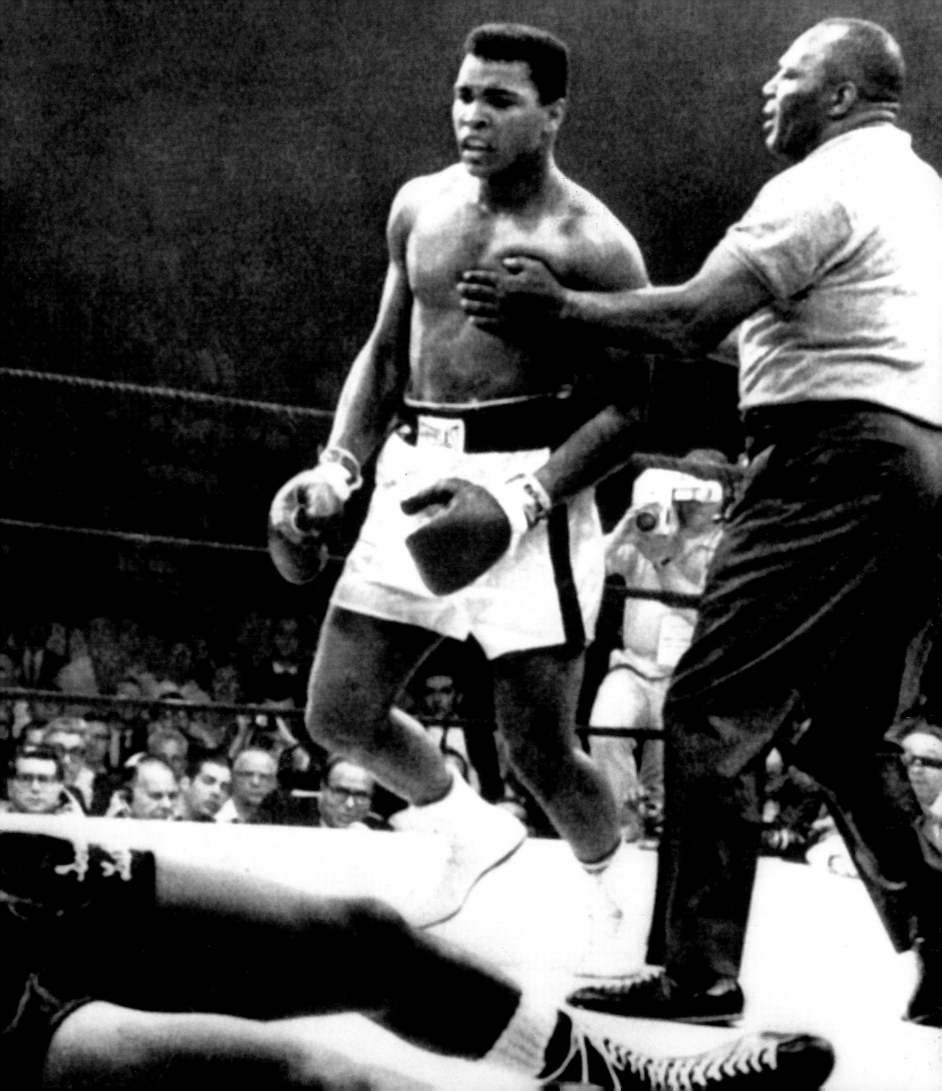

ABOVE: Ali with Hollywood comedian Stepin Fetchit, the man Ali claims had taught him his "secret anchor punch." The reporters keep insisting that it must have been a non-existent "phantom" punch because they hadn't seen it. "Don't feel bad," replies Ali. "Sonny was closer and he didn't see it either."

OPPOSITE: Ali screams at the fallen Liston to get up and fight. "I was afraid he was going to kick Liston in the head," says referee Jersey Joe Walcott afterwards. "Clay was like a wild man." Muhammad Ali: "Once he went down, I got excited; I forgot about the rules. I was having fun, and wanted to give people their money's worth. Also, people forget it now, but Liston said he lost the first fight because he had a bad shoulder. Other people said maybe the first fight was fixed. So the second time, I wanted to whup him bad. I didn't want him making excuses or quitting. I wanted him to get up, so I could show everyone how great I was."

After the fight Ali proved his commitment to the Nation once more by banishing Bundini. Since Ali's conversion the Muslims had been pressuring Bundini to enlist. Elijah Muhammad was quoted as saying he would rather convert Bundini than 12,000 ordinary men. But not even Ali could persuade Bundini to shift allegiance from Solomon to Islam.

The rift finally came when Ali's Chicago apartment was gutted by fire. Bundini saved the championship belt from the flames, but by then the relationship between the two men had so deteriorated that he didn't bother to return it. Instead he hocked it to a Harlem barber for $500. Ali opened his door one day to find the barber trying to sell him back his own belt. Bundini was fired.

With the uproar over his Muslim affiliations, non-combatant Army status, and "fixed" rematch showing no signs of abating, Ali turned on his detractors. His target was Floyd Patterson. "Freud Patterson," as his nickname suggests, was boxing's most complex and curious champion.

On one side of Patterson's deeply split personality lay a humble, self-effacing man who would meekly retrieve an opponent's gum shield after belting it out of his mouth. His most painful childhood memory was of being ridiculed for wearing his father's outsize shirts, and the experience left a permanent scar on his character. One writer claimed that, given a choice, Floyd would sign his name without capital letters. When he defeated Ingemar Johansson he apologised for his zeal. "I never want to get that angry again," he said shamefacedly. "It's wrong to hate a man the way I hated." Defeat drove him to seclusion and depression and so injured his psyche that he could only face the world in disguise.

The other Floyd Patterson—the antithesis of humility—was a jingoistic crusader who dedicated his gloves to America each time he entered a ring—"I love the United States despite all the things that we may have here…the prejudice," he told anyone who would listen. "This is my country, and the one that I'll fight for." Such super patriotism, coupled with his historic success in regaining the heavyweight crown from a "foreigner," made

Floyd a national hero. His disastrous but patriotically inspired efforts against the "gangster" Liston did nothing to detract from this heroic image.

Floyd was also a recent convert to religion, but his God was a Roman Catholic. Ali's "un-American" Islamic doctrine infuriated him. "I am willing to fight for nothing if necessary", he promised, "just so I can bring the championship back to America."

Ali was outraged. "I wish you would print for Patterson to read that if he ever convinces my managers to let him in the same ring with me, it's going to be the first time I ever trained to develop in myself a brutal killer instinct," he told *Playboy* before the Lewiston rematch.

Some weeks after the fight had been scheduled for Las Vegas, Ali gate-crashed Patterson's training camp accompanied by an expectant crowd of reporters and photographers. He ranted at the embarrassed Patterson, whom he had christened "The Rabbit." "Don't be mad at me," he shouted, thrusting a bunch of carrots at Floyd. "I'm not the white man who chased you out from that white neighborhood." (Patterson had recently been forced to sell his new house in a white suburb. Neighbors had proved intractably hostile.)

The morning of the fight Patterson was summoned to Frank Sinatra's suite in the Sands Hotel. "Sinatra told me I could win," reported Floyd later, "[told me] how so many people in America were counting on me to win back the championship from Clay." Floyd had become the first black "White Hope" in history. "I am going to punish him," Ali predicted coldly, choosing his words slowly and deliberately. "I'm going to beat him so bad that he'll need a shoe-horn to get his hat on."

In his prime, Floyd Patterson had been a formidable opponent. His trademark was the "peekaboo" defense—gloves held high and close to the head. Floyd would lure his opponent into trying to penetrate this leather shell. Suddenly he would lash out with a devastating wave of combination punches. His gloves moved so fast that he would continue punching by reflex as his opponent was on his way down. He couldn't stop himself. In Las Vegas, Ali set out from the opening bell to bury that legend for ever.

"I boxed well in the first round," recalled Patterson in *Esquire* nine months later. Perhaps the passage of time had dimmed his memory. While it was true that all three judges awarded Patterson the round, their decision was based more on Ali's negative performance than Floyd's mastery of the ring. For the full three minutes Ali did not deign to attempt a single punch. He was after humiliation, which took time. "Uncle Tom!" taunted Ali as he danced around the hapless Patterson, "…white man's nigger!" At the end of the round he looked at Joe Louis seated just below his corner and asked, "Why can't they get me a real challenger?"

In the second round Ali started fighting. Leaning back, effortlessly avoiding any rare counter-punches, Ali's left jab beat a relentless rhythm on Patterson's swelling face. As Ali danced and jabbed, danced and jabbed, the enormous gulf between the two boxers became painfully apparent. Ali hit Patterson at will, sneering at his target and petulantly shaking his head if one of his punches happened to fall short. Outclassed in every respect, Floyd was reduced to courage alone. But all courage could do was keep him on his feet.

In the third round Patterson's back collapsed. It was, he said later, a recurrence of a muscle spasm which had dogged him for the past ten years. Between rounds his corner man tried in vain to relieve the agony by hoisting Floyd's shoulders in the air. By the fifth

OPPOSITE: Ali, at 210 lbs and 6ft 3in, towers above Patterson in his peekaboo stance. By the fifth round Floyd is a shuffling wreck, crippled by a strained back.

BELOW: Accompanied by Bundini and the press, Ali invades a bemused Floyd Patterson's training camp in Marlboro, New York. Patterson insists on calling Ali "Cassius Clay"; Ali calls Floyd a rabbit. Things turn nasty from there. "Cassius Clay is disgracing himself and the Negro race," opines Floyd. "No decent person can look up to a champion whose credo is 'hate whites'. Cassius Clay must be beaten and the Black Muslims' scourge removed from boxing." Ali responds by calling Floyd an "Uncle Tom," and vows:
I'm gonna put him flat on his
*   back*
So that he will start acting black.
Because when he was champ
*   he didn't do as he should.*
He tried to force himself into an
*   all-white neighborhood.*

he had difficulty walking. In that round Ali jabbed Patterson's face 19 times before retiring to catch his breath. He then stepped forward and hit him again four more jabs before the bell. Patterson did not return a single shot. "I hit him so many times I got tired," commented Ali. "I had to rest to be sure I'd go the rest of the way."

"You don't feel pain," author Peter Heller quotes Patterson as saying in his book, *In This Corner!* "To me it's a very lovable feeling. Maybe it's like dope. I don't know. I've never taken it. It's like you're floating. You feel like you love everybody, like a hippie, I guess." By round six, Floyd had overdosed. "I really wanted to be knocked out," he recalled. "I wanted to be knocked out with a good punch…or a good combination of punches. I wanted to go down with something that would be worthy of a knockout." Even that was denied him, although Ali did come within seconds of losing his whipping boy in the sixth. Under a particularly vicious barrage of jabs, Patterson wilted to the floor. Referee Harry Krause reached "five" before he stopped the count to force Ali into a neutral corner. A dozen seconds elapsed before Krause counted out the mandatory eight. By that time Patterson had regained his shaky footing.

After the 11th Krause asked the mangled Patterson if he wanted to continue. Floyd said yes, but two minutes into the 12th Krause stepped between the fighters and declared Ali the victor. Recalled Floyd: "You may remember seeing me turn to the referee, shaking my head. 'No, *no*.' Many people thought I was protesting his decision to stop the fight. I *really* was protesting his stopping those punches. I wanted to be hit by one really good one. I wanted to go out with a great one, to go down that way. It never happened…"

The next day, Patterson was humble Floyd once more. "I was beaten by a better fighter," he mumbled through pneumatic lips. "Mr Clay will be a great fighter when he gets more experience." "There are always excuses when I fight," retorted Ali. "I can't box and I can't hit and I need experience, but here I am. I'm the Heavyweight Champion." Turning to the cameras he said in his best stentorian voice, "Patterson was fighting for you folks. He was fighting for America. I was fighting for the championship. I pay taxes. They can't talk about you Floyd. You're the good clean American boy, and I'm that bad Muslim."

Later Ali was more magnanimous. When a *Ring* magazine reporter asked what he had been saying to Patterson during the fight, he replied, "Let's forget it. Floyd's a good fellow. He's a man." But the sports fans and writers couldn't forget. At the end of the bout the crowd had cheered the loser and hooted the winner. Next morning the papers called Ali, among other things, "a sadist, a tormentor and a fighter obeying the vile orders of a discredited organization." It was unanimously agreed that Ali had propped up Patterson during the early rounds to prolong his agony.

Wrote Joe Louis: "I would have been ashamed to do it. Clay wasn't doing his best as a fighter. He was putting on a show, like wrestlers. He could have knocked out Patterson any time he really went to work, certainly no later than the sixth, when he had Floyd on the floor. Let's face it. Clay is selfish and cruel."

Ali denied he had pulled his punches. "I hit him with my best punches, and he didn't fall," he said. Perhaps so, but at the expense of Patterson, Ali had revealed a ruthless, wolfish side to his nature, which unsettled many of those admirers who saw it. He had succeeded in making his point. But it had won him few friends.

Patterson's popularity also faded. When he was ushered into Sinatra's suite to deliver his customary apology, the singer rose and walked to the far end of the room almost out of earshot. "I got the message," said Floyd. "I left." The boxing press was more tactful, offering its condolences before publishing his epitaph. But Patterson had no intention of retiring. For years afterwards he hovered around boxing rings like a battered black tragedian, soaking up punishment and pay-checks with equal enthusiasm. However he always remained humble Floyd. In August 1966 he appeared on *Esquire*'s front cover under the heading "In Defense of Cassius Clay, by Floyd Patterson."

Ali's New Year began badly. On January 7th, the courts at his own request dissolved his fragile marriage. The divorce came as no surprise; separation rumors had been circulating since soon after the first Liston fight. Ali's increasing involvement with the Nation had provided the final impetus. Sonji was "a party girl, a good-time girl", remembers one close friend, who ignored the austere and chauvinistic Muslim sense of propriety. In court Ali claimed his wife had failed to meet Muslim standards. She wore skimpy dresses, he told the judge. "You could see all the slits in her body." The judgement cost Ali dearly. Sonji won alimony of $15,000 a year for ten years and an additional $22,500 to her lawyers, a total of $172,000. "I am the only one to beat him," she crowed before leaving to sing the blues in a Pittsburgh nightclub. "He'll remember that for the next ten years while he's making my payments." In future when asked which of his opponents had been the hardest, Ali would invariably answer, "My first wife".

On February 17th, Ali was relaxing on the lawns of his Miami home when a local reporter hurried over to tell him he was now eligible for Army service. The Pentagon had discovered that two million college graduates—as well as Muhammad Ali—were classified 1-Y. Desperately striving to meet the demands of an escalating war, it had dropped its Army pass percentile by 15 points. Ali's previous score of 16 now meant that he was shortly to be reclassified I-A—eligible for induction. "How can they do this without another test to see if I'm wiser or worser than last time?" he cried impulsively. "Why are they gunning for me? I ain't got no quarrels with them Viet Congs."

PRECEDING PAGES: Ali connects with the crippled Patterson. "I hit him so many times I got tired," says Ali later. Angelo Dundee: "Muhammad did a number on him. I would've liked to have seen the fight stopped, because his back went out and everything else. I didn't like it. But a lot of people forget that, when that bell rings, Ali is a fighter, a tough guy."

OPPOSITE: "What's my name!" Ali brutalizes the detested Ernie Terrell. Terrell: "I had a great chance to win that fight. But during the second round, he took his thumb and he poked it in my eye and the muscles that turn the eye got caught in that bone and the eye wouldn't turn. I would see one guy over there and one guy over here whenever he moved around. It looked like I was fighting two Alis."

BELOW: Ali nonchalantly explains to reporters why Floyd had to be punished: "Patterson was fighting for you folks. He was fighting for America."

Ali could hardly have picked a more inopportune moment to criticize his country's involvement in Vietnam. At that time, America was gearing itself for war on a grand scale. In 1964, 147 American "advisers" had died in combat. A year later the death roll had jumped to 1,400. Suddenly in 1966 there were 400,000 troops in Vietnam, and in that year 5,000 Americans were to die. The extraordinary speed of this escalation stifled protest; the few voices raised against the war were considered to be jeopardizing lives. The same day that Ali coined his famous "Viet Congs" remark, General Maxwell Taylor warned dissident senator Wayne Morse that protest could benefit only the enemy. Both stories appeared side by side in the morning papers and by implication Ali became a "tool of Hanoi". Ali refused to recant. Instead he coined a second, equally quotable riposte: "No Viet Cong ever called me nigger!" Its effects were immediate.

For almost a year the sportswriters had been urging Ali to face Ernie Terrell, a 6ft 6in boxer from Chicago who held the WBA's version of the heavyweight title. Terrell was anxious to resolve the anomaly and had already brought a suit against Ali for calling himself champion. The WBA was also eager to end its ludicrous position. The Nevada Boxing Commission—a WBA member—had approved the Patterson bout on the condition that Ali would meet Terrell next. In March the contracts were signed. What followed soon became the most convulsive promotion since the much-travelled Jack Johnson vs. Jess Willard match of 1915.

Ironically it was Terrell, a confirmed patriot, who initiated the trouble. Terrell numbered amongst his friends and business associates a Mr. Bernard Glickman whose dubious activities had earned him the attention of the FBI. Glickman had assisted Terrell with nightclub bookings for his rock and roll group, The Heavyweights. He had also appeared in Terrell's corner during his fight against George Chuvalo in Toronto. When Terrell applied for a license to meet Ali in Madison Square Garden the New York commissioners deplored the liaison. "The association of Ernie Terrell with Bernie Glickman in the entertainment field and in professional boxing over a period of years is detrimental to the best interests of professional boxing," ruled General Melvin Krulewitch in denying the licence.

With New York barred, the promoters turned to Chicago, where it was Ali who came under investigation. His Vietnam protests had outraged the American Legion and the Veterans of Foreign Wars. Together they campaigned to have Ali banned from the ring.

From Chicago the fight travelled to Louisville where Ali was once again persona non grata. The South has been the chief recruiting area of the American armed forces since the Civil War, and Louisville's streets contain an inordinate number of billboards advertising the Army, Navy, Air Force, and Marines. Louisvilleans were fiercely proud of their sacrifices and unforgiving to "draft-dodgers." Nine years after the abortive Terrell promotion the city fathers changed a downtown side street named Armory Place to Muhammad Ali Place. The new sign stood for a day until pressure from the ubiquitous veteran groups forced its removal. Armory Place remains Armory Place.

From Louisville the fight moved to Pittsburgh, to Bangor, Maine, to Huron, South Dakota before, like his mentor Jack Johnson, Ali realized he would have to leave the United States to follow his profession. Across the Canadian border the fight was almost as unwelcome. Four different sites were chosen and refused before Toronto grudgingly accepted.

It was left to Ernie Terrell to complete the charade. While training at his camp near Atlantic City, Terrell announced he was abandoning his challenge. His excuse was contractual commitments, but most critics believed he was gambling on Ali's eventual disqualification or imprisonment. From Terrell's viewpoint there seemed no point in risking his WBA title when he was almost certain of gaining everything for nothing in a matter of months. *The Ring* magazine later speculated that Terrell had been warned against the match by the FBI who were still investigating Bernie Glickman. Whatever his reasons, Terrell passed up a $75,000 purse plus expenses and left Ali with a date (March 19th), a site, but no partner. Main Bout, the harassed promoter, scoured the rankings for available opposition and finally settled for local fighter and Canadian Heavyweight Champion George Chuvalo.

Chuvalo had been previously considered as a possible challenger. Between the Liston bouts, Ali had visited Chuvalo's camp prior to the Canadian's match with Floyd Patterson. (The visit was not a success; during the journey Ali drove his bus—Big Red—into a ditch while chatting over his shoulder to newsmen.) Ali had been impressed enough by Chuvalo to change his nickname from "Washerwoman" to "Washerman." After the Liston rematch Ali remembered the Canadian. "Chuvalo may be the best man for my next fight," he had mused. "He's tough and he's crazy. He pushed me twice after the fight and no man does that unless he's out of his mind." But in Toronto everybody—including Ali—was well aware that he was merely Terrell's substitute. In his 42-bout career Chuvalo had been beaten a dozen times—the last time at the hands of Terrell. His strongest boast was that he had never been knocked out.

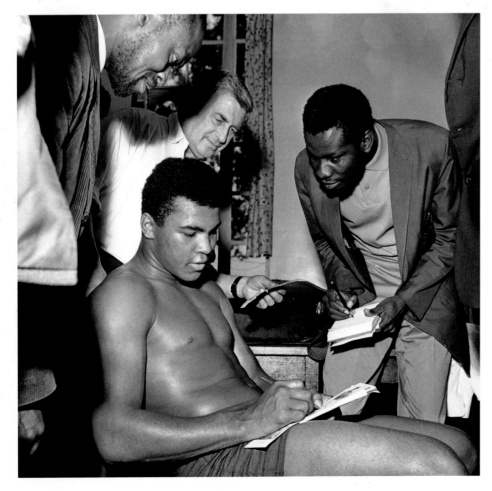

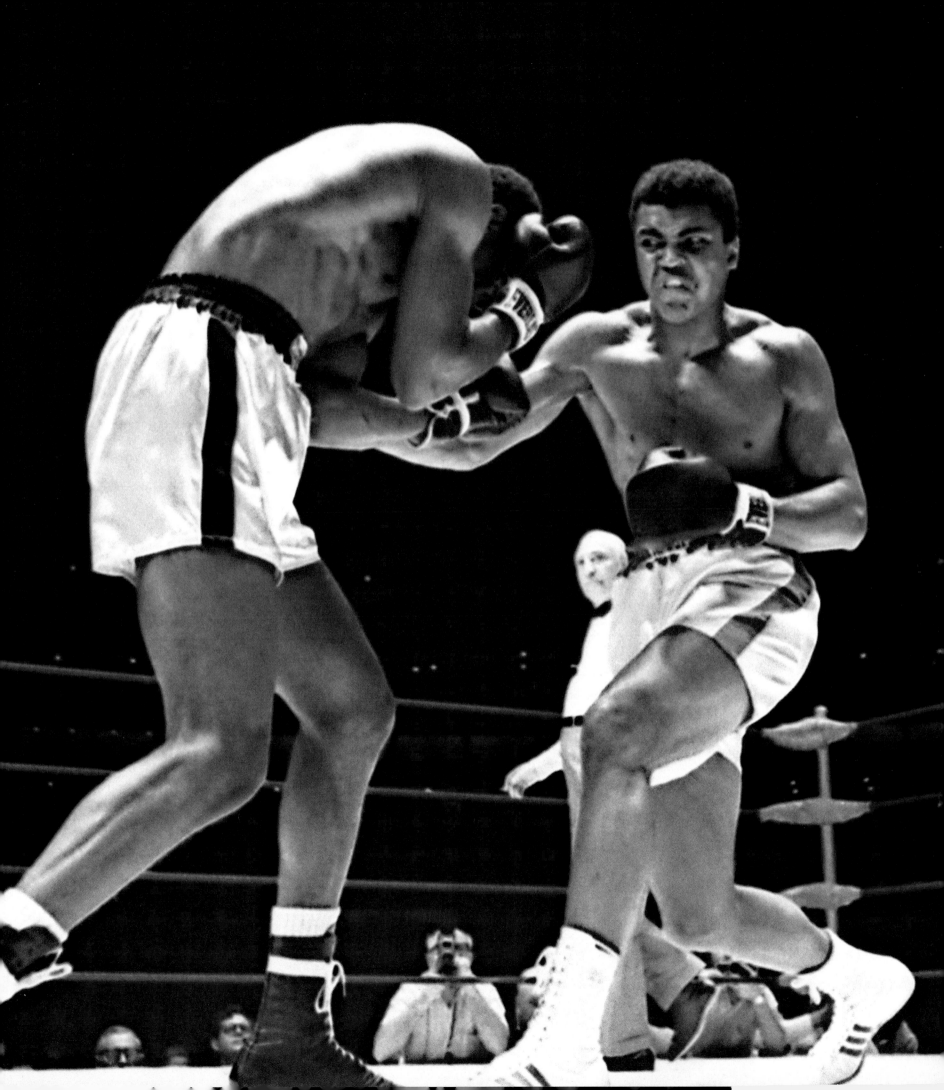

ABOVE: Ali pulls on army boots for training. The press finds his choice of footwear ironic.

RIGHT: Although he tries, Ali fails, like all Chuvalo's other opponents, to knock his challenger down. "I bruised my knuckles on him," complains Ali after the gruelling 15 round battle.

OPPOSITE: Monticello, NY. Ali trudges up a country road after crashing his bus on the way to George Chuvalo's training camp. When he finally reaches the camp, he is quite impressed by his opponent, so much so that he changes his nickname from "Washer-woman" to "Washerman".

Exile palled on Ali. Although Toronto offered a more sympathetic climate than his homeland, he became morose and dispirited in the days leading up to the fight. Lying on his motel bed he lamented: "They maketh me fight out of the country. They leadeth me down the path of bad publicity. I shall be bewailed in the history of sport forever. The sports fan shall follow me all the days of my life." The approaching fight he dismissed contemptuously. "All this is child's play," he scoffed, "this stuff ain't nothing."

Chuvalo's trainers had advised him to bulldoze his way past Ali's jabbing left glove and exploit the champion's weakness at in-fighting. From the bell he followed his instructions to the letter, barging across the ring in his awkward crouching gait and hurling punches at Ali's midriff. Many of the blows fell below the belt, but referee Jackie Silvers turned a blind eye and allowed the local hero to continue his assault unreprimanded. Although he was hit hard, and often, during the first four rounds, Ali made light of Chuvalo's belligerence. At one point he stood still with his arms raised, inviting the Canadian to punch him harder. The risk frayed Dundee's nerves. "Why he does it is beyond me," he later confessed. "I was afraid he was going to get hit in the pit of the spine and be immobilized."

By the middle rounds Ali appeared firmly in control. His left jab repeated its work against Patterson, scattering Chuvalo's shuffling attacks and rendering his face almost unrecognizable. At the final bell one writer noted that the challenger's face looked as if it was composed of Ping-Pong balls. The only time Ali seemed in any danger was when he became wedged in a corner and was unable to dodge Chuvalo's blows. But although he tried, Ali could not break his opponent's spotless knock-down record. "I bruised my knuckles on him," said Ali, and still Chuvalo kept taking the fight up to the champion. In the later rounds his seemingly suicidal resolve was vindicated when Ali began to tire visibly. Bundini, who had defected to Chuvalo's corner—as he had to Patterson's four months earlier—pleaded for a last effort. "Think of yo' babies, George," he urged in his unmistakable foghorn voice. In the final round Chuvalo did manage to brush past the jab and land a stunning right on Ali's chin, rocking the champion back on his heels. It was the closest the Canadian came to victory, but he had needed a clean knockout. Ali shook off his weariness and dourly slugged it out to the bell, earning a unanimous decision. Chuvalo had taken Ali for the first time in his career to the full 15 rounds. "This was my toughest battle," admitted Ali. "I have a sore kidney from the pounding Chuvalo gave me when he cornered me. He was tougher than Patterson or Liston. He's tougher than Terrell!"

As a concession to WBA intransigence, the Toronto Commissioners had insisted on labelling the fight a "Heavyweight Showdown." 'Muhammad Ali, The People's Champ vs. George Chuvalo, Canadian Heavyweight Champion," read the posters. The new title was virtually the only reward Ali gained from the match. Certainly the $160,000 gross takings barely compensated for the weeks spent traipsing across two countries. "Clay in the US is a dead piece of merchandise," pronounced Main Bout's Bob Arum. "He's through as far as big-money closed-circuit is concerned."

ABOVE: Ali arrives at the United States Armed Forces Examining and Entrance Station in Houston on April 28, 1967, where he is scheduled to be inducted into the army. When his name—Cassius Marcellus Clay—is called out he refuses to step forward. After being warned that he faces a five-year jail sentence, he is called to step forward a second time. Again he refuses. He then hands over a written statement, reading "I refuse to be inducted into the armed forces of the United States because I claim to be exempt as a minister of the religion of Islam." One hour later, before he'd even been charged with any crime, the New York State Athletic Commission suspends his boxing license and strips him of his title. The other bodies soon followed suit.

OPPOSITE: With a possible five-year jail sentence hanging over his head, a preoccupied Ali enters the ring against Zora Folley.

A t home in Louisville, Ali's case dragged slowly through the interminable Draft Board and Justice Department bureaucracies. He had appealed against reclassification on three grounds: he was a conscientious objector, a minister of God, and a family man who would suffer financially if inducted. On his return Ali learned the FBI was investigating him, and that several prominent boxing officials had been questioned about his activities. To escape the impossible situation he now found himself in, he agreed to tour Europe, signing as his first contender Henry Cooper. He applied to his draft board for an exit visa. It finally arrived on the very day of his scheduled departure.

The tour was no gilded swing through the friendlier suburbs of international boxing. The truth was that Ali desperately needed a respectable payday. Toronto had been a financial disaster and already the newspapers were reporting that he had applied to the courts for time to pay Sonji back alimony. Europe promised a perfect opportunity to revive his flagging bank balance. The British promoters, for example, offered Ali £100,000 plus ancillary rights. When percentages from the American closed-circuit venues and England's now defunct Pay-TV network were added in, the final total amounted to a sizeable temptation.

Ali found that Britain had warmed to him since his last visit, primarily because of the champion's genuine admiration for Cooper and his unexpected left hook. "An English gentleman," said Ali of his opponent, "who I think is a worthy challenger for my title." The British public knew little of the Black Muslims and cared even less.

Ali basked contentedly in the hospitality. "I am happy here," he told the children at the London Free School. It was a comment he was to repeat on several occasions. At a press conference shortly before

the fight Ali was positively effusive in his praise for the British Government, the British public and even "the bus and taxi drivers I have met on my way to and from the gym." He hurriedly added his thanks to the President, US Government officials, and the Louisville Draft Board for consenting to the match.

Cooper entered the ring a 10-1 outsider. Although he was still the British and Empire Heavyweight Champion and his left hook had lost little of its force since 1963, at 32 he was giving away eight years and 16 pounds to his competitor. Also his eyebrows had worn to tissue paper; the local joke was that 'Enery started bleeding before he got up off the stool.

For the first three rounds Cooper, overawed by the 20 foot square ring, which Ali had stipulated in the contract, found difficulty in reaching the champion. Ali was content to remain a step ahead of the stalking Cooper, who nursed his left glove like a loaded missile. The next two rounds saw a quickening of the pace as Ali allowed Cooper to come closer. In the sixth he achieved the inevitable. Soon after the bell he caught Cooper a slashing right cross to the eye. There followed a sharp exchange of punches and when Cooper finally stepped back blood was streaming from his transparent left eyebrow. In his autobiography Cooper had this to say about the people who paid to watch him: "The boxing public generally are a bloodthirsty lot. They like to see a good, hard fight, and if there's plenty of gore and snot flying around they love it." If his judgement was sound, Henry scaled a new summit in boxing entertainment the night he fought Ali in London's Arsenal Football Ground. His cut was a truly sickening wound. Cooper's prominent bones and brittle scar tissue had once again conspired to produce his premature downfall. "It was the worst cut I ever had in boxing," he remembered, "deeper and longer even than in my first fight with him…I knew at once it was a bad cut with the warm blood gushing onto my body. I could feel it on my shoulders and chest; it was really blinding me." The crowd, which until that moment had confined itself to chanting "Hen-ree, Hen-ree" between rounds, screamed for Cooper to unload his left. Everyone realized he had only seconds left in which to win. Ali stayed clear. A minute later referee George Smith stepped in and stopped the blood bath.

Encouraged by the profits from the Cooper match, British promoters enticed Ali back to Britain and into the ring on August 6th with the other English heavyweight, Brian London. Like Cooper, London was 32 and seemed to have been around British boxing since the bare-knuckle days. For all his years he had enjoyed little success. Henry Cooper had beaten him three times, the first as far back as 1956. In 1959, when London was in his prime, Ingemar Johansson had laughed, "London could not beat my sister." His one world-title bid had been aborted by Floyd Patterson in the 11th, seven years before. He had lost 13 of his 48 professional fights. Ali's entourage titled him "the human punching bag". The half-filled Earl's Court Stadium summed up British opinion of the "Blackpool Rock."

Apart from two delicate taps early in the fight, London failed to lay a glove on Ali. For two rounds Ali danced circles around his bedazzled partner, jabbing at his prominent jaw while Dundee yelled, "Finish him off…Finish him off!" At the beginning of the third Dundee ordered, "Enough, Muhammad. Take him out in this one." Ali immediately landed a right followed by a one-two combination onto London's inviting chin. London backed into his own corner and Ali followed. With his quarry on the ropes, the champion unleashed an astonishing succession of

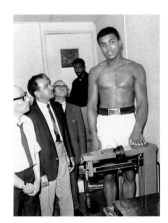

ABOVE: Ali weighs in before the second Cooper fight in London, May 18, 1966.

OPPOSITE: Many consider Ali's fight against Cleveland Williams one of his finest performances. Not only does he dispel the myth that he cannot punch, he also unveils the "Ali Shuffle" for the first time.

PRECEDING PAGES: The Champion reigns supreme. Left: (Clockwise from top) The elusive Ernie Terrell is beaten for the full 15 rounds by a merciless Ali; Brian London fails to make it to the fourth; Karl Mildenberger survives until 12; Cleveland Williams is dispatched in three. Page 149: British hero Henry Cooper goes down to bloody defeat for the second time. Cooper: "They were the worst cuts I ever had in boxing, the ones I got in the two Ali fights, and that second one was perhaps worse than the first one. I had to have 60-odd stitches in that. It was like plastic surgery."

quick-fire left and right punches at London's face. The blows weren't particularly hard, just incredibly fast. London slid slowly onto his side. Towards the end of the count he gave a few kicks like a dying rabbit and then lay still. Eleven thousand fans jeered in disgust.

Afterwards, fully clothed, cleaned up, and set to return to Blackpool less than three-quarters of an hour after the beginning of the fight, London confessed he had no desire to meet Ali again. "He hits you so often you're dizzy," he said before picking up his easily earned $100,000 paycheck. The papers headlined the affair a disgrace and a black eye for Britain. London was pilloried as a cowardly "lumbering, bumbling, unskilled worker." One writer described the fiasco as "a lamb trying to bite a dog!"

Accompanying Ali on both his British trips had been Elijah Muhammad's son Herbert. Initially Herbert was introduced as Ali's "spiritual adviser and public relations officer." After the London episode he became Ali's manager. The announcement caused little surprise. Bill Faversham had retired as active manager in mid 1965 following two heart attacks. As *The Ring* magazine disdainfully reported, "Black Muslim control of Cassius long since had been established."

Ali flew home to Louisville to plead his case for exemption. His controversial appeal had been shuffled back and forth between the various judicial bodies like a time bomb and the strain of waiting for a decision was beginning to show. "At times he seemed preoccupied and almost disinterested during his training for the London fight," reported *The Mirror*, "…a champion fighting on two fronts."

Uncertainty about his future, coupled with the hectic pace of his title defenses, finally caught up with Ali in Frankfurt. Against Karl Mildenberger, another 10-1 outsider, he contributed a lackluster performance in a match which seesawed for 12 rounds. Mildenberger's unfamiliar southpaw stance disconcerted Ali in the early rounds and it wasn't until midway through the fourth that he was able to shrug off the German's savage liver punches and open a cut under his right eye. Towards the close of the fifth a right sent the challenger to the canvas. Three times he went down, but each time recovered his feet and fought on gamely. In the ninth, peering through bulging eyelids, Mildenberger rallied and took the fight up to the champion. For two rounds Ali tried his hardest to end the battle, but failed to do so. Halfway through the 12th, with Mildenberger propped against the ropes unable to defend himself, the referee pulled Ali off. Ali seemed relieved it was over. It had not been a championship display. Ali returned to Chicago nursing a damaged right hand, the first injury in what was to be a painful and protracted history of hand ailments.

During Ali's American absence much had been written about Texan Cleveland Williams, a formidable slugger in the Sonny Liston tradition. Bad luck had constantly undercut Williams' potential. On the eve of his 1964 match with Ernie Terrell in the WBA elimination tournament, a Texas Highway Patrolman had shot him in the stomach with a .38 magnum. The bullet seemed certain to prematurely end Williams' career, but after a 5½ hour operation the chief surgeon was moved to comment, "This man has an iron constitution, a body of steel. I believe he will be fighting again." Williams, who had already survived a girlfriend's cleaver assault, did recover. In doing so he paved the way for Ali's return to American rings.

After his three impressive comeback fights, Texas was anxious to see Williams try for the heavyweight title. This desire outweighed the state's strong links with the American Legion and the Veterans of Foreign Wars, and when an Ali vs. Williams match was scheduled for Houston, there was little local protest. Boxing commissions in other states looked on with interest. New York Commissioner Eddie Dooley hinted at a possible Ali vs. Terrell match in Madison Square Garden if all went smoothly in Houston. "We are not inclined to rush into giving Cassius a licence," he said. "We must wait for the reaction to his return to the United States, and the Williams affair in Houston."

On the night, Ali had no trouble with either hostile demonstrators or Cleveland Williams. From the bell Ali pranced around, ducking and slipping the bemused Texan's brutish punches. He even found time to unveil his tribute to Fred Astaire—a flashy but ineffectual quick-step that he named the "Ali Shuffle". In the third round Ali changed gears almost audibly, came down off his toes and stood in the center of the ring slugging it out with Williams. In five punches he had split his opponent's face and pummelled him to the floor for the fourth time, but this time for the count. It was hailed by many as his finest performance.

Early in the New Year Ali finally caught up with the elusive Ernie Terrell. It was the match critics and fans had been eagerly awaiting for more than a year, and 37,321 people packed the Houston Astrodome—an indoor record. The WBA champion added to the suspense by claiming to have perfected a "secret weapon" with which to beat Ali. Perhaps he had a psychological weapon in mind: at every opportunity he pointedly referred to Ali as "Cassius Clay". If so, it backfired disastrously. As with Floyd Patterson, Ali marked Terrell down for a slow death.

Ali found difficulty both in overcoming Terrell's height and reach and in penetrating his defense, which consisted largely of gloves held tightly over the face. But by the middle rounds he had established his superiority. Terrell's eyes were razor slits as he stumbled hopelessly after his evasive opponent. Ali was content to stay one step ahead, sniping at Terrell's swollen face. "What's my name?" he demanded after each punch. "Tell me my name!" Referee Harry Kessler recalled later that the deciding blow was a vicious left hook Ali landed in the eighth round. "The fight ended then and there as far as Terrell was concerned," said Kessler. As far as Ali was concerned, it was to last the full 15 rounds. In the later stages he did stop taunting Terrell and made a concerted effort to satisfy Dundee's plea to "put him out". On failing to do so, he resurrected the doubts about his punching ability, which he thought had been buried with Cleveland Williams. The final decision, however, was unanimous. Exhausted, Terrell was led to his dressing room and from there to hospital for an emergency operation on his left eye. Like George Chuvalo, his face was a battlefield.

Ali was now undisputed ringmaster of heavyweight boxing. Outside the ropes, the net was drawing tighter. The Army had already set a date for his induction; if he refused to comply he faced prosecution and a five-year jail sentence. A month before the induction deadline he met the WBA's top ranking contender in Madison Square Garden. Zora Folley, approaching 35, was a perennial challenger but never champion. He had been fighting professionally since 1953 and in his youth had shown considerable potential. (In 1958 he had been paired with Archie Moore as leading challengers for Patterson's title.) Yet somehow fame and the wealthy

OPPOSITE: The last waltz–Zora Folley. "The right hands Ali hit me with just had no business landing, but they did," says an overawed Folley afterwards. "They came from nowhere. He's had 29 fights and acts like he's had a 100. He could write the book on boxing, and anyone that fights him should be made to read it." Angelo Dundee: "When they stripped him of the title, that was when he was in his prime years. He had looked the best he ever looked to me in the Folley fight."

BELOW: Ali is surrounded by the press as he leaves the Federal Court House on June 20, 1967, after an all-white jury finds him guilty of unlawfully refusing army induction. While the prosecution stated that it had no objection to Ali's receiving a lesser sentence– "The only record he has is a minor traffic offense"–the conservative Judge Joe Ingraham gives him the maximum sentence of five years in prison and a $10,000 fine.

bouts had eluded him. "The man deserved a title shot a long time ago," said Ali at the signing. "He has fought everyone and ducked nobody, just like me." Ali said he was happy that Folley–"such a nice man"—would be taking home an unusually large paycheck to his eight children. In deference to Folley's geniality, Ali promised to end the fight painlessly as soon as the home-movie makers had filmed a worthwhile amount of footage.

Folley was one of boxing's genuine scientists. Before the match he meticulously studied all of Ali's fight films, memorizing each jab and thrust and developing his own counter-punches. As he climbed through the ropes he was confident he knew everything there was to know about his opponent. He was wrong. Ali opened with a style Folley had never seen before.

Ali toyed with Folley for the first three rounds, standing with his hands by his sides daring his opponent to attack, as he had done with Liston in Maine. In the fourth, at Dundee's insistence, he hit Folley a short, chopping right to the jaw that left the veteran spreadeagled on the canvas. People began streaming to the exits and with Ali standing with his arms raised in a victory salute, the fight looked at a tame end. But on the count of six Folley regained his feet and, blood streaming from his nose, tore into attack. Folley doggedly stalked Ali for the next two rounds until once again the champion closed his opponent's eyes with a lethal left jab. At the start of the seventh Folley tried to rush Ali. Carefully maneuvering his target to center-ring, Ali buckled Folley's defenses with a left and finished him off with a sharp right cross to the jaw. It was thrown so swiftly that to

many present the knockout blow was another of Ali's phantom punches. When Ali stepped back, Folley was lying on his stomach. He attempted to rise, rolled over, and was counted out. "The greatest fight he ever looked was against Folley," said Angelo Dundee seven years later. "Cleveland Williams, that was a great fight….But against Folley he was fantastic. And if he had gone on from there? Well, there's no telling…"

Folley's eclipse meant the end of worthwhile challengers to Ali's title. The only course open to him was Joe Louis' Bum of the Month Club. Ali already had his eyes on Louis' record of 27 title defenses before retirement. His choice of opponent for his ninth defense indicated his intentions—Floyd Patterson. On April 5th the contracts were signed. Five years later the two actually met in the ring.

On April 25, 1967, Ali's chief attorney Hayden Covington filed a 67-page petition in the Federal Court stating his grounds for appeal. Ali claimed he should be regarded as a minister in the Nation of Islam under a precedent established by a radio/TV technician named Dickenson. The Supreme Court had ruled that Dickenson was legally a Jehovah's Witness minister because he had expounded the faith to such a degree. (Soon after Covington lodged the plea, Ali preached in a Houston mosque on the evils of pork. He told the congregation that eating pork damaged the brain.)

Three days later, on April 28, 1967, Ali walked past a battery of reporters and cameramen into the Armed Forces Induction Center in Houston. There, in a back room, Ali refused to recite the oath of allegiance administered by an Army sergeant. Instead he proffered a note stating that he was a Muslim minister and that "I find I cannot be true to my belief in my religion by accepting such a call." With that, he left and returned home to telephone his mother.

New York Commission Chairman Edwin Dooley did not bother to wait for the courts to decide on Ali's plan. Immediately, he withdrew title recognition. The WBA followed suit and once again retrieved its truant title. Two months later on June 20th Ali was convicted in Houston's Federal Courthouse of unlawfully refusing induction. Covington argued unsuccessfully that, "the head of the Church, the Honorable Elijah Muhammad, has appointed and designated him (Ali) to fill the position somewhat like a travelling bishop." Judge Joe Ingraham ruled that the court was not to question the 1-A draft classification, nor was it privileged to decide on Ali's ministerial claim. The jury had virtually nothing to decide. Judge Ingraham fined Ali $10,000 and sentenced him to the maximum punishment of five years imprisonment. Ali lodged another appeal, but the conviction had effectively wrecked his career. All that was left to the ex-champion was the last word:

Clean out my cell
And take my tail
On the trail
For the jail
Without bail
Because it's better in jail
Watchin' television fed
Than in Vietnam somewhere dead.

To Fall Like Lucifer

"I'm black. They never let me forget it. Sure, I'm black. And I'll never let them forget it!"

Jack Johnson, first black Heavyweight Champion

For three and a half years the elders of the boxing fraternity conspired to exorcise the spirit of Ali from their profession. Removing Ali's title was merely the opening broadside in what became the most inflexible boxing lockout since John L. Sullivan's turn of the century "color line." Branded a disgrace to boxing, Ali was effectively blackballed from the ring. His bureaucratic colleagues then arranged a series of elimination tournaments—mainly comprised of Ali's past victims and former sparring partners—to determine their respective champions. Finally the two leading pretenders to Ali's crown were played off against each other to produce the new Heavyweight Champion of the World.

But Ali refused to be exorcised. "Let them have the elimination bouts," he decreed. "Let the man that wins go to the backwoods of Georgia and Alabama or to Sweden or Africa. Let him stick his head in an elementary school; let him walk down a back alley at night. Let him stop under a street lamp where some small boys are playing and let him say: 'What's my name?' and see what they really say. Everybody knows me and knows I am the champion. You see they know who the real champion is and all the rest is sparring partners."

For once Ali and his public were in harmony. Despite every effort by the WBA, the NYBC, boxing commissioners across the country and the more stridently "patriotic" members of the press, Ali's supporters survived, and indeed multiplied. At each WBA bout a persistent chant would float down from the terraces to sour the victor's moment of glory…*Ah-lee. Ah-lee!* Whenever Joe Frazier, the new Heavyweight Champion of the World, swaggered onstage to sing songs before his Caesar's Palace audience, there was always someone to shout from the back seats, "Ali 'ud whip your ass!"

In time, what had begun as a hard-core minority of Ali fanatics keeping "the faith," swelled to a solid majority of sympathizers. Ali was publicly transformed from villain to cult-figure to hero until, in the late summer of 1970, he entered Angelo Dundee's 5th Street Gym to prepare for his sanctioned return from the wilderness. Surrounded once again by the familiar faces of Bundini, Dundee, Youngblood and the rest of his courtiers, Ali knew he had finally triumphed. But at a price. "It's been so long," he murmured, wistfully surveying the termite-ridden floorboards and grimy windowpanes of Angelo's "honest" gym. "I never thought I'd be back again, here again. Back in my old life again. All those years…!"

The reasons behind Ali's Lazarus-like revival were inextricably woven into the broad social fabric of America in the late 1960s. Protest was the keynote of that period, and Vietnam its focus. 1967, the year of Ali's Federal conviction, marked a turning point in public reaction to a war which was becoming a bloody nightmare. Ten thousand of the half million American troops stationed in Vietnam died that year—double the number killed in 1966. In college campuses and coffee bars across America, the Days of Rage gave way to the Days of Dissent as the Peace Movement began in earnest. Three years later this tide of protest breached the establishment barriers blocking Ali's return to the ring.

It was more by circumstance than choice that Ali found himself swept along at the head of this current, a hero to an unfamiliar following of white liberals, students and hippies. To these new supporters, Ali was an irresistible example of the free-thinking individual crushed by a repressive power structure: while businessmen convicted of massive swindles were permitted to continue trading until every avenue of appeal had been exhausted, he had been deprived of the right to work

OPPOSITE: "If you want to see a man at his best, take a look at Ali in his prime."—US football star, Jim Brown.

OPPOSITE: Ali and Belinda in later years at Fighter's Heaven. Pictured are (clockwise from front) twins Rasheda and Jemilah, Ali, Belinda, Muhammad Iben and Maryum. "When we got married, he was an innocent guy, but he changed during the course of our marriage."

on conviction; whereas other celebrities with "the right complexion and the right connection' easily avoided the draft, he had been singled out for martyrdom. The government had even confessed to wiretapping his telephone conversations with Martin Luther King.

In March 1968, boxing fans arriving at Madison Square Garden, to watch Frazier fight Buster Mathis for the NYAC version of the heavyweight title, were forced to cross a predominantly white picket line of anti-Vietnam demonstrators clutching blown-up portraits of Ali. By the end of the decade, following in Malcolm X's footsteps, Ali was the third most popular speaker on the college lecture circuit after Eugene McCarthy and Bobby Kennedy.

Ali readily accepted his unsolicited role of anti-war hero, grateful for any friends he could find in his hostile world. (Today he still lists "hippies" among his most ardent supporters.) But to him, Vietnam was a sidetrack which had little bearing on the struggle as he saw it. Whereas the young, white protesters accepted the Black Muslims as merely another fraternal anti-war group, conveniently forgetting Elijah Muhammad's statements that "the whole Caucasian Race is a race of devils", Ali continued to view the world in black and white. He was far more attuned to black poet LeRoi Jones than the Vietnam marchers outside Madison Square Garden when Jones remarked, "Even though Buster Mathis and Joe Frazier might tell white people that they are the heavyweight champion after this fight, they will never come in the black community claiming they are the Heavyweight Champion. They know that little kids would laugh them out of the streets." To Ali, race was really the only issue at stake. "…No Vietcong ever called me Nigger!"

"I love my people," Ali explained to a delegation of well-known black athletes hopeful of persuading him to accept military service. "The little Negroes, they catching hell. They hungry. They raggedy. They getting beat up, shot, killed, just for asking for justice. They can't eat no good food. They can't get a job. They got no future. They was nothing but slaves and they the most hated people. They fought in all wars, but they live in the worst houses, eat the worst food and pay the highest rent, the highest light bill, the highest gas bill. Now I'm the one's catching hell, too. I could make millions if I led my people the wrong way, to something I know is wrong. So now I have to make a decision. Step into a billion dollars and denounce my people or step into poverty and teach them the truth. Damn the money. Damn the Heavyweight Championship. Damn the white people. Damn everything. I will die before I sell out my people for the white man's money."

Although adopted by his wide-eyed supporters as a symbol of resistance, Ali's religious beliefs never allowed him to become a fully-fledged spokesman of a Peace Movement protesting what he believed was essentially a "white man's war". The young, white students—Abbie Hoffman, Jerry Rubin, and the SDS leadership—together with white liberals such as Kennedy, McCarthy, and McGovern, took care of that.

As the black struggle submerged beneath the struggle over Vietnam, the nation's changing priorities left Ali stranded. Whereas black integrationists—Martin Luther King, Ralph Abernathy—could in all conscience throw themselves into the Peace Movement and use it to fight oppression in the name of all people irrespective of race, Ali found himself relegated to the wings, a speaker without a stage. And life outside the spotlight, he soon discovered, was a singularly unattractive proposition.

During the first months of his exile, Ali was invited to speak at Elijah Muhammad's University of Islam in Chicago. Among the students who gathered around to greet him was a 17-year-old Muslim sister from Blue Island, Illinois, named Belinda Boyd. "I didn't like Ali at first," she recalls. "All the other girls ran up to him and giggled and everything but I didn't. Well, I did get his autograph—but that was only for other girls. I guess he picked me out because I didn't act like anything special. I was different."

Belinda had been brought up as a strict Muslim. She refused to use "stuff" on her face and had never been to the movies. In her spare time she worked as a waitress in the Shabazz Restaurant next door to the Chicago mosque on 71st Street. Belinda was also strikingly beautiful with the deportment and flawless features of a model. On August 17th, the couple were married at Ali's home by Dr Morris H. Tynes, Minister of the First Church of the Master in Chicago. Herbert Muhammad was the best man.

Belinda, and the family which followed, helped fill the hole knocked in Ali's life by the courts and Commissioner Dooley. But it was a huge hole. His life was reduced to a spasmodic succession of small events, centered on the Chicago Muslim community and in particular the *Muhammad Speaks* office on 79th and Champlain. Indeed, religion held his life together. At daybreak, he and Belinda would rise, wash, wrap themselves in shawls and pray to Allah. For at least three hours each day, Ali studied the Qur'an, the Bible, and the dictionary, catching up on his overlooked education. For much of the time he pottered about the house helping Belinda, emptying the garbage, taking clothes to the cleaners, buying groceries. Once out of the house he could

BELOW: Anti-war demonstrators picket Madison Square Garden before the Buster Mathis vs. Joe Frazier match in protest at Ali's treatment at the hands of the boxing hierarchy.

ABOVE: An afro-ed Ali in *Big Time Buck White*. "I'm talking. I'm talking. I'm talking about history…"

OPPOSITE: The exiled Ali on the lecture circuit. "If I had to give up my fighting or my religion, I already know what I would do. I would give up boxing and never look back! No Vietcong ever called me a nigger. I am not going to war. Every day, they die in Vietnam for nothing. I might as well stay right here for something! If going to war—and possibly dying—would help 22 million Negroes gain freedom, justice, and equality, I would not have to be drafted. I would join tomorrow."

not resist indulging in street theater, blocking sidewalks by raising his arms over his head and shouting out such challenges to his delighted black audience as, "Who's the baddest man around here? I'm looking for a fight!" Other times he would burst into a store and repeat the performance, while the startled shoppers looked on in disbelief.

"Good luck, champ," they would say when they suddenly realized who it was.

"I'm not the champ no more."

"Don't you worry what they say. You still champ!"

George Plimpton tells how Ali once crept up behind a beefy truck driver hunched over a flat tire. "I hear you're talkin' around town that you can whup me," boomed Ali. "Well, here I is." The truck driver whirled around and then, recognising Ali, his jaw dropped and the tire iron he was holding clattered to the ground. Ali grinned, got back in his Cadillac, and sped off. "It was the speculation of what happened afterwards that caught Ali's fancy," wrote Plimpton. "How the truck-driver would come home that evening and look across the kitchen table at his wife and say, 'Hey Martha, I was changing a tire today…I know you're not going to believe this, but I was changing this tire…'"

Fun, however, was thinly spread. Most of Ali's pleasure was derived from driving aimlessly around town, around 800 miles a week on average. "Know what I do sometimes?" he asked *Esquire*'s Leonard Shecter. "Drive up to Milwaukee. When I get there I turn around and come back."

In November 1969, Ali turned his hand to acting, choosing as his debut a shoddy piece of hip Broadway exploitation titled *Big Time Buck White*. Based on the activities of the Beautiful Hallelujah Day Organization (BAD), a black political group of dubious conviction, the play purported to be a Black Power musical satire. Ali had already refused a reported $400,000 offer to play Jack Johnson in the screen production of the black champion's biography. ("I wouldn't appear on no screen with no white women," Ali had bluntly told the producers.) Buck White he considered fitted his circumstances. During the second act, Ali strode up through the crowd, sporting a fake beard and an Afro wig, to deliver his show-stopping soliloquy:

"…I'm talking. I'm talking. I'm talking about history, history 50,000 years ago, and it seems like today, because today man is filled with useless laws…Lord knows, a Whitey obeys laws. He drinks his water from pure white fountains, excretes that good food he eats in lily-white toilets, and he walks the white sidewalks and tells us that Law is a thing he created that teaches him against death. But the walking mud of Mississippi is staining those shoes. Your life is the most precious thing you'll ever have…so crush those useless laws and let man create his own universal form so that men can stand and walk their own little dark areas in life."

Unfortunately the show did not live up to its star. Even Ali had to admit, "It was pretty bad," hastening to add, "but I was great." Within a week it folded and Ali was once more in search of a job. After Broadway, Ali concentrated on his campus lectures. Initially he had been called upon to discuss his views on Vietnam and the draft, but over the years he developed his own ambitious themes: "Education of the Infant," explaining "how children go through three or four or five different colleges within themselves, even before they're three years old"; "The Art of Personality": "Personality's not something you're born with. We're born as individuals. What I'm trying to say is that personality is the development of individuality"; The Power of Suggestion": "In it I say that if you suggest failure to yourself, then you'll be a failure. Some

people say 'I'm timid' or 'I'm forgetful' or 'I'm stupid'. And once you repeat this two or three times, it deepens your stupidity or forgetfulness." (Conversely, if one endlessly repeats "I'm the greatest"…!)

The lectures provided Ali with a stage, and he enjoyed them immensely. "Durin' all the years I was away, I was never lonely," said Ali after his return. "Oh, I had a ball, drivin' to the colleges and stayin' at the inns and meetin' students and Black Power groups, the white hippies, and we'd all have sessions on what we was gonna talk about and dinner was then planned in the hall, and we'd go to the student union buildin' and have the meetin' and they'd ask me questions, all the boys and girls, black and white. Like what should we do, or what do you think is gonna happen here, you know just like I was one of those sleepy-lookin' senators up in the Capitol."

Ali's tutorials also helped swell his sagging finances. At the Federal hearing in Houston, Ali had told Judge Ingraham that he was broke. Without ring earnings, he had pleaded, he was without any form of income. The newspapers hinted that the Muslims had siphoned off the estimated $3,135,302 Ali had earned from title fights. He could not even pay his household bills, they said. Lawyer Hayden Covington filed a $250,000 suit for unpaid salary.

Several of Ali's associates agree that his finances did at times touch rock bottom. Harold Conrad: "He was broke, very broke. He survived doing lectures, which wasn't enough to keep him going…pickups on television, *What's My Line?* kinda crap. It was a terrible situation." Bundini, readmitted to the fold in early 1967, often travelled with Ali to the various mythical venues which always evaporated before they could be pinned down on paper. "…him [Ali] and his wife and me didn't have no money at all," he told José Torres. "We was eatin' out of the same pot. And sometimes the champ couldn't afford to pay me." British boxer Joe Bugner hired Ali as a sparring partner while touring the United States. "We paid him $1,000," he recalls. "He seemed glad to oblige. I know he was broke because he tried to sell me a portable radio-telephone gadget for $1,200. 'It's just what you need, Joe,' he said."

Ali himself confessed to being, if not exactly on the breadline, at least on the ice cream line. "I take my wife out and we eat ice cream," he told *Esquire*. "My wife is such a good cook I never go to a restaurant. I give her $20 for a whole week and it's enough for her. We can eat on $3 a day."

But as romantic as the poverty-stricken exile image may be, Angelo Dundee is possibly closer to the truth when he says, "He wasn't exactly rolling in money, but he never hurt. He always had money." The day Ali was stripped of his title, he received a 60 percent share in a San Antonio oil well, which paid a monthly royalty check. He was involved in a "Champburger" franchise and a publisher advanced him a considerable sum for his life story, *The Greatest*, that was published in 1977. The lectures brought in upwards of $2,000 a piece.

In a Louisville vault he had $76,000 banked in his name by the Louisville Group. By 1970, Ali had recovered sufficiently to purchase a $75,000 split-level home in Philadelphia equipped with thousands of dollars worth of added attractions—five color television sets (including one in the bathroom), a gold table service, a swimming pool and 22 telephones. Outside in the garage, a $32,000 Rolls-Royce convertible stood alongside three lesser American models on the wall-to-wall carpet. In January of that year, Ali had to be escorted from the

ABOVE: Despite the cars in the garage, exile for Ali is financially crippling, although he shrugs it off. "What do I need money for? I don't spend no money. Don't drink, don't smoke, don't go nowhere, don't go running with women. I take my wife out and we eat ice cream."

OPPOSITE: The slings and arrows of outrageous fortune —*Esquire*'s famous Ali cover, "The Passion of Muhammad Ali," May 1970. Inside the magazine, the disgruntled former champ says he is hanging up his gloves. "I'm sorry, but I'm through fighting now. Y'all keep it all. If they ever want me to fight again, the boxing commissioners of this country will literally have to beg me…They'll have to crawl on their knees in front of the television cameras and tell everybody they were wrong."

lecture hall of Mahlenberg College when black militants attacked him over the house. "You niggers give me more trouble than the whites," he told the unsympathetic audience.

However, his $75,000 house notwithstanding, Ali's premature dismissal from the ring undoubtedly robbed him of an unassailable bank account. It also robbed boxing of its richest draw-card. Jimmy Ellis, Ali's long-standing sparring partner, had finally triumphed in the WBA's risible elimination tournament. (One sports magazine labelled the playoff a "three ring circus.") Just how tenuous a grip Ellis had on the crown was shown four months later by his first title defense, against Floyd Patterson in Stockholm. The much-battered Patterson took Ellis the full 15 rounds and broke his nose into the bargain. Many ringside spectators in fact considered Floyd the winner. The NYAC champion, Olympic gold-medallist Joe Frazier, was a more formidable pretender to Ali's title. But neither he nor Ellis could muster anything like Ali's box-office appeal.

From 1968 to 1970, dozens of promoters, Ali supporters, and fortune hunters, tried vainly to arrange Ali's return bout on scores of sites ranging from Madison Square Garden to the Gila River Indian Reservation in Sacaton, Arizona. All were doomed to failure, their plans scuttled by officials either outraged at the suggestion they play host to Muhammad Ali, or fearful of a veteran backlash. Even the Gila Indians refused Ali their land, claiming that their "military and historical heritage" would not allow it.

Of all those working for Ali's reinstatement, the most persistent was former New York author and screenwriter Harold Conrad. "Honest to God, we worked through a dozen states," he remembers. "Couldn't move anybody. We got close twice. Once in Seattle we got a split

decision on the board; one voted to give the license, one was on the fence, and the other—an old man who was on the Draft Board up there—naturally he turned him down. In the last second they turned him down! In Las Vegas, the Commission agreed to license him [to face Floyd Patterson]. As I was walking into the meeting—they'd already given the okay—the Governor came in and said, 'What are you doing here?' I said, 'It's an important meeting.' 'What do ya mean?' he said, 'I'm not going to give him a license.' I said, 'but the Commission…' and he said, 'The Commission works for me…they do what I tell 'em!' I then subsequently heard it was Howard Hughes who was the big man in Nevada who didn't want the fight. Hughes was an administration guy and they didn't want the draft dodger connotation. But we were in, you know…up to the last second!"

Ali was asleep when Conrad told Dundee the fight had been cancelled. Dundee crept in and broke the news to Ali. "'Muhammad,' I says, 'it looks like the fight ain't gonna take place.' 'Well,' he says, 'it isn't gonna make no difference. What's gonna be is gonna be. They think they're doing the right thing.'" Later, Ali enjoyed the irony that a "clean-livin'" Muslim boy should be barred from Nevada because he might "corrupt" a town built on Mafia money. "Me," he asked wide-eyed, "corrupt Las Vegas?"

Unlike Jack Johnson, who jumped bail to fight on foreign soil, Ali remained a prisoner in his own country. When he was offered $250,000 to fight in Yokohama, his lawyers asked the courts for permission to make the trip, guaranteeing that Ali would report to the American authorities on his arrival and would return to the US immediately after the fight. The judge vetoed the idea. As an afterthought he ordered Ali's passport confiscated. An attempt to allow Ali to cross the border for one hour to fight in Tijuana on Mexican soil was similarly disallowed. Even Ali's offer to fight in Oakland, California, and donate all but $100 of his purse to feeding the poor in the South was ignored. "It was impossible," remembers Ali's business associate and camp follower, Gene Kilroy. "Impossible! Hate from all sides."

Ali did actually appear in two major fights during his exile—on computer printouts. The first bout, in which James J. Jeffries defeated him, so enraged Ali that he filed a million dollar suit against the computer firm. "They won't let me fight to earn a living anymore and my name is all I've got", he snapped. "Now somebody is trying to ruin that too." In the second match, filmed in August 1969, Rocky Marciano knocked Ali out in the 13th round. Marciano was killed in an air crash three weeks before the fight was shown. He never learned the outcome.

At first, Ali had managed to take each new rebuff in his stride. "This just makes me a bigger man," he would say to Gene Kilroy. But by mid-1970, he had had all he could take. That May, in an *Esquire* article headlined "I'm sorry, but I'm through fighting now," Ali resigned from boxing.

"Y'all keep it all," he railed at the boxing hierarchy. "I don't need no prestige at beating up nobody. I'm tired. And I want to be the first black champion that got out that didn't get whipped.

"Fighters are just brutes that come to entertain the rich white people. Beat up on each other and break each other's noses, and bleed, and show off like two little monkeys for the crowd, killing each other for the crowd. *And half the crowd is white*. We're just like two slaves in that ring. The masters get two of us big old black slaves and let us fight it out while they bet, 'My slave can whip your slave.' That's what I see when I see two black people fighting.

OPPOSITE: After only one year in exile Ali says of boxing, "It is a barbaric European sport… the more religious I get, the more I don't miss it." The glaring contradiction in his words doesn't escape everyone's notice, "When he catches a glimpse of himself in a mirror as he walks by, he'll whirl, strike a fighting pose, and start throwing his lightning punches. He likes the way it looks and the way it feels and he does roadwork to keep his belly in bounds. If he looks forward to anything at all, it's climbing into the ring with the winner of the heavyweight elimination now being staged to replace him as champion," comments one reporter.

BELOW: Ali is asleep when Angelo Dundee breaks the news to him that his return bout with Patterson is off, the latest in a long line of disappointments. "Well, it isn't gonna make no difference," he replies. "What's gonna be is gonna be."

"If they ever want me to fight again, the boxing commissioners of this country will literally have to beg me and to apologize publicly for all that they've done to me. They'll have to free me from all their threats. They'll have to crawl on their knees in front of the television cameras and tell everybody they were wrong."

Ali had been building up to this unequivocal resignation for more than two years, mainly through the pages of *Esquire*. (The liberal New York magazine adopted Ali as its own cause célébre. In 1968 it devoted its front cover to a picture of Ali shot through with the "slings and arrows of outrageous fortune"; a year later, a dozen celebrities demanded from the cover that Ali be permitted to fight. Inside, 90 other notables, ranging from Elizabeth Taylor to Allen Ginsberg, agreed.) "It's a barbaric European sport," Ali had said of boxing after only a year in exile. "The more religious I get, the more I don't miss it." But the reporter noticed a glaring contradiction in Ali's professed hostility towards his sport. "On the other hand, when he catches a glimpse of himself in a mirror as he walks by, he'll whirl, strike a fighting pose, and start throwing his lightning punches. He likes the way it looks and the way it feels and he does roadwork to keep his belly in bounds. If he looks forward to anything at all, it's climbing into the ring with the winner of the heavyweight elimination now being staged to replace him as champion." So too was it with Ali's resignation. After likening his years of ring life to a slave dancing for his master, he still could not resist boasting how easily he would demolish Joe Frazier, given half a chance:

It might shock and amaze ya.
*But Ali **destroyed** Frazier.*

Light-heavyweight Willie Pastrano, one of Angelo Dundee's seven world champions, summed up the hypnotism of the ring for fighters in Peter Heller's book: "After I got started, man, it's like kicking the habit, junk, or cigarette smoking, or some people get on Coca-Cola habits. Well, this here's a heavy habit, man. It becomes your way of life…the taste of the applause, the taste of being in condition, the last round while the other guy is getting tired and knowing you're looking good and doing a beautiful job. That's where it's at. It's like show business."

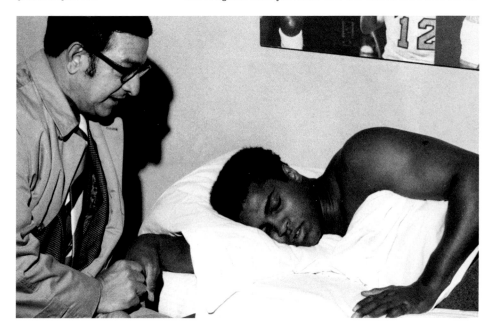

Ali had tasted boxing at its richest. Little surprise that when given a second chance he waived his demand that the commissioners crawl on their knees to him.

While Ali had been losing battles in court, Joe Frazier had been winning them in the ring. On February 16, 1970, two months before Ali's resignation, he had met Jimmy Ellis in Madison Square Garden to finally settle the championship tangle. Ellis, coached by Angelo Dundee, leaped into action at the bell, throwing his best punches at Frazier's bullet head. Frazier did not so much as blink. Ellis' heart sank as he realised he could not win. For the next two rounds the WBA champion kept punching, but he was chiselling Stonehenge with a nail file. In the fourth, Frazier gave an audible grunt and hit Ellis in the stomach, almost breaking him in half. Two more left hooks and Ellis was on the canvas. He regained his feet for as long as it took Frazier to rewind his left hook. "It felt like when you hit a baseball and you send it sailing out into the open field," said Frazier later. Ellis instinctively protected his face with his gloves. He did not seem to realise that he was lying prone on his back. As the bell rang for the fifth, Dundee threw in the towel. The boxing press heralded the second coming of Sonny Liston.

After the fight, Ali made it his business to become more closely acquainted with Frazier. Both men had homes in Philadelphia, a city lenient on taxation problems—and Ali cultivated a habit of calling Frazier on the telephone. "You just keep whuppin' those guys in the ring," he would tell Joe, "and I'll keep fighting Uncle Sam and one day we'll make a lot of money together." It is debatable whether or not Ali seriously believed he would ever fight again, but he made it clear that if he did, Frazier would be his first opponent. Both athletes trained in Philadelphia's Fairmount Park and during one run happened to meet. Ali challenged Frazier on the spot. "I walked away from him," Frazier said in Phil Pepe's biography *Come Out Smokin'*. "He wasn't going to do that to me. Not until they put up the money. I told him, 'I ain't fightin' you now, Clay, I don't want to waste it in private. I want the whole world to see what I'm gonna do to you…'"

Ali embarked on a well-publicized war of attrition. "Smokin' Joe" he derided as an ugly, flat-footed chump, a pretender to a crown he had never legitimately won. Eventually Ali's campaign was successful. Frazier cracked and angrily offered to fight Ali at a local gym. Ali leaped at the invitation and arrived accompanied by close to 1,000 supporters. The police suggested the brawl be staged outdoors in Fairmount Park. News of the match flashed around Philadelphia and by the time Ali appeared in the park, more than 2,000 excited fans had gathered in expectation. Frazier, however, failed to keep the appointment, again refusing to fight unless money was on the table.

Ali's campaign, the abortive run-ins and an endless string of media-assisted name-calling matches built enormous interest in an Ali vs. Frazier championship bout. Hopeful promoters increased their efforts to win Ali a reprieve. Most imaginative was Miami's Murray Woroner, the inspiration behind the "Woroner Dream Bout" computer fights. One of his plans was to slip the fight into a 500-seat South Miami arena, charging astronomical prices for each exclusive ticket. Another involved secretly filming the match at an undisclosed venue, thereby avoiding veteran harassment and reprisals. As it would have taken a fortnight to process and distribute the footage, Woroner proposed locking up everybody involved—fighters, corner men, camera crew—until the film had reached the cinemas.

ABOVE: The computerized "fight" against Rocky Marciano. Marciano purportedly knocked out Ali in the 13th.

With the assistance of Detroit mayor Jerry Kavanaugh, the fight was tentatively scheduled for September 21, 1970 in Detroit's Cobo Arena. Ali returned to Dundee's Miami gym and began training. "I'd say he's about 75 per cent of what he was," commented Dundee. I don't know if this Frazier match will ever come about. I'll believe it when I see it." Dundee's skepticism was well founded. Like so many of their colleagues before them, Michigan's boxing commissioners caved in under the weight of patriotic pressure. Harold Conrad, obsessed with the thought of a Frazier vs. Ali "Super Fight," gambled again, this time in Montana. It too went awry.

Despite the continuing hostility of the boxing authorities, Middle America's commitment to Vietnam was visibly slackening. The bloody and protracted "unwinnable" war had soured all but the most fervent hawks. Richard Nixon was voted into office on a promise of finding a way out of the quagmire. The people who had once written letters to the Louisville Draft Board saying, "You are nothing but a yellow bellied Negro lover, and apparently a cheap Jew," and "How much has Clay paid you to keep him out of the Army?" began to have second thoughts. Super-patriotism was a tarnishing commodity.

Ali read these signs of growing disillusion and realized that, barring a massive reversal of public opinion, he would never be imprisoned for his beliefs. In 1968 he had actually been jailed (in Dade County jail), serving eight days of a ten-day sentence for a 1967 traffic offense before being released in a Christmas amnesty. The experience shook him and he shuddered at the thought of a five-year sentence. But in his 1970 resignation he all but dared the authorities to put him behind bars:

"You done rolled the dice on me. Now we're going to have to finish the game. You can't cop out now. We done gone too far to turn around. You've got to go on and either free me or put me in jail, because I'm going to go on just like I am, taking my stand."

On June 15, 1970, the first crack appeared in the judicial rock face opposing Ali when the Supreme Court ruled that conscientious objector status could apply to those motivated strictly by religious beliefs. The ruling attracted little attention at the time, and few people related it to Ali's case, which had yet to be heard by the Supreme Court.

It was Harold Conrad who worked this crack and the shifting sands of public opinion to achieve the breakthrough. Ironically, the state which finally lowered its guard to Ali was, of all places, Georgia, domain of Governor Lester Maddox who had won national notoriety by chasing blacks out of his restaurant with a pistol in one hand and a pick-axe handle in the other. While promoting the Frazier vs. Ellis bout, Conrad had intimated to his partner Bob Kassel that if Ali were licensed he would have no hesitation in accepting Atlanta, Georgia, as a venue. Kassell passed on the news to his father-in-law Harry Pett, head of an Atlanta spice firm who in turn told Senator Leroy Johnson, the first black to be voted into office in Atlanta for 92 years. Johnson was a major Atlanta vote-catcher, and as such had virtually unlimited political clout. His patronage of Ali, reinforced by Atlanta's traditional liberalism (it is often said that the only thing wrong with the city is that it is surrounded by Georgia), immediately won over Mayor Sam Massell in a crucial victory. As Atlanta had no boxing commission, licenses were granted solely by the mayor.

On August 11th the promoters—acting under the name House of Sports, after Pett's House of Spice trademark—announced to the press that Ali had been granted a license and that the fight would

take place on October 26th. When Maddox learned the news he was furious. Harold Conrad: "Maddox, that jerk with the pick-axes, he didn't know what the hell was going on. He thought Ali had been cleared by the Supreme Court. He was so confused we sneaked the fight in. And it was a helluva good promotion. *Great* promotion!"

Ali was understandably guarded about the match. "I'll believe I have a fight when I'm in the ring and I hear the bell," he said. His pessimism was almost rewarded. Just when it looked as if the "Super-fight" would actually occur, Frazier's management pulled out. To be fair, Joe and his trainer-manager Yank Durham had been all but forgotten in the stampede to host Ali's return, an event that Frazier was certain would never come to pass. When the date was fixed, Durham complained that money had not yet even been discussed, let alone contracts signed. Frazier had left for Caesar's Palace with his band and was completely out of shape, said Durham. In any case, he was already committed to meeting the Light-Heavyweight Champion Bob Foster on November 18th.

Conrad and the House of Sports were not about to let the Atlanta opening pass them by. Jerry Quarry, a burly Californian white hope who had previously stayed on his feet for seven rounds against Frazier, was substituted at a price of $300,000, netting $95,000. Ali was offered exactly double that amount.

In early September, Ali returned to Angelo Dundee's grimy little gym, where he fought eight rounds with three sparring partners. The last time he had boxed in earnest was in June 1967. Crowed *Sports Illustrated*: "The roof did not fall in. No one threw a bomb. Fire and brimstone did not rain down from heaven and no one was turned into a pillar of salt. Thus were confounded a horde of timid politicians in some 70 communities from one end of the US to the other."

Ali was far more subdued, fearful of jeopardizing the coming match by an overt display of self-righteousness and mindful of the daunting fact that only one Heavyweight Champion—Floyd Patterson—had ever really succeeded in coming back, and that after a lay-off of less than a year. Sitting in Angelo's back room after the workout, studying a photograph of himself taken five years before on the eve of the Liston fight, Ali quietly spoke his mind in the hypnotic, singsong voice he reserved for off-camera profundity:

"They're all waitin' for me. Fans call me up, write me letters, telling me they worry about me, like will I or won't I be able to beat Jerry Quarry. People tell me it can't be done. You can't come back. I get letters from black brothers beggin' me to be careful. Like Quarry's too tough, he's been active and Ali you've been away too long. Take another fight first, they say. All that just makes me more stubborn, and I know I've got to do it. And all those people who say I was over-rated and Jerry Quarry will prove it now. All this leaves no time for poems, jokes and gimmicks. Nobody has to tell me this is a serious business. I'm not fightin' one man. I'm fightin' a lot of men, showin' a lot of 'em here is one man they couldn't defeat, couldn't conquer, one they didn't see get big and fat and flat on his back.

"Lose this one and Quarry'll be a movie star… Like the man who shot Liberty Valance. It won't be just a loss to me. So many people'll be rejoicin' and jumpin' up and down and hollerin' and just rollin' under beds and chairs. Then again so many millions of faces throughout the world will be sad, so sad they'll feel like they've been defeated. All of this, just over a bout.

OPPOSITE: While promoters work every angle to get Ali's license reinstated, the former champ continues to train, more in hope than expectation.

ABOVE: Ali displays his unique artistic prediction regarding the outcome of the Jerry Quarry bout. "Stop, Ali, it's all over," says the referee, as Quarry sees stars. "Go to your corner now." An enraged Lester Maddox rushes down the aisle shouting "Stop the fight. Stop it!"

OPPOSITE: The return of the king. The Quarry fight proves an irresistible magnet for America's black elite. Even Ali's corner boasts, in addition to Bundini, a youthful Jesse Jackson.

"If I lose I'll be in jail for the rest of my life… So I'm fightin' for my freedom."

This said, Ali glanced up at his small audience, grasping for an image to encapsulate his past 3½ years. "The artist returns, like, say, what ya call him?…yeah, Rembrandt, back from exile…"

Two weeks before the fight, Ali quit the Dundee gym and moved his camp to a cottage perched on the edge of a lake outside Atlanta, the property of Senator Leroy Johnson. There, watched by an ever-present armed guard on duty outside his door, he began the final preparations for his return. Rising at 5am, he denied himself breakfast and lunch—"my stomach burnin' with hunger in an effort to lose the extra pounds." (Flab has long cursed Ali who finds it extremely difficult to refuse cakes, pies, and especially ice cream. "Some people lose, some people gain," he shrugs resignedly. "I gain.") After roadwork, Ali moved across to a crowded gymnasium on the campus of Atlanta's Morehouse College, the university from which Dr. Martin Luther King graduated. Watching Ali's ring performance, Dundee swore his fighter was back on original form: "Big man…he moves like silk, hits like a ton…like lightning!"

On the day of the fight, Ali at last consented to make a prediction of sorts. During his exile he had devoted time to cultivating his unique artistic talents, and on a square of cardboard he painted his version of the coming event. The picture showed the referee pushing Ali towards his corner with the words "Stop, Ali, it's all over—go to your corner now" as a spiky-haired Jerry Quarry stood stunned in the middle of the ring, a small galaxy of stars buzzing around his head. Lester Maddox was depicted rushing down an aisle shouting, "Stop the fight. Stop it." Angelo Dundee also tendered a prediction. Before lacing up Ali's gloves he wrote "third round" on the inside.

There had never been a fight crowd like the audience that witnessed the return of Muhammad Ali. As Ali sat through the third showing of a rediscovered Jack Johnson film back at his cottage, his extraordinary black supporters were filing to their seats from their psychedelic white-chauffeured Rolls-Royces. "From every corner of the country and the world they came in brilliant plumage," reported *Sports Illustrated*, "the most startling display of black power and black money ever displayed." Ali's return was an exclusively black celebration, studded with such luminaries as Mrs. Martin Luther King and the Reverend Jesse Jackson, Sidney Poitier, Bill Cosby and Henry Aaron, the Temptations and the Supremes. "He win and it's medicine for everyone," explained Bundini. "He's sellin' pride. Medicine. And he's sellin' it down here in Klan Land. The ol' Slave Master is lettin' him rumble. He do everyone some good if he win." Downstairs in his dressing room, Ali unveiled his obligatory poem: "Quarry sorry".

The screaming began as Ali walked towards the ring, shadow-boxing the air ahead of him. By the time he had climbed through the ropes and peeled off a gratuitous "Ali Shuffle," it had reached concert pitch. When Johnny Addie picked up the microphone to announce Ali's name, his lips moved but any sound he may have uttered was drowned in the crescendo. Ali had definitely returned.

Jerry Quarry was a slugger, a hard-punching Irish-American who worked stolidly at carrying the fight to his opponent. One writer described his fight with Joe Frazier, whose style overlapped Quarry's, as like two Mack trucks meeting in a narrow street. "They would smash into each other, then back up and smash into each other again," he wrote.

ABOVE: "Quarry Sorry "–Jerry Quarry, tears rolling down his cheeks, lunges at Ali in frustration as the fight is stopped. Referee Tony Perez: "I'd never seen a cut like that before. You could see the bone. Quarry wanted to keep going. He was screaming, 'No, no, Tony. Don't stop the fight!' But I had to stop it. His own trainer wanted me to."

OPPOSITE: The Ali of old dances (top left) to the delight of the partisan Atlanta crowd, until (top right) Quarry bulldozes him to the ropes in the second. Round three (bottom left) sees the two fighters exchange a flurry of punches, and with Quarry's eye gushing blood, it is all over (bottom right) to the obvious joy of a jubilant Bundini.

In the first round of his return, Ali was what his audience wanted him to be—the old Muhammad Ali. Dancing around Quarry, he peppered the rugged face with pistol-shot jabs. Not once did he present a stationary target for his opponent's lurching left hooks. At the bell Ali had turned the expected tables, forcing Quarry onto the defensive.

But in the second round, Quarry reverted to form and began relentlessly to apply the pressure. Several times as he bore in he caught the elusive Ali with his short, powerful hooks. Midway through the round he bulldozed Ali onto the ropes, where he lay pinned by wild but furious punches. Ali seemed to make little attempt to extract himself from the trap. Three days before the fight, José Torres had criticized Ali during training for deliberately lying on the ropes, which traditionally form a sort of halfway house between a standing boxer and the canvas. Ali had at the time shrugged off the maneuver as merely an experiment. "Now he was at a competitive level still doing what he did in the gymnasium," wrote Torres after the fight. "He can't do otherwise. He can't help what he's doing. He fell into a habit." This "habit" of deliberately courting the ropes was to form a continuous and, to many, worrying thread through Ali's post-exile career. Certainly in the second round against Quarry, it seemed uncomfortably close to causing his downfall.

Early in round three the two fighters closed and traded a flurry of inside blows. When Quarry stepped back he was brushing his left eye with his glove. A moment later blood gushed from the burst skin; Ali flew at his disabled opponent, aiming a steady stream of jabs at the widening gash. At the bell, Quarry's trainer Teddy Bentham, like Angelo Dundee a cut specialist, hurried in to work desperately on the eye. Well within the prescribed minute he had realized it was

hopeless. Ignoring his fighter's protests he motioned over referee Tony Perez. Perez inspected Quarry's anguished face, turned and waved an end to the match. Quarry, with tears rolling down his cheeks, lunged in frustrated rage at Ali before Bentham could restrain him. The ecstatic crowd went wild.

Much of the old Ali had been apparent in Jerry Quarry's opponent. At times, especially during the first round, Ali's brief second honeymoon with the square ring impressed the critics. But the cut had stopped the combat prematurely, leaving unanswered several crucial questions. Ali himself sounded less than confident when he admitted that, "If he didn't get cut I think it might have gone ten rounds." Joe Frazier was scornfully unmoved by Ali's fortunes, as was Yank Durham. "I thought Quarry would put up a much stronger fight," commented Durham. "We won't let him run around the ring. We'll make him run."

Ali's detractors were, however, firmly in the minority. Twenty-three days later, as Frazier proudly raised his gloves after knocking Bob Foster stone cold in the second round, the same, familiar, infuriating dirge he had been hearing for the past two and a half years fairly boomed down from the balconies…*Ah-lee. Ah-lee!*

Oscar Bonavena was a solid mass of off-white Argentinian muscle whose imposing demeanour both on-stage and off brought out the animal similes in boxing writers. Christened "the Bull" by the press and "Ringo" by his devoted countrymen (after his vaguely Beatle-esque hairstyle), Bonavena was the only man alive to have lasted 25 rounds with Joe Frazier over two fights, and to have knocked him down twice in the process. In his 53 fights he had never been stopped. More than one critic felt that Ali was either a brave man or a fool to have chosen Oscar Bonavena as his second opponent after a 3½ year absence.

For most of the weeks leading up to the bout Ali ignored Bonavena, casually dismissing "the Beast" as easy meat. Psychology he reserved for other targets: the luckless Eddie Dooley, for example. At the contract signing, Ali was seated next to the commissioner, the leader of the vigilantes who had clawed at the heavyweight title on Ali's conviction. While Dooley lamely tried to explain why his New York Athletic Commission had performed a perfect about-face by licensing Ali to fight at Madison Square Garden ("We can take away a fighter's title for any acts which we consider not conducive to the best interests of boxing…"), Ali whipped himself into a self-righteous rage. "You took my title away," he stormed at the florid-faced commissioner. "I'm gonna make you give it back!" History had been horribly reversed for Dooley; whereas he had once been the acclaimed savior of heavyweight boxing, he was now its court jester.

However, at the weigh-in it was Ali's turn to be upstaged. Unlike the Atlanta promoters who had taken pains to keep the two fighters separated until the bell, the Garden officials allowed Ali and Bonavena to meet face-to-face at the scales, providing Ali with his traditional theater for psychological warfare. Instead it was Bonavena who seized the initiative. "You cheekeen," he shrieked at Ali in his broken English and near-castrato voice. "You no go in Army." Bonavena blurted on, calling Ali a "black kangaroo" and implying that Ali had a hygiene problem. He even lifted an old Liston line and accused Ali of homosexuality, anathema to Ali's straight-laced Muslim ethics. Ali, angry underneath his outward calm, was reduced to making gestures indicating that Oscar was crazy, as Sonny Liston had done seven years before.

ABOVE: The return of the exile. "I'm not just fighting one man. I'm fighting a lot of men, showing them here is a man they couldn't conquer. If I lose, for the rest of my life I won't be free. I'll have to listen to all this about how I was a bum, how I joined the wrong movement and they misled me. I'm fighting for my freedom."

OPPOSITE: At the opening bell, Ali is everything the crowd hopes for against Jerry Quarry. But to more experienced observers, there are lingering doubts about the state of his boxing skills.

FOLLOWING PAGES: The still ring-rusty Ali stages a Lazarus-like return from the dead with a perfect left hook to Oscar Bonavena's jaw in the final round. Ali goes on to knock Bonavena down another three times, but after the first it is all academic.

Ali retrieved some of his stolen thunder after the weigh-in when he burst unannounced into the Argentinian's dressing room. Gripping the door with tensed knuckles, his body rigid, he fired a hysterical broadside at the startled Bonavena. "I knew he was going to do that," moaned Dundee, who genuinely feared for his fighter when he launched into histrionics. "I begged the Garden to put Bonavena on the other side of the building." Eventually Oscar's handlers managed to shove Ali out of the room.

"I've never wanted to whup a man so bad," proclaimed Ali on the day of the fight. "I'm gonna put some soul on his head. I tell you that the Beast is mine. And tonight he falls in nine." His actions, however, belied his words. Author Budd Schulberg trailed Ali that day, following his criss-crossing path through downtown New York. By evening, Schulberg was exhausted. Ali did not let up. On the way from his Motor Inn to the Garden he leaped out of his Cadillac and dived into the subway. "This is being free, staying down to earth and nature," sang Bundini as he skipped happily down the steps into the dirty black tunnel. The passengers in his carriage crowded around Ali and with the same regal benevolence he employed in his pre-championship days before the Doug Jones fight, he invited them all to the match. At a Garden side entrance, Ali propped open the door while his freeloading fans ducked in over the frantic protests of the box office officials. The People's Champ!

Bonavena was relegated to the background in the wide-screen version of a triumphal New York return being projected in Ali's mind. It was an unhappy piece of miscasting which he was shortly to regret.

For three rounds Ali dispelled the rumors that he had irretrievably rusted in exile, bemusing Bonavena with all the élan of his championship years. Once again Ali sneered at his opponent as he had done against Patterson, Liston, and Terrell. Once again he invited his opponent to punch him, easily slipping Bonavena's crabbed, ungainly lunges. At first Bundini had howled from the sidelines, "The world is watching you, champ. Go to war. You the boss. Kill the bull!" But with a quarter of the fight gone, Ali's disdain moved him to scold, "Stop that clowning! Box like Sugar Ray. Get vicious!"

A minute or so into round four, Ali's tightly coiled mainspring seemed to snap, leaving him drop-shouldered and flat-footed in the center of the ring. Automatically he retreated to the ropes, presenting the mechanical Bonavena with the stationary target he had been praying for. Unlike Ali's black constituency in Atlanta, the Garden crowd was deeply divided, roughly according to color. As Bonavena lashed wildly at Ali, the white hope contingent rose to its feet, chanting "Ringo, Ringo!"

The fight pattern remained constant for the next four rounds. Occasionally Ali reverted to Cassius Clay, cycling around Bonavena's ugly stance and cracking his set face with stylish jabs and combinations. But most of his time was spent either back-pedalling in the face of Bonavena's dogged pursuit, or leaning across the ropes relying on his reflexes rather than his feet to avoid the blows whistling past his nose. The numerous body shots the Argentinian landed, Ali had no option but to absorb. Bonavena remained Bonavena, a fighter with an infinite reserve of determination and patience and an almost masochistic disregard for pain, but lacking the sophisticated technique needed to eliminate a

master like Ali. The fight degenerated into a dreary, muddled brawl. By round six the crowd was stamping its feet in frustration, booing Ali each time he managed to wriggle out of Bonavena's ham-fisted grasp.

In round nine—Ali's self-proclaimed three minutes of triumph—it was Bonavena who salvaged the fight from its own lethargy. Soon after the bell, Ali shook Bonavena with a stunning right to the jaw. Keen to realize his ninth-round promise, Ali moved in purposefully, but the indestructible Argentinian pressed ahead undaunted. The fight became a furious slugging match with neither man yielding an inch. Suddenly, during the melée, Bonavena hooked and found Ali's jaw.

Ali, remembering the incident: "Funny, when I was predictin' the ninth round, I never thought I came close to predictin' on myself. I made a lot of mistakes in that fight, and it cost me. I got careless with him in the ninth round, and you can't do that with Oscar. In that ninth round I got hit by a hook harder than Frazier could ever throw. Numb! Like I was numb all over. Shock and vibrations is all I felt, that's how I knew I was alive. I mean, I was jarred. Even my toes felt the vibrations. The first thought that came to mind — another good one or two might have dropped me. So the minute I'm hit — two steps backwards and I'm on the other side of the ring."

Both fighters were still desperately punching after the bell. The crowd shrieked solidly for Ringo.

The hard-fought ninth appeared to be the last flash of inspiration in a moribund battle. From the tenth the fight returned to its former course, running sluggishly downhill on fatigue and stale sweat. Ali had grossly underestimated the Argentinian. Drugged by the easily earned acclaim from the Atlanta match, he had trained lightly for what he had considered was a foregone conclusion, if he had considered it much at all. Now he was paying the price. The wide margin of points he had built up coming into the last round was no accurate reflection of the fight.

But Bonavena knew he had to cap his attack with a knockout to rescue the match, and the final round opened with his long, looping left hook backed up by his right. Several more shots and he lined Ali up with his right. From the blue, Ali reached out and won the fight. A hard, deadly accurate left hook caught Bonavena with his defenses open and sent him to the floor. From canvas to knees to feet, the glassy-eyed Bonavena rose, only to be knocked down once again. Working by memory he struggled upwards towards the lights as his corner threw in the towel. Standing over his victim, Ali waited until Bonavena was upright on his jellied legs before landing a left and a right. Bonavena toppled for the third time and lay crumpled against the referee's knees. The third knockdown in one round gave Ali the fight.

Bundini headed the rush into the ring. Pressing his cheek to Ali's he sobbed, "The world will know. The whole world will know!" Grabbing a microphone, Ali shouted between gasps, "I have done what Joe Frazier couldn't do—knocked out Oscar Bonavena. Now where is he? I want Joe Frazier!"

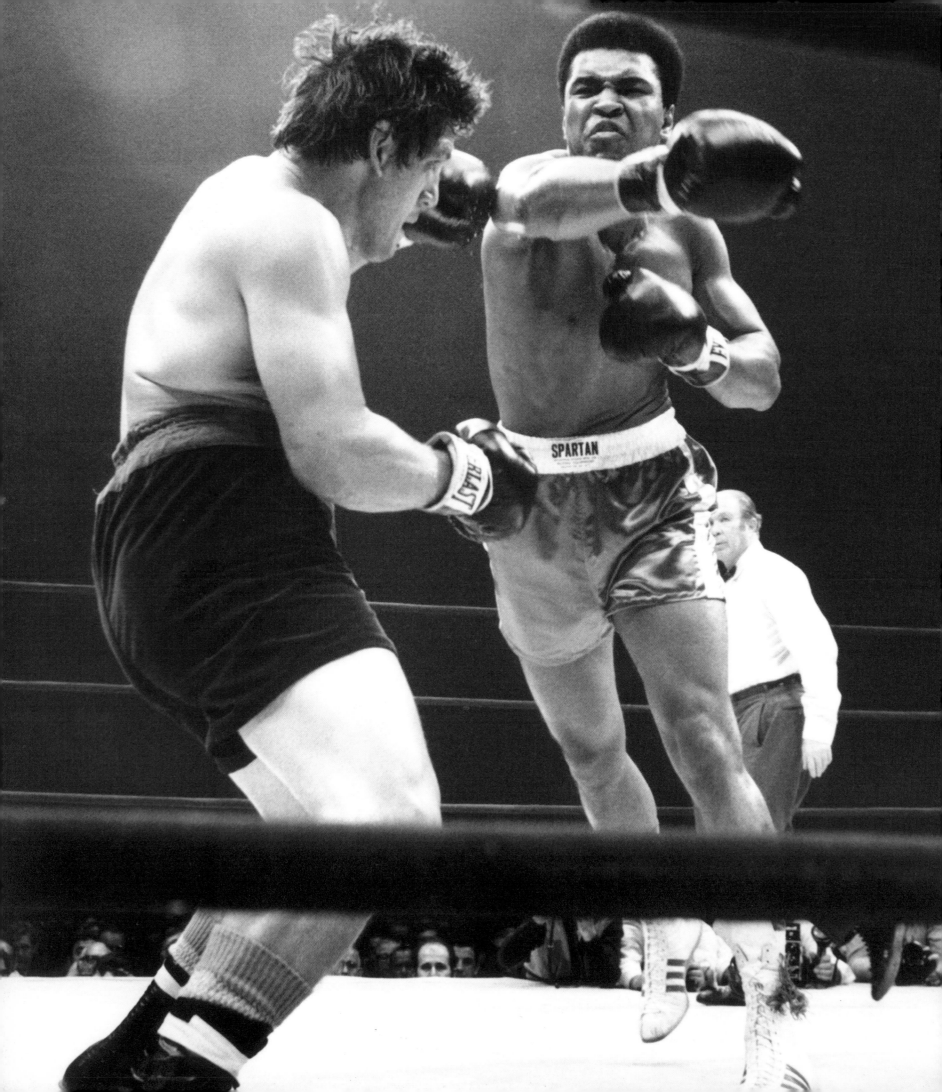

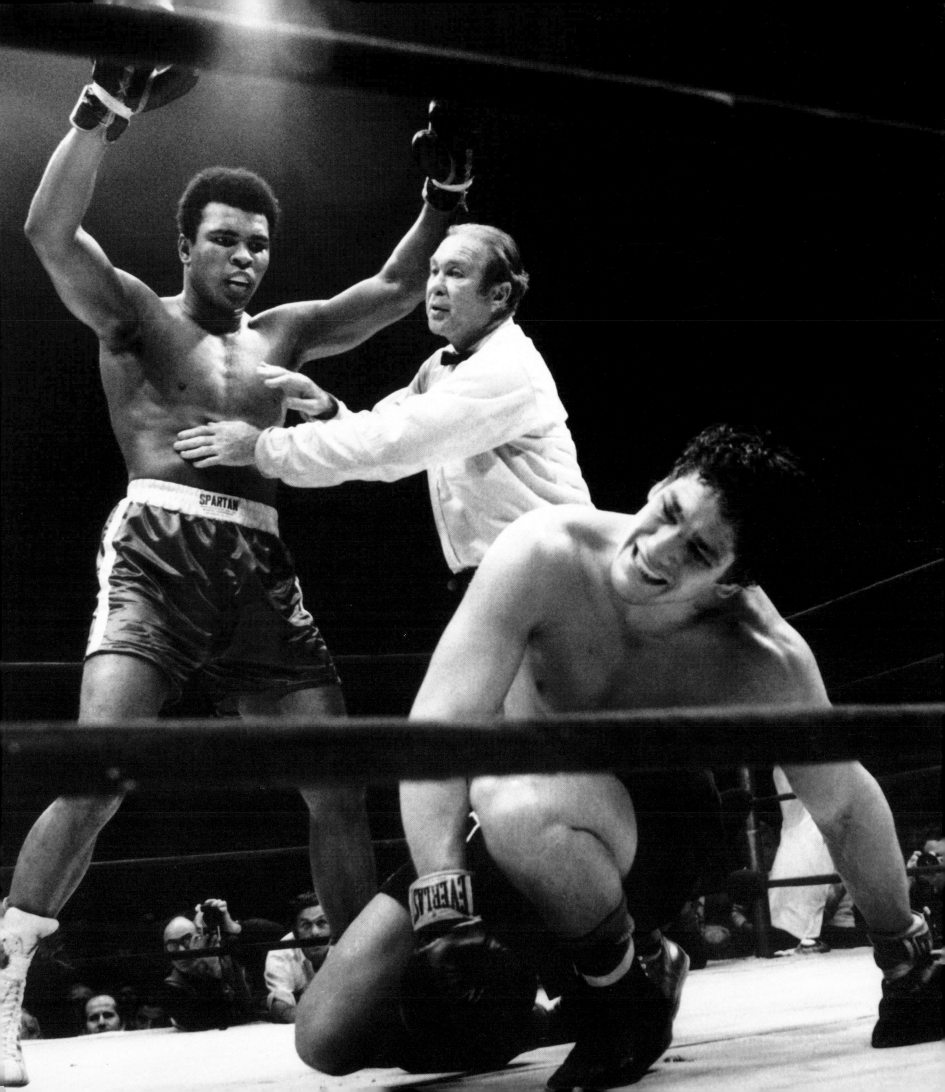

If At First...

"I'm not excited about fighting anymore. You people are the ones who're excited, not me. I've been fighting since I was 12. It's just another night to jump up and down and beat up somebody."

Muhammad Ali

Joe Frazier was a master slugger, a throwback to the days when men fought each other with bare fists face-to-face across a chalk mark on the floor. His nickname "Black Marciano" was an apt description, for like "The Rock," any finesse Frazier possessed in his squat, chunky body was entirely eclipsed by his unshakeable determination to knock out his opponent.

Every day, Joe Frazier soaked his head in rock salt and water. "It makes me mean and toughens my skin," he would say, and indeed, whenever he was hit he would instinctively smile. He christened himself "Smokin' Joe," after his habit of steaming from his corner at the bell until he was crouched head to chest against his opponent. "I'll be so close to him they'll have to dig the hairs from my beard out of his chest before they pick him up," he had sworn before demolishing Jimmy Ellis in the fifth round of their championship bout.

In his autobiography, veteran British boxer Henry Cooper paired Frazier with Sonny Liston. "They were slugger-killers from the hard American school," he wrote. "You could hit Frazier with your Sunday punch and you could break your hand. He'd shake his head and come on after you. Those guys can also break your heart." By 1971, Frazier had consecutively broken 26 professional hearts—23 by clean knockouts—and was the Heavyweight Champion of the World.

Joe Frazier should have been an All-American legend. Born in the swamplands of South Carolina, his childhood as the son of an impoverished dirt farmer was a running battle for survival. Four of his 12 brothers and sisters died of worms, scurvy, and starvation. In the few spare moments he was allowed between work and sleep, Joe slung a flour sack over a beam and trained to become "the next Joe Louis." His favorite chapter in the Bible he laboriously read a page at a time each night was the Book of Judges "because it's about war, and fighting puts me in mind of war."

Married at 15, Frazier headed north, first to New York and then to Philadelphia and a job in a slaughterhouse (prompting one later critic to suggest he fought like he worked, "up to his elbows in entrails and tripe"). In 1962 he dropped by a local gym to lose weight and was persuaded to resume boxing. Although an unlikely candidate for ring success, with his sawn-off reach and barrel-shaped legs, within two years he had reached the trials for the Tokyo Olympics. In the final he was beaten by a 300-pound Buster Mathis. As consolation he was offered a position on the team as a sparring partner.

Frazier's Olympic hardships make Ali look by comparison as if he won his gold medal in a raffle. Prior to Joe's departure for Tokyo he fought an exhibition with Mathis in San Francisco. Buster broke his finger on Joe's rugged skull and was dropped from the team. Frazier became the American heavyweight hope in a field stacked with Russians. In his qualifying fight it was he who broke a thumb on his opponent's head, but mindful of Buster's fate, stoically kept his injury to himself. As with all legends, he went on to win the gold medal.

On his return to Philadelphia he was laid off from the slaughterhouse because of his thumb. For the next year he lived a penniless existence as a janitor at the Bright Hope Baptist Church. In 1965 his luck changed. Under the auspices of his trainer Yank Durham, Frazier became a corporation—Cloverlay Inc.—owned by 40 respectable Philadelphians. After 13 consecutive victories—all knockouts, barring a hard bout with Oscar Bonavena—the press recognized him as a serious heavyweight contender. Durham

OPPOSITE: Uncle Muhammad wants you, Joe Frazier!

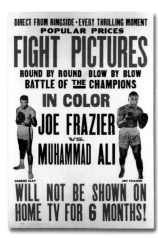

DIRECT FROM RINGSIDE · EVERY THRILLING MOMENT
POPULAR PRICES

FIGHT PICTURES

ROUND BY ROUND   BLOW BY BLOW
BATTLE OF THE CHAMPIONS

IN COLOR
JOE FRAZIER
vs.
MUHAMMAD ALI

CASSIUS CLAY   JOE FRAZIER

WILL NOT BE SHOWN ON HOME TV FOR 6 MONTHS!

ABOVE: Frazier vs. Ali at Madison Square Garden pulls in over 19,500 fans who watch ringside. Tens of thousands more watch the "Battle of the Champions" on closed-circuit screens in local theatres.

OPPOSITE: Ali trains in his Deer Lake retreat under the watchful gaze of his entourage and a paying public. From left: Wali "Blood" Muhammad, Bundini, Gene Kilroy, Angelo Dundee, Luis Sarria, and Ali.

shrewdly held his fighter back from the scramble for the WBA title, vacated by Ali's exile. Instead he matched Frazier with Mathis for the NYAC crown, which he won in the 11th. Later he picked off Jimmy Ellis, who had emerged as the WBA champion.

Frazier's life outside the ring was at once solidly respectable yet enviably glamorous. While continuing to read the Bible and worry publicly about preserving the reputation of his title, he became rich, bought a mansion in Philadelphia, and drove a gold Cadillac. Occasionally he rode a large Harley Davidson motorcycle (with hand-tooled boxing gloves for handlebars), and wore tailored wet-look leather ensembles. Between fights he sang—albeit poorly—inoffensive rock and roll with his backing group, The Knockouts, at such desirable nightspots as Caesar's Palace. Affable enough for a man who had been hit as often and as hard as he had, his social image was a far cry from Sonny Liston's inarticulate chain-gang charisma.

Joe Frazier had it all—fame, fortune, and the Heavyweight Championship of the World. And he had built it all himself out of nothing. He should have been a legend. But he was not.

The fly in Frazier's ointment was of course Muhammad Ali. In another time he would have been universally hailed as a boxing colossus. As it was, to all but serious students of the sport, he was either regarded as a second-stringer who had usurped the title, or overlooked entirely. Even his admiring biographer Phil Pepe subtitled his book *Come Out Smokin'* with *Joe Frazier—The Champ Nobody Knew*.

At first Frazier bridled at his assigned role. "What do I have to do?" he wailed. "I've beaten everyone they've put in front of me!" After winning Ellis' WBA title he shouted ecstatically, "I'm free at last!" Nine months later, after eliminating Bob Foster, Ali was still at his shoulder, in the shape of 1,000 chanting fans. It was then that Frazier realized if ever he was to be popularly recognized as Marciano's legitimate heir, he would first have to beat Muhammad Ali.

The biggest draw card in heavyweight boxing is a match between a consummate boxer and a master slugger. Jess Willard vs. Jack Johnson, Dempsey vs. Tunney, Joe Louis against Billy Conn, Marciano and Ezzard Charles… all of them results of what *Sports Illustrated* termed "the classic confrontation." On March 8, 1971, a fifth classic bout was nominated to the list when Joe Frazier met Muhammad Ali at Madison Square Garden in yet another Fight of the Century.

The Frazier vs. Ali promotion was almost as much a boxing milestone as the fight itself. "Contrary to what some people say, boxing isn't show business," snorted one disgruntled would-be promoter who had been left by the wayside in the race to engineer the match. A Beverly Hills celebrity agent named Jerry Perenchio proved him wrong. Perenchio had met neither Ali nor Frazier until he signed them. In fact, he had never even seen Frazier throw a punch. "I really don't know the first thing about boxing," he candidly told the press. What he did know was show business, and under the very noses of the cigar-chewing, smoky-backroom boxing barons, he stole the sport's choicest plum.

"You've got to throw away the book on this fight," he said. "It's potentially the greatest single grosser in the history of the world. It's like *Gone With the Wind*. And that's why I'm involved. I know how to book Andy Williams into Salt Lake City. Well, this fight is like booking Andy Williams into 500 Salt Lake Cities all at once."

Perenchio backed his beliefs by offering the two fighters the unprecedented sum of $2.5 million apiece. Both Frazier and Ali—who had originally priced themselves at $3 million—accepted, discarding

ABOVE: FRAZIER FALLS IN SIX—Ali delivers his prediction for the fight that will be the biggest event in boxing history. Both fighters are to receive an unprecedented $2.5 million apiece. Madison Square Garden is completely sold out with a month still to go.

OPPOSITE: Shades of Sonny Liston—Ali baits Frazier on his home turf. "Joe Frazier is too ugly to be champ. Joe Frazier is too dumb to be champ. The Heavyweight Champion should be smart and pretty like me. Ask Joe Frazier, 'How do you feel, champ?' he'll say, 'Duh, duh, duh.'" Replies Joe: "He can keep that pretty head; I don't want it. What I'm going to do is try to pull them kidneys out." And so begins one of the most venomous and enduring enmities in sporting history.

FOLLOWING PAGES: (Left) The end of the dream—Frazier's left hook finally achieves the unthinkable in the 15th. The challenger's right leg buckles, his left leg shoots from under him, and he falls to the canvas for a count of eight. (Right) The punch that did it. Ferdie Pacheco: "Ali was tired; he was hurt, just trying to get through the last round. And Frazier hit him flush on the jaw with the hardest left hook he'd ever thrown. Ali went down, and it looked like he was out cold. I didn't think he could get up. And not only did he get up, he was up almost as fast as he went down. It was incredible. That night, he was the most courageous fighter I'd ever seen. He was going to get up if he was dead." (Over) Slugger's revenge—Frazier smashes Ali with a right.

tenders from Madison Square Garden and the Houston Astrodome. Perenchio then set about stumping up the cash. After scanning a list of some 70 potential backers, he settled for a Los Angeles based sports buff who owned a basketball team, a hockey teams, and part of a football team as well as the Inglewood Forum stadium. Jack Kent Cooke put up $4.5 million. Madison Square Garden, which agreed to stage the fight, guaranteed the rest. As return on their money they hoped to gross $20 million.

The publicity leading up to the fight was as one would expect for such a massively financed venture. Both Ali and Frazier were always on hand to growl the requisite threats for the press. But there was little real venom on either side. In an unguarded moment Frazier actually admitted to liking Ali, although he reserved doubts about Ali's commitment to the black man when "a lot of guys around him are white". Ali himself, as far back as 1970, had spoken warmly of his opponent, dreaming how one day they would both get together and discuss "freedom for black folks", visit the ghetto to help "the old wine head, sitting on a doorstep, drunk", and generally "wake up the black people".

"Me and Joe Frazier will be buddies," he had said. "I just want it to go down in history that I didn't sell out or Uncle Tom when I got famous, and I don't think Joe Frazier's going to do that, either. He ain't dumb."

Given these past statements, Ali's jibes about Frazier's wits, looks, and awe of whites sounded slightly hollow. Even Ali seemed unconvinced and it was left to the public to provide the malice—the NAACP demonstrators who threw up a hostile picket line around Frazier's Cloverlay Gym; the New York cabbie who told Phil Pepe when he learned about the fight, "Good, Frazier will kill that draft dodger!" Just how emotionally charged an issue the fight had become was indicated by an incident during the Philadelphia screening of the Ali vs. Bonavena bout. A 40-year-old black crane operator named Leslie Scott became involved in a heated argument with a white man over who was superior—Ali or Frazier. According to police records, Scott pulled a knife on the white man, who then identified himself as a policeman. Scott fled and the policeman shot him dead. Ali visited the funeral parlor where Scott lay in his coffin. "I ain't worth dyin' for," he said, shaking his head.

Ali's pronouncements during training also sounded slightly off-key. "It's gonna be the champ and the tramp," he boasted to the sports writers. "I hit so much harder now. I hit Bonavena so hard it jarred his kinfolks all the way back in Argentina. Joe Frazier ain't a great fighter to me. He's a great fighter to the fans been reading his clippings. But to me he can't even dance. I'll be dancing on March 8th. I'll be dancing, moving and hitting, and Frazier won't be able to find me."

But Ali appeared to be taking his training lightly. Although he talked often of "dancing", he spent most of his ring time lying on the ropes, content to cover his face with his gloves and absorb punishment like a punching bag. Several critics wrote him off as lazy.

Privately, he confessed that training was now more of a job than enjoyment. "Ain't in my lungs—they all right," he gasped between breaths. "It's in my muscles. They get tired. Ain't like when I was a young man. Now I'm older, gonna be 29."

As the fight date drew nearer, Ali's thoughts seemed to stray further from the job in hand. A month away he had caused concern by saying he needed one more bout before Frazier, against Jimmy

Ellis. However, as the weeks passed, he grew increasingly blasé about the World Champion. Almost every day he would cut short his training to mingle with the celebrities who dropped in to the gym. With a week to go, Ali flew to New York for the physical and was mobbed every time he set foot out of his hotel. He positively basked in the glut of multi-racial adoration, and it was only Angelo Dundee's subtle persuasion which managed to coax him back to the 5th Street Gym. Wrote Budd Schulberg of the challenger's apparent serenity: "Perhaps Ali had come to believe in his own perfection instead of his perfectibility. Losing was simply not in his lexicon."

While Ali was showboating, Frazier was holed up in his Cloverlay retreat, relentlessly pounding the big bag. He trained as if he had more to lose than Ali, and to him he had. The stakes were made painfully obvious when Frazier broke training to attend a fight in Philadelphia. As his name was announced from the ring, the hall echoed with boos…in his own hometown! While Ali fiddled, Frazier grew more sullen by the hour. "He's getting mean," said Yank Durham happily. "That means the fight's getting close. That means he's ready."

By 9pm on March 8, 1971, Seventh Avenue from 31st Street to 33rd Street was choked with the mandatory black limousines of boxing's newest and most exclusive fans. "I lost count of the number of famous legs I tripped over," reported one British writer. These legs belonged to luminaries such as New York Mayor John Lindsay, Frank Sinatra, Ed Sullivan, Hugh Hefner and Barbi Benton, Hubert Humphrey, George Raft, the Teddy Kennedys, Ethel Kennedy, Bernadette Devlin, astronaut Alan Shepherd, and literally dozens more. If they were fortunate, these famous faces had snapped up their ringside seats at the official price of $150. If they had resorted to the black market, they may have paid $1,000.

As with the Bonavena fight, the question on everybody's lips was not, who do you think will win, but rather who do you hope will win. But unlike the Bonavena audience, which split on the issue of color, the Frazier house was a house divided over ideals. If you were for Ali you were for ecology, women's liberation, and peace in Vietnam. Conversely, if you were for Frazier, you supported Law and Order, Spiro Agnew, and the status quo.

The Garden officials, fearful that Ali would be torn apart by his fans if he arrived outside the stadium on the night, had set up a makeshift apartment for him in a third-floor press room. At 9pm he awoke and wandered across the room to look down on his brother Rahaman lose a six-round preliminary against British fighter Danny McAlinden. At the bell, seemingly unperturbed, he caught the elevator for his dressing room. Several blocks away, Joe Frazier put down his guitar and made his way from his hotel room to the Garden.

Downstairs in his dressing room, Ali tore open an envelope and produced a scrap of paper on which he had written a week before his prediction: "FLASH. I predict first of all, that all the Frazier fans, and boxing experts, will be shocked at how easily I will beat Joe Frazier, who will look like an Amateur Boxer compared to Muhammad Ali, and they will admit I was the Real Champion of all time. FRAZIER FALLS IN SIX."

At 10:30pm, Frazier threaded his way through the crowd wearing a green and gold brocade robe emblazoned with the names of his five children. A moment later, Ali, resplendent in white satin, red velvet trunks, and white "Ali-Shuffle Shoes" adorned with red tassles, also appeared. The two men reached the ropes almost simultaneously.

TRAINING HDQTS.
FOR JOE FRAZIER
HEAVYWEIGHT
CHAMPION

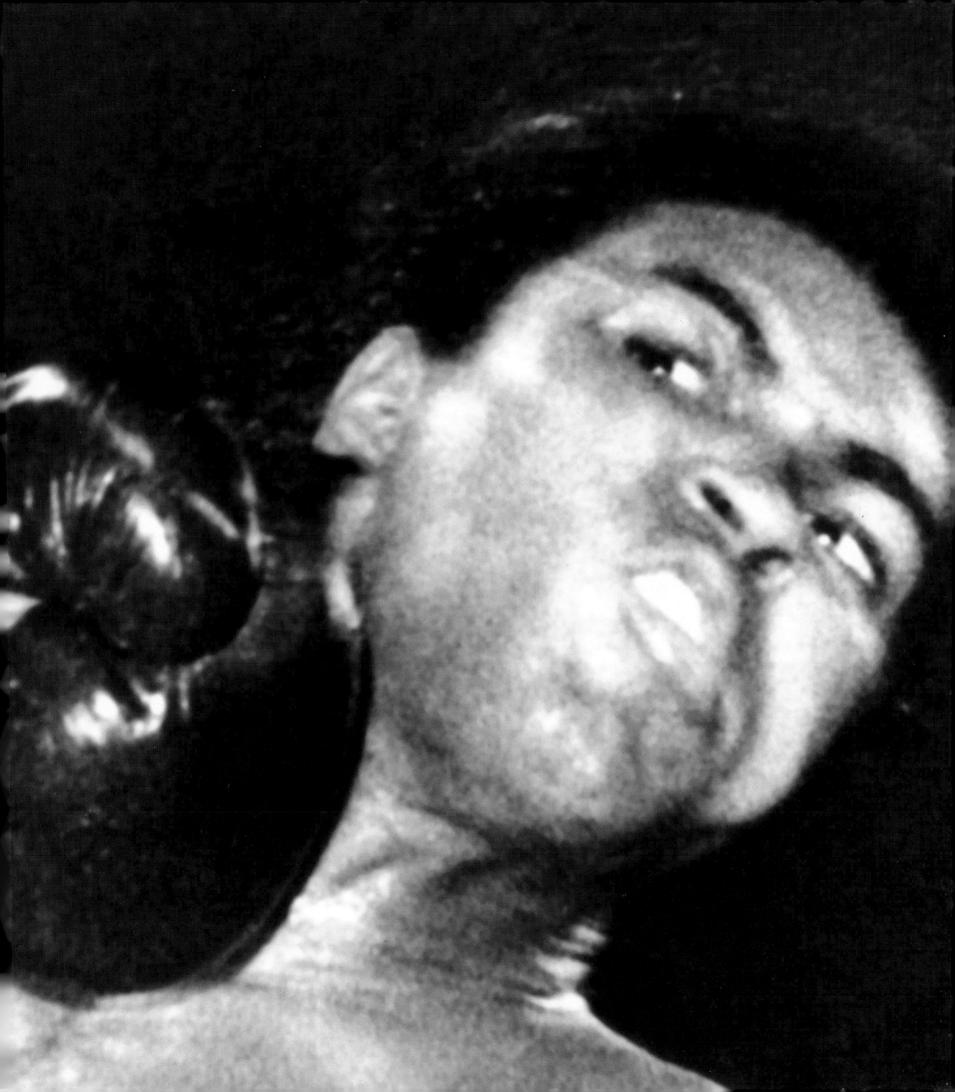

The roar from 19,500 throats was overwhelming. In the ring, Ali immediately began shadow boxing—dancing and flicking at the air until he had edged his way into Frazier's corner. There he leaned over and patted Joe's head. "Chump," he said. At center-ring, while referee Arthur Mercante ran through the rules, Ali continued his verbal cold-warfare. Frazier replied just once. Looking up into Ali's face he hissed, "I'm gonna kill you!"

For two rounds Ali managed to erase the doubts lingering in the minds of the critics who had witnessed the Bonavena marathon. Once again, the Ali who opened the match was the old Ali, dancing and jabbing as fast and as frequently as ever, the red tassels flying about his feet. Joe Frazier was, as always, Joe Frazier, a fighter with a seemingly boundless capacity for absorbing punches. Like Oscar Bonavena, his style was ugly and awkward, "a wild beast tangled in a thicket," as one magazine put it. Frazier depended on his telephone-box legs taking him in as close to his opponent as possible to land his leaden blows. (Frazier's reach measured just 71in, compared with Ali's 80in.) But even when he managed to force Ali back against the ropes, his hooks swished by as Ali swayed from the waist like a cobra.

In the third round, the pattern began to go awry. At the bell, Ali slid from his corner and inexplicably backed onto the ropes before Frazier was anywhere near. It was a red rag to a bull, and the champion needed no further encouragement. Frazier was on his toes as he hurled his hooks at the immobile target. Ali snapped his head clear split seconds before each one could land, but the hooks and rights falling on his arms and body were no pulled punches. At one point Ali half turned towards the crowd and laughed, shaking his head in an elaborately mimed "no". But when he tried returning his own jabs, they skittered off Frazier's skull like so many Ping Pong balls thrown against a brick wall. It was Frazier's turn to smile. Crouched before Ali, pinning him like a butterfly in a display case, he took the round with ease.

Back in the corner, Dundee implored Ali to stay away from the ropes. For the first time in the fight, Ali accepted a stool.

After surviving two rounds of one-sided brutality, Ali regained sufficient composure in the sixth and seventh to partly rebuild his scorecard. He still favored the ropes, but instead of merely ducking and absorbing Frazier's bullets, he fought back. Soon his jabs had begun drawing blood around Frazier's eyes and lips. By the end of the fight, the champion was to look like a butchered product of his former employment.

But although Ali was taking the points, he was nowhere near winning the fight. As emphasized by Bonavena three months before, points are of small value against a slugger with a sweet tooth for the grand knockout. It was only Ali's talent for avoiding the crucial Frazier punches to the jaw that kept him on his feet. How long this talent could continue was the vital question.

Round eight saw Ali promise, with a laugh in Frazier's face, that he would stand forever. Dropping his hands to his sides, he haughtily disdained to make any attempt at defense. The promise held good for round nine, perhaps Ali's best ever. Back on his feet he circled and jabbed at his opponent's head. Frazier halted and, for the first time in the fight, stepped back. Ali's showboating vanished as he stood off the ropes, trading short, solid uppercuts with his opponent. Step by step, Frazier was driven back. *Ah-lee, Ah-*

lee, chanted the crowd. Near the bell, Ali landed three consecutive right-left combinations. Frazier sagged, and as he walked back to his corner he was wobbling.

Round ten. Frazier charged from his corner, bunched up in fury, straight into Ali's glove. Ali worked on Frazier's raw face and then slid back onto the ropes. Frazier followed, but to ringsiders he seemed punched out, exhausted. Ali did not catch a single dangerous blow, while several times he visibly jolted Frazier. Ali shouted confidently to Dundee, Bundini, and old Fred Stoner huddled in his corner, "He's out!"

But in the next round the tide turned again. At the bell, Ali moved from his corner straight to the ropes. Frazier pressed forward and swung a left. Ali dodged, slipped, and fell. Referee Mercante ruled no knockdown, but Frazier closed in all the same as if to deliver the coup de grace. Pushing Ali back he landed two left hooks to the head. Ali countered with a right and Frazier stepped away. Ali remained with his back against the ropes and imperiously waved Frazier back. The champion moved forward a step and landed a perfect left hook to the jaw. The wild, wolfish look in Ali's eyes vanished; in its place appeared the fixed, glassy stare of a shell-shock victim. Ali's legs turned to jelly as he reeled around the ring avoiding Frazier's onslaught. Bundini sent an arc of water flying through the air, an act that earned him NYAC suspension. "Trying to revive my soldier," he explained later. Somehow, Ali survived.

For two rounds Ali hung on, avoiding as many shots as he could and smothering what he couldn't with desperate clinches. Frazier ignored exhaustion and tried his hardest to destroy the shadow which had haunted his entire championship career. In the final round he succeeded. With a long, grim left hook dredged up from the depths, the fighter with the autopsied face conjured the unthinkable on his opponent's immaculate features.

Ali was standing out from the ropes when the blow landed. Unsupported, his right leg buckled, his left leg shot out straight ahead and he fell spread-eagled to the canvas where he lay with his feet pointing to the roof. In the three seconds Ali was on the floor his cheek swelled obscenely. At three he had climbed up from the bottom of the pit and stood shaking the mist from his eyes. At the bell he was still standing. Whatever else his critics seized on gleefully after the fight, cowardice was not included.

When it had ended both fighters collapsed exhausted. Somebody at ringside shouted, "draw", and the chant was taken up *draw, draw*. But there was only one winner. The tears coursing down Bundini's cheeks told the story; the three judges merely provided the figures in the record book. Muhammad Ali was the fourth boxer in prizefighting's five classic bouts of skill against strength to have his talents sabotaged by a slugger.

In the dressing room, Joe Frazier sneered through his battered face at the reporters. "What can you say about me now?" he demanded. "I always felt like the champ. I fought everyone they put in front of me. God knows!" Softening, he paid Ali his dues. "You've got to give him credit," he said. "He takes one good punch. That shot I hit him with in the 15th round, I went way back to the country to throw. God, he can take it!" Afterwards Frazier slipped out the back door of the Garden into a waiting limousine. Only a handful of fans waited to see him off. Some weeks later, Frazier was admitted to a Philadelphia hospital. His biographer Phil Pepe attributed his three-week convalescence to emotional and physical exhaustion. Rumors circulated that Ali had effectively ended Frazier's fighting career.

OPPOSITE: An overweight Buster Mathis—"the dancing elephant"—enlists in Ali's Bum of the Month Club. "I'm gonna do to Buster what the Indians did to Custer," taunts Ali. In the end, Buster gets off a lot more lightly than the Colonel does.

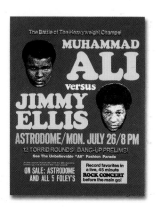

BELOW: Ali finally manages a 12th round TKO over his boyhood opponent and long-time sparring partner Jimmy Ellis. "I thought that I could get him, but hey, in that last round, with only 58 seconds left, he comes in with some good shots. When you got hit by him, it's like, you wake up and say, 'What hit me?' He could hit you so hard with a right punch. After you've been in a fight with Ali, the next morning, you're all swelled up."

Ali did not stay at the Garden for the press conference. Dr. Ferdie Pacheco drove him to New York's Flower Hospital Fifth Avenue to have the grossly swollen jaw X-rayed. Ali slumped in the back seat exhausted during the long ride. At one point he focused and muttered, "Must have been a helluva fight 'cause I'm sure tired." The jaw was not broken; it was only a cheek hemorrhage. The injury did not surprise Dr. Pacheco. What did astonish him were Ali's hip joints. Forced to bear the brunt of Frazier's blows, these joints—the toughest in the human frame—had swollen up to such a degree that they almost paralysed Ali.

Floyd Patterson considered losing to be the fighter's perennial dread. "We are not afraid of getting hurt but we are afraid of losing," he once told *Esquire*. "A prize-fighter who gets knocked out or is badly outclassed suffers in a way he will never forget. He is beaten under the bright lights in front of thousands of witnesses who curse him and spit at him, and he knows that he is being watched, too, by many thousands more on television and in the movies, and he knows that the tax agents will soon visit him—they always try and get their share before he winds up flat broke. The losing fighter loses more than just his pride and the fight; he loses part of his future, is one step closer to the slums he came from."

Floyd, who went into hiding for nearly a year after losing to Johansson, may have been overstating the ignominy of defeat. But other fighters also recall failure as a particularly bitter pill. Rocky Graziano: "They look at you different. How soon they forget. It's no longer hi ya, champ! It's hello…You feel self-conscious. You go to the old places, the old joints, and you walk in and it's completely different." After Joe Louis lost to Ezzard Charles, Louis arrived at the New York address where his post-fight parties were traditionally held. The only other guest turned up at 3am the next morning.

Defeat for Ali, the man who had proudly promised "If I lose, I will crawl across the ring on my hands and knees and tell him, 'Joe Frazier, you are the greatest,'" would seem to have almost certainly been an intolerable humiliation.

Shakespeare reserved tragedy for kings and princes, believing only they truly had the capacity to suffer the necessary fall from grace. Ali was unquestionably a latter-day king, and the press had no hesitation in ascribing tragic proportions to his failure.

But Ali appeared curiously unaffected by his misfortune.

"Oh, they all said about me that if I ever lose, he'll shoot himself, he'll die," he told reporter George Plimpton the day after the defeat. "But I'm human. I've lost one out of 32, and it was a decision that could have gone another way. If I'd gone down three times and got up and was beat real bad, really whupped, and the other fighter was so superior, then I'd look at myself and say I'm washed up." If defeat meant the end of all the reporters, cameras, and crowds, he said, then he didn't mind. "I remember thinking that it would be more relaxing to be a loser."

Of course the press and its public had no intention of forgetting Ali, and despite his words to the contrary, he seemed relieved by the continuing attention. The next day he was eagerly guiding an army of fans through his still-unfinished $250,000 house in the New Jersey suburb of Cherry Hill. Later he bolstered his spirits with a conspicuous new $15,000 Oldsmobile trimmed with $7,500 worth of gold plating.

Defeat did have its compensations. For the first time in many people's eyes, Ali looked human, sitting propped up in bed telling the world's press, "I'm not going to cry." Frazier's fists went a long way to defusing the frustration Ali's critics had suffered for almost a decade. Besides blotting his unblemished record book, the defeat marked the end of "Ali, the Man They Love to Hate". Coincidentally, three months after the fight, the eight judges of the Supreme Court voted unanimously to overturn Ali's draft conviction and five-year sentence.

Only a few months after his defeat, Ali began preparing for his second comeback. His choice of opponent hardly came as a surprise. Jimmy Ellis was definitely no "unrated duck". Although Joe Frazier had beaten him in five rounds, Ellis had won the WBA tournament and as he had matured as a fighter relatively late in life, at 30 he was not far from his prime. Under Angelo Dundee's tutelage, Ellis had developed into a hard-punching, stand-up boxer whose sneaky right hand had knocked out six opponents in the first round. "My guy," said Dundee, who elected to work in Ellis' corner against Ali (Ali adopting Sugar Ray Robinson's old trainer Harry Wiley), "is the best first-round banger in the heavyweight division."

Beating Ali had become almost an obsession for Ellis. "I don't care if I never win another fight as long as I live—if I win this one," he said. "I lived in the shadow of Ali too long." Ellis had grown up in Louisville with Ali and claimed to have beaten the former champion as an amateur. "Beat him with ease!" As Ali's long-term sparring partner, Ellis had had the benefit of 1,000 plus rounds with his opponent. The experts noted that if anyone knew Ali's faults and weaknesses, it was Jimmy Ellis.

But conversely, Ali had also come to know Ellis like the back of his glove. In selecting him, Ali knew that the fight might become gruelling, but would hold no dangerous surprises. Entering the ring, Ali was like a student who knew before an exam, if not the answers, at least what questions were on the paper.

Although he admitted to being "a little pulpy", Ali looked close to top form on the night. After surviving Ellis' promised scorching first round, he laid the foundation for his victory in the fourth. Jimmy Ellis: "It was a right hand in the fourth round hurt me so bad I couldn't

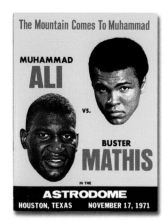

The Mountain Comes To Muhammad

MUHAMMAD **ALI**

VS.

BUSTER **MATHIS**

IN THE

ASTRODOME

HOUSTON, TEXAS   NOVEMBER 17, 1971

ABOVE: Muhammad Ali sends Buster Mathis to the floor three times before coasting to an easy points victory in their bout at the Astrodome, Houston. Television networks didn't bother showing the fight save for a ten minute edited clip set to a soundtrack composed of *Waltz Me Around Again* and *I Want To Hold Your Hand.*

OPPOSITE: Ali chopping trees to build Fighter's Heaven. Angelo Dundee feared that the camp was just another of Ali's whims. In fact, he throws himself wholeheartedly into the project, chopping down hundreds of trees himself for the exercise.

FOLLOWING PAGES: Training at Fighter's Heaven.

really fight my best after that. I knew about that right hand. After all, I been seein' that right hand for a long time. When it came it sneaked up on me and it ruined me."

Ellis was reeling as the round ended and from then on the fight followed the unspectacular pattern of virtually every other Ali vs. Ellis sparring session. Ali moved easily, changing direction at will, a master instructing his prize student. "He wanted to prove he could go 12 rounds on his feet, and he did," said Dundee. In the 12th, Ali caught his opponent with a fatal left uppercut and followed through with a combination, leaving the groggy Ellis sagging on the ropes. Ali did not attempt to finish him off and the referee stopped the fight. "Ain't no reason for me to kill nobody in the ring," explained Ali later in the dressing room.

After the Ellis bout, Ali began his own version of Joe Louis' Bum of the Month Club. Joe Frazier's old partner, Buster Mathis, was the first contender. Mathis, who was still desperately trying to live down a humiliating capitulation to Jerry Quarry two years before, was a great overweight whale of a man with a belly like Santa Claus. The day before the match, Ali did not even bother to train, although he himself weighed in at his heaviest fighting weight to date—227 pounds.

The fight was broad farce. For ten rounds, Mathis floundered after the former champion, trying to land his "speciality," a wild left hook. Ali calmly avoided most of Buster's attempts, although at one point when he was trapped against the ropes, a fist did bounce off the top of his head. "He's hurt, Buster. He's hurt!" screamed Mathis' trainer, Joe Fariello. Ali turned to the frantic Fariello and shot him a wink before coolly gliding away.

In the 11th, Ali loosed a short right to the side of his opponent's jaw and Mathis flopped down on to his hands and knees, shaking the floor with his weight. The bell saved him. During the break, Fariello considered throwing in the towel. He should have. It was only Ali's new merciful image which saved Mathis from a brutal beating. As it was, even Ali's half-hearted punches caused Buster to wobble and sent him to the floor three times. Despite Dundee's insistence that he "Take him out, damn it Ali! Take him out!", Ali preferred to coast to an easy points victory. The television networks passed over the opportunity of televising the fight, save for a ten minute edited clip which showed Ali and Mathis performing to a soundtrack composed of *Waltz Me Around Again* and *I Want To Hold Your Hand.*

Back in the dressing room, Ali defended his new pacifism. "I see a man in front of me, his eyes all glassy and his head rolling around," he said. "How do I know just how hard to hit him to knock him out and not hurt him? I don't care about looking good to the fans or to Angelo. I got to look good to God. I mean Allah." Somebody asked if he was in the wrong business. Yes, he agreed, there was enough killing and hurting in the world. After deposing Frazier he would retire. But wasn't his professed non-violence a trifle incompatible with past bouts, such as the Patterson and Terrell bloodbaths? "Them was the days of the draft thing and the religion thing and black against white, all that," was the reply. "Now them days have gone forever. I don't need to do like I did then. I'm more educated and more civilized."

The Bum Club continued just days after Buster's embarrassing exit when Ali signed to fight a German heavyweight named Jurgen Blin on December 26, 1971. Blin, a blond ex-butcher from Hamburg, appeared to make a reasonable showing in the early rounds until the fight degenerated into a dull series of clinches, with Ali resorting to

the ropes much more than in his two previous bouts. In the seventh, Ali regained his composure and put Blin on the canvas. The German staggered to his feet, but it was obvious even in the cheap seats that he could barely stand. His corner threw in the towel. "It would have been easier for him to have been knocked out cold," said Ali. Such was the mismatch that even Ali's admiring Swiss fans could not be inspired to attend the fight in large enough numbers to provide the promoters with a profit.

On March 2nd an arrest warrant for Ali was issued in Chicago for his failure to comply with a court order directing him to deposit $44,000 guaranteeing Sonji her alimony. Ali paid up and then travelled to Tokyo to recoup his loss by outpointing big Mac Foster—another former sparring partner—on April Fool's Day.

Ali continued his international season by meeting George Chuvalo in Vancouver a month later, the same George Chuvalo he had easily outpointed six years before. In 1970, Chuvalo had been so badly beaten by boxing's rising star George Foreman that his wife had pleaded with the referee from ringside to stop the fight in the third. Ali could only manage a decision over 15 rounds. Another month and he was in Las Vegas facing Jerry Quarry, the same Jerry Quarry he had beaten in three rounds in the first fight after his exile. This time the meeting lasted until the seventh.

Next Ali went to Dublin where he had agreed to fight a near-225 pound Al "Blue" Lewis of Detroit. Only Ali's mother, whom he took along to see Ireland and the English crown jewels, seemed at all excited by the arrangement, apart from the Irish boxing fans who were to see their first major world heavyweight match in 64 years. Ali had a cold and confessed he had grown weary of too many fights in too many cities. The only time he cheered up was when Peter O'Toole knocked on his hotel door ("Hiya, Lawrence, come on in").

But for a protracted "Irish Count" which annoyed Ali, "Blue" would have been back in his dressing room long before he actually was. After the fifth, Ali settled for punching practice until referee Lew Erskine stopped the fight in the 11th. "Thank you," said the relieved Lewis. Ali collected his standard $250,000 paycheck (for exhibitions he charged $6,000, with opponents thrown in) and returned to New York to meet another old foe, Floyd Patterson.

Before he did so, Ali purchased a Pennsylvania hilltop, which, as "Fighter's Heaven" or "Muhammad's Mountain," came to exert a considerable influence on future events. Ali had heard about the mountain from Gene Kilroy, who persuaded him to drive the 30 miles from Reading, Pa., along Highway 61 to the township of Deer Lake. Ali camped in the open, breathing the country air, viewing the rolling Pennsylvania farmlands and dreaming of the spartan life of ancient fighters. When he returned to civilization, he bought Fighter's Heaven for $200,000.

Angelo Dundee feared Ali would spend thousands clearing the land, putting up buildings and so on, only to lose interest in the project halfway. "And once Muhammad's lost interest, there's nothing you can do about it." But Ali had been well and truly seduced by the natural life. He cleared the land—chopping down hundreds of trees himself for the exercise— drew up the blueprints, built a collection of log cabins, and unearthed several huge boulders, which his father painted with the names of the boxing greats. Swooping down on the surrounding farms, Ali bought up as many artifacts as he could from his phlegmatic Dutch-stock neighbors. One of his prize acquisitions was a massive iron bell, made

in 1896 and costing $2,000. An antique ironclad quarry wagon stood in stark contrast to Ali's Rolls-Royces and Cadillacs. Long benches cut from whole tree trunks lined the courtyard. The gymnasium that he built, Angelo likes to think was modelled on his own spartan 5th Street establishment. "A real place," Ali would tell the visitors who flocked to the camp each weekend, "a valid place for fighters to come and work and sweat like fighters should, not like all those places with chandeliers and thick carpets and all those pretty girls around."

As much as the clean air, long country runs, and the honest sweat helped Ali, Fighter's Heaven was equally important for Ali's psychological outlook. Since long before the Ellis fight he had been cutting a despondent figure in the gymnasium. "Used to be, before the Liston fights, all I thought about was fight, fight, fight, be the greatest, be the champion," he would tell the reporters. "Now it's like I go to work, put in eight hours a day, do my job. I got other things on my mind, heavy things." His "Uncle Tom's Cabin" at the new retreat afforded Ali the opportunity of collecting these "heavy" thoughts. His output of philosophic lectures increased and his poetry changed from boxing doggerel to odes extolling freedom, destiny, and truth:

> *I am riding on my horse of hope,*
> *Holding in my hand the rein of courage.*
> *Dressed in the armor of patience,*
> *With the helmet of endurance on my head,*
> *I start out on my journey to the land of love.*

Welded together, these thoughts became what Ali and Bundini referred to as "The Mission," a rather hazy but implicitly believed philosophy of life for the black man. "We are both sons of God," said Bundini. "We feel we are on a mission to do good for all people, bringing people together through understanding. The black man is the onliest one can save this country. If the black man pack up and leave, this country will fall, because there's a sin on it already. We got to overcome this sin, forget it, straighten up from today on. The young people know this and the champ is their hero."

OPPOSITE: If at first you don't succeed…the 37-year-old Floyd Patterson tries once again, and this time around puts in a surprisingly spirited performance.

At 37, Floyd Patterson had made a profitable success out of failure. Since his Las Vegas massacre at the hands of an avenging Ali, he had made two abortive efforts to win another crown for the third time: first he was eliminated from the WBA tournament and then outpointed by title-holder Jimmy Ellis in Stockholm. Going in for a second time with Ali made no boxing logic at all, but with 17,378 people willing to pay $512,361 to watch him try, Floyd was not especially daunted by his impending humiliation. And as *Sports Illustrated* pointed out, he was decidedly more fortunate than many of his former colleagues—Sonny Liston, dead; Zora Folley, dead after striking his head in a swimming pool; Hurricane Jackson, last seen shining shoes in the Garden; Eddie Machen, dead after falling from his balcony.

For Ali, the bout was little more than Broadway show biz. As the two fighters performed pre-fight callisthenics in their respective corners, Joe Frazier was called up into the ring to be introduced to the crowd. Immediately Ali forgot all about Floyd and launched into a long harangue at his nemesis. Frazier chuckled, avoided Ali's attempts to throw off his restraining cornerman, and sat down.

Surprisingly, Patterson put up a spirited performance before his exit. Ali, who had trained lightly, found himself losing the third, fourth, and fifth rounds to his determined elder. With his opponent landing his famous combinations and, especially in the fifth, several snappy rights, Ali had difficulty penetrating Patterson's unique defense. In the sixth round, Ali opened up with uppercuts and chopping rights, one of which sliced open Floyd's left eyelid. Ali concentrated on the eye and within two rounds had worried it to an open wound. At the bell for round eight, Patterson did not leave his stool. After the fight, Ali praised Patterson for his grit, Floyd apologized for not doing better, and everyone tried to forget what had taken place.

Two months later, Ali's Bum of the Month Club reached a new nadir when he faced Light-Heavyweight Champion Bob Foster. Although his record of 42 knockouts in 54 fights indicated that Foster could perhaps be expected to provide some stronger opposition than Patterson, "Blue" Lewis, and Blin, the mismatch was made obvious at the weigh-in where Foster surrendered 41 pounds to his opponent. What made the fight even more depressing was the venue, a nightclub in a gambling casino in Stateline, Nevada, the poor man's Las Vegas! The sign in the lobby of the Sahara Tahoe Hotel which read "Live November 21 Muhammad Ali vs. Bob Foster. Next Attraction November 23 Isaac Hayes" summed up Ali's situation. He had become a cabaret act, performing amidst slot machines, blackjack tables and waitresses in orange boots.

Ali himself was disgusted by the event. The day before the fight, Bundini and Dundee tried to wake him for training. Ali refused to get out of bed. "I'm not excited about fighting anymore," he said when he finally arrived for the weigh-in, 20 minutes late. "You people are the ones who're excited, not me. I've been fighting since I was 12. It's just another night to jump up and down and beat up somebody."

Ali toyed with Foster at the beginning, obviously content to string out the mismatch until his dutifully predicted fifth round. A ringside spectator shouted "Phony", and Bundini urged his man to stop playing. Ali turned fully away from Foster and snapped "Shut up!" The match glimmered in the fifth when Ali unseated Foster four times. Foster survived the round, in the process nicking Ali's left eyebrow, the first time he had ever been cut in his 12 year professional

career. Foster went down twice more in the seventh, after jolting Ali several times with his right, before finally staying down 40 seconds into the eighth round.

Ali had five stitches in his eyebrow. "Now people know he's got blood," cracked Dundee. "I don't know if the cut came from a butt, a thumb, or a punch, but the important thing is Ali won and we can go home."

1972 had been a frankly uninspiring year for Ali. But at least he had kept busy, which was more than Frazier had accomplished. Indeed, compared with Smokin' Joe's performance as Heavyweight Champion, Ali's year looked positively interesting. Frazier's embarrassing slaughter of unknowns Terry Daniels and Ron Stander spoke volumes for his negative view of his role as champion.

Frazier also had a negative view of Ali. The promised rematch was delayed for months, firstly because of Frazier's hospitalization and then by financial complications involving the rematch agreement held by Jack Kent Cooke. But as the months passed, it became obvious that Frazier was avoiding Ali. Five million dollars apiece had been discussed as the price of the rematch, but even this could not tempt Frazier. Instead, he signed to meet Olympic gold medallist George Foreman in Kingston, Jamaica, for less than a million.

On January 22, 1973, Frazier charged across the ring at the bell and caught his challenger with several of his left-hook specialities. It was the only moment in this extraordinary fight that Frazier looked anything like the Heavyweight Champion of the World. Foreman's first counter-punch was a sickening body blow, which stopped the

champion in his tracks. The second caught Frazier flush on the jaw and sent him skating across the canvas. Foreman hit him again on the jaw and Frazier resumed his position on the floor. He regained his feet and charged in; Foreman reached out and pushed him off as if he were an over-enthusiastic female fan. Another punch and Frazier's head and shoulders shot under the bottom rope. Only the bell saved him.

Soon after the start of the second round, Foreman crashed yet another right into Frazier's jaw. When he staggered back up he was wobbling and the challenger lifted him clean off his feet. After the sixth knockdown, Foreman glanced inquiringly at the referee and when Frazier had recovered his feet he was led off to his corner. George Foreman was named the new Heavyweight Champion of the World one minute and 35 seconds into the second round.

Ali was asleep when Frazier surrendered his title. "They woke me up to tell me," he recalls. "I thought: My, my, there goes $5 million out of the window."

Frazier's savage defeat spurred Ali into the toughest training session he had undertaken for months. He contracted to fight British champion Joe Bugner and low-ranked Ken Norton a month later, but his eyes were set on higher stakes. "There's too much involved for me to lose," he said when questioned about his intensive workout. "We're too close to the big one. There's something around the corner. Wait and see."

At 22, Bugner had already seen much of Ali, sparring with him on four occasions and appearing on the same card when Ali fought "Blue" Lewis. He was something of a black sheep in British boxing after having relieved Henry Cooper of his title, but Ali was a Bugner fan and had often predicted a glowing future for his young opponent. The fight, held in Caesar's Palace, lasted the full 12 rounds. Although Ali looked fresh and fit, he declined to despatch Bugner sooner. Several critics suggested he was baiting a hook for Foreman, whose management had shown a marked reluctance to consider Ali as a possible contender.

It was left to an unknown fighter whose last match was before an audience of 700 for a $300 purse to shatter Ali's careful plans. Ken Norton was ranked seventh in the heavyweight hierarchy but, as one magazine noted, he seemed to have sneaked into the listings. A former marine built like an hour-glass ("He'll break in half," laughed Dundee), Norton had yet to meet even a reasonably rated heavyweight when he signed with Ali. Ali was Norton's big chance, and he was not about to pass it by. Assisted by a hypnotist (Dr. Michael Dean), trainer Eddie Futch—who had plotted Frazier's victory over Ali—worked to implant ring tactics in Norton's subconscious.

Dundee said he realized it in the first round; Ali said he knew in the second. Whichever round it occurred, by round three the dark red blood trickling from Ali's mouth confirmed that Ken Norton had broken Muhammad Ali's jaw, and with a punch no one had even seen. Dundee believes that the injury was a fluke; a one-in-a-million combination of two missing back teeth and Ali's opening his mouth at the precise moment Norton clipped him. "In the third round I asked him to let me stop the fight," remembers Angelo. "'Let me stop it,' I said. 'Your jaw's broke.' He says, 'No, I can beat this sucker…he won't touch my jaw.' What bigger thing can you have thrown in your face than a guy boxing with a broken jaw for 12 rounds?"

SEE IT LIVE ON BIG SCREEN CLOSED CIRCUIT TV

MUHAMMAD ALI
FORMER WORLD HEAVYWEIGHT CHAMPION

Mon.
10th
Sept.

KEN NORTON
NO.1 WORLD CHALLENGER

12 ROUNDS

THREE LOCATIONS!
FLAGLER KENNEL CLUB
AUDITORIUM
MIAMI BEACH
CONVENTION HALL
DIPLOMAT HOTEL

ABOVE: Just five months after Norton broke Ali's jaw in their first fight, Ali faces him again, this time determined to prove himself once and for all. He does, but with the narrowest of margins.

OPPOSITE: New York, 1974, and the fight everyone has been waiting for—Ali vs. Frazier II. It didn't matter that there is no title at stake, this is a grudge match of heroic proportions. By the time fight night arrives, the pre-match niceties have already degenerated into a public brawl.

Norton's unrefined style paled beside Ali's experience, but his strength, and the broken jaw, compensated. At one point in the tenth, Norton darted up under Ali's guard and literally lifted him off the floor. Nevertheless, the match was a close-fought contest with the judges narrowly awarding it to Norton. As the doctor wired Ali's jaw later that night, he was amazed at Ali's courage. "There was a quarter-inch separation," he said. "The pain must have been unbelievable."

Sitting at home alone (Belinda was in the hospital after trying to fight her way past three security guards to reach her injured husband in the ring), slurping ice cream through his clamped jaw, Ali said he had nursed a twisted ankle during the fight, an injury which had forced him to abandon his training a week before the match. According to Ali he had suffered the sprain while revolutionizing the game of golf. "I don't stand there an' look at the ball and wiggle the club like Arnold Palmer and Jack Nicklaus and them cats," he said straight-faced. "I was walkin' up to the ball and hittin' it while I was walkin' and knocking it 300…350 yards. Then I figured I'm gonna do even better. I was gonna run up and hit the ball. First time, I hit the grass. Second time I lost my balance and swung all the way round and fell down and twisted my ankle." The excuse was so outrageous that the listening press found it impossible to disbelieve.

Ali was philosophic about his broken jaw. "Funny, the jaw didn't hurt so much in the fight. Under all the heat and excitement, you don't feel it. Like a man in a street fight, he get cut in the stomach, fights on with his guts hangin' out and don't feel nothin' until he gets to the hospital." Resourcefully salvaging some capital from the disaster, he said the injury had been sent as a test from Allah. "What happened is Muhammad Ali ate a lot of ice cream and cake," he confessed. "He didn't do his running, he didn't punch the heavy bag. I'm ashamed Ali let himself get into such shape. He won't do it again. Going back to the old Golden Glove days, I was too busy puttin' on a show, talkin', laughin', making jokes. When I start trainin' again all that is out. I'm gonna get up at five, say my prayers and run three miles. Train up at my camp in the Poconos, just me and my manager and a sweaty gym, like in the old days." After that, he said, he would "bump off" Norton in four, Frazier in six, and then tackle Foreman. "But I won't knock him out. I'll beat him so bad they'll have to stop the fight!"

Many critics were unwilling to give Ali a second chance, heralding once again the end of the legend. Recalled Bundini: "Some guy comes up to me in the hotel with 2,000 Ali buttons, the ones with THE PEOPLE'S CHAMP written on them. He says, 'Well. I guess these aren't good anymore. He's had it.'"

Ali also revealed after the fight what the "something around the corner" that he had referred to while training for Bugner had been. He had, he said, cancelled himself out of a record $5 million payday.

When his jaw had healed, Ali barnstormed across the US drumming up ticket sales for the return match. Then he closeted himself away in Fighter's Heaven for a rigorous work-out. "He's never concentrated this hard on a fight," said Harold Conrad. When he emerged, Ali was a fit man. Even Dundee claimed to have lost ten pounds.

Ken Norton was also not about to rest on his laurels. His windfall (Ali referred to him as "The man who shot Liberty Valance") had rocketed him into the major league and he was already hungrily eyeing Foreman's silver belt. At his training camp in the ominously named Massacre Valley, 80 miles from Los Angeles, Norton worked to secure his overnight stardom.

Interest in the rematch ran high as the scheduled date approached—September 10th, five months after the first bout. Indeed, Ali's spirited tub-thumping succeeded in eclipsing George Foreman's first title defense against Joe "King" Roman, a boxer even less well known than Ken Norton had been before his San Diego triumph. England, for example, readily agreed to closed circuit coverage of the rematch, but refused to touch the championship fight. "No interest," explained British impressario Jarvis Astaire. "Yes, yes," babbled Ali, delighted to be back at center-stage, "they are all talking about Muhammad Ali like it's his life or death on the line. Is he through, or is he not? Is he still the fastest and most beautiful man in the world, or is he growing old or slow? It shows you what they think of Ali that this question would come up."

The rematch may have posed the question, but its result provided no answer. Before the fight, Ali promised to thrash Norton. "I took a nobody and created a monster," he said angrily after being told that Norton was maligning him. "I put him on *The Dating Game*. I gave him glory. Now I have to punish him bad." By the middle rounds Ali was clearly ahead and seemed set to administer his punishment. But then Norton's enormous strength and youth turned the tide. Ali continued to dance and jab, proving once again that the ropes were not necessary for him to survive 12 rounds, but as the final round approached he seemed less and less capable of remaining one step ahead. Also, Norton's style was unsuited to Ali's jabbing. Whereas a George Foreman left hook could remove the ex-marine from the ring in no time at all (and later did), Ali had difficulty in fathoming Norton's peculiar habit of leaning back off his splayed right foot.

In the 12th Ali tried a desperate gamble. Coming down off his toes, he met Norton at ring center and slugged it out, stopping the Californian's monotonous advance. Ali's last-round combinations proved sufficient to win him the nod from referee Dick Young, a decision that really could have gone either way.

Ali was so upset by the bout that a few seconds after the bell he turned and swung at Bundini, who in turn took a frustrated poke at camp photographer Howard Bingham. Ali's lawyer Bob Arum was equally disappointed. He was carrying a $10 million offer for a Foreman vs. Ali match from a British promoter as well as a rematch plan for Frazier in December. Ali's close shave against Norton cast a considerable shadow over both proposals.

While Arum resumed negotiations with the Frazier and Foreman camps, Ali wound up his minor league commitments by flying to Indonesia to meet Dutchman Rudi Lubbers on October 20th. Although Ali padded out the event to the full 12 rounds, the only remarkable aspect of the match was Ali's capacity to draw international crowds. Thirty-five thousand Indonesians showed up for the fight, and at an exhibition bout Ali charmed another 45,000 onlookers. "They never had a fight there before in Jakarta, yet he's adored there," said Dundee. "Places we would go that people you would think never heard of him, they heard of him!"

Ali returned to Fighter's Heaven nursing his hands. The old bursitis inflammation, which caused shooting pains up into his shoulders every time he landed a solid blow, had reappeared after the first Norton bout, restricting Ali's training program. He compensated by sparring with his snarling $2,000 German shepherd, Shadow.

Joe Frazier was the opponent eventually chosen to replace Shadow, at a price of $850,000 (the same as Ali's purse). Locked away in the ghetto neighborhood of North Philadelphia, Frazier

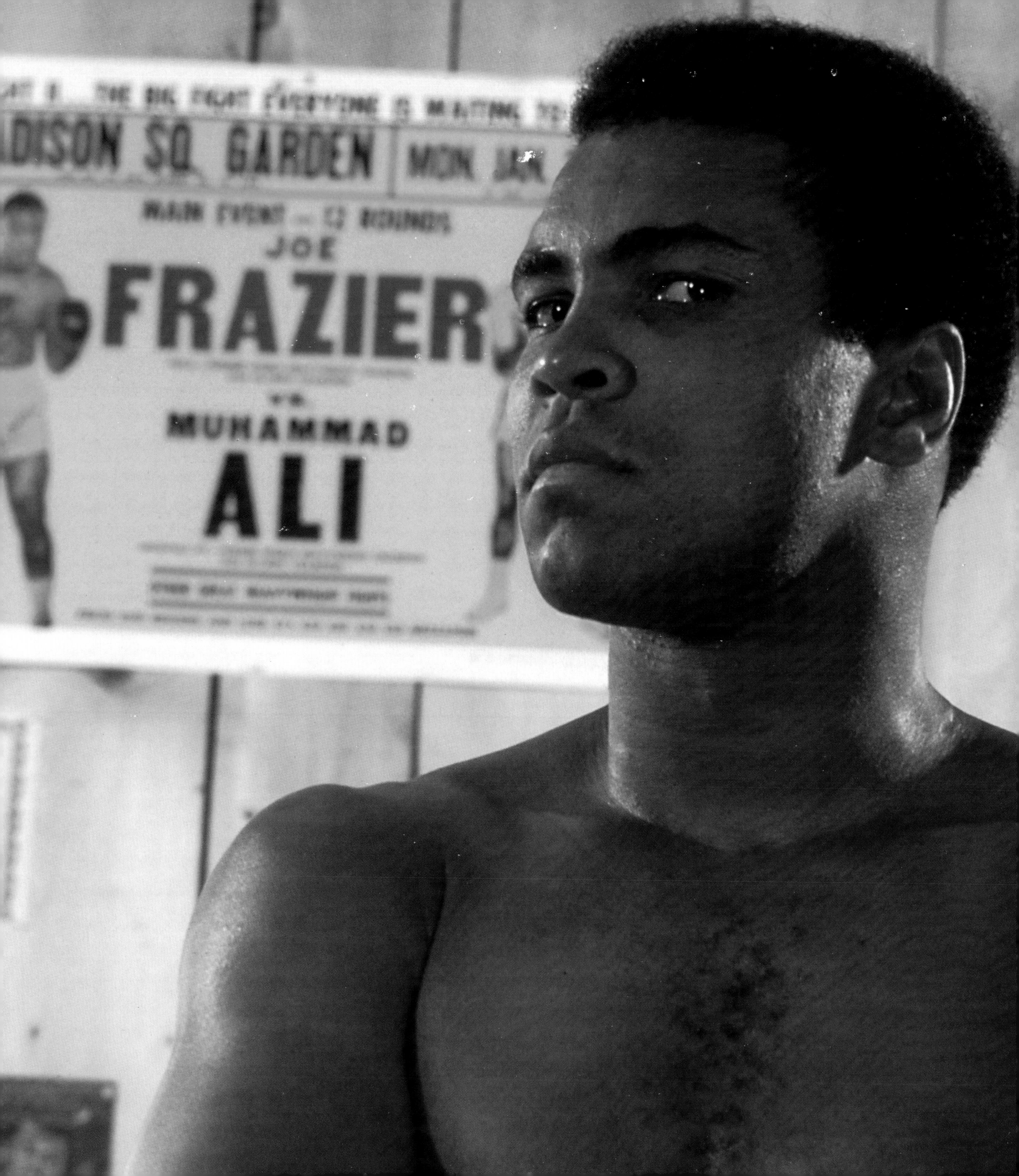
THE BIG FIGHT EVERYONE IS WAITING
ADISON SQ. GARDEN
MON JAN
MAIN EVENT — 12 ROUNDS
JOE
FRAZIER
vs.
MUHAMMAD
ALI

OPPOSITE AND FOLLOWING PAGES: Ali's "ring artistry" defeats Frazier's "one-man war of attrition".

sweated long hours honing his body to a high-tensile 210 pounds. He worked without the watchful eye of his "creator," Yank Durham, who had recently died in his fifties. The formidable Eddie Futch, fired by a willfully confident Ken Norton, now presided over Frazier's former ballroom of a gym, with its secretary, wall-to-wall carpeting and baby-blue telephones.

Frazier, training under a giant photograph of the left hook which sent Ali to the canvas during the Fight of the Century, impressed the boxing writers with his determination. "He acts like a man who has lost something he thought he did not love, only to discover soon afterwards that he did truly care," reported *Sports Illustrated.* Frazier was also desperate to dispel suspicions that Ali had ruined him, that his kidneys were badly injured and that he had lost part of the sight in his right eye. "I can't remember when I been in better shape," he rounded angrily on doubting pressmen, "and I kin give a whole list of doctors who'll say the same thing." He talked little about the Foreman disaster ("That was in the past. That was yesterday. That is finished") except to admit he had fought a dumb fight. His big mistake, he said, was in getting up immediately after the first knock-down instead of resting and clearing his head.

Once more the publicity machine was cranked into action as befitted a genuine "Superfight." Frazier, like Sonny Liston, was a perfect foil for Ali's caustic tongue. Everything about Smokin' Joe provided Ali with ammunition: his self-effacing Middle-American lifestyle; the ugly, awkward way he fought; the terrible punishment he masochistically soaked up (which made Ali recoil in horror and conclude Frazier was punchy before his time). But the litany had such a soggy familiarity about it that it served to remind the fans just how long the two had been at each other's throats.

Then, in finest Ali tradition, it all boiled over. Seated beside each other in front of the television cameras, the ritual mud slinging had almost run its course when Ali touched an unexpectedly exposed nerve. The two opponents had been bickering over who had come off worse after the first fight.

"You went to the hospital," sniped Frazier.

"I went to the hospital for ten minutes and you went to the hospital for ten months," retorted Ali.

Frazier: "Just for a rest. In and out."

Ali: "That shows how dumb you are…that shows how ignorant…"

With that Frazier snapped. Pulling out his studio earplug he leaped up and reached across to yank Ali from his seat. Both men grappled, heaved and eventually rolled off the stage into the audience where they were pried apart by alarmed spectators.

Ali, of course, had been separated from almost as many fights outside the ring as inside, and there was nothing to suggest that he regarded this particular piece of photogenic horseplay as anything special. Frazier was a different matter. When he issued his half-cocked challenge he was livid, as he was on most other occasions when Ali scorned his racial allegiances ("white man in a black skin", "Uncle Tom"), snapped personal insults ("soooo ugly"), and slurred his intelligence.

Such was the unassuming nature of the man that Frazier was unable to take Ali's act anywhere but to heart, and it consumed him to the extent that he was prepared to pay a $5,000 fine to button Ali's lip on the floor of a television studio. Once again Ali had succeeded in psyching an opponent into unreasoning hatred.

It was in this strained and bitter atmosphere of genuine enmity that Ali and Frazier climbed into the Garden ring before 20,788 witnesses on the edge of their chairs. From the word go it was Ali's fight, "ring generalship," as *Sports Illustrated* put it, "over a one-man army fighting a war of attrition."

Ali took the first round in arrogant, peacock fashion, dodging and slipping Frazier's best shots, bottling him up when he pressed too close. In the second, Frazier rediscovered his familiar two-fisted drumbeat rhythm, only to have it shattered by a stunning right—a slugger's punch—which visibly shivered him to his toes. The referee saved him by diving between the hunter and his kill in the mistaken belief that the bell had sounded.

Ali won the first six rounds with ease, his combinations and left jabs keeping "The Bull" at bay. He avoided the ropes like a disease and Frazier could not work his way close enough to land his short, heavy punches. But Ali failed to smother either Joe's juggernaut charges or remove his death's-head smile. Later he estimated he was throwing four times the number of punches Frazier could manage— a conservative estimate—yet his opponent never relented.

By the end of the seventh round, Frazier's grit appeared about to bear fruit. In the eighth, he strode across the ring into the opposing corner and unleashed a battery of left hooks at Ali's head. Ali stayed on the ropes, apparently arm-weary and capable only of looping his arm around his opponent's neck and dragging him down into a clinch. The ninth continued in the same vein until Ali dropped to his heels and moved forward to slug it out at Frazier's invitation, as he had done in the closing round of the Norton bout. Again the gamble paid off. Frazier never recovered and Ali never looked back.

Celebrating his 12-round victory in his dressing room, Ali happily berated the press with, "I told you so." The press' general pre-fight scenario had held that the match was to be a double tragedy, a showdown between two fading, aging gunslingers from which only one would emerge, badly shot up, but still able to announce his retirement with at least a modicum of dignity. The press was perhaps half right. In his dressing room, Frazier was claiming he had won every round…in fact every minute of every round. The reporters crowding around appeared to be taking down his fuzzy logic. Actually they were writing his obituary.

The victor, gnawing a frozen popsicle on a stick, was by no stretch of the imagination badly battered. "Can you see a mark on it?" he demanded, thrusting his face at the line of cameras and writers. "Can you believe that this is the face of a 32-year-old man who has just fought Joe Frazier 12 rounds?" Then he sat back and smiled, content in the knowledge that once more he stood poised to enter his name in the boxing record.

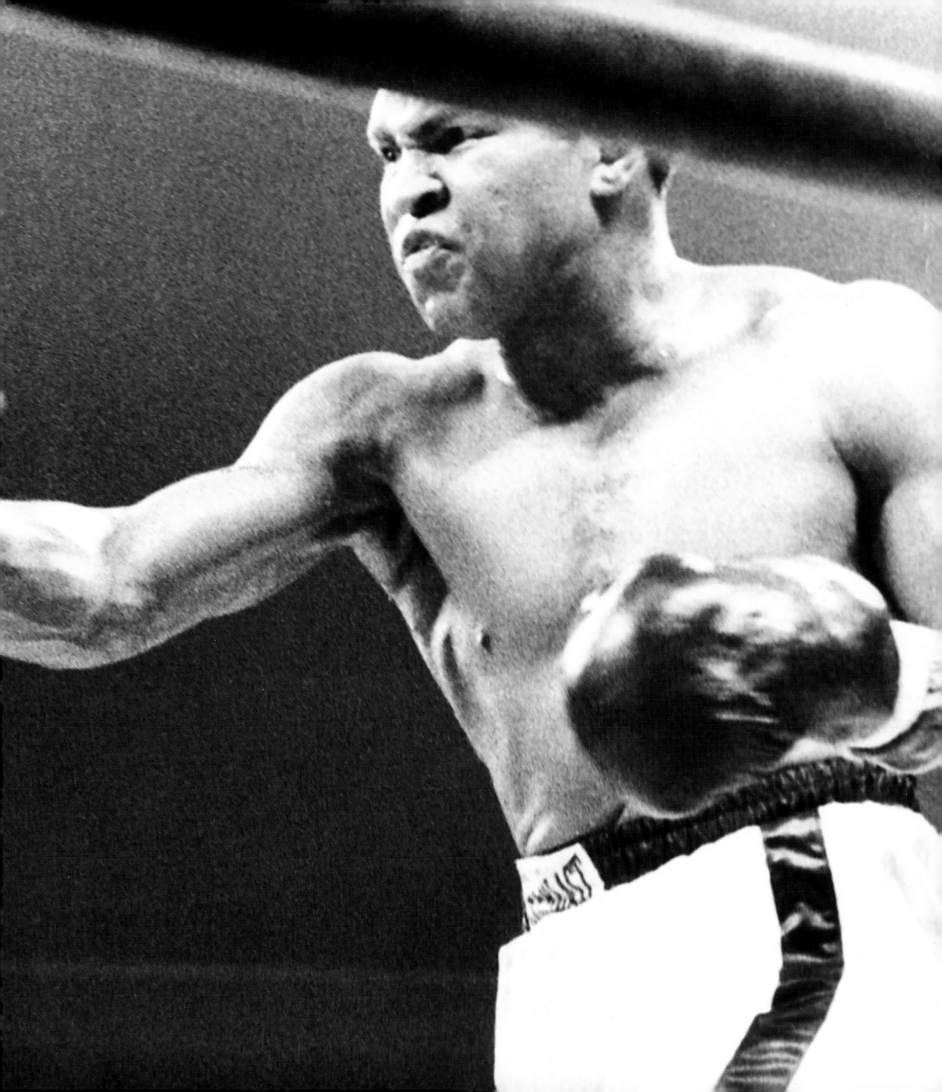

Rumble In The Jungle

"It's a divine fight. This Foreman—he represents Christianity, America, the flag. I can't let him win. He represents pork chops."

Muhammad Ali

Zaire, 1974. Muhammad Ali squats on the steps of his bungalow blinking at the dark waters of the second-largest river in the world moving swiftly past him some 50 yards away. In the deceptive half-light before the African dawn, the broad expanse of water looks filled with hundreds of floating crocodiles. Ali knows that what he is seeing is merely jungle flotsam, great clumps of matted vegetation being swept down to the sea from the rain forests of the north. But it nevertheless intrigues him to imagine all the exotic creatures of his professed homeland.

Ali fiddles with the battered pair of black hiking boots he insists on wearing even when the midday sun is frying Zaire's other visitors. Then he jumps to his feet, twists his head to relieve the neck muscles, and sets off at a steady jog along the road separating the silent row of unlit bungalows from the river. He turns left beside the riverboat *President Mobutu* (whose propellers, according to rumor, once sliced into little pieces a political opponent of Ali's patron), and heads on up the hill, past the experimental plots tended during the day by Red Chinese agricultural experts, past the dead flower beds neatly ruled off in concrete, until he reaches an extraordinary oriental building known to Ali as the Chinese House and to the more cynical journalists as The Laundry.

Ali pauses beside this elaborate showpiece and looks back across the flats to the river, which marks the end of Zaire and the beginning of the Republique Populaire Du Congo. As he stands there in the gloom he's thinking heavy thoughts, thoughts which force him out of bed and onto the road while his critics 50 kilometers away are still playing blackjack and ordering nightcaps.

Ali is not training simply to win back the Heavyweight Championship of the world. There's much more at stake here than just a silver belt and a $4,500,000 paycheck. Once again, as in the heady days more than a decade ago when Cassius Clay battled Sonny Liston in the name of Allah, Muhammad Ali has talked his way into another Holy War. The difference this time is that instead of race, Ali now talks in terms of nations; instead of a red-haired demagogue named Malcolm X, Ali's mentor is now a shadowy despot who rules his African state with a rod of steel.

As he jogs along the road past the huts of the citizens of Zaire, Ali's head is filled with dreams of the future—how he will be able to speak with authority once he has regained "his" title, how he will help "resurrect our people so they can look after themselves", how he will be on an equal footing with the great rulers of the world. The harder he runs, the closer he gets to realizing these dreams, and when he arrives back at the still silent row of bungalows, the sweat stands out in beads on his forehead and trickles down his broad brown shoulders. The soldiers in their steel helmets seated beside the house grin at his return, and shift their guns to more comfortable positions. Satisfied with his effort, Ali glances at the Zaire River and its wooden crocodiles, then turns and enters the dark bungalow. A moment later he is asleep.

In his camp on the hill rising above the Chinese House, George Foreman is also asleep, happily ignorant of the plans bubbling in Ali's mind.

President Mobutu Sese Seko (literally "the all-powerful warrior who, because of his endurance and will to win, will go from contest to contest leaving fire in his wake") is also, as his name implies, a man of ambition. Formerly Sergeant Joseph Mobutu of the Belgian Congo Armed Forces, he survived the bloody civil war which broke out after his country seized its independence

OPPOSITE: Ali looks out over the Zaire River at N'Sele, dreaming the impossible.

ABOVE: Zaire is where the electric-haired Don King will make his mark. At the time it seems to many that King's credentials as the black man's promoter are genuine. However, as one of Ali's entourage will later remark, it soon becomes apparent to others that "the only color Don cares about is green."

OPPOSITE: Ali relaxes at his training camp in N'Sele under the omnipresent eye of The Great Leopard, Mobuto Sese Seko. Ali's camp is an extraordinarily casual affair, open to all-comers day or night. It stands in marked contrast to the isolation of the glowering George Foreman, barricaded away in his Kinshasa hotel room.

from Belgium in 1960, and five years later assumed power via a bloodless coup. Since then, Mobutu has enjoyed unprecedented success in unifying the 200 impossibly divided tribes which make up Zaire's 22 million population. Besides the strong-arm tactics employed by most absolute dictators, much of Mobutu's success stems from his passionate black power program—*Authenticité*—which he has used to remove the traces of colonial rule. The Congo River he renamed the Zaire; neckties, women's wigs, and short skirts are taboo; Western Christian names and Santa Claus are banned. "Mobutuism rehabilitates black people" and "Black power is sought everywhere but it is already here in Zaire" read the yellow and green billboards lining the route from the airport to the capital, Kinshasa.

According to the ubiquitous officials of the Foreman vs. Ali Commission D'Organisation, Zaire has purchased the Heavyweight Championship of the world as the crowning glory of *Authenticité*, a view heartily endorsed by Don King, the most obvious of the uneasily allied Western promoters. "All the elements are here, man," says King, whose special concern is the doomed Afro-American rock festival From Slaveship to Championship. "This is the most beautiful situation that ever could be. You have a black venue, a wealthy black nation that's emerging, coming out of the struggle, shaking off the shackles and the fetters. If the fight comes off, which it will, with sophistication and dignity and effectiveness, then this adds dubiousness to all those who have been taught that blacks are retarded, that blacks are slothful, they can only sing and dance, they have nothing else but rhythm."

But the reasons for Zaire's involvement are more complex than the promotion of black power in an obscure African state. Largely, they boil down to the finances and ego of Mobutu Sese Seko, other-wise known to his subjects as Le Guide, Le Clairvoyant, Le Redempteur, and The Great Leopard (after the national football team, The Leopards). Mobutu is everywhere in Zaire's capital, Kinshasa. His portrait gazes sternly down from countless billboards and peers from the front page of the newspapers virtually every day. Television programs are regularly interrupted by a five-minute vignette which begins with a small speck whirling out of a cloudy sky; as the martial music rises to a crescendo, the speck inflates into Mobutu's head. The national costume appears to be multi-colored shirts and saris depicting this same head. The songs chorused by the schoolchildren who serenade Ali and Foreman after workouts are mostly about Mobutu. When he travels abroad, Le Guide commandeers the Air Zaire jumbo jet; when his wife accompanies him she takes a DC-10, leaving the airline without its two largest planes.

After Foreman, Ali, and the visiting journalists have left, Mobutu will launch an anti-Christianity campaign on the grounds that, whereas the local churches display photographs of Pope Paul, there are none of the nation's ruler. "The President is a Messiah himself and the savior of the Zairese people," a government spokesman will say.

Like Chairman Mao, Mobutu encourages this crude personality cult as a means of consolidating his power base and unifying the people. (Although it is never admitted, some tribes are still unhappy with his leadership. In 1975 fighting once again broke out in the former Katanga Province.) Buying his own World Heavyweight title fight, an attraction expected to draw the highest television viewing figures ever, is at once a gigantic boost to Mobutu's

ballooning ego and an international feather in his leopard-skin pill-box hat. It is also a daunting show of power to his would-be successors. The official Zaire fight poster, translated from the domestic French, reads "Ali-Foreman, a gift from Mobutu to the People of Zaire". Later it is replaced by the sterner "Ali and Foreman trust Mobutu… So should YOU!"

How Mobutu cornered world sport's richest prize has more to do with *The Wall Street Journal* than *The Ring* magazine—as have all post-Perenchio heavyweight productions. Hank Schwartz of Video-Techniques Inc., a three-year-old closed-circuit television company whose arrival on the heavyweight scene coincided roughly with the arrival of George Foreman, set the promotion in motion. After Foreman's Caracas defense against Ken Norton, which Video-Techniques handled, Foreman's energetic trainer Dick Sadler casually put the champion's price for fighting Ali at $5 million. Schwartz didn't bat an eyelid. Instead, he enlisted Don King to help assemble the package.

King is unique, even among the larger-than-life characters that surface around big time boxing. An impressively large black man from Ohio, sporting an uncontrollable Afro which stands out from his skull like electrified chicken wire, he was once known to his associates as the "Numbers King" of Cleveland. His numbers empire collapsed following an assault in which a man died, and while Ali was languishing in exile, King was serving a four-year prison sentence. The two men had known each other casually since Ali's Olympic victory and had developed an amicable relationship. By cleverly out-maneuvering Ali's lawyer Bob Arum, who also represented a rival closed circuit firm (Top Rank Inc.), King persuaded Herbert Muhammad to agree to the match. After weeks of frantic pursuit, King finally caught up with Foreman in a Californian parking lot. He clinched the deal, he says, by pointing to his skin and saying, "This is my promotion. And I'm black!" Foreman signed. What King offered both fighters was $4.5 million apiece, the largest payout ever for a single sportsman and perhaps the highest per minute wage in history.

With both signatures on his option contract, Schwartz began scouting for backers. Like Jerry Perenchio, he found no immediate takers. Desperate, he approached the Hemdale Group, a British entertainment organization with stakes in the film and music worlds, founded in 1965 by actor David Hemmings and John Daly. Daly had an hour to decide whether to put up $1½ million risk money to keep the option open. He decided and accepted.

This time both men went stumping for financing. Madison Square Garden was approached and discarded because of New York's uncompromising tax laws. Kuwait and its unlimited supply of petrodollars was considered but also abandoned when Foreman blanched at the thought of fighting Ali on Allah's home ground. Another idea, shades of South Miami's Murray Woroner, was for the match to be staged on an ocean liner in the mid-Atlantic.

At the 11th hour a Swiss-based investment company named Risnelia expressed interest. Risnelia was a holding company set up to transact deals for the Republic of Zaire. ("Countries are bidding for me now!" Ali would later crow.) Talks in Paris led to an agreement: Hemdale was to receive 38 per cent of the action, Video-Techniques 20 per cent, and Risnelia, in return for letters of credit guaranteeing $10 million, was to pick up the rest, as well as the proceeds from the live gate. "Our mathematics tell us that the very least the promoters

ABOVE: Ali throws a headlock on his old trainer Dick Sadler, the light relief of the Foreman camp. Sadler, who once was driven mad by a twist-obsessed young Cassius Clay on a train journey across America, happens to be the only member of Foreman's camp on hand after Foreman gets cut. Ali instantly leaps on the uncomfortable-looking Sadler, shouting, "if Foreman won't fight me, then I'll fight you!"

OPPOSITE: The Mummy Walks—George Foreman, accompanied by his ever-present bodyguards and his dog Daggo, leaves the N'Sele gym for the seclusion of his impenetrable hotel room. "There was a time in my life when I was sort of unfriendly, and Zaire was part of that period," recalled Foreman years later.

FOLLOWING PAGES: Ali's mother and father embrace their boy at the N'Sele gym.

can expect to receive is $20 million, which would mean an $8 million profit," said Daly at the time. "With anything over $20 million we'll be laughing all the way to the bank."

Mobutu's one string was that the fight be held in Zaire. Which seemed an acceptable proposition to all parties. Just 25 miles from Kinshasa there was a brand new satellite relay station. And the city couldn't be any less convenient than a ship bobbing in mid-Atlantic. Could it?

Which explains why the cream of the world's sporting press is congregated in this equatorial tank town which rises from the dusty plains of what used to be called Darkest Africa. Kinshasa and its startling lack of amenities has bewildered the journalists from the minute they arrive. Compared to the Garden—or even Lewiston, Maine—the town is a tourist's nightmare, complete with rats on the pavement, cobras in the drains and whisky at $4 a shot. "Give it a new coat of paint and the place would be sheer hell," comments one of them after their first day in town.

Ali and Foreman are housed in more well appointed accommodations 50 kilometrers away at N'Sele, Mobutu's version of Camp David. Several reporters elect to join them. But whereas life beside the Zaire is a more comfortable experience, the boredom is overwhelming. One noted correspondent retreats almost completely to his air-conditioned villa, spending his time huddled over a bottle or a typewriter, filing stories with exotic datelines and opening paragraphs which begin, "As I sit here, elephants crashing through the jungle not six feet to my right…" Boredom is to play a major role in this fight.

But more than the boredom of N'Sele or the dubious comforts of Kinshasa, what particularly infuriates the press is the iron grip Mobutu, through his Commissioners, holds on the fight. When Zaire's overloaded communication facilities inevitably begin to break down in the hands of the eager but inexperienced Foreman-Ali officials, the reporters turn their frustrations into a steady stream of unfavorable copy, deriding life in Kinshasa and, in particular, the president's opulent existence.

Such stories are exactly what Mobutu has striven to avoid. (Before any foreigners arrived, he publicly executed more than 40 petty criminals randomly selected from Kinshasa's prisons as a warning to his subjects that they had better be on their best behavior during the fight.) The Commissioners react swiftly to the hostile reports, altering copy while it is on the teletypes, or simply tearing stories from the machines. At least one journalist who leaves the country is refused a re-entry visa. The bad feelings between the press and its hosts boil over with only hours to go before the bout when writers, cameramen, and officials fight desperately over the inadequate number of allotted press seats.

Ensconced in his presidential compound, Ali hears little of such minor irritants, and probably cares even less. Ever since mid-September when he stepped from his all-black Air Zaire 747, he has been adopted by the Zairese, as a prodigal son, an advantage Ali is not slow in exploiting. "This is my country," he tells the crowds, lumping Elijah Muhammad, Mobutu, *Authenticité*, and himself into a socio-religious black brother-hood package. "George Foreman, he's a stranger in this country and I'm givin' him until high noon to saddle up his horse or his plane or whatever and get outta here." Seizing on a few well-chosen words of the native *lingala*, he has his

enchanted audience chorusing *Ali, bomayé. Ali, bomayé*, which means, literally, '*Ali, kill him*'. Ali's publicist Bob Goodman: "He's the promoter's best friend—he's been a dream to me."

George Foreman, on the other hand, is a promoter's nightmare. "George couldn't draw his breath at the gate," sums up the PR view of the world champion. Although he is on record as saying he likes talking to reporters, he spends little time with the press, confining himself to two post-training conferences a week. Like Sonny Liston he appears tongue-tied and inarticulate, perhaps even shy, which does not ingratiate him with the copy-hungry journalists. "He's a mean son-of-a-bitch," says a veteran AP reporter. "I've never had a good talk with him…no one has."

Shortly after his arrival, Foreman locks himself away on the slopes above N'Sele, reportedly behind pillboxes manned by armed guards. Whereas Ali's fame has long since been established in Zaire before his visit, virtually no one has ever heard of Foreman, a state of affairs which apparently does not bother the champion. Ali aggravates George's unpopularity by calling him a Belgian, a nationality unloved in "liberated" Zaire. As Foreman's name sounds suspiciously like "Flemish" in *lingala*, many people believe the champion is a black Belgian. Foreman's $25,000 prize German shepherd also reminds the Zairese of colonial rule.

So overwhelming is the locals' support for Ali that the *feticheurs*, Kinshasa's highly paid witch doctors, are deluged with requests to "fix" Foreman and the fight. Voodoo is not to be taken lightly in Zaire. The city's nightwatchmen light open fires after dark despite the heat and the airport night shift is paid danger money, all because of the fear of *N'dokes* (Zombies…the Living Dead). Rumor has it that Mobutu regularly consults his own personal pygmy *feticheur*. The Commission becomes so concerned for Foreman's safety, not so much because of the spells, explains one official, but who knows just how the *feticheurs* and their clients would react if Foreman accomplishes the expected and levels Ali in the early rounds? A public relations campaign is hastily mounted to sell the champion to the people of Zaire. A fresh billboard appears on the road to N'Sele: "The fight between Ali and Foreman was not a battle between enemies, but a competition between friends."

But it would take more than *N'dokes* to frighten George Foreman. And unpopularity is certainly nothing new. As with so many of boxing's heroes, Foreman was not born with a silver gumshield in his mouth. His early life in Houston's Fifth Ward—one of the oldest ghettos in the South—as the fifth of seven children born to a railroad construction worker, was a harsh mixture of pills, cheap booze, and street fights. "The juvenile people were after me all the time," he remembers. "The cops knew me…you name it, I've done it. One week I broke 200 windows and didn't get caught, but the next week I'm walking down the street with a rock in my hand and the cops picked me up."

At 16, while shooting pool, George saw two of his football idols (Jim Brown and Johnny Unitas) advertising the Job Corps, the government's dropout training program, on television. His mother had recently collapsed while trying to hold down two jobs ("In the Fifth Ward we used to call it 'bad nerves', but really it was a case of total exhaustion"), and so George joined up. In Oregon he learned bricklaying and carpentry. "That was the greatest feeling I ever had. I felt I was somebody." In Pleasanton, California, he

OPPOSITE: Until Zaire, Ali has avoided working with the heavy bag for fear of inflaming his hands again. Some weeks before the fight he begins punching solidly, but compared to Foreman's onslaught on the heavy bag, his blows look almost feeble.

learned electronics assembly and met the Corps' vocational guidance director, Nick "Doc" Broadus. Broadus persuaded George to take up boxing. In his first fight on January 26, 1967, he scored a first-round knockout.

Within a month Foreman had won the Golden Gloves junior heavyweight title; within another month he had the senior title. Broadus set his sights on the Mexico City Olympics, just 18 months away. "Doc kept telling me about the 1968 Olympics and how I'd win the gold medal, but it didn't bother me a bit. But after he told me about Floyd Patterson, Cassius Clay and Joe Frazier, and what the Olympics did for them, my interest quickened."

Mexico City saw the return of political posturing to the Olympic arena. Not since Hitler's pre-war tantrums over Jesse Owens had politics overtly stolen so much of the athletic limelight. As American track stars Tommie Smith and John Carlos were proclaiming Black Power with clenched fists from the victory dais, George Foreman was steeling himself for his title bout with the Russian favorite Lonas Chepulis. The betting was firmly behind Chepulis, a crafty veteran of several hundred bouts, but Foreman pounded him so badly that the fight was stopped in the third round.

Fame, however, came after he had left the ring, as George stood waiting for his medal. America sat wondering if he too would raise his fist for Black Power. In that instant, George dipped his hand into the pocket of his gown and produced a tiny American flag. "I can't believe it," shouted the television commentator. Said George later: "I did it because, first, I am an American, second, because I'm

George Foreman, and third, because I was proud to represent my country. I knew that I was proof the American system could be made to work."

At that time, Ali was losing his battle to continue his ring career. When Smith and Carlos outraged the Olympic officials, Ali commented that they hadn't gone far enough. Foreman's gesture he would remember bitterly.

After the Olympics, Foreman signed with Dick Sadler, Archie Moore's old trainer. Assisted by Moore and his brother, Sadler unleashed the gold medallist on the lesser names of professional heavyweight boxing. By January of 1973, he had won 37 consecutive matches, the last 21 by knockouts, 15 in three rounds or less. That month he destroyed Joe Frazier.

The boxing press had been criticizing Foreman for months before his championship victory. Besides the Sonny Liston aura he had adopted, it complained loudly about the quality of his opponents. After Frazier the grumbling began afresh when he massacred an unknown, Jose "King" Roman, for his first title defense. George was upset by the criticism. "I knocked Roman out in one round. Yeah, they said he was no good," he growled. "Yeah, he was no good because I hit him in the ribs and then I hit him in the head. That's why he was no good." Seven months later he reinforced his claim by knocking out Ken Norton in two.

In Zaire, the boxing press walks in awe of George Foreman. It is not merely the daunting knockout record or the brief performances against Frazier and Norton that impresses the reporters;

RIGHT: Angelo Dundee and "my fighter" at N'Sele.

KINSHASA _ ZAIRE
CHAMPIONNAT DU MONDE DES POIDS LOURDS
MERCREDI 30 OCTOBRE 1974 A 3H. DU MATIN
15 ROUNDS

GEORGE FOREMAN — MUHAMMAD ALI

CE MATCH DU SIECLE EST UN CADEAU DU
CITOYEN·PRESIDENT MOBUTU SESE SEKO
AU PEUPLE ZAÏROIS

OPPOSITE: Rumble, young man, rumble! –- Bundini and Ali in N'Sele.

*…his hands can't hit what his eyes can't see.
Now you see me, now you don't.
George thinks he will, but I know he won't.*

whichever way you look at him, the man is a monster. Although their Tales of the Tape are roughly the same, the champion appears to dwarf his challenger. Stripped to his trunks, he looks capable of stunning a draft horse.

Foreman's training sessions are tense, ominous affairs lightened only by the antics of Dick Sadler, a former vaudeville tap dancer. They open with the champion striding grimly to the ring surrounded by his bodyguards, where he performs a tight, awkward dance to the accompaniment of ethereal music. After ten minutes of calisthenics he is ready to fight. Usually he takes on three sparring partners, two trained to dance Ali-style, the third (ranked heavyweight Henry Clark) to act as a sort of retaliatory punching bag. Clark invariably leaves the ring proclaiming Foreman as the "greatest heavyweight ever". George's training speciality is the heavy bag. With Dick Sadler leaning against the bag to give it added resistance, he literally crushes it in half with shot after shot. As each punch lands, Sadler is jarred back several paces. After a spell on the fast bag, Foreman puts on his robe, collects his dog, and disappears, usually without uttering a word. "I don't like fights," he once remarked. "I just land the right punch and everything is over. Nobody gets hurt and nobody gets killed."

Ali's workouts are, by comparison, like a preliminary bout to the main event. Instead of piped music, his entrance is heralded by a spirited fanfare on conga drums by a California musician named Big Black. With a wave to his applauding audience (who pay two dollars a head to see the show), he begins exercising, flicking drops of sweat in a circle around his feet. Ali also uses the heavy bag, but his punches are feather-light against Foreman's pulverizing blows. (Prior to Zaire, Ali has avoided the heavy bag, fearful of aggravating his painful bursitis.) By the time he moves on to the speed bag he has started a running conversation with himself, insulting Foreman and pillorying the "suckers" of the boxing press for their skepticism. When he climbs through the ropes to dance around the ring by himself, this conversation becomes an endless monologue on the state of his health, his prospects, past career, opponents, and so on. Bundini delivers the responses from the corner.

Ali: Oh man. I'm ready. I been trainin' for six months. I'm in shape.

Bundini: *In shape!*

A: Couldn't do this when I was 22. Think my legs are goin'?

B: *Thirty-two years old and he's still dancin'. Tip on him, champ!*

A: I've started gettin' points here…that jab has cut him…he's bleedin'…see the blood…stand and sting him.

B: *You ain't started floatin' yet. You can't fly, your wings are wet.*

A: Can't do no dancin'! I'm the fastest of all time. I'll be dancin' every round. First eight, stickin', movin', no stoppin', no cornerin', bouncin' off the ropes. Be ready for the first eight…nothin' for certain, nothin' for certain…every round hittin' and movin'. I danced 12 rounds with Joe Frazier.

B: *Twelve!*

A: …twelve rounds with Ken Norton—ain't no way for this man to dance to rounds…he's a flatfooted man…he ain't no dancer!

B: *I'm gettin' drunk here tryin' to follow you. We gonna mug him when we get him drunk. We gonna make a lot of money…make all of you rich, you won't feel bad.*

A: Is this fast enough for a big man? Round ten an' I'm still dancin'.

B: *Round ten! Put the double clutch on him.*

A: What we gonna do, Boo-dini?

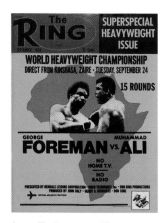

ABOVE: The front cover of *The Ring* magazine before Foreman's cut.

OPPOSITE: The surprisingly confident Ali in full vocal flow during training at N'Sele. "George moves like a slow mummy, and there ain't no mummy gonna whup the great Muhammad Ali. See, you believe all that stuff you see in the movies. Here's a guy running through the jungle, doing the hundred-yard dash, and the mummy is chasing him. Thomp, thomp, thomp. 'Ooh, help! I can't get away from the mummy! Help! Help! The mummy's catching me!' And the mummy always catches him. Well, don't you all believe that stuff. There ain't no mummy gonna catch me."

BELOW: "Ali and Foreman trust Mobutu…so should YOU!" The Great Dictator gets his money's worth out of a cut Foreman (left) and Ali.

Both:
Float like a butterfly, sting like a bee
His hands can't hit what his eyes can't see
Now you see me, now you don't
He thinks he will, but I know he won't
They tell me he's good, but I'm twice as nice
Gonna stick to his butt like white on rice
B: *Rumble, young man, rumble!*

With this combination of ring antics and light-hearted banter, Ali stresses his point each day: on The Night he will be dancing as well as he ever has, dazzling Foreman with his pace until he finishes him off sometime after the eighth. Moving around the ring alone he looks impressively fit, but when he faces sparring partner Roy Williams, the hulking bearded champion of Pennsylvania, his promised strategy falters. Again and again Ali falls back onto the ropes as Williams pounds away at his midriff. The dancing evaporates, save for the occasional shuffle for the benefit of the cameras. The reporters shake their heads, shuddering at the thought of Foreman catching Ali on the ropes as easily as Roy Williams. Ali is unfazed by his mauling; even as Williams is attacking him he reiterates his dancing plan.

Ali slips out of the ring, leads his adoring audience in an *Ali, bomayé* chorus, and leaves with his hands held high over his head. It is an irresistible performance. But of the dozens of experts and past champions polled by the boxing magazines, less than a handful rate him a chance.

O n September 17th exactly a week before the scheduled fight date, Foreman runs into an elbow during training and gashes his right eye. Bill McMurray, the 6ft 5in truck driver whose elbow it is, breaks down in tears. Foreman curses and the fight is postponed until the end of October. Although the cut is not deep and will heal quickly and satisfactorily, the incident is a major upset. For the harassed promoters it is a godsend. Preparations for the fight have bogged down in a mass of Commission red tape and inexperience. If it had gone ahead as planned, the closed-circuit picture might have got out, but few other facilities would have been operating. "Politically for Zaire it would have been a disaster," says John Daly.

For Foreman, the cut is another link in a chain of disasters which started before his arrival in Africa. First his wife Adrienne won a divorce settlement of $235,000—virtually the entire purse he earned for his Tokyo defense. Next, a $5 million suit by a 19-year-old Oakland girl, Pamela Clay, charging sexual assault made headlines before it was quietly dropped. A promoter filed a $100 million suit claiming that Foreman had previously signed with him. In Zaire, Foreman's cook fell ill with a skin rash. On the road from N'Sele to the capital, his fast-moving limousine convoy crashed, injuring a member of his entourage.

Even more worrying is the champion's financial situation. Foreman was reportedly carved into more pieces than a wedding cake: Dick Sadler owns a third of his earnings; Leroy Jackson, George's personal agent, has ten per cent; a Philadelphia syndicate 25 per cent; a Las Vegas organization another 33⅓ per cent; Barbra Streisand's manager Marty Erlichman has cornered half Foreman's ancillary rights for the following decade. It is little wonder that the champion carries a pocket calculator wherever he goes. Before the Norton bout, he admitted to being $200,000 in the red. In Zaire, Foreman's financial problems become acute. In fact, they will come perilously close to cancelling the fight.

With another five weeks in which to brood, Foreman's self-control begins to crack. He has survived the loneliness of his hillside retreat by watching the sunsets and writing a diary "Just some thoughts." But after the cut he becomes even more bad-tempered than usual. Finally he uproots his camp, to the chagrin of his hosts, and moves downtown to the Hotel Continental, Kinshasa's only four-star hotel. It is a mistake.

Apart from a daily stroll around the hotel pool—accompanied by his guards, his dog and his court jester Elmo Henderson (an occasional sparring partner who monotonously tries to whip up support for the champion by shouting through a megaphone, "Oyez, George Foreman, this is your lucky day")—there is even less diversion in Kinshasa than at N'Sele. Surrounded by four hotel walls, Foreman is rumored to be going stir crazy.

Even for Ali, the prospect of another five weeks at N'Sele is not a pleasant thought. When Foreman was cut, Bundini rushed back to tell Ali the news. "I've done it, I've done it," he shouted happily. "I've put the curse on Foreman." "You've *what*?" snapped Ali. "You mean we've got to stay here another *month*?" Bundini's face fell. "It wasn't me," he pleaded, "honest."

But unlike his 24-year-old opponent, Ali has long since mastered the tensions of a title fight. Even on such unlikely ground as Zaire, he tries to follow as closely as possible the pattern of his Fighter's Heaven lifestyle. Ali thrives on people. He is without doubt the most accessible of superstars, and the living room of his N'Sele bungalow is a permanent crossroads for the most diverse visitors—journalists, fans, Muslims, and officials.

Ali conducts his court slumped in a plush green velvet chair facing a gilt-framed portrait of Mobutu. Away from the cameras he is curiously quiet, still frankly voicing his thoughts as soon as they enter his head, but in a soft, restrained voice. As the famous faces who are almost permanent fixtures at Ali fights—the Mailers, Schulbergs, and Plimptons—call by, he takes pains to draw them into the conversation, testing out

his ideas on them. Surprisingly, he listens as seriously as he talks. When a British expedition leader who spent several months charting the Zaire River drops in to shake his hand, Ali deliberately spins out the conversation. Prodding and prompting like a professional interviewer, Ali has the staid British man recounting such information as how elephants, when sated on a particular jungle fruit, passed so much wind that they forced the crew below decks to escape the stench.

Boxing, he says, bores him. He often talks about retirement, of getting out while he still has a pretty face and an unscrambled brain. Foreman is to be his swan song, he says. Away from the gymnasium Ali fends off questions about his fitness and ring abilities. "I'm not like other boxers like Joe Frazier," he says, reeling from side to side in a parody of a fighter who has taken one too many punches.

Angelo Dundee believes that Ali's life is a series of struggles towards new goals, which he is continually setting for himself. The cherry-pink Cadillac was the first goal, followed by the championship, the grand mansions, the $110,000 bus, Fighter's Heaven, and so on. In Zaire, his goal does not appear to be Foreman's championship belt. What does preoccupy him is his future after he has regained the title. Zaire, with its expertise in Western technology, has opened his eyes, he says, and he feels it is his duty to take the message back to "his people" in the American ghettos. But more than that, he dreams of becoming a great leader of his people, a sort of black Kissinger, roving around the world telling other nations about black America. The government would be foolish, he says seriously, not to appoint him ambassador to the Third World.

When he mentions Foreman, whom he has nicknamed The Mummy after a slow-moving character in the horror movies he watches nearly every night, it is merely as an extra in the Holy War Ali has firmly in his mind. He first made this crusade plain at the 49th Annual Boxing Writers' Dinner in New York's crusty Waldorf-Astoria Hotel long before his arrival in Zaire. Ali, as guest speaker, directed his barbs at the also-present Foreman. Finally Foreman had had enough and stood up to leave, saying, "I don't know how you people can stand this." Ali made a grab at Foreman's newly awarded plaque. George retaliated by tearing Ali's jacket, and suddenly the 49th Annual

Boxing Writers' Dinner was a ringside event. "I'm gonna beat your Christian ass, you white flag-waving bitch you!" screamed Ali, hurling glasses erratically at "that nigger". Later, when he had cooled down, he amplified his thoughts: "I'm fightin' to represent Elijah Muhammad. It's a divine fight... Armageddon on a miniature scale. This Foreman, he represents Christianity, America, the flag. I can't let him win. He represents pork chops."

And the Holy War is just the start. "You don't know how serious I am," says Ali softly, hunched down in green velvet. "This fight ain't nothing... All this is just for my new job. What I say after this people will believe. There's another power in this."

Ali speaks with such quiet conviction that it is a struggle not to believe him. But the journalists in the room are not really listening to his words, they're sadly hoping that they won't have to spend too much time with Ali after George Foreman's left hook shatters his dream.

I t is 2am on October 30, 1974. Muhammad Ali stands in the darkness on the grass below his bungalow facing the Zaire. He stretches, removing the kinks in his body left from his catnap. It is the morning of the fight. In less than an hour he will be facing a predicted billion viewers. By now George Foreman is also awake in his hotel room 50 kilometers away.

Ali comes alive in the black Citroen on the journey to the stadium. Bob Goodman: "We'll have to do an interview or a press conference, say, and we'll sit around the hotel room watching TV until the time. We get in the elevator and you can see his face change as he's watching the numbers. At three his eyes open. At one he's lit up like a Christmas tree. You can see it." When he reaches his stark white dressing room in the new concrete bowels of the Stade Du 20 Mai, Ali is glowing. "What's wrong around here?" he demands, surveying the tense expressions in mock horror. "Everybody scared? This ain't nothing but another day in the dramatic life of Muhammad Ali." As he strips he sneaks backward glances at himself in a mirror, his singsong voice reminding himself and those around him of what he has been through in the past and what he has accomplished.

Through a maze of riot-proof concrete tunnels, in another bleak vault, George Foreman is lying on a bench swathed in towels. Only his eyes show. The tension in the room is electric.

These last few days immediately prior to the fight have weighed heavily on Foreman. His financial worries reached a head and, through Leroy Jackson, he demanded an extra half million dollars from John Daly. Daly held off the crisis by sending Jackson on a wild goose chase to London. When he returned empty-handed, Foreman exploded. Daly was summoned to the champion's hotel room. "George, you know, is menacing enough when he is in the ring, but golly he was menacing out of the ring that evening," recalls Daly. "He just said to me, 'You know you have tricked me. You have made me look a fool. I am telling the government you tricked me, and I am not going through with the fight.' I said, 'Well, George, I can't tell you what to do. I can only say that I haven't tricked you and your problem is your problem and it is just too late for me to do anything.' After about ten minutes sitting there with his dog growling I was allowed to leave." Three hours later Daly was again summoned to negotiate with Foreman and the Commission officials. "I was getting an awful feeling, you know, that the white man was about to be sacrificed and it got very awkward."

Daly managed to defuse the situation by asking if the government officials would perhaps like to pay the extra half million, an offer they hastily refused. Foreman eventually backed down.

(After the fight, Foreman reiterated his demand, and it transpired that he had been promised the additional payment if the fight grossed $18 million. In fact it barely grossed $10 million. As with Ali's first Liston bout, the public was unwilling to pay high closed-circuit ticket prices to watch what they considered would certainly be a lopsided Foreman victory. Nevertheless, Commission officials had Daly pulled off his homeward flight and his passport confiscated until the matter had been settled. "With hindsight," said Daly, "I would put on something like Ali vs. Foreman again. But with hindsight I would never have gone into business with certain people, and I don't think I would have ever stayed in Zaire.")

Back through the tunnels in Ali's dressing room, Bundini is sulking. All along he has expected Ali to wear a robe he—Bundini—has designed, a white silk garment with a map of Zaire stitched over the heart which matches Bundini's own jacket. Ali has rejected the robe in favour of an African-style gown made in London. Bundini refuses to look at the offending garment. Ali is piqued and slaps Bundini hard on the cheek. Later he attempts to soothe his disappointed cornerman. "Ain't we gonna dance, Bundini?" he wheedles. "You know I can't dance without you." Bundini wavers. "Are we gonna dance?" says Ali. Bundini cracks. "All…night…long!" he smiles.

George Foreman unwinds his towels and stands in the middle of the dressing room, holding hands with his cornermen—Dick Sadler, Sandy Saddler, and Archie Moore—to perform a ritual they have been practising ever since George won his title in Jamaica. What they do is pray for success, only this time Archie Moore is praying for something else. Later he tells George Plimpton: "I was praying, and in great sincerity, that George wouldn't kill Ali. I really felt that was a possibility."

Ali is ready. "Now," he says, shouting the war cry which mortified his progress-conscious hosts and which Kinshasa's hotel keepers blame for the total lack of foreign fight fans, "Let's rumble in the jungle."

Ali has discarded his robe and is jogging around the fringes of the ring, sparring at the air under the glare of the overhead television arc lamps. Already the sweat is beaded on his forehead. Bundini stands in the centre of the canvas talking non-stop, his eyes never wavering from his master's face. Ali half-shuffles and the 60,000 Ali supporters in the stands roar their allegiance.

The minutes tick by and still there is no sign of Foreman. Ali shoots dark glances across to the empty tunnel-mouth. At ringside, John Daly is also sweating, praying that at this moment George Foreman is not demanding that unless Leroy Jackson's briefcase is filled with half a million dollars, he's not fighting.

Ali stops jogging. He leans across the top rope and pumps his arm in the air, mouthing the familiar chant Ali, bomayé. Suddenly he looks up at the official stand and in that instant the crowd's chant dissolves into a roar. Flanked by flags and cornermen, and wearing a long red gown with "Heavyweight Champion of the World" emblazoned on the back, George Foreman strides into the arena. As Foreman clambers through the ropes, the two contestants' eyes meet and lock, until Ali dances off.

During the Star Spangled Banner, Ali trembles like a leaf, shuddering in his shoes under Foreman's cold glare. Suddenly he jerks to attention and laughs. "Shit," he mouths across at George, dismissing him with

a casual flip of his bright red glove. "Sheeeet." Foreman flexes his jaw muscles. At the end of Zaire's national anthem the crowd begins to chant Al-lee bomayé. Below Ali's corner is a lone Foreman fan, Elmo Henderson, shouting through his megaphone, "Muhammad Ali, you'll flee in three." Dundee whirls around and screams, "Get that bastard outta here!"

Ali glides across the ring to where Dick Sadler is lacing the champion's gloves. Foreman shoots the intruder a grim Liston glare as Ali begins his verbal cold-warfare. The one-sided tirade continues as referee Zack Clayton repeats the rules at center-ring. Finally Foreman hisses, as Joe Frazier hissed in Madison Square Garden back in 1971, "I'm gonna kill you!"

The reporters at ringside are certain of the blueprint about to unfold: Foreman will stalk Ali, trying his hardest to catch him on the ropes to deliver the coup de grace; Ali will move and jab—"stick 'n' dance"—desperately avoiding the blind alleys to stay one crucial step ahead.

For the first few seconds of the fight the expected floorplan holds true. At the bell, Foreman strides out purposefully and Ali dances up to him, landing two neat, hard jabs to the face. Then everything falls apart. Of his own accord, Ali moves to the ropes, inviting Foreman to move in for the kill. The champion's corner cannot believe its luck. The whole Sadler-Moore-Saddler strategy has been tailored towards cutting the ring on Ali and bullying him to a corner or the ropes. Now, with less than 30 seconds of the fight gone, he is right where they want him. Foreman does not hesitate. He moves in swinging his long, loaded left-hooks. Between blows, Ali reaches out and grabs Foreman's neck, forcing him down into a clinch. But as Zack Clayton pries them apart, Ali makes no effort to move from the ropes. Rahaman is on his feet two rows away imploring his brother to box. "One-two, Ali," he shouts. "One-two." Bundini begins an unbroken wail.

Foreman directs his fire at Ali's head, but his punches are so pregnant that Ali sees them before they start and calmly twists out of danger. If Foreman catches him he won't survive. But Foreman doesn't. Frustrated, he concentrates on the body, smashing Ali's arms and ribcage. The crunch carries out of the ring over the crowd.

Seconds before the bell, as the champion steps back to gather himself for a renewed assault, Ali darts out and hits him with a copy-book combination of lefts and rights. Ali's face is a madman's mask, complete with slack jaw and bulging eyes, as he catches Foreman bang on the nose. Immediately the champion's eyes redden and begin to puff.

At the sound of the bell, Dundee tumbles into the ring demanding that Ali box, that he keep clear of the ropes, that he dance! "I know what I'm doing," says Ali coolly, walking away from the corner to pump his arm at the chanting crowd.

The second round is a brutal replay of the first. Foreman backs his challenger into a neutral corner, pushing with his gloves until he has lined Ali up to his satisfaction. A long, looping haymaker catches Ali in the throat and the sweat flies off his head to form a halo in the glare. Ali returns with a left and right to Foreman's bruised face before clinching. Foreman shakes him off, backs away, and then plows in again. Another clinch. Ali's eyes have that crazed look, and as he pulls Foreman's head down he shouts in his ear. "C'mon, champ, you can do better than that. They told me you were a big hitter."

Foreman pushes his opponent back onto the ropes and catches him on the jaw. Pain flashes across Ali's face and Foreman hurls everything he can muster into a series of bone-crushing body-punches. "*Ali, c'est fini*," moans a Zairese reporter. The crowd chants, urging him on, and Ali manages to snake a left into Foreman's face. Foreman shrugs it off like an ox flicking away a tick. Each time Ali aims a punch he scores directly on the button. But beside Foreman's raw blows, he looks as if he is juggling eggshells. Ali lashes out towards the end of the round, shouting at the champion as he lands a hard left. Foreman swings wildly and Ali shakes his head, telling the crowd he is home safe, at least for the moment.

From his stool, Ali shouts defiantly across the ring at the Foreman camp. Angelo begs him to hush while he massages his stomach and chest and Ali sits still, clicking his tongue against the roof of his mouth. Then he leans through the ropes and demands of the reporters who have predicted his downfall, "You think he's hurtin' me? Hey?" Later he admits, "I can't lie, he shook me twice. Once I took a right hand and I could feel my toes shaking. I was out on my feet but you couldn't tell." Almost certainly he was remembering the second round.

Round three sees the turning point in a fight which the champion has dominated. The pattern remains the same: Ali against the ropes courting Foreman's hammer, retaliating at intervals with jabs and clinches; Foreman trying his utmost to finish the fight with one punch. But as each second of the round passes it becomes more and more apparent that Foreman is tiring, winding down like a mechanical music box. His arms refuse to respond the instant his brain commands. He leans into each punch, top-

pling forward in the clinches. For long periods all he attempts are body shots. By the end of the round he must know he will never knock Ali down.

As George squanders his energy, Ali's strategy becomes clear. The journalists at ringside slowly realize they will not see Ali dance; that in fact he has never intended to dance from the start. The Ali-Bundini "*dance all night*" duet is a calculated fraud, a hoax fed to the press to fill the minds of Foreman and his cornermen with the vision of Cassius Clay. "The newspapers couldn't have helped me more than if I'd paid them," he later confessed. Ali performed his fraud with such guile that the critics ignored a host of clues indicating his true intentions. Ali had been training for this moment since 1970 when he returned to Angelo Dundee's Miami gym after 3½ years in exile. Trainer Ollie Wilson, who had spent a lifetime studying boxers, told *Sports Illustrated* at the time: "He's like nobody else I've ever seen. He does what he wants in the ring. He trains the way he wants. He'll lay over the ropes day after day and allow the sparring partners to beat him to the body, and as a result he takes the best body shot I've ever seen. You got to say the big man knows what he's doin'."

José Torres saw Ali's strategy before the Frazier fight, but dismissed it as a habit Ali had picked up in exile. Budd Schulberg noticed it too: "Sometimes he would dance as he hoped to against Frazier, and sometimes, to the puzzlement of writers passing through, he would lie back on the ropes and let strong, squat spar mates pummel him in the body. He had already proved he could take hard shots to the body from Liston and Quarry, Chuvalo and Bonavena. If he had practiced sliding off those ropes and getting back to the center of

OPPOSITE: By the fifth, Foreman, his face puffed by Ali's lightning jabs, is himself on the defensive.

the ring where he had dancing and punching room, these workouts would have made more sense… 'I'll be dancin', movin', jabbin', punchin' Joe and he won't be able to find me', Ali had been telling us. Yet against a heavy muscled brawler from Jamaica he frequently stood flat-footed and let the hired hand flail away.' Schulberg could have been writing about Zaire.

The two corners at the end of round three tell the story. As soon as he sat down, Ali was up again, stumping along the ropes to berate ex-footballer turned film star Jim Brown, who is commentating the fight from the first row. Brown, a friend of Ali's, has offended the challenger by predicting a Foreman victory. Across the ring George Foreman slumps on his stool as Sadler and Moore patch his face and rub his weary body. The worry shows on their faces; they know that in none of George's past eight fights has he been forced to box more than two rounds.

Round four. Foreman moves out and Ali retreats to the ropes. "Box him, Ali. Box him!" shouts Rahaman, and Ali remains a foot off the ropes keeping the champion at bay with his left jab. Foreman is standing full face to us not a dozen feet away, and as each blow connects we see his eyes shut and his head snap back, showering the canvas with drops of sweat. Ali's punches have nothing like the power of Foreman's own, but their speed and frequency upset and disorient the champion. Finally he lunges forward, hurling a devastating but wide haymaker. The momentum carries him forward against Ali and into another clinch.

Apart from Ali's perfect jab, it is not a clean fight in the classic sense. Often it is little more than a wrestling match on the ropes. Angelo Dundee has predicted this. While studying Foreman's past fights, he noticed the champion's habit of placing his left glove on his—usually smaller—opponent's shoulder to position him for a knockout. A big man like Ali, thought Dundee, would have no difficulty in countering this habit. The fight proved him right. When the two fighters close, Ali invariably loops his arm behind George's head, pulling him down and smothering any chance of in-fighting.

Foreman presses on, swinging and missing, catching his breath and swinging again. "Come out…don't lie on the ropes," directs Rahaman, but Ali doesn't hear. Leaning out over the top rope like a crew-member in the jib harness of a racing yacht, he sways out of reach of George's gloves, riding the blows until their power has dissipated. The only time he stands upright is when he flicks a jab into Foreman's face. "Good round, good round," applauds Angelo as the bell sounds.

The fifth marks the beginning of George Foreman's long drop to the canvas. Once again Ali moves to the ropes, but this time he presents an open target for his opponent. Barely moving, gloves covering only his face, he invites Foreman to do his worst. For a moment Foreman appears to be actually damaging Ali, then Bundini lets out a hoot of laughter as Ali peeks through his gloves and spurs the champion on. "Punch, sucker," he taunts. "Punch, you pussy." The harder Foreman flails the more Ali shouts. "Punch… punch!" He ends the torment by opening his gloves and spitting, "Now it's my turn," words which must have sounded devastating to his almost-spent opponent. At once he is off the ropes, smothering Foreman's face with leather. The crowd, which until now has been unsure of Ali's ability to withstand the battering, becomes

frenzied. Rahaman turns to the stands grinning broadly. "Two more rounds," he shouts, waving a V sign. "He didn't hurt me," Ali is telling Dundee in the corner. "Believe me, he didn't hurt me."

Round six. Foreman catapults from his corner in desperation. Ali, seeing his approach, also rushes forward. The two bodies smack resoundingly at center-ring. Ali remains on the ropes for the rest of the three minutes, Foreman still attempts to land the final right, but it is obvious his power has short-circuited. After each punch he literally falls into Ali's arms. "Fight now," goads the challenger. The crowd senses that the end is approaching. Herbert Muhammad, seated directly behind us, is displeased with Ali's taunts. Between rounds he sends his runner to warn Ali against playing. Dundee spots the man as he is climbing the stairs. "Get the hell out here," he snaps. Ali hears the disturbance and pokes his head over the ropes. "It's okay," he shouts to Herbert, thinking his manager is concerned for his safety. "No way is he hurting me." Then he walks to the center of the ring to orchestrate his supporters.

The seventh is a carbon copy of the sixth, with the addition of Ali's now-relentless jabbing. Foreman gives perhaps one good blow for every half dozen he receives. He is reduced to throwing the whole bulk of his body at his opponent. At one point Ali grabs him around the neck and almost throws him through the top two ropes. Shortly before the bell, Ali places his glove against his own jaw and invites the champion to, "Hit me… C'mon, hit me."

Early in round eight, Foreman is on his knees tangled in the ropes. He had swung at Ali, missed and staggered forward in exhaustion… He regains his feet and swings again. Suddenly, Ali is off the ropes and smashing the champion's unguarded face with two straight rights and a left hook. Foreman recoils stunned, and Ali catches him with a chopping right to the side of the head. Foreman jack-knifes at the waist and begins to topple. He falls so slowly that Ali has ample time to hit him on the way down. He resists the temptation. There is no need.

Archie Moore moves along the ring apron to attract Foreman's attention, trying to tell him to roll over onto his stomach and push himself up with his knee. Foreman almost makes it. At the count of nine he is nearly standing. Then Archie winces as Zack Clayton waves his arms over the former champion's head. Dundee, Bundini, Youngblood, and Kilroy dive through the ropes as one to reach their man, who is standing with his gloves raised over his head. "You fooled us," sobs Dick Sadler, before the ring is engulfed by a surge of fans, officials, and baton-wielding police. Ali fights his way through the crush to the ropes. For the first time tonight he looks scared.

The hysteria continues outside Ali's dressing room as fans battle police around horrified pressmen. Inside, the room is an oven. Ali emerges from an antechamber, takes one look at the crush and disappears. Angelo Dundee squats on the floor in a corner telling reporters he was surprised the fight ended as soon as it did. He had expected it to last at least another round. Ali reappears and moves to a chair hurriedly placed on a trestle table at one end of the room. There he sits, silently looking down at the cameras until the chaos dies to a din. At last he speaks.

"You didn't see me tonight," he says in the same tone of voice Moses must have used when he delivered the Ten Commandments. "Tonight you saw the power of my God, Allah. Allah was in the ring tonight."

OPPOSITE: It's all over in the eighth. Ali catches Foreman with a right, and the champion jack-knifes and executes a perfect swan dive to the canvas. He struggles slowly to his feet to beat the count. He does not make it.

The reporters are unimpressed by this religious sidetrack. They are after the facts, Tale of the Tape talk. Ali leaves their questions hanging. When he resumes there is the hint of a smile on his lips. "You know it wasn't me…because I have no punch, remember? I told you what I was going to do before I did it! I told you this man don't have no class! I told you this man don't have no skill! I told you this man don't have no punch! I told you this would be a TOTAL MISMATCH!"

By now Ali is shouting. But although the words he uses are virtually the same, he is a different man from the newly crowned champion who leaned out of a Miami ring more than a decade ago and told the press to "Eat your words". This time he laughs as he talks; this time the writers laugh with him. His closing words are a token of this hard-earned respectability. Holding up a sponsor's packet with his picture on the front, he urges all the viewers to hurry on down to their corner drug store and purchase some "Saint John's 100 percent natural ice cream."

The ride back to N'Sele is like a scene from the liberation of Paris. As the Ali convoy passes, hundreds of cheering people spill out of their houses and line the roadside waving frantically. In the bus behind Ali's Citroen, Dr. Ferdie Pacheco shakes his head over the man he has been following since before Sonny Liston. "Ali didn't even tell his inner circle about this strategy of laying on the ropes," he muses. "It was a complete surprise even to Herbert Muhammad. He's been saying this stuff about dancing and boxing for six months and then he goes and does something people would

have shouted him down for…lying on the ropes! He does it and suddenly it's right for Ali and wrong for Foreman. Everything he does is like that. He said he was going to build the camp in the hills and everybody told him no. But he did it and it's great. They told him not to avoid the draft and it turned out to be the best thing he ever did."

Outside, the night skies open and the rain pours down in sheets. Within minutes the whole of the Stade Du 20 Mai is knee deep in water. An hour earlier and it would have wiped out the fight. "Allah knows what he's doing," says Rahaman.

Dr. Pacheco looks out the bus window at the people dancing in the rain. "They just lucked out here in Zaire," he says. "They just happened to score the greatest fight of the last 20 years."

Back in his bungalow, Ali disappears into the bedroom. The rest of the house appears to be filled with Muslims toasting the world with Coca-Cola. Rahaman is rolling around on the carpet, demonstrating how Foreman fell. "That's some brother I've got, y'know," he tells the room. "You all witnessed history."

Next door in Angelo Dundee's villa, the non-Muslims are celebrating with something a little stronger than Coke. Only Bundini is absent. Two days later we see him burst into Ali's living room with great tears rolling down his cheeks, sobbing that no one will honor the $10,000 in bets he claims to have won on the fight.

Gene Kilroy: "You know what the turning point was? It was at that fuckin' press conference in New York when Foreman ripped Ali's coat and Ali ripped his shirt and started throwing glasses. It was then that Foreman realized he couldn't buffalo this guy. And

RIGHT: Pandemonium in the ring. For the first time that night, Ali looks scared.

ABOVE: *Ali, bomayé*—a bare-chested Ali with "his" people, whose support undoubtedly makes a difference on the night. "All them people shouting A*li, bomayé*, it takes something out of you, makes you mad. He's the champ and they're screaming *Ali, bomayé*."

OPPOSITE: Foreman watches in disbelief as referee Jack Clayton waves him out, and the new Heavyweight Champion of the World raises his hands in victory. Foreman: "After the fight, for a while I was bitter. I had all sorts of excuses. The ropes were loose. The referee counted too fast. The cut hurt my training. I was drugged. And then, finally, I realized I'd lost to a great champion; probably the greatest of all time."

Ali wasn't even serious! A little old lady grabbed Ali by the arm and handed him a candlestick and said, 'Here, hit him with this.' Ali just laughed and said, 'No, I'm only playing.' "

Angelo Dundee: "It was that last workout of Foreman's that made me very happy. I watched the guy closely and when he was hitting that big bag, hitting it with all he had, his head stayed still. The guy don't move! He just asks to be hit!" And was Dick Sadler correct? Was it all just a trick? "Aw, there was no trick. It was all very simple…it was just Muhammad doing his thing."

At 8am, after three hours sleep, Ali wanders out into the morning sunshine swinging his walking stick Mobutu-style. The only clue to his nocturnal activity is a bloodshot right eye – as if a few moments before he has rubbed away a small flying insect – and a slightly puffed jaw-line. He is greeted by a dozen or so of his N'Sele staff and a handful of reporters.

Ali chats for maybe an hour on his lawn beside the river, his soft voice covering a host of topics ranging from the number of people who die after an Ali fight to the physical benefits of a teaspoon of potassium. He appears totally unbothered by his victory. It was always a foregone conclusion, he says. He had done nothing more than follow his destiny. The matador will always triumph over the bull; a dog's jawbones "don't mean nothin'" if the squirrel is up a tree.

"You know you destroyed this man," he tells the reporters. "The press destroyed Foreman. He's a humble, normal fellow, George Foreman. He would come to my camp when I was champ and lay on the ground and say I am the greatest. But it wasn't the same man walking through the lobby of the Intercontinental Hotel with his dog and his bodyguards. He was proud, wouldn't talk to the press. I'm glad he's gone. He couldn't draw flies now."

Ali pauses to hear a tape-recording of Foreman's comments in the dressing room after the fight. George sounds dazed and lost. He can't remember the last seconds of the fight, but he knows he wasn't tired and was in full control until, to his surprise, his cornermen were there beside him in the ring. Ali is moved to pay his opponent

some dues. "I know I make a man look bad, but he's strong. He met the world's greatest and fastest heavyweight and you just don't knock out the world's greatest Heavyweight Champion in the first round."

Much of his victory he attributes to his training and diet. He swallowed salt tablets—ten a day—had his own cooks, took potassium, ate lots of sugar. "At eight o'clock, my last meal before the fight, I ate a big bowl of peach cobbler. I was taking sugar water during the fight. He (Foreman) sweat too much and didn't put it back. He dried himself out. He was overstrained and overworked."

His attitude during the delay was crucial. While Foreman was so bored he had to move to a hotel, Ali kept himself occupied. "Days have gone by where I had to find something to do…the laundry… something…a schedule. I walked six miles the day of the fight. I walked to the Chinese House three times. By 3pm I had so much energy I didn't know what to do with it." The crowd also helped tilt the balance. "All them people shouting *Ali, bomayé*, it takes something out of you, makes you mad. He's the champ and they're screaming *Ali, bomayé*."

And the trick? "The trick was no dancin'. I was a little winded after the first round and I thought 'I can't dance for 15 rounds at this pace. If I dance from the beginning after nine or ten he starts taking over. When I saw him in Caracas I knew I had my title back…all those big, wild swings!"

As the morning wears on and the fact that he has the title back grows on him, retirement slips further and further from Ali's mind. He still wanted to retire and become a Minister for Allah, "converting our prostitutes, helping the poor people…I can talk about them because I am so much bigger now." Also, he is carrying "the burden of the world", he says. "In some countries—these Muslim countries like Egypt—the women weep if I lose…nations go into mourning…Egypt…some of them scratch their faces…Benghazi…these people really grieve. It's too much burden."

But in the same breath his mind is captured by the sheer enormity of this adoration. "The US which is predominantly white… they are all for me…the hippies, the young people…England…Switzerland Ireland…Morocco…Venezuela…they are all Muhammad Ali countries. I can go to any country in the world and they know me. I am the most well-known person on earth!" And as he smiles happily at the thought of a Muhammad Ali world, both he and his small audience know that it will be a long time before he exchanges his title and fame for social work in the service of Allah. "Don't I look like I've got a few more years left?" he grins.

Ali moves off to stroll around his grounds. We are alone with him. As he rounds the corner of the bungalow he spots a big yellow and red lizard sunning itself on a bare patch of earth. Ali gives chase with his cane, herding the reptile along the side of the house and back again. "You gotta tire it," he shouts over his shoulder, "just like I did George." The lizard dives into a shallow hole and tries frantically to bury itself. "You can't hide, lizard," laughs Ali. Bending down he deftly plucks off its tail, which wriggles between his fingers. With the heel of his old black boot he savagely crushes the creature into the earth. On his face is that same wild, wide-eyed, open-mouthed expression George Foreman had seen the previous night. For the first time that morning he is the Heavyweight Champion of the World. Then he turns and grins, and once again he is Muhammad Ali.

The Harder They Come...

"Nobody ever told Muhammad what to do."

Angelo Dundee

Probably the most mythic moment in world sports," wrote Robert Lypsyte in the *New York Times*. Certainly the fight in Zaire was Ali's finest hour and in boxing terms it was a victory of historic proportions, a David and Goliath triumph which was hailed by even his bitterest foes in the boxing world. *The Ring* magazine, which only a few short years before had withheld its top award to Ali on the grounds that "Cassius Clay is most emphatically not to be held up as an example to the youngsters of the United States", now named him "Fighter of the Year," one of many such awards both nationally and internationally. Even his hometown of Louisville—where Ali had encountered his share of racism—named a street after him; Walnut Street in downtown Louisville became Muhammad Ali Boulevard. By now it was indisputable; the decade that began with Sonny Liston and ended in Zaire with George Foreman was a golden era for heavyweight boxing, and Muhammad Ali was its King Midas.

But boxing was only a part of it. The extraordinary wave of good will which greeted Ali post-Zaire was not just for his athletic prowess, but for Ali the man. It was as if all the rancor and resentments of the past—the draft dodging, the race hatred—had simply evaporated overnight. Ali was a hero, not just to blacks and the Muslim nations of the world at large, but to many in the constituency that had constantly reviled him—white Middle America. As a columnist from the *New York Post* put it: "It is time to recognize Ali for what he is; the greatest athlete of his time and maybe all time and one of the most important and brave men of all American time. The time has come to end the bitterness and forget the past."

In a symbolic gesture by the White House, Ali was invited to meet Nixon's successor, Gerald Ford. On December 10, 1974, Ali was making small talk with the President of the United States, an event absolutely unthinkable a decade before when Georgia Senator Richard Russell had sworn that "Cassius Clay will never be invited to the White House to see the President of the United States." It was official: Muhammad Ali was now an All American Hero.

And he revelled in it. "Now that I got my championship back," he told the *New Yorker*, "every day is something special. I wake up in the morning and no matter what the weather is like, every day is a sunny day." But for Ali, this universal acceptance, while welcome, must have seemed somewhat bizarre. After all, it was not Ali who had changed position; he was still an ardent follower of a religion which loudly proclaimed separatism and which routinely dismissed the white race as blue-eyed devils. The change had all been one way.

And then came an event which did change Ali's position, and profoundly. On February 25, 1975, the spiritual leader of the Nation of Islam, Elijah Muhammad, died. His son, Wallace Muhammad, was elected leader in his place. The move signalled a new direction for the movement, which would in time split it in two. Wallace had long considered his father's beliefs to be out of step with the teachings of "true Islam," especially his attitude towards race. Wallace adopted a far more liberal outlook on the Nation's old enemy, the white man, instructing that color didn't matter as much as an individual's character. While some followers, under the leadership of Louis Farrakhan, rejected Wallace's new direction, Ali, together with his manager Herbert Muhammad, embraced it. In private, Ali had long been uncomfortable with the "white devil" proclamations. In doing so he removed many of the contradictions between his beliefs and his actions. Now at the moment that the establishment was embracing him, he was able to respond with far less ambivalence.

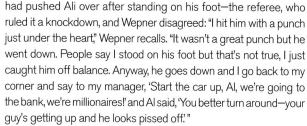

FOLLOWING PAGES: Ali lands a stunning right to the chin of Ron Lyle in the ninth. Two rounds later, Ali wins a TKO.

OPPOSITE: Ali and brother Rahaman (left) meet the US President Gerald Ford at the White House.

BELOW: Chuck Wepner hangs on against all the odds until the 15th. Wepner: "Sylvester Stallone was watching the fight in a movie house in Philadelphia and it gave him the inspiration for Rocky. Stallone said, the night before the fight in Rocky, 'Even if I don't win this fight, I just want to prove that I belong in there.' That was one of my lines, and that was what it was all about."

Later, in October 1976, Wallace would announce that his organization was no longer the Nation of Islam, but the World Community of Islam in the West. He also denounced his father's claim to divine messenger status, bringing the organization closer to more orthodox Muslim beliefs. Louis Farrakhan and Ali's old mentor Jeremiah Shabbazz left the Nation at this point to set up their own Nation of Islam, which still to this day adheres to Elijah Muhammad's belief in black nationalism.

"I don't hate whites," Ali told the *New York Times*. "That was history, but it's coming to an end. We're in a new phase, a resurrection. Elijah taught us to be independent, to clean ourselves up, to be proud and healthy. He stressed the bad things the white man did to us so we could get free and strong. Now his son Wallace is showing us there are good and bad regardless of color, that the devil is in the mind and heart, not the skin."

A month after the death of Elijah Muhammad, Ali stepped into the ring for the first defense of the crown he had regained in Zaire. Billed as "Give the White Guy a Break," Ali was matched against a 35-year-old liquor salesman from Bayonne, New Jersey, Chuck Wepner. Wepner's nickname was the "Bayonne Bleeder"; in his 30-win, 9-loss career he'd suffered more than 300 stitches to his face alone. While the match was not far short of Joe Louis' Bum of the Month Club, it proved a massive payday for Ali; desperate to wrestle a hold on the heavyweight division, and on Ali in particular, Don King guaranteed Ali $1.6 million. Given Wepner's huge underdog status, the bout was a financial disaster for King. It did, however, help him establish a stranglehold on the sport.

The bout, held in King's hometown of Cleveland, was certainly not worth King's money. "Before the fight I was edgy," Wepner recalls. "I wasn't worried about getting hurt, I was tough. But everybody thought it was a mismatch and I didn't want to let myself down. I said to my manager (Al Braverman), 'Ali is the king of boxin'.' 'Yeah, yeah, Chuck,' he said, 'but in the ring you're the king of dirty fighting. You're both royalty'."

With his vast arsenal of fouls and dirty tricks and no small amount of courage and stamina, Wepner was no pushover, even putting Ali on the canvas for only the fourth time in his career. Although photographs later appeared to confirm what many at ringside thought—that Wepner

had pushed Ali over after standing on his foot—the referee, who ruled it a knockdown, and Wepner disagreed: "I hit him with a punch just under the heart," Wepner recalls. "It wasn't a great punch but he went down. People say I stood on his foot but that's not true, I just caught him off balance. Anyway, he goes down and I go back to my corner and say to my manager, 'Start the car up, Al, we're going to the bank, we're millionaires!' and Al said, 'You better turn around—your guy's getting up and he looks pissed off.' "

Embarrassed by the flash knockdown, Ali punished Wepner for the rest of the fight. Seconds before the final bell, he caught the exhausted Wepner with a sickening cluster of punches and he slid into the ropes to be counted out for the first time in his career. Later, Ali said that Wepner "was dirty and fought like a woman". However, Wepner's effort was enough to inspire a young Sylvester Stallone to base his character Rocky on Wepner, and Rocky's opponent, the loquacious fictional champ Apollo Creed, on Ali.

Ali had weighed 223½ pounds for the fight, his heaviest ever. Asked later why he didn't train hard for the fight Ali replied, "An old man was once asked by a young man, 'How is it that you look so good and stay in such fine condition at your advanced age?' The old man replied, 'It is the preserved energy of youth which is now maintaining my life.' That is why my boxing career spanned twenty years. I didn't burn myself out training for guys like Al Lewis, Jurgin Blin, and Chuck Wepner."

Ali could have added the names of his next two opponents to the list. In stopping a game but limited Ron Lyle in 11 rounds, Ali was rarely stretched, while in Kuala Lumpur Ali sleepwalked to victory over Britain's gun-shy Joe Bugner. Bugner's non-performance prompted the *Observer*'s Hugh McIlvanney to write: "Bugner is built like a Greek statue but, unfortunately for Joe, a Greek statue has more moves." Later Ali would confess that he hadn't knocked out Bugner because he rather liked him.

Maybe so, but serious doubts were beginning to be raised about Ali's abilities post-Zaire. At 33, age and the constant struggle against his ballooning weight were conspiring against him, and it was beginning to show. "He should have quit after Bugner," Ali's long-time doctor Ferdie Pacheco told Ali biographer Thomas Hauser. "The time was right; he had his health. If Ali had retired after Malaysia, he'd be far ahead of the game today."

What possessed Ali, at 33, to step into a Manila ring against his nemesis Smokin' Joe Frazier is anybody's guess. Perhaps it was the size of the purse, put up in large part by Philippine despot Ferdinand Marcos (Ali was offered $4.5 against 43 per cent of all fight-generated income—in the end he went home with six). Perhaps he needed the money—by now Ali's travelling circus of dubious friends and hangers-on numbered over 50. Perhaps it was, as American boxing writer Jerry Izenberg put it, a final opportunity to settle the ultimate grudge match. "What it came down to in Manila wasn't the Heavyweight Championship of the World," wrote Izenberg. "Ali and Frazier were fighting for something more important than that. They were fighting for the championship of each other." Perhaps—almost certainly—he foolishly underestimated Frazier. Many in Ali's camp believed Frazier, who had struggled in his last fight against Jimmy Ellis and about whom there were persistent rumors concerning damaged eyesight, was not the Smokin' Joe of old. After all, hadn't Foreman destroyed Frazier? Perhaps, in the end, Ali had genuinely come to believe he was invincible:

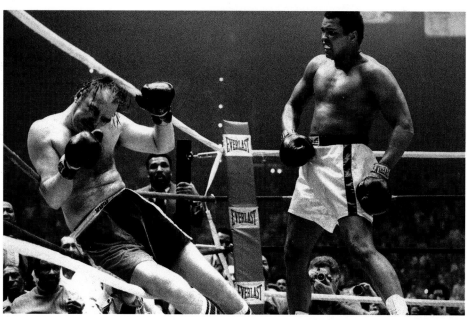

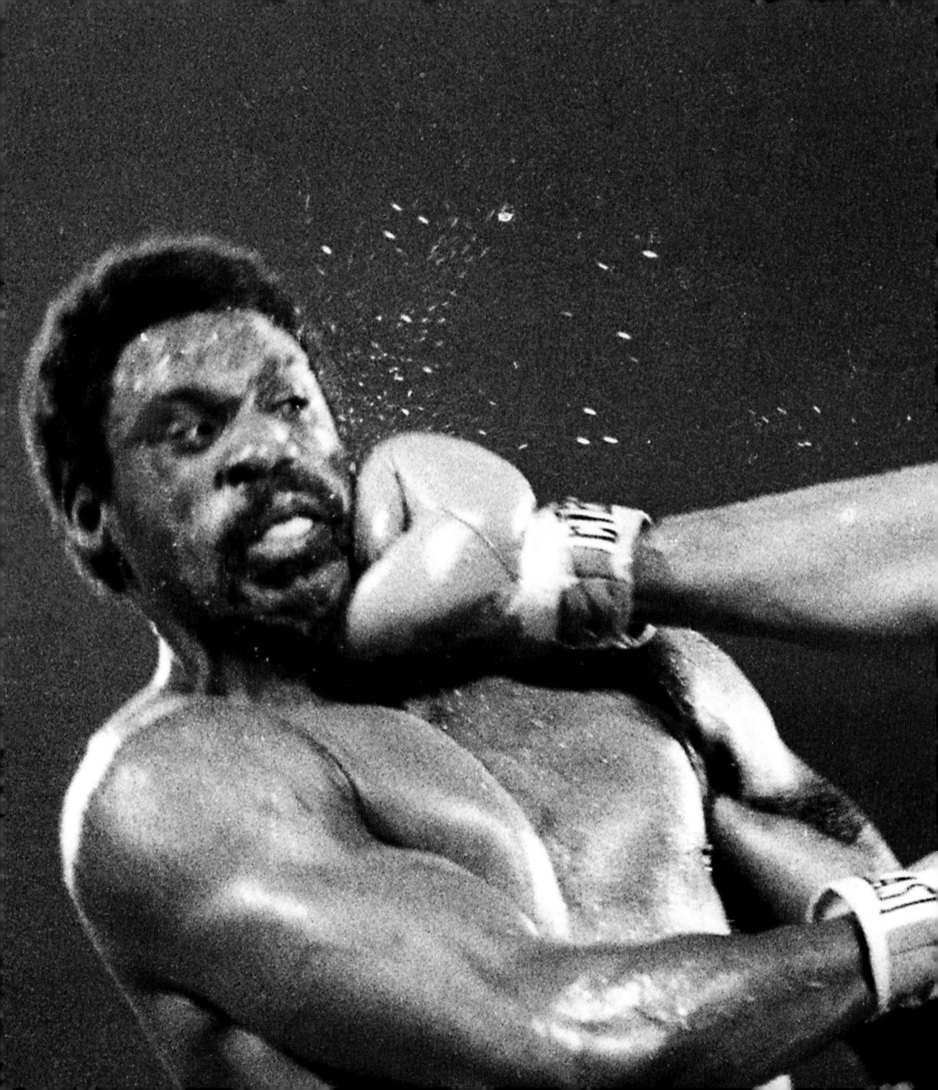

"I must be the greatest," he crowed to reporters over the top rope as a shattered Ron Lyle was led back to his corner. "Am I immortal too?" Whatever Ali's reasons for going to the Philippines, Manila at least provided an answer to that.

It was an ill-tempered affair from the very outset. The bad blood that existed between the two fighters had been well documented, particularly on the part of Frazier who felt that he had never been given his due recognition as Heavyweight Champion because of Ali's constant shadow. Now, with an increasingly arrogant Ali taunting an increasingly surly Frazier, the pre-match rhetoric degenerated into mutual hatred. At a joint press conference in Malaysia the day after the Bugner fight, Ali ridiculed Frazier mercilessly for his appearance, his intelligence, and even his lack of education. By Manila, Ali had dubbed Frazier a "gorilla," an image loaded with racial overtones. Mimicking Frazier's ungrammatical way of speaking, he proclaimed over and over:

It will be a killer
And a chiller
And a thrilla
When I get the gorilla
In Manila

"Ali waged unrestricted warfare on his [Frazier's] subconcious and his pride," says Ferdie Pacheco, who was with Ali in Manila. "Nobody had ever done that and got away with it. Frazier was an extremely proud man and extremely tough, a man of the streets. If you insult him he is going to deck you, but Ali came and did the worst thing you can do to a tough guy—he made fun out of him, made him look foolish. And worse than that, he made fun of him as a black man."

Things degenerated even further when Ali took to pummelling a dishevelled toy gorilla at press conferences. On one occasion he whipped out a toy gun and pointed it at Frazier, shouting that he was going to "shoot a gorilla", provoking uneasy laughter from the crowd. Most were disturbed by the personal nature of Ali's attacks. Ferdie Pacheco: "Ali had that sort of childhood capacity to deliver evil thoughts in the form of humor. Gradeschool kids have that to the max because they have no inhibitions. There's no sensibility with kids. They will find out the funniest things to say. They are cruel and they will rip out your heart and that's what Ali did to Frazier."

Initially, Frazier tried to shrug it off, telling reporters he would "carry on like a gorilla in the ring, and Ali knows what that's all about." But as the fight drew closer, Frazier's mood turned murderous. "It's real hatred," he said. "I don't want to hurt him. I don't want to knock him out. I want to take his heart out." Decades later, Frazier's opinion of Ali had not much altered. "I hated Ali," he told Thomas Hauser. "God might not like me talking that way but it's in my heart. I hated that man. First two fights he tried to make me a white man. Then he tried to make me a nigger. How would you like it if your kids came home crying, because everyone was calling their daddy a gorilla? The way I feel, I'd like to fight Ali—Clay—whatever his name is again tomorrow. Twenty years I've been fighting Ali, and I still want to take him apart piece by piece and send him back to Jesus."

For Ali's part, the lead up to the fight was soured by a very public rift with his wife Belinda. Since his split with his first wife Sonji, Ali had garnered an insatiable appetite for women. Over the years their attentions grew to rock star proportions. And, despite the tenets of the Nation of Islam, Ali could not resist. "I used to chase women all the time," Ali confessed to Thomas Hauser years later, "and I won't say it was right, but look at all the temptations I had. I was young, handsome, Heavyweight Champion of the World. Women were always offering themselves to me." In fact, Belinda (now called Khalilah) insists that many in his group, including Muslims, encouraged Ali's infidelities: "There were men in the camp who had wives and they wanted to get a piece of Ali, to use Ali to get women. They would say, 'You're Muhammad Ali, do what you want. You're a man and all them women are chasin' you anyway,' and they would use that because they knew it was his weakness. They'd manipulate him that way." Even though they were common knowledge among the press corps, Ali's peccadilloes—like John F. Kennedy's—were never reported. Manila changed all that.

A year earlier Ali had met a beautiful model called Veronica Porche, who had entered a contest to be a "poster girl" promoting The Rumble in The Jungle. Although she didn't win—"I was considered too light-skinned to represent the black race"—the organizers still took her to Zaire where, despite the formidable presence of Ali's long-suffering wife, she and Ali began a surreptitious affair. "We spent a lot of time together in Zaire," she recalls. "I used to come over sometimes and we'd walk along the Zaire River and talk and then I'd go back. Then, one day, when he was at his training camp in the presidential compound just outside of Kinshasa, he was reciting one of his lectures and it was on friendship and love and all his ideals, and I fell in love with that and started falling in love with him, too. That's the beginning of it." After his success in Zaire, the relationship blossomed, and when Ali went to Manila, Veronica went too, staying with him in his suite on the 21st floor of the Manila Hilton. While Ali passed her off as his "cousin" the affair went unreported. However, when, ten days before the fight, Ali took Veronica to a reception at the presidential palace and allowed President Marcos to believe that she was his wife, the story broke with a vengeance. An unrepentant Ali tried to shrug off the scandal. "I got three or four lady friends here," he told the press. "I can see some controversy if she [Veronica] was white, but she's not." As for his wife Khalilah, she would simply have to live with his lifestyle. "My wife rides around in two Rolls-Royces, two Eldorados," he said. "We have a 16-room home in Chicago, beautiful children, a couple of farms. She should have no complaints." For Khalilah it was the last straw. She took the next flight to Manila, stormed past the waiting reporters in the hotel lobby, burst into his suite during the filming of a television interview, and had a flaming row with Ali in the bedroom.

"I knew he was in Manila with Veronica, that's why I stayed at home," recalls Khalilah. "I would let him have his fun. I knew he was going to do it anyway and I felt it was part of my religious principles to keep the family together, no matter what. But Ali got too cocky. He started bringing them home and he even had a child by another woman at this point. But with Veronica I just had to go over there and tell him how I felt."

Twelve hours later Khalilah returned to the US on the same plane that had brought her. Veronica stayed. Among the bookmakers, Ali's odds were widened. He went into the fight 2-1 favorite.

OPPOSITE: Ali and Frazier sign for their third and final bout, the Thrilla in Manila. The money is enormous—$6 million for Ali; $3 million for Frazier—but by the end of one of boxing history's most brutal bouts, it's doubtful either fighter will think it's enough.

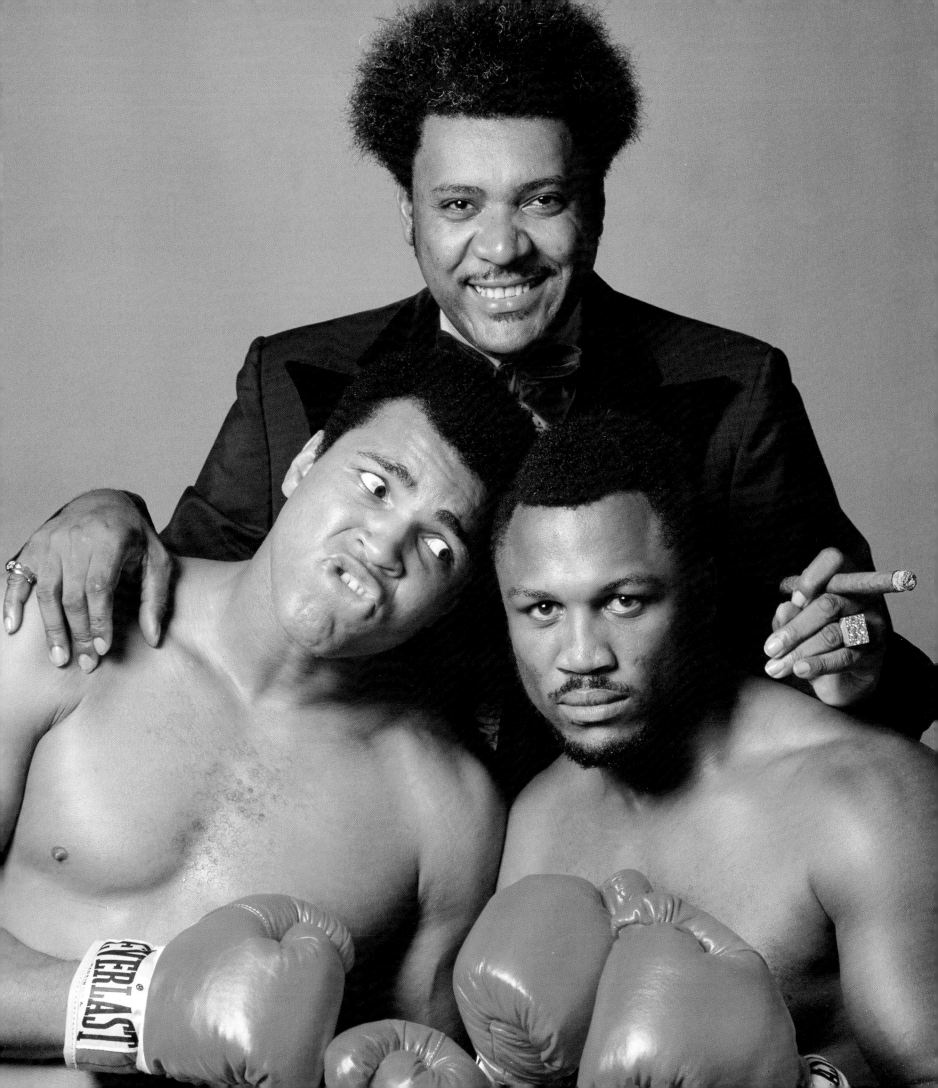

OPPOSITE: Ali and Frazier slug it out head to head in the sweltering Manila heat.

By any measure, the third Ali vs. Frazier fight was one of the most brutal title bouts of modern times. It took place in Quezon City on the outskirts of Manila, in temperatures of over one hundred degrees. While Ferdinand and Imelda Marcos sat fanning themselves in bejewelled seats, the two greatest fighters of their generation came within an inch of killing each other.

Like all great drama the fight unfolded in three acts. The first act was Ali's. A confident-looking champion came out fast, taking the center of the ring and rapping Frazier with sharp combinations as the challenger searched for an opening. "There he is!" shouted Bundini at ringside. "Bring it on home, Champ!" As Ali tattooed Frazier's head with jabs, it looked like it was only a matter of time for the challenger; several times Ali shivered Frazier with hard rights. But as Jerry Izenberg had noted, this was more than just a title fight, particularly for the humiliated Frazier, who continued to advance regardless. Time and again the 25,000 fans packing the Manila Coliseum rose to their feet as the advantage ebbed and flowed.

It was Frazier's pet punch, the left hook, that finally began to turn the fight in his favor. He landed two in the sixth round that had Angelo Dundee wincing. "The hardest punches I'd ever seen," said Dundee later. It took all of Ali's will for him to stay on his feet. He wrestled Frazier, trying to hustle some time and gulping for air, but it was as one of Ali's cornermen, Booker Johnson, who said of Frazier: "Here's the man who wouldn't let you breathe because every time you breathe he's on top of you." By the tenth it looked as if it was Ali who was finished. At the end of the round he sat slumped on his stool—thinking about dying, as he confessed later—while Bundini wept in the corner.

Then, somewhere amongst the chaos, Ali managed to find the reserves to regroup, and by the 12th round he was miraculously back in control, firing jabs at Frazier again from center-ring. Frazier kept trying to burrow under Ali's reach looking to land a last big left, but the arms were leaden, the snap was gone. Worse still, his left eye was closing fast. "Joe's eye was up like a half a grapefruit," remembers Ferdie Pacheco. "And every time Ali landed you could here the squish! squish! of the fluid in his face." The 14th round sealed Frazier's fate. At the bell, Frazier walked into a barrage of lefts and rights which

BELOW: The pre-fight insults are just as rancorous as before, with Ali's slurs on Frazier's intellect making even his own camp cringe. "How would you like it if your kids came home crying because everyone was calling their daddy a gorilla?" complains the simmering Frazier.

knocked him almost unconscious on his feet. In all, Ali landed with nine straight right hands in that round. It was a small miracle that Frazier, exhausted and probably blind, was still on his feet when the referee guided him back to his corner at the end of the round.

Both fighters were spent. In his corner Ali was mumbling for someone to cut the gloves off him. He didn't want another round. Nobody made the move. In the opposite corner Frazier was flopped on the stool. His trainer, Eddie Futch, realized that his fighter was in bad shape. He had to make a quick decision: one last throw of the dice, or throw in the towel before permanent damage was done. The oppressive noise and heat only added to the confusion. Frazier's son Marvis, who was sitting at ringside, recalls that one of Joe's entourage, Willie Monroe, who was sitting near Ali's corner, had been frantically trying to attract Futch's attention over the pandemonium. "He was shouting, 'Ali's finished! Ali's finished!' but nobody heard him. It all could have been different if we'd heard Willie Monroe."

Futch, a wise and decent man, made the choice to stop the fight. "I didn't want Joe's brains scrambled," he said later. Frazier stood up and protested through swollen lips, but the fight was over. For a moment the crowd was puzzled as to what was happening. Then came the announcement and Ali's entourage leaped into the air around him. Ali stood up and then collapsed. "Frazier quit just before I did," he said afterwards. "I didn't think I could fight anymore."

"Ali asked for me to come to his dressing room before any of the press arrived," recalls Marvis Frazier. "I went in there and Ali was real tired and he hugged me and apologized for what he'd said about my father before the fight. He said, 'Tell your father he's a great man.'"

At the post-fight press conference, Ali, relatively unscarred compared to his near-blind opponent, wearily admitted: "I'm so tired I want to rest for a week. My hips are sore, my arms are sore, my side is sore, my hands are sore. There's a great possibility that this may be my last fight. Tonight you may well have seen the last of Ali. Going into rounds 14 and 15 you're going to faint. It's a bad feeling. I want to get out while I'm on top. I want to get out unscarred and let these young fellows fight." But Ali had left something behind in Manila that he would never retrieve, his health. In later life he would attribute his damaged health to the third Frazier fight.

After the warfare in the Philippines, Ali felt that he was entitled to a few easy matches, and in heavyweight terms they didn't come much easier than his next opponent, Jean Pierre Coopman, the Heavyweight Champion of Belgium. A 29-year-old sculptor of religious statues, the Puerto Rican promoters christened him the "Lion of Flanders" in a desperate bid to drum up ticket sales. "The only lion Coopman resembles is the lion in the *Wizard of Oz*," remarked one writer. Unfortunately for the worried promoters, Coopman was an unabashed fan of Ali; it was all his trainers could do to stop him kissing his idol at the press conference. "How am I gonna get mad at this guy?" asked a bemused Ali.

In the end he didn't have to. After the first clinch, Ali burst out laughing. At the end of round one Ali leaned through the ropes and shouted down to one of the CBS television executives: "You guys are in trouble; ain't no way you're gonna get all your commercials in." Coopman, who was happy just to be there, sipped champagne between rounds until Ali knocked him out with an uppercut in the fifth. Coopman had failed to land a single effective blow during the entire contest. "I

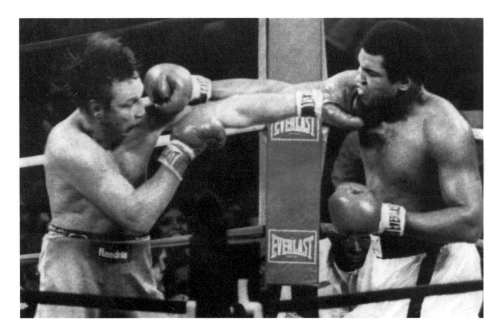

ABOVE: The champagne-swigging Lion of Flanders throws a rare blow in his farcical mismatch with Ali. "Nothing to brag about," admits the Champ.

OPPOSITE: Ali works on Frazier's closed eye. Ferdie Pacheco: "Every time Ali landed you could hear the squish, squish of the fluid."

FOLLOWING PAGES: A woefully unprepared Ali takes on a fit Jimmy Young and leaves with a lucky points victory and a broken eardrum.

enjoyed it," said Ali disarmingly after the bout. "Everything was nice". The next day a more objective Ali agreed the fight had been "nothing to brag about". "I'll admit now I wasn't trying to knock him out at the beginning," he told reporters. "I wanted all the 12,000 spectators to get into the arena."

While Ali, accompanied by Veronica Porche, was on his way back from Puerto Rico, Khalilah Ali announced that she and her husband were separating. "My interest is now in the Nation of Islam," she said, "not in boxing and not in my husband." Soon after, Ali made an announcement of his own: Veronica was pregnant. On September 2, 1976, citing desertion, adultery, and mental cruelty, Khalilah finally filed for divorce.

"He didn't grow up on principles," she now says of her former husband. "He was just winging it. I told him, 'You are a big elephant in the jungle and you can't hide. You're too big to mess around and nobody notice. This is the sacrifice you have to make when you are famous. How are you going to teach your children not to screw around with everybody?' But, you know, it wasn't the women that finished it all for me. Around that time I was really devoted to my religion because Ali was doing many bad things, and one morning I was knelt down praying and he says, 'What are you doin'? Are you tryin' to make me look bad?' and he picked up some vegetables and he threw them at me. When he started disrespecting me and my religion, that was it."

Following the Coopman farce, Ali outlined his future fight strategy for the press: "We're working on Jimmy Young," he said, referring to the plodding journeyman who had just scraped through on points over a local boxer during a preliminary bout on the same Puerto Rican bill. "Young, then I must get Norton. I gotta have Norton, then Foreman. Then I retire." The rematch against Foreman was to be held in the Sudanese capital of Khartoum the following autumn, and Ali intended it to be a spectacular climax to cap his career. Mollified by the promise of great bouts to come, the press was not too hard on him when he stepped into the ring against the game but decidedly average Jimmy Young.

Expecting another walkover (Young was a 15-1 underdog), Ali trained sparingly and let his weight balloon to 230 pounds, the heaviest of his career. It was a grave mistake. Young was a more accomplished and determined fighter than Coopman and he was there to cause an upset, not to sip champagne from his corner-man's bucket. The 27-year-old challenger took the fight to Ali, landing far more effective blows than the champion, whose timing was off. It wasn't so much that Young was good; it was far more that the out-of-shape, flat-footed Ali was just plain awful. The occasional flashes of the old Ali were enough to scrape a very dubious 15-round points decision, but Ali left with one broken eardrum and boos ringing in the other ear. Afterwards he conceded he had been shaken by some of Young's punches and that he had not trained hard enough. "Getting old," he said. "That used to be me, the young man popping about like that. It could be I'm through, finished."

Others agreed. In a prophetic article *The Economist* wrote that Ali "may be about to make the mistake of boxing on for too long". "Since boxers started wearing gloves only four heavyweights, James Jeffries, Gene Tunney, Joe Louis, and Rocky Marciano, have retired as undefeated World Champions and only two of these (Marciano and Tunney) resisted the temptation to make a comeback. Several of these have fought on for much too long. Joe Louis, a pathetic wreck of the once unbeatable 'Brown Bomber,' was knocked out in eight rounds by an up and coming Rocky Marciano. Ezzard Charles stayed around to get beaten by men he would not have hired as sparring partners while champion, Floyd Patterson to fight has-beens and never-wasers. True, Archie Moore was nearer 50 than 40 years old when he lost his title, but Ali, on his performance against Young, is already past his peak... Only pride plus the lure of the resin and the roar of the crowd can explain why Ali has not yet hung up his gloves."

Nevertheless, only a few weeks later, a much slimmer Ali travelled to Munich to fight British and European Heavyweight Champion Richard Dunn. The match proved so unappealing to the public that the German promoters were on the verge of cancelling two weeks before the night. Their American partner, a 28-year-old novice named Butch Lewis who had managed to persuade Herbert Muhammad and Ali that he could handle the promotion (his first ever), suddenly found himself in the middle of a nightmare:

"We had given Ali half a million dollars already on his purse which was all non-refundable shit. When we got there the German guys said, 'We ain't got the money'. There wasn't much interest in the fight. And there wasn't a lot we could do. So I'm up in my hotel room trying to figure out a plan and Bundini Brown knocks on my door and says, 'The champ wants to see you.' I was trying to work up the courage to tell him. I'd talked to Herbert on the phone about the difficulties and he said, 'You're coming home. I'm telling Ali to pack his bags and everybody is getting out of there. If you want to be in the business that's the way it is.' So I go up to Ali's room and he says, 'I know what's happened. I've been talking to Herbert.' I'm looking for what to say because he's given me this chance when everybody told him not to and I fumble the ball on the one yard line. I say, 'I'm sorry. I don't know what to do.' So Ali says, 'How much are you short?' It was about half a million dollars. He calls Herbert and he says, 'I'm not leaving Butch here like this. I'm gonna cut my purse and you will still

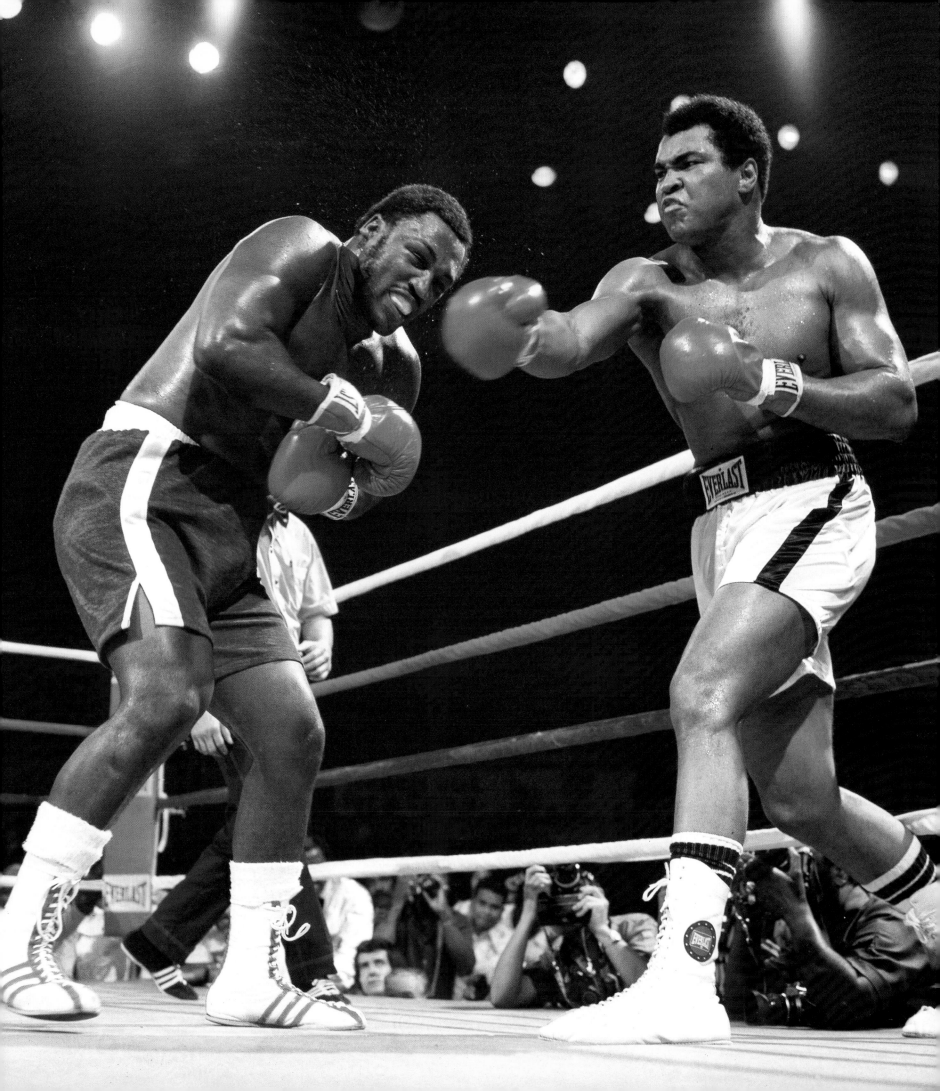

ABOVE: A return bout with a real contender—Ken Norton known as 'the man that broke Ali's jaw'—is eagerly awaited by fans and pundits alike.

OPPOSITE: By now the Champ is finding it increasingly difficult to get in shape. The London *Daily Telegraph*: "Muhammad Ali's reign as Heavyweight Champion is drawing sadly to a close as old age creeps relentlessly through his body."

BELOW: Ali and British and European Champion Richard Dunn in the fight that almost never was.

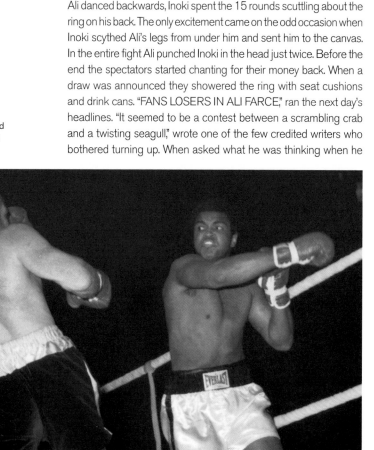

get the same cut 50:50 as if it was never done.' And I'm crying when I hear this. I don't know what to say. So after he does that he says, 'How much are the best ringside seats?' I say, 'I don't know, maybe $500 dollars.' He says, 'There's a major army base here.' He says to somebody, 'Write a check out for $100,000.' He gave me the check and said, 'Buy as many tickets as you can with this and give them to our soldiers stationed here and have them at ringside.' Then he says, 'Hold on! One other thing—when I get in the ring I want to hear every soldier who bought a ticket shouting "Ali! Ali!" That's the deal.' He could have walked away from that fight and still have done everything he could for me, but what he did was incredible."

Unfortunately, the fight itself fell far short of incredible. Despite Dunn's surprisingly gritty performance, he was hopelessly outmatched and was knocked down five times before the referee stopped it in the fifth. Although Ali was to fight another five-and-a-half years, Dunn was the last opponent he would knock to the canvas.

After the Coopman, Young, and Dunn disappointments, Ali pushed the public's patience even further by agreeing to a bout against Japanese professional wrestler Antonio Inoki in Tokyo. Inoki, nick-named "The Pelican" by Ali because of his large chin, billed himself as the world martial arts champion. According to the promoter Bob Arum, the contest was meant to be tightly scripted, like all professional wrestling bouts. Unfortunately Ali's conscience got the better of him and he threw away the script. When both fighters entered the ring, neither knew what the other was going to do. What followed was one of the most tedious spectacles in "entertainment" history. While Ali danced backwards, Inoki spent the 15 rounds scuttling about the ring on his back. The only excitement came on the odd occasion when Inoki scythed Ali's legs from under him and sent him to the canvas. In the entire fight Ali punched Inoki in the head just twice. Before the end the spectators started chanting for their money back. When a draw was announced they showered the ring with seat cushions and drink cans. "FANS LOSERS IN ALI FARCE," ran the next day's headlines. "It seemed to be a contest between a scrambling crab and a twisting seagull," wrote one of the few credited writers who bothered turning up. When asked what he was thinking when he

was lying on the canvas, Ali said, "I was just letting time go by while I collected my six million dollars." (In fact he wound up with just over two.) When he returned to America, Ali was admitted to a hospital in California with blood clots on his leg, the result of Inoki's kicks.

And then came the moment everybody had been waiting for—a real bout against a genuine contender, Ken Norton, the man who had broken Ali's jaw and lost the rematch by a whisker. The bout was a gamble for Ali at this stage of his career, but, unlike many other fighters, Ali had never ducked challengers. This time, Ali did not underestimate his opponent (despite Norton having been destroyed by Foreman in under two rounds). With more than a month to go before the bout, he hid himself away in Arizona with only Dundee, Bundini, his masseur Luis Sarria, and three sparring partners for company. He returned to the limelight only after the New York promoters begged him to move nearer to Yankee Stadium to promote the fight.

But despite all the preparation and isolation, the gamble almost didn't pay off. Norton didn't pressure fighters with the same ferocity as Frazier and he didn't have the power of Foreman, but he was always a puzzle that Ali could never really solve. A bright, good-looking guy with a reasonably successful film career, Norton had no obvious psychological flaws Ali could work on. Norton also had the clever and experienced Eddie Futch in his corner who helped him develop a style that Futch knew would always give Ali problems—a forward motion, cross-armed, peek-a-boo stance.

On a warm summer night in 1976, Ken Norton outfought Ali for much of the 15 rounds. Ali, approaching his 35th birthday, was by now unable to fight for the full three minutes of each round. He would retreat to the ropes as he had done in Zaire, ending each round with a flurry of activity to catch the judges' eyes. Unfortunately for Norton it worked; the judges often scored more for Ali than he deserved.

Perhaps Norton's biggest mistake was not winning the final round with a flourish. Thinking he had the fight won, he spent the 15th trying to evade Ali, and in doing so lost the round. The fight went to the judges' cards and the 15th round proved crucial. Ali won a split decision and Norton, who cried all the way back to the dressing room, was convinced he'd been robbed. "I know I won and he knows I won," he said bitterly. A large portion of the 30,000 crowd agreed. Ali, though, was unrepentant. "To be a World Champion you have to whip the world champion, and he couldn't do it," he said. Then, almost apologetically, he added: "This is getting tough."

On one thing everybody did, however, agree: the old Ali magic had all but vanished. As the London *Daily Telegraph* put it: "Muhammad Ali's reign as Heavyweight Champion of the World is drawing sadly to a close as old age, an adversary whose ultimate superiority even he cannot deny, creeps relentlessly through his body into the far corners of his mind." A week later, while on a good-will mission in Turkey, Ali formally announced his retirement from boxing. Of course it wouldn't last long.

Outside the ring Ali's life was becoming even more tumultuous, with numerous goodwill missions to foreign countries, myriad public appearances, the production of a woeful Hollywood movie in which Ali played himself, and the publication of his even more depressing "autobiography"—*The Greatest.* This was in fact, little more than blatant propaganda for the Nation of Islam—Herbert Muhammad had the final say on the entire editorial content.

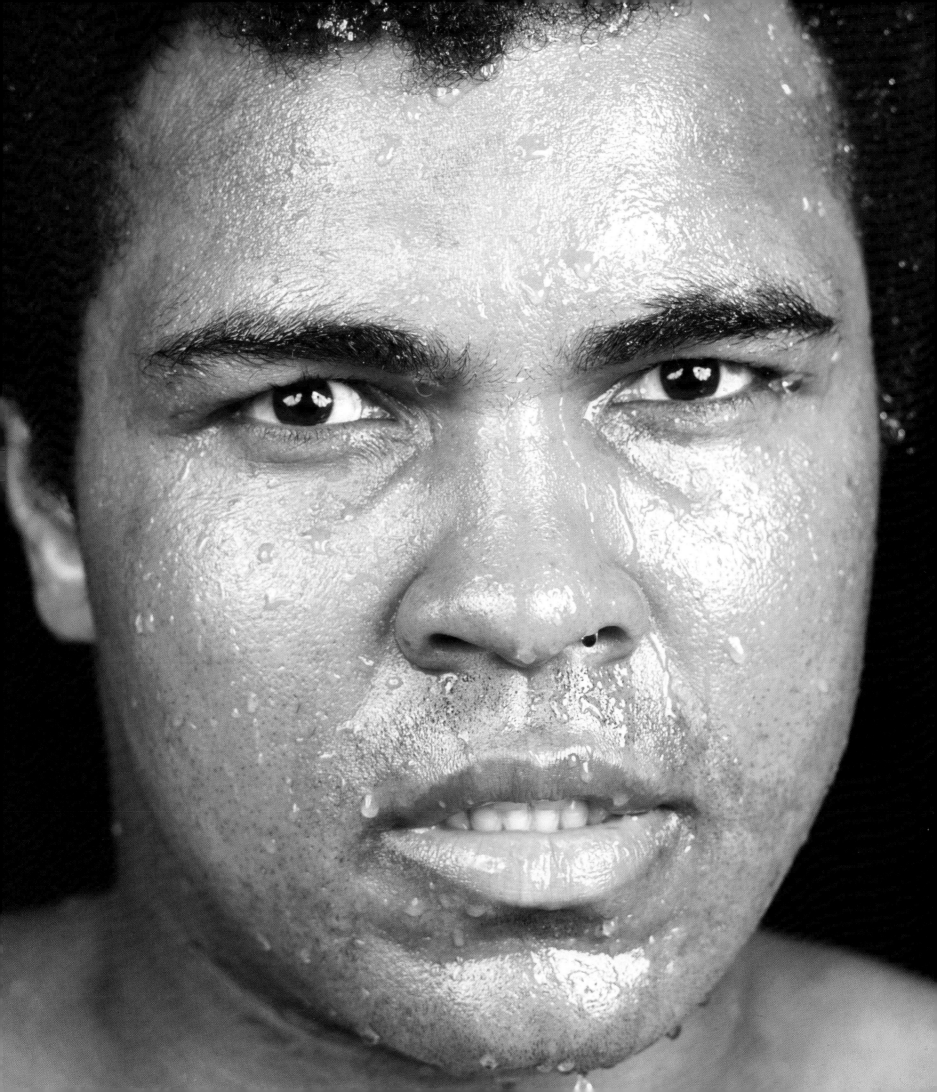

OPPOSITE: The Champ hangs on to win a split decision against Ken Norton. "I know I won and he knows I won," weeps the disappointed Norton.

BELOW: The fight that never should have been. Japanese wrestler Antonio–The Pelican –Inoki lets fly crab-style. Ali stays out of range. "I was just letting time go by while I collected my six million dollars."

Also, in January 1977 Ali's divorce from Khalilah finally went through. Khalilah reportedly received $670,000 payable over five years, a home in suburban Chicago, and miscellaneous personal property. Ali also placed one million dollars in a trust fund for their four children.

With all these distractions, it was little wonder that Ali was less than focused on his next opponent, a 22-year-old Uruguayan named Alfredo Evangelista who had been plucked from the depths of the boxing rankings. In fact, so lowly was Evangelista that even his manager was unsure of his professional record. "He's come from so far down he may have the bends when he gets in the ring," quipped one comedian. The paying public was similarly unimpressed; once again Ali had to give away $200,000 worth of tickets "to the poor" in order to fill even half the seats in Landover, Maryland. Once again the bout was terrible, with a hopelessly outclassed Evangelista chasing an uninspired Ali for 15 rounds. Ali was awarded a lopsided points win as the crowd booed.

A few weeks later, Ali married Veronica in front of 240 guests, including Joe Louis and Sugar Ray Robinson. To the strains of a harpist and a string ensemble the guests sipped fruit punch. Ali, uncharacteristically silent during the event, appeared nervous but happy. In private, however, friends were becoming seriously concerned about his health. It was becoming alarmingly clear to many of them that not only had Ali slowed in the ring, but that his speech sometimes slurred almost to the point of incomprehension. Ali's next choice of opponent gave them little comfort.

Earnie Shavers was no Evangelista. A seasoned pro of 33, he possessed one of the hardest right hands in heavyweight history, a fact amply illustrated by his record of 52 knockouts. It promised to be a genuine contest and people paid to see it. The 20,000-seat Madison Square Garden sold out, and NBC, which showed the fight live across America, attracted 70 million viewers. Ali received $3 million and Shavers $300,000, the highest of his career.

During training Ali pretended to take it easy, rather lamely giving Shavers the moniker "The Acorn" because of his bald head. "That ugly bald-headed acorn doesn't belong in the same ring as The Greatest," he told the press at his Deer Lake training camp. In reality, though,

he trained hard; wisely, as it turned out. In the second round Shavers caught Ali with a stunning right hand; Ali's legs turned to jelly and it took all his extraordinary strength of will just to remain upright. "I loved Ali," said Shavers later. "He'd helped me out at his training camp, given me advice. Maybe that's why I didn't finish him when I had him in that second round. I had too much respect for him, maybe. When I saw him stagger back I looked at his eyes and they seemed clear, I thought he was playing possum." But Ali wasn't fooling; once again he retreated to the ropes for much of the fight. By finishing rounds strongly, Ali managed to tip the judges' pens in his favor, but after a ferocious onslaught from Shavers in the 13th and 14th rounds, the fight was too close to call. A big rally from Shavers in the 15th, and the title would certainly have been his. But it was Ali who once again turned the tables. In a quite remarkable last round, Ali was off the ropes and taking the fight to Shavers with a two-handed attack which had Shavers reeling. In the end only the bell saved Shavers from a dramatic stoppage. It was an incredible turnaround and more than a few veteran Ali watchers consider it one of his finest ring achievements.

Despite the unanimous decision for Ali and the brilliance of the final round, the match had still been a brutally close-run thing. "Battling Shavers Takes Ali To The Limit" ran the next day's headlines. Watching Ali post-fight, battered and exhausted, the calls for him to quit grew louder. Even Teddy Brenner, the head of boxing at Madison Square Garden, told a press conference he thought it was time for Ali to hang up his gloves. The statement was quite amazing given the ruthlessness of the boxing business and the kind of money Ali was generating at the time. "I shouldn't say this—he's been our biggest money maker—but the Garden won't make another offer to Muhammad Ali as long as I'm here," he said.

Ferdie Pacheco, Ali's physician, was also ready to close the door behind him. "The Shavers fight in the Garden was so hard," says Pacheco. "I said to whoever would listen: 'Don't you know that this guy is really hurt? These are the sort of fights that send you off into punch-drunk land!'"

Pacheco, who had been in Ali's corner continuously for 14 years, had been worried about Ali since the last Frazier bout. "That's when it really started to fall apart," he told Thomas Hauser years later. "He began to take beatings, not just in fights but in the gym. Even sparring he'd do the rope-a-dope because he couldn't avoid punches the way he did when he was young. And I don't care how good you are at rope-a-doping; if you block 95 punches out of 100, the other five are getting in."

For Pacheco, the final straw came after the Shavers fight when the New York State Athletic Commission gave him a copy of a lab report that showed Ali's kidney's were in bad condition. "By that time, it was evident to others, not just me, that he was losing blood after the fights. Stacks of the cells that filter the blood were going out. It means that blood is going straight from blood to urine." Pacheco said he forwarded the report to Ali's camp, but that he heard no response. So he quit. "Boxers can look all right on the outside," he explained to reporters, "but they wear out inside."

The press, on the other hand, was keen that Ali defend his title once again against Ken Norton, who had established himself as the top contender after beating Jimmy Young. However, after the Shavers fight, Ali's management was intent on pursuing "easy" bouts. It was

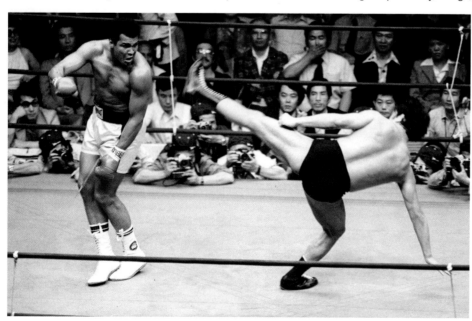

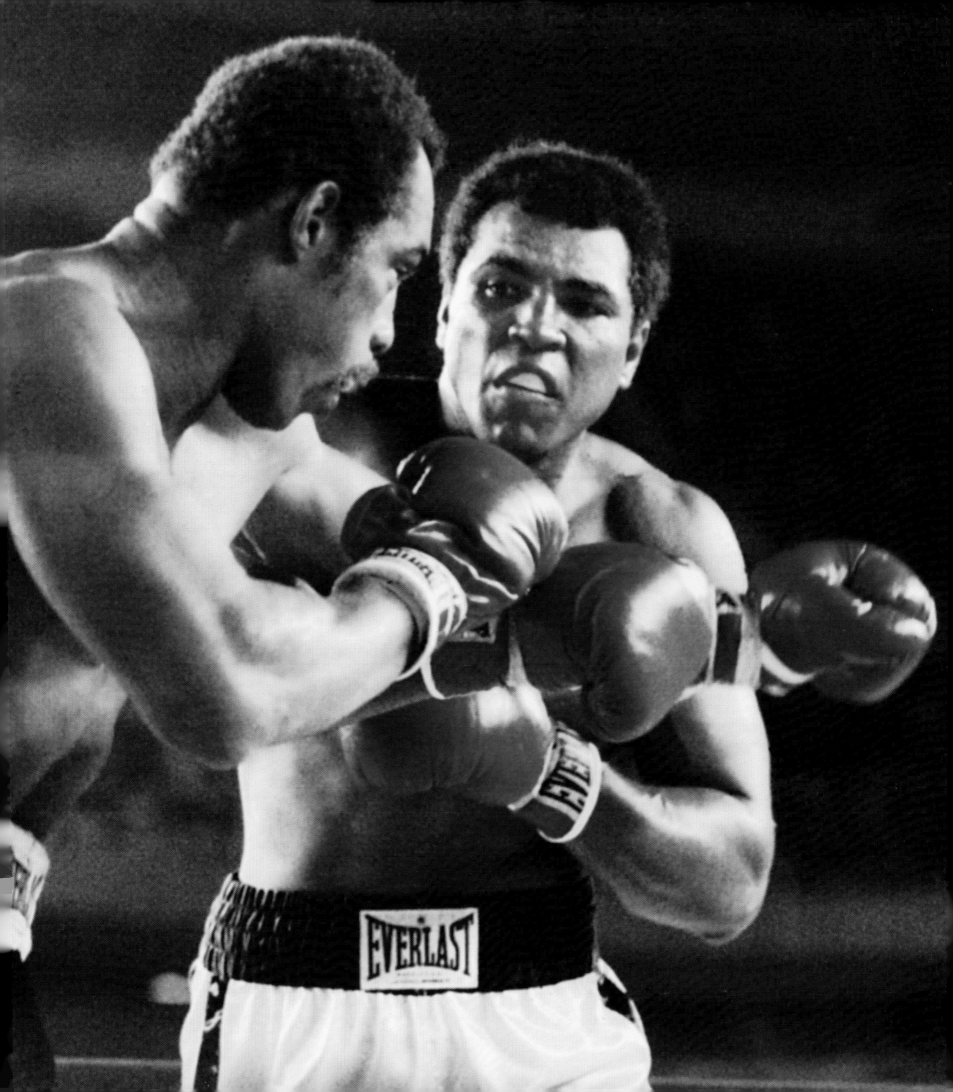

OPPOSITE: The writing is well and truly on the wall for Ali when he can only manage a points victory over Uruguayan Alfredo Evangelista, a fighter so unrated even his manager is unsure of his professional record.

BELOW: During a trip to Turkey following his painfully narrow escape from Ken Norton, Ali announces his retirement from boxing. But as usual, it is all for the cameras.

only under pressure from the WBC, which threatened to strip him of the title within 60 days if he didn't sign, that Ali finally agreed in December 1977 to face Norton. But he pushed back the fight date for as long as possible—September the following year. In the meantime he agreed to take on a rank outsider, Leon Spinks. According to Herbert Muhammad, Ali would retire after the bout regardless of his commitment to Norton and a $12 million purse.

It's difficult to overestimate what a huge underdog Leon Spinks was when he climbed through the ropes at the Hilton hotel in Las Vegas on February 16, 1978. Although, like Ali, he was an Olympic gold medal winner, he had had only seven professional fights. And in his previous fight, against journeyman Scott Le Doux, he could manage only a questionable draw. At 24, he was such a novice that even Ali was embarrassed. "I can't fight this kid," he told Spinks' manager Butch Lewis. "It would make me the laughing stock of the world." After briefly trying to hype the bout as a "battle of the gold medallists," Ali eventually fell silent, refusing to talk to the press even at the weigh-in. "What am I gonna tell people, that I'm gonna destroy him?" he admitted to Butch Lewis. "Talking that way makes me look stupid, so I ain't gonna talk." But the press saw through it. Wrote the *Washington Post* after the silent weigh-in: "The suspicion is that he slickly evaded persistent questions of how he could justify a defense against a youngster with only seven professional bouts."

Indeed, the press was unanimous the fight was simply an event cynically manufactured solely for television. Spinks, it transpired, was part owned by the television network CBS. "Leon Spinks is a product of the television age," opined Norman Giller in the London *Telegraph*. "He has had a total of only seven professional contests, but because each of them have been screened 'live' in 60 million American homes he is considered to have the right grounding and projection for a world championship challenge. Promoters used to look at a boxer's ring record before deciding whether to put their money into a fight. [Now] when they talk about ratings they mean the kind you get from the TV monitoring services rather than *The Ring* magazine." When the young Cassius Clay, after 20 paid bouts, was given his first title shot against Sonny Liston, noted Giller, "it was widely

suggested that he had been rushed to the top with indecent haste. "Well, if his progress was indecent then Spinks' sprint to championship status has been positively obscene."

Given this universal disparagement of Spinks, it was little wonder that Ali, already long bored with the rigors of training, barely broke sweat in the days leading up to the fight. Each day at his Miami Beach camp he waded through an hour-long routine in complete silence, seizing every excuse to take a breather. Ten days before the bout he even showed up in New York to publicize a new comic book, *Superman vs. Muhammad Ali*. (Ali won on points.) Eventually Ali stopped sparring entirely. When reporters quizzed promoter Bob Arum on Ali's dour demeanor, he conceded: "I think it may be because he's having a hell of a time training to get in shape at this stage of his career."

By contrast, Spinks was revelling in the attention. He skipped and danced through his training sessions to a blaring pop soundtrack, obviously enjoying himself.

"Watching this happy young man at work takes my mind back down through the ages to Miami Beach in 1964," wrote boxing correspondent Donald Saunders, "when I saw another fresh-faced, impudent youngster preparing to challenge for the Heavyweight Championship of the World. His name was Cassius Clay—and a few days later he was the champion."

Explaining why 5,500 spectators had paid $200 apiece to see such an obvious mismatch, and CBS $4 million to screen it, Angelo Dundee told reporters on the eve of the fight, "You never know when the eve of the rainbow will cease." For Ali, the rainbow ceased 15 rounds later when the judges crowned Leon Spinks the new Heavyweight Champion of the World by a 2-1 majority decision. While some die-hards at ringside thought Ali was unlucky to have lost, the ex-champ did not. "I have no excuses," he conceded. "I wasn't robbed."

At the start it seemed even a poorly prepared Ali would be able to outmaneuver the novice from St Louis. For the first half of the fight Ali—as he had done since Foreman—lay on the ropes and let Spinks flail away. But any thoughts that the eager young fighter would punch himself out soon faded. Round after round, Ali found himself pinned under a barrage of leather. Spinks did not stop throwing punches the entire fight and in the end it was the aging champion who was the one to run out of steam. In the final round, Ali attempted a Shavers-style comeback, but this time there was nothing left. For the first time in his career, Ali had lost a title in the ring.

After the fight the sense of sadness amongst the press and veteran fight aficionados was almost palpable. "I went into his dressing room and I nearly cried," admitted Bob Arum. "It takes a lot to make a boxing promoter cry, especially in Las Vegas." To most it seemed an inglorious end to such a glittering career, but Ali disagreed. "It's a funny thing," he told reporters through a bruised and swollen face. "I should be sad, but I'm not. We all have losses in our lives. I just lost." Retirement was not on the cards. "After a couple of months you get the feeling," he said. "You start thinking that you fought wrong and could do better next time. Something tells you you've got to take one more gamble."

"When Leon upset Ali, I had mixed emotions—with Leon being my fighter and me admiring Ali so much," recalls Butch Lewis, who was key to Ali's receiving an immediate rematch with Spinks, and with it a chance to bow out on a high note. "We were going to fight Norton because the WBC had him as their mandatory challenger and my

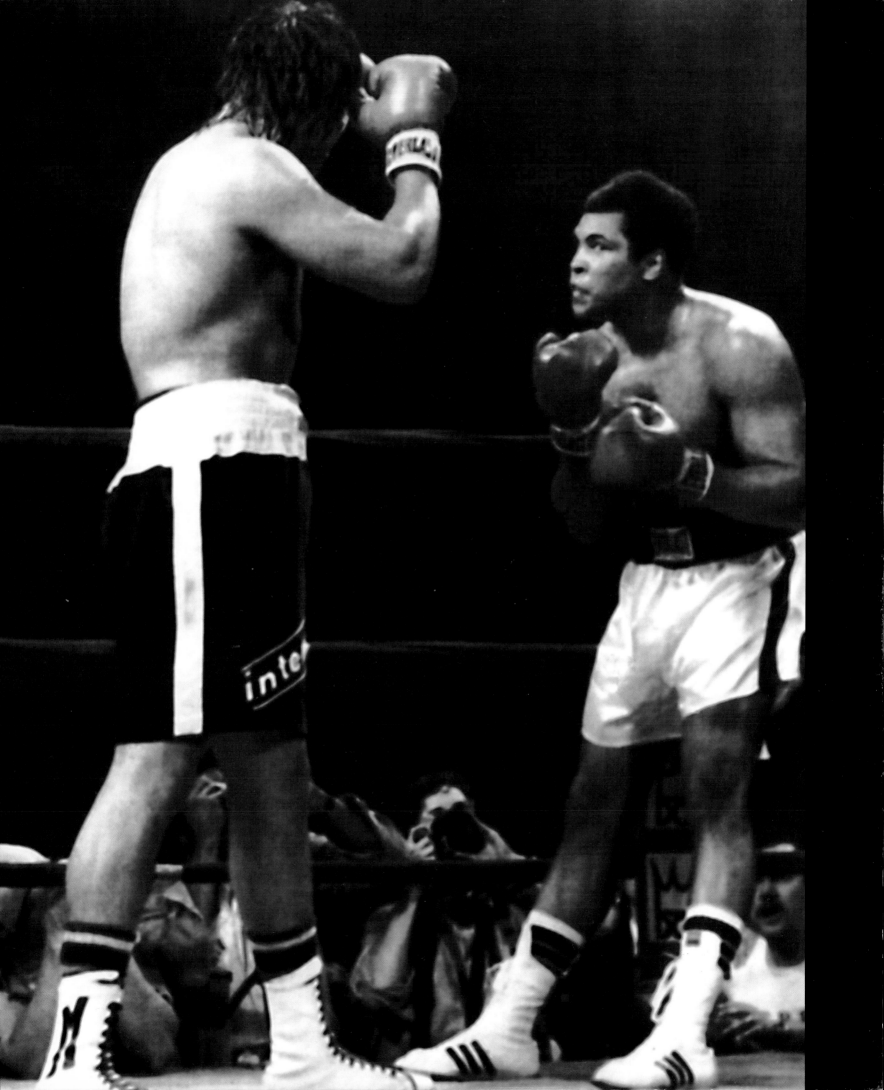

partner Bob Arum wanted to go that route. Arum was so overwhelmed with the fact that he didn't have to deal with Herbert Muhammad anymore. He was like, 'Fuck Herbert Muhammad and fuck Ali!'"

Unfortunately for Arum, Spinks was Lewis' man and Butch had a soft spot for Ali, who had done him a favor in Germany. It was also a fact that a Leon Spinks vs. Ken Norton fight was hardly the most enthralling match up. The real money fight was with Ali. Butch Lewis: "Ali calls me and he came to see me on his own without Herbert at a hotel on Central Park South. He says, 'I'm getting old and I don't have a lot of time…can't really box another year, year and a half to get to the title…' I say, 'Champ, fuck what Arum says, I control Spinks. Arum can go shadow box himself with fucking Ken Norton.'"

The WBC stripped Leon Spinks of its version of the title, but the WBA agreed to sanction the rematch seven months later in the New Orleans Superdome. This time around, however, it was a vastly different Ali and Spinks who stepped through the ropes. This time around there had been no underestimations in the Ali camp. Apart from the occasional obligatory foreign jaunt—to Bangladesh and to the USSR, where he trained in Red Square and bear-hugged Brezhnev in the Kremlin—Ali had trained relentlessly during the seven-month layoff, pushing his body to the point where he was in constant pain. As well as his aging body, which was taking longer to burn off the fat, Ali had been having problems with his hands for many years. Over 20 years of beating heads and heavy bags had taken its toll on the knuckles and the relatively delicate pterodactyl webbing of the hands. Ali had been taking pain-killing injections in his hands for years. They often ached and swelled terribly, but he was prepared to suffer the pain one last time to make up for the disappointing display in

Vegas. "I hate it," he confided to reporters, "but I know that this is my last fight, and it's the last time that I'll ever have to do it. I don't want to lose and spend the rest of my life looking back and saying, 'Damn, I should have trained harder.'"

Spinks, on the other hand, was a different story. Since winning the title, the new World Heavyweight Champion had been on a seven-month-long party, earning him the nickname "Neon Leon." He drank, he smoked dope, and he was even busted for possession of cocaine. He disappeared for months at a time and not even his trainer knew where he was. When he arrived in New Orleans, he highjacked a limousine on the drive from the airport to his training camp and disappeared for another round of partying. According to his long-suffering manager Butch Lewis, Spinks trained at most ten days for the return bout. "Ali didn't win that fight. Leon lost it," Lewis says. "Forget all that stuff about Ali going back and working hard and being better the second time around. Ali wasn't better… Ali was worse. Ali had slipped even more than before, but Leon went against him with nothing at all."

Muhammad Ali created history in the New Orleans Superdome on September 15, 1978, in front of nearly 64,000 delirious paying customers and an estimated one billion television viewers. Ali dominated Spinks for much of the 15 rounds (the judges eventually scored it 10-4 to Ali), hardly surprising considering Leon had left most of his strength behind in bar-rooms and bedrooms. Ali's superior fitness allowed him to outwork and frustrate his younger and smaller opponent. It was a drab fight compared with Ali's heroic triumphs of the past, but this was a night where the boxing was overshadowed by history. As one paper reported, in the

OPPOSITE: Ali, sporting a moustache which he claims makes him look like "Dark Gable," together with Blood and Bundini at Caesar's Palace before the tragically ill-judged bout against Larry Holmes. In the pre-fight war of words, it's Holmes' prediction which proves eerily prescient: "Ali was a great fighter, but he stepped out of his time into my time. I know all there is to know about how he fights. Whatever he tries, I'll beat him. At a distance I'll out-jab him. If he covers up, I'll break his ribs or murder his kidneys. If he wants to wrassle, I'll show him a few holds. I'll beat him to death. He's in trouble. You know it; everyone knows it. They just feel sorry for the old man. He thinks he can pull a rabbit out of a hat, but there's no more rabbits."

BELOW: With Bundini.

closing stages of the fight when it became apparent that Ali would win, "70,000 half-crazed spectators screamed 'Ali! Ali! Ali!' from the floor, the stands, the boxes and seemingly even from the huge dome that dominates the largest and highest arena in the world". After a reign of only 214 days, the shortest in heavyweight history at that point, Leon Spinks was no longer champion and Ali had become the first fighter to win the Heavyweight Championship for a third time.

If ever there was a time for Ali to finally retire, it was now. He had, as he had sworn he would, achieved the impossible. What else was there left to achieve in the ring? "Did I look like I needed to retire?" he taunted the press after the fight. "Did I look like I was all washed up? Did I look like a 37-year-old?" As the Irish featherweight Barry McGuigan once said, "Boxers are always the first to know when they are finished and always the last to know when to retire."

Over the next few months a variety of opponents were touted: some were credible, like British champion John Gardner; others, like Kent Green, who'd beaten Ali in the amateurs as a kid, were not. The closest he came to signing was with white South African Gerrie Coetzee, for ten million dollars. However, a week later he scotched the plan following a phone call from Nigeria's United Nations Ambassador who begged Ali not to give a white South African the chance to become world heavyweight champion. "Satan has been tempting me," said Ali. "It's not easy, to turn down $10 million—that's six million after tax—for six weeks' work and a 40-minute fight."

But turn it down he did and, nine months after winning back his title, he announced his retirement. He had, he said, passed up an offer of 50 million dollars to fight WBC champion Larry Holmes in South Africa. "I know I could beat that boy, but the wear and tear on my body and other things I'm involved in make that offer seem awfully small," he told reporters. In the main the press believed that, this time, he was sincere about quitting. The *Washington Post* pointed out that he had recently been caught by a British cameraman "in droopy boxing drawers overlapped by a stomach of Falstaffian flab that appeared to add up to an unsightly 240 pounds or more". That, it said, would have offended him deeply, to "see himself in the morning papers as others saw him, not only out of shape but grotesque".

Whatever prompted him, Ali wrote to the WBA and vacated his title. A few months later, American heavyweight John Tate beat Gerrie Coetzee in Pretoria to win the last vacant part of Ali's crown.

For Ali, it was his chance to fulfil his dream of stepping out onto the world stage in something other than boxing gear. He threw himself into an even more frenetic round of international goodwill missions, criss-crossing the globe from Paris to Peking as a sort of roving ambassador—"the black Henry Kissinger"—for the United States and American Islam in particular. He had talks with Col. Gadaffi in Libya about using his name to promote the sale of Libyan oil, the profits to be used by Ali to promote Muslim education in the US. A group including "film stars, millionaires and civil rights leaders" formed an "Ali for Senator" committee to persuade him to run for the US Senate. When the Iranians overran the US Embassy in Tehran in November 1979, Ali offered to exchange himself for the 60 American hostages. "I'm a Muslim and I don't think they would hurt me," he said. Although nothing came of it, it was reported that both Washington and the Iranian government were considering the offer.

His big diplomatic chance came two months later when, following the Soviet invasion of Afghanistan, President Jimmy Carter appointed Ali as a special envoy in an attempt to solicit support among African and Islamic nations for the US-led boycott of the Moscow Olympics. Ali cut short a tour of India and flew to Africa on what he called "a delicate mission". Just how delicate became abruptly apparent at his first port of call—Tanzania—where he was grilled for 45 minutes by the local press about America's failure to support the African boycott of the Montreal Olympics over apartheid in South Africa. And when the journalists pointed out that the USSR actively supported African liberation movements, Ali seemed genuinely surprised. "They didn't tell me in America that Russia supports these countries," he exclaimed as nervous State Department officials tried desperately to intervene. "Maybe I'm being used to do something that's very wrong. If I find out I'm wrong I'm going to go back to America and cancel the whole trip." At his next stop in Nairobi, instead of delivering his boycott message, he rounded on Carter, accusing him of "sending me around the world to take the whupping". As the US officials squirmed, he told the Kenyan press that he probably would have not accepted the Carter assignment if he had known beforehand "the whole history of America and Africa and South Africa". He said he was turning the tour into a "fact-finding mission" so that he could report African grievances against America to President Carter. It was only at the end that he finally got to the point of his visit: "The Russians have made a move and if we don't show no protest they may say: 'Hey, the Olympics is going. The Africans came. Nobody worried about what we did. Let's go and take Iran tomorrow.'" Later, he leaped out of his embassy car to tell the crowd: "I'm here to stop a nuclear war". "If these two white men start fighting," he announced, "all of us little black folks are going to be caught in the middle." When he was cold-shouldered at his next stop, Nigeria, it was obvious the mission had been an embarrassing failure. Instead of showing Ali's potential as a diplomat the trip had exposed him as being childishly naive in matters of international politics.

Ali returned to the US to face derision—*Time* magazine dubbed it "the most bizarre diplomatic mission in recent US history"—his dreams of diplomatic greatness shattered. Three weeks later, in an exclusive interview with a Cleveland paper, Ali announced he was making a comeback to recapture the title for the fourth time. The

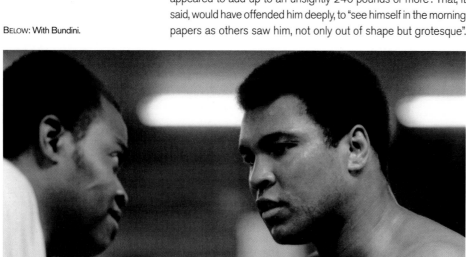

ABOVE: While still refusing to give up his day job, Ali returns to acting—this time with Kris Kristoffersen in a four-hour television mini-series *Freedom Road*. Ali plays a former slave named Gideon Jackson, to bad reviews.

OPPOSITE: Ali and Veronica. "He was a hard man to live with."

following day, Bob Arum officially announced that Ali had signed to fight WBA champion John Tate in late June. The retirement had lasted all of eight months.

The ignominious failure of Ali's diplomatic mission to Africa was not the only reason for Ali's return to the ring. Ali's brief sojourn outside of boxing had been somewhat capricious. Another acting role—starring alongside Kris Kristofferson in *Freedom Road*—was panned by critics. His business ventures—never of much interest to Ali to begin with—lurched from financial disaster to financial scandal. There was a line of Ali sports apparel which went belly-up, a doomed "Champ Burger" fast food chain, an Ali candy bar, a "Champ's Soda," and so on. At best, Ali would see a few meager dollars in return; at worst, he would end up in a messy fraud case.

Ali's generous and forgiving nature had been a target for conmen for years. Pat Patterson, who was Ali's chief security guard, recalled: "I remember there was one guy who came up to camp and he asked Ali for some money to bury his mother. Ali gave him the money and then about a year later this guy was there again asking Ali for money to bury his mother. Ali gave him the money without hesitation and I said, 'Ali, that guy was here last year asking you the same thing. He's taking you for a ride!' And Ali said, 'He might be, but I'd hate to say, "You're mother isn't dead" and be wrong.' Having lots of money and fame can be liberating, but it can also imprison you. I think Ali just liked to be free to do what he wanted."

Even more worrying were the persistent rumors that Ali himself was in severe financial difficulties. Ali's management had commanded the largest purses in boxing history; up to this point Ali had earned an estimated $50 million dollars. Just how much he had actually managed to keep had for long been the subject of intense press speculation. The rumors had first surfaced in February 1978 before the Spinks fight when Ferdie Pacheco revealed that Ali was fighting only for the money. "If Muhammad were financially able he would quit when this fight is over," he said. "Indeed, if he had been financially able, he would not have taken the fight in the first place." Ali tried to quell the rumors by saying he was in fine financial shape. "Who told you that?" he snapped after persistent questioning. "That's just another lie, another smear like the smears about my divorce and me changin' my name, all that kind of stuff people say to get me mad. Boy, if I sold all my property tomorrow I'd be worth better than 10 million dollars. Does that sound like a man who's broke?" But below the surface, the financial reality was somewhat different.

Over the years, many questions have been asked about how much Ali earned and lost. There has been much finger pointing, many explanations, many villains—Ali's management, the entourage of hangers-on, the bogus "financial advisors" and charlatan business partners who were always on hand with another real estate deal or movie investment opportunity, a host of promoters and even some of his closest "friends." Suffice it to say, much of Ali's fortune amassed during his boxing career was undoubtedly robbed and squandered, reducing his financial position to a perpetual state of chaos which was always threatening to erupt into scandal. The worst came when Ali, who had sold the rights to his name—Muhammad Ali Professional Sports—to a sometime boxing promoter, became embroiled in a $23 million bank fraud—then the biggest case of bank embezzlement in American banking history. Although the prosecutors did not believe that Ali was involved, as the courtroom drama unfolded it became

painfully apparent that Ali had, once again, been used.

But just how much all of this weighed on Ali's mind or was a factor in forcing him back into the ring is highly debatable. "To be able to give away riches is mandatory if you wish to possess them," Hana Ali quotes her father in her recent book *More Than a Hero*. It was a philosophy he followed to the letter. His own personal acts of generosity were by then legion, ranging from the $100 tips to the beggars on the street to, famously, a $100,000 donation to save a Jewish old folks' home whose plight he'd seen on the television news that night. "They say I've given all my money away," he told reporters. "Sure, I've given away lots of money. I've given it to old folks, to crippled people, to people who needed it for schools and I've given it to churches. That's what money is for, that's what it's needed for."

And as he gave himself, he forgave those around him whom he knew were stealing from him. It drove his financial advisors to distraction, but he would simply shrug and say: "Everyone deserves a second chance." Most had many chances. In reality, the money, although a factor, was definitely not the sole factor for Ali's fighting past his sell-by date. As Ferdie Pacheco told Thomas Hauser: "People say, and it's true, that Herbert [Muhammad] made a fortune off Ali. And it's also true that Ali might not be as well off financially as he could be today. But the bottom line is, if Herbert had never taken a penny, if he'd worked for 20 years for free and brought in every dollar possible for Ali, Ali would have given it all away." "I'm not excited by money," he said before his next bout. "Whether I'm rich or poor it doesn't matter. I passed that point long ago."

Perhaps the best explanation for Ali's ill-judged comeback is that he missed the limelight, missed the excitement, and missed boxing. In early 1979, he and Veronica moved into an outrageously grand mansion in the Hancock Park district of Los Angeles. Veronica furnished it like a museum. Oriental rugs covered the marble floors, and expensive paintings and antiques adorned the enormous rooms. To visitors, Ali—the man who liked to lounge around his log cabin training camp in shirt, trousers and working boots—seemed rather adrift, lost amidst all the splendor. Author George Plimpton reported that despite all the beautiful things, the house seemed "so empty and bare". Another visitor, Floyd Patterson, agreed that Ali seemed surprisingly lonely: "He goes out in the morning in his Rolls Royce with the top down, looking for people to recognize him," said Floyd. Ali was like a king estranged from his kingdom.

As the *Washington Post* wrote: "Out of the ring, Ali is an actor without a play. Ali can talk forever about Allah and peace in the world and helping starving nations, but without the Heavyweight Championship, he is an out of work actor mouthing hollow words...As long as Ali is physically able to fight, he will. It is his world that square ring. Only there is he honest and complete. He needs the satisfaction that comes from his work there. He can talk about ambassadorships and missionaries and ministries, but Ali from age 12 has been a fighter creating his own world in the ring and without that world he is a man at a loose end. All he needs, even now, even in official retirement, is the hint that he can still do it." That hint was the apparent weakness in the new crop of heavyweights who laid claim to the title.

John Tate, who had been touted as a possible Ali opponent, had lost his WBA title to the erratic but hard-hitting Mike Weaver. If Ali were to go straight for the title it would be Weaver or Larry Holmes who held the WBC version of the title. Holmes was the fighter with

ABOVE: Requiem for a heavyweight – the greatest boxing career ever shudders to an ignominious end in the Bahamas. Angelo Dundee: "The fight with Berbick, that was a disaster. I tried so hard, but he had promised some guy in Nassau that he would come there…the last guy he shakes hands with, that's his buddy. Anyway, this guy was having an ego trip, and Muhammad went there in no kind of shape. None. He looked like Chubby Checker."

OPPOSITE: Beaten, bruised and broken, the drugged Ali, surrounded by Angelo Dundee (left) and Bundini, contemplates the final curtain after the horror of Larry Holmes. Angelo Dundee: "The Holmes fight…that was something that should not have happened. The doctor gave Muhammad thyroid pills, which sapped his strength, although they made him look beautiful, physically. He looked like a picture of health. He never looked better. But the tank was empty. The thyroid pills ruined him. I thought he was taking vitamin pills. In the end, it was me who decided to stop the fight. He couldn't do nothing. He wasn't punching back. He wasn't pulling out that special Ali formula."

the most credibility and he was also the more accomplished of the two. Ali knew him well, having sparred hundreds of rounds with him at Deer Lake, which is possibly why Ali chose to fight him.

As he began training at Angelo Dundee's Miami Beach gym, Ali cut a pathetic figure: "eyes glazed, mouth slack, fat bubbling at his waist," as one reporter wrote. At around 250 pounds, he was grotesque. The press was incredulous. "No-one believes there will be a comeback," wrote Donald McLachlan in the London *Observer*. "The black Cadillacs are still drawn up outside, but where once there would have been police cars with lights flashing and patrolmen holding back the crowds, there is only the sunswept street and a group of old men talking in the shade. Muhammad Ali. Sure, they say, and jerk their heads towards the seedy stairs that lead to the big room above the drugstore. A scrawled notice flaps on the door outside: 'See Ali train—$1.'" Other voices joined the chorus urging Ali not to risk a comeback, including that of his mother, Odessa: "I don't want to see him fighting anymore. I talk to him on the phone two or three times a week and I've told him every time." Ali dismissed it all and promised to "shock the world". Even after a sparring partner drove one of his teeth through his lip, he remained outwardly unfazed. "My mother's scared, my wife's scared, my best friends want me to quit, but I ain't finished yet." However, even the notoriously lax boxing authorities were worried. The Nevada State Athletic Commission ruled that Ali must undergo a full physical before the bout could go ahead in Las Vegas.

They were right to be concerned. Ferdie Pacheco was again raising doubts about Ali's health and more than one reporter had commented on Ali's slurred speech, although they put it down to fatigue. There were those close to Ali who said that even during his prime Ali would often speak slowly and quietly in private, especially if he was tired. Ali checked into the prestigious Mayo Clinic on July 23, 1980 for a check-up. Despite ambivalent findings, the clinic's report was taken by the Nevada authorities as clearing Ali to be able to fight. The match was given the go ahead.

And then something quite remarkable happened—Ali started to look good. His weight plummeted from 251 pounds to under 220 pounds, only a few pounds heavier than when he fought Foreman. When he arrived in Las Vegas he pranced around the training ring like the Ali of old, preening for the growing crowds. "I look ten years younger," he crowed. "I'm ready. Tell them Ali is trim, lean, mean…and dancing." Reporters who had previously written him off now gave Ali a chance as he berated them for their lack of faith. "I can't lose to Holmes, I'm superior physically and mentally," he swore. The odds on Ali dropped dramatically.

Some reporters remained skeptical. "For all the dramatic improvements in his appearance (black dye has given him a head of hair to go with his youthful muscle definition)," wrote Colin Malam in the *Sunday Telegraph*, "there are unmistakable signs of physical and mental deterioration. Whether it is simply a matter of age taking its toll, as Angelo Dundee insists, or the legacy of too many hard fights, Ali's speech is definitely not as clear as it used to be and his movements are appreciably slower." Despite all the crowd-pleasing antics during training, Ali's sparring sessions did not bear up under close scrutiny. On the very eve of the fight, one of his sparring partners, Marty Monroe, caught him badly over and over again during a furious exchange of punches. "What Monroe can do, Holmes can do better," wrote Malam ominously. "At nearly

31, he is as fit as a butcher's dog, and he has been punching in training with the sort of power and precision which have kept him unbeaten in 35 fights."

It was a massacre. The 24,740 fans, who had paid a record-breaking six million dollars to sit in a converted parking lot next to Caesar's Palace, had been led by the pre-fight hype to expect the Muhammad Ali of old. Instead they saw his shell. From the outset it was apparent something was drastically wrong with Ali. After fruitlessly trying to taunt Holmes into an early indiscretion, Ali simply retreated onto the back foot, hiding behind his gloves. Holmes hit him at will, round after round. After the sixth round—by which time many thought the fight should have been stopped—even Holmes looked concerned as he continued to pound Ali with little resistance. Between rounds Holmes sat down and asked his cornerman, "What am I going to do with this guy?" His trainer said that it would be better for all if he knocked Ali out. But Ali kept coming back for more. In the ninth, Holmes caught Ali with a sickening hook to the kidneys, which had him doubled over in agony. Round ten was worse. At the end, Herbert Muhammad, who had been staring at the floor throughout the fight, signalled to Angelo Dundee to stop the fight. Bundini Brown begged him to let it go one more round. "Fuck you! No!" snapped Dundee. "I'm the chief second. The ballgame's over." It was the first time Ali had ever failed to finish a contest.

It had been a shameful event. Ali had not thrown a single effective punch the entire fight. Even Holmes was disgusted. "I feel no gratification," he confessed. The press was stunned. "It is difficult to accept that the tired old man, seated dejectedly on his stool, had once been the arrogant master craftsman who dominated professional boxing for most of the last 20 years," wrote Donald Saunders in the London *Telegraph*. "This once superb athlete looked like a frail geriatric setting out blank-eyed and tottery on a one way journey to the old folks home. Indeed, when they helped him out of the ring 15 minutes later, I fervently wished I had not been there to see the pathetic end of a glorious era." As Ali was led back to the dressing room through the largely silent crowd, he passed Joe Louis sitting in a wheelchair at ringside, "staring unseeingly ahead, unheedful of the chants of 'good old Joe', his body wrecked, his mind seemingly frozen by a series of strokes."

Four days after the fight a listless Ali was admitted to the UCLA Medical Center. After two days of tests it was discovered that he'd been taking large doses of thyroid pills in the weeks leading up to the fight. The drug, Thyrolar, had been prescribed by Herbert Muhammad's personal physician Dr. Charles Williams, for what he had diagnosed as a "hypothyroid condition." However, none of Ali's tests, including the recent Mayo Clinic medical examination, had shown any indication of thyroid problems. The medication could have proved disastrous. Thyrolar is a drug with potentially lethal side effects; while it has the propensity to induce rapid weight loss, used incorrectly it can lead to fatigue and heart damage. No boxer who has taken Thyrolar should be allowed to fight. To make matters worse, Ali had been taking double doses of the drug each day in the belief that they were like vitamins. The UCLA tests also showed traces of the powerful stimulant Benzedrine in Ali's system.

In its aftermath, the fight provoked a wave of rancor and revulsion throughout the sporting world. Many column inches were devoted to the apparent exploitation of Ali and the greed that had brought him to such an ignominious and humiliating end. Although it was generally

ABOVE: Ali announces his retirement after the Berbick fiasco.

OPPOSITE: The Greatest.

BELOW: With President Bill Clinton. In retirement, Ali moves from sporting hero to national icon.

acknowledged that it had been Ali's decision to fight—"Nobody ever told Muhammed what to do," said Angelo Dundee—the furor over how it had been allowed to take place at all gained a life of its own. The Nevada Commission and boxing's hierarchy came under fire, as did Dr. Williams, Ali's manager Herbert Muhammad, and the promoters, in particular Don King. Indeed, it was after this fight that serious questions first began to be asked about King's operation and his treatment of fighters, questions that are still being asked today. In one shameful night, boxing was revealed as the sordid, tawdry, brutal spectacle it had always been, a fact that Ali's greatness had disguised for the past 20 years. Ali had elevated boxing out of the gutters and into respectability; with him on the ropes, boxing, and most of those associated with it, reverted to type. As former Chicago newspaperman John Schulian said: "They sacrificed Ali. That's all it was: a human sacrifice for money and power. And it was more than a matter of Ali getting beaten up. That night went far beyond Ali. One of the great symbols of our time was tarnished. So many people—blacks, whites, Muslims, Americans, Africans, Asians, people all over the world—believed in Ali. And he was destroyed because of people who didn't care one bit for the things he'd stood for his entire life."

But still it didn't end. Ali managed to convince himself that the Thyrolar was to blame for his disastrous performance against Larry Holmes, not his physical and mental deterioration, a delusion reinforced, accidentally or wilfully, by those around him. "He seems perfectly normal to me now," said his wife Veronica a few weeks later. "I'm convinced that he had lost too much weight too quickly and on top of that he was taking more pills than he was supposed to." But looking better was one thing; fighting a heavyweight bout, as others in his camp were urging him to do, was something else entirely. Eventually, he agreed to fight British heavyweight John L. Gardner early in the following year (Gardner's camp seemed to regard Ali merely as a stepping stone to greater glory—a sort of Bum of the Month), but the British Boxing Board refused to issue a license. "Our position is clear regarding Ali," said its secretary. "We are strongly opposed to him continuing in boxing." Hawaii was briefly considered as a possible venue, but eventually the match just fizzled out.

Ali was quiet for several months, but just when it looked like an overdue retirement declaration would be made, Ali was once again preparing to fight. His opponent was Canadian and Commonwealth Champion Trevor Berbick, a man 11 years his junior. But the press was not concerned with the credentials of Ali's challenger; the overriding issue was Ali's health, and the fact that just one year shy of his 40th birthday Ali would again be taking heavy shots to the head. Ali claimed doctors had given him a clean bill of health, "even the best white doctors". But the fight venue—Nassau in the Bahamas—belied the bluster; no American state was willing to grant him a licence after the Holmes disaster.

The man behind this shameful promotion was a convicted felon named James Cornelius, who had connections with the Nation of Islam. Cornelius and his company, Sports International Ltd, had finally managed to secure the Nassau venue. However, there were problems to come. Don King had signed Ali to a three-fight deal and he was determined to secure a piece of the action. Cornelius, however, was not impressed by King or his reputation. When King arrived in the Bahamas he was met by two karate-trained friends of Cornelius and given a sound beating. King took the hint and left to nurse his wounds. Foolishly, Ali stayed.

If Holmes was an execution, Berbick was a farce. In training, Ali looked terrible—in the words of one reporter, like "the Michelin Man". His weight was back up to 236 pounds and this time he failed to lose it. The fans were not impressed. There was no pay per view television, and none of the American networks even bothered to bid. Ticket sales were so slow that the promoters eventually resorted to cut-price deals in the local Nassau supermarkets. On the night, tickets could be had for less than $10. In the end, the "Drama in Bahama" attracted less than 7,500 spectators to the half-finished Queen Elizabeth Sports Centre. When they arrived they couldn't get in because no-one could find the key to the main gate. When the officials did manage to get in they discovered there were no gloves in the stadium. Nor was there a bell to signal the end of each round; eventually someone rustled up a cowbell. The show eventually began over two hours late. Because of the lack of paying customers, Berbick had refused to perform until he was paid.

Events in the ring were equally dismal. Ali—"just a tired old fighter, his belly bouncing," as one writer had it—tried in the early rounds to live up to the crowd's chants of "Ali, Ali" by putting together some combinations. Berbick simply brushed them aside and forced him back on the ropes, his arms flailing. In the fifth he showed some flashes of the old Ali, catching Berbick with some solid left jabs and then scoring with a right-left-right combination. But by the sixth all the magic had vanished. Berbick, not the world's most skillful boxer, hammered on Ali at will. By the last round, Ali was completely drained. It was all he could do to hang onto Berbick.

After the final bell, Berbick anxiously paced the ring as Ali slumped in his corner. When the unanimous decision was announced in his favor, Berbick ran across to Ali, and hugged and kissed him. "I love you, I love you," he said over and over again. It was a sentiment, which in the years to come would grow and multiply to extraordinary dimensions. But on that sad, squalid, sorrowful night in Nassau, the greatest career in boxing history was finally at an end.

King Of The World

"He way up there now. Like an eagle. Where he gonna land, how he gonna land?"

Sonny Liston

ABOVE AND OPPOSITE:
Muhammad Ali was the
lifeblood of boxing for
decades. With his departure
the sport disappears from
magazine front covers and
respectability, and returns to
the shadows.

Ali was sitting in a New York hotel suite. It was getting late and he was tired. He'd spent another day with his wife, Lonnie, helping to raise funds for his legacy—the Muhammad Ali Center in Louisville, Kentucky. A schedule that would tire a far younger man was taking its toll on Ali's 59-year-old body, but his aging and ailing limbs were about to be enlivened by a familiar face.

A knock at the door was answered by Lonnie. She opened it and Don King—a rhinestone grin spread across his face—strode into the room. "Every knee must bend," said King, "every head must bow, every tongue must confess…thou art the greatest, the greatest of a-a-a-all times! Muhammad. Muhammad. That's my man. The history." "Yeah, but I a bum," Ali said. "You ain't never be a bum, man," King replied.

The two embraced affectionately. It had been a while since they had spent time with each other. He had a soft spot for Don King, but the changes in Ali's life meant that the promoter was no longer a particularly welcome guest. Lonnie, together with Ali's life-long friend Howard Bingham, had instigated the successful remolding of Ali's image. His once murky business affairs had been polished. The shady characters, the infidelities, and the bad deals that were as much a part of his fighting days as his poems and his right-hand jab, were gone. Now, Ali was recognized, alongside Nelson Mandela, as one of the true heroes of the 20th century. The 60s symbol of defiance and self-determination was now a silent statesman of tolerance and peace. There was no room for the likes of Don King and his tarnished reputation anymore.

Under the watchful gaze of Lonnie, King and Ali swapped old jokes. For King's benefit Lonnie slipped on a promotional video for the Ali Center. An earnest young Cassius Clay appeared on the screen:

"Where's freedom? Where's God? Where is the church? These are the questions that stand at the heart of man…" announced the young Cassius. Lonnie, in turn, asked Don for a donation towards the center and he agreed to give them $100,000.

As they talked and joked Ali's mobile phone rang. It was the actor Will Smith, who had just played Muhammad in the Hollywood movie about his life. Ali talked briefly with Smith and then Lonnie took the phone. "Will? You gotta do the voice for Don," she said, passing the phone to King. "Float like a butterfly, sting like a bee! Rumble, young man, rumble!" rejoined Smith. King howled with laughter. He told Will he was proud of him, playing the role of the great Ali. Said he wanted Will to go to China with him. Wanted them all to go to China, where King was promoting a heavyweight title fight. A trip to China would be good for the movie, he said. "Three hundred million as a fan audience!" Smith gave his number to Don and then rang off. Don smiled. The room was quiet.

Ali broke the silence. "I'm gonna make a comeback," he announced. "That'd be great," said King. "We gonna bring him back at 60! This is gonna be our major comeback, from the ashes to the phoenix, Muhammad rises again!"

"Sixty!" Ali exclaimed, and repeated it to himself and to the room, as though the idea seemed faintly ridiculous. The mouthy young kid from Kentucky was getting old. "Sixty!" he said again, softly.

The first years of retirement were very difficult for Ali. Boxing had been his native language; now he was going to have to become fluent in another tongue. Amidst the splendor of his Hancock Park mansion, Ali would sit and read the Qur'an and the Sufi teachings, teachings of peace and love from a sect of the Muslim

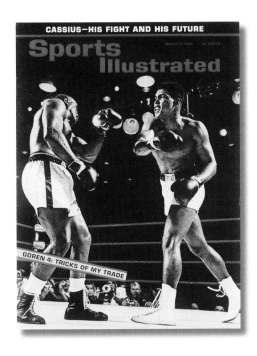

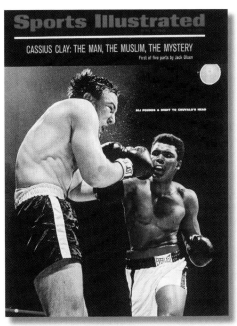

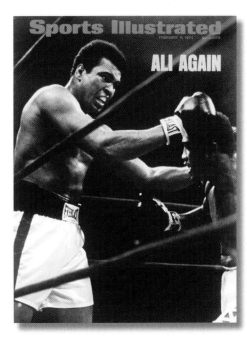

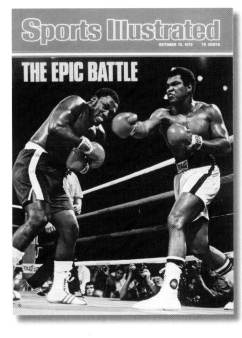

religion, looking for answers. He tried to busy himself, travelling as much as he could and spending time with his children and friends. Observers thought he looked lost and disconnected.

His relationship with his wife, Veronica, was also become increasingly frayed. Ali's unbending belief that his woman should be a loyal servant rankled with Veronica, who was young and ambitious and tired of being the doting Muslim wife. "I wore long clothes and I covered my head a lot of the time," she recalled later. "Eventually I stopped doing that, but I did adhere to a lot of his wishes. But it was pretty much an old-fashioned way of living." She had hoped to pursue her own career now that Ali was no longer fighting, but he insisted that she stay at home.

Ali and Veronica argued. They argued about the house always being full of strangers (she complained she couldn't walk downstairs in her nightgown). They argued about what school the kids should go to. "He was a hard man to live with," she said. "He could be very stubborn sometimes." The arguments were exacerbated by Ali's increasing worry and frustration over his physical condition. Ali would often feel fatigued and it was obvious that his speech was slow and slurred at times. He complained to his doctor that he was "walking like an old man".

In July 1982, Ali checked into the UCLA Medical Center. A series of tests were carried out—including a CT scan on the brain—but the doctors found nothing serious. Ali's fatigue was attributed to his hectic lifestyle. However, Ali's condition did not improve and during a trip home to Louisville he called Lonnie Williams. Lonnie was the 25-year-old daughter of Odessa Clay's best friend, Marguerite Williams, and had been close to him for many years. They met downstairs in the

hotel where Ali was staying and Lonnie was shocked by Ali's condition. The man, once so agile on his feet, stumbled out of the elevator to meet her. On several occasions during their time together he staggered and nearly fell. It was like he was drunk, only Ali didn't drink. Something was horribly wrong. Ali asked Lonnie if she would move to LA to help him. She later explained her decision to Thomas Hauser: "I was aware that I would be taking a risk—giving up a good job, not to mention what people might say about being in Los Angeles because of Muhammad. But I didn't feel I could place a lot of emphasis on that. I felt, wisely or unwisely, that Muhammad's well-being was more important than the sum total of anything negative in my going."

With Veronica's consent, Ali set Lonnie up in an apartment near to the mansion and he soldiered on. "My mind is made up to promote the Islamic religion and be an evangelist for Islam," he said. "That's all I want. Like Billy Graham is a Christian evangelist, I want to be an Islamic evangelist." Late in 1983, Bob Greene of *Esquire* magazine met with Ali at Chicago's O'Hare Airport. It was a cold day, but Ali was wandering around wearing a short-sleeved shirt and carrying a salesman's sample case stuffed full of Muslim pamphlets. Ali was waiting for his manager, Herbert Muhammad—they were to attend a Muslim rally—and as he waited people flocked to him for autographs and a few words. Ali looked bored with it all. Greene asked him why he thought he was so popular. Ali, barely audible, gave him an unusually forlorn reply that betrayed his melancholy state of mind. "I don't know. I'm not smart. I'm dumber than you are. I can't spell as good as you, but people don't care. Because that shows I'm a common person. Just like they are." Ali later told Greene, "Life is not real. I conquered the world and it didn't give me satisfaction. The boxing, the fame, the publicity, the attention—it didn't satisfy my soul. It's all nothing unless you go to heaven."

His speech and gait worsened by the end of 1983 and he complained of tremors in his left hand. Suspecting Parkinson's disease, his doctor prescribed him with Sinemet—the most potent drug used to treat Parkinson's—but it wasn't until September 1984 that an official statement was made regarding Ali's possible Parkinson's. After eight days of tests at the Columbia Presbyterian mMedical Center in New York, Dr. Stanley Fahn said Ali showed clear signs of Parkinson's and damage to the brain stem. The diagnosis was a post-traumatic Parkinson's due to injuries from fighting.

However, at that time, Ali did not want Dr. Fahn to reveal that his condition may have been caused by boxing. It wasn't until Ali gave his biographer Thomas Hauser access to his medical records that the facts were revealed. The statement given at that time said that Ali was not suffering from Parkinson's disease, but did exhibit some mild symptoms of Parkinson's syndrome.

Ali also had problems on other fronts. By 1984 his relationship with Veronica was practically over and his financial situation was a constant cause for concern. Although he owned several pieces of real estate worth several million dollars, most of his business ventures were failing or had failed. Wanda Bolton (now called Aaisha), who had an affair with Ali in the 70s and had given birth to his daughter, Khaliah, told *Sports Illustrated* writer, Mark Kram, that she called Ali in 1984 for some money to help fix a furnace in her home, but she was rebuffed. "I'm going broke," Ali told her. "I take care of my parents, my brother and his family, Veronica and her family... I can't take care of everyone. I'll try to help you." Aaisha said he never did.

ABOVE: In retirement, Ali spends much of his time responding to the daily avalanche of correspondence from around the world, as well as signing hundreds of autographs a day.

OPPOSITE: Physically still formidable, Ali works out on the big bag in the gymnasium in his home in Berrien Springs, August 2001. Ali, a notoriously lazy trainer in his later career, rejected the modern equipment installed on his doctor's orders. Instead, he replaced it with the minimum—a speed bag and a heavy bag. These are now all he uses.

On top of all that, Ali pledged his support to Ronald Reagan's 1984 re-election campaign, which appalled many of his supporters. How could Ali endorse such a hawkish candidate? Prominent civil rights campaigner Andrew Young was clearly disappointed when he said that Ali was supporting "candidates whose policies are harmful to both blacks and whites." Like Ali, Reagan's reading matter didn't extend much beyond bad film scripts and the Bible. Reagan was keen that more religious education should be taught in schools, and Ali agreed with him. Mike Marqusee, an expert on the politics of Ali, commented on Ali's lack of political scruples: "Ali was untroubled by intellectual contradiction. One minute he's meeting with Colonel Ghadafi, the next with President Ford. He really didn't feel that it was his job to connect the dots. He felt that it was his job to speak out against injustice and generally meet with and be polite to anyone who would talk to him." In 1988 he pinned his colors to George Bush's mast, but neither his links to Bush nor to Reagan could be seen as any sellout or disturbing shift in Ali's thinking. Ali gave an election about as much time and thought as he would the Superbowl. He would pick a team and tune in while doing other things. Ali had never been enthralled by politics. He probably didn't even vote.

Despite his seemingly misplaced political allegiances, Ali was still in demand and much loved throughout the world. "I don't think Ali ever spent more than seven days at a time in his house," said Omer Ahmed, a friend of Ali's who spent time with him in Asia. He travelled extensively in Europe, Asia and Africa. He opened a football stadium in Pakistan in 1986 in front of 78,000 people, and visited China. He also travelled throughout the US, performing magic tricks and handing out Muslim pamphlets in schools, old people's homes—even a women's prison. Ali would always sign the pamphlets. "They might keep them and read them if I sign them," he explained.

Ali would also occasionally be seen ringside at a big fight. Don King paid him $10,000 an appearance and more often than not he would get a bigger cheer than Mike Tyson or Sugar Ray Leonard or whoever else was topping the bill. However, the deteriorating state of his health at these appearances was causing increasing concern among the boxing press, and some less enlightened scribes wrote cruel reports about Ali's physical condition. A journalist from *The Ring* magazine described Ali as looking like "a zombie from *Night of the Living Dead*". Joseph D. O'Brien, from the same magazine, wasn't quite so crass when he wrote: "I have also sat close to him at a couple of fights when he was not a featured attraction, and the poor bugger just sat there like a sack of flour, barely aware, it seemed, of where he was or what he was doing there. The only conclusion I can draw from all this is that while the man is occupied he's okay. Given no occupation, he's what the rumor-mongers say he is."

The rumor-mongers were still unsure exactly what Ali was suffering from, as was his former physician, Ferdie Pacheco. As late as 1988 Pacheco was still unconvinced by the Parkinson's diagnosis. During an interview with *KO* magazine in 1988, Pacheco claimed it was all "bull!" "He had a very long career," said Pacheco. "His condition isn't unusual for anybody who takes years of pounding in the head, both in the gym and in the fights. Remember, he sparred with three former World Champions, three young guys, strong guys. He had Tim Witherspoon, Larry Holmes and Jimmy Ellis punching him. All the time, every day. That's not exactly a therapeutic benefit."

In September 1985 it was announced that Ali and Veronica had filed for divorce. The statement read: "The decision to dissolve the marriage was mutually agreed upon by Muhammad and Veronica. Both parties maintain the utmost admiration, love and respect for each other, and their deep friendship remains intact." The divorce became final in July 1986. A prenuptial agreement had been signed, but Ali had torn it up during their marriage. Veronica would allegedly come out of the divorce in a healthier financial state than Ali. She kept the house in LA and received $750,000. Ali tried hard to have the children, Laila and Hana, stay with him after the split, but Veronica wouldn't allow it: "He really wanted to have the kids with him, but he knew it wasn't practical because he was travelling so much, and I was very tentative about sending them across the country without someone there because he wasn't remarried then."

His poor health and the break-up of his third marriage made headlines around the world and seemed to strike a sentimental chord. When Johnny Carson mentioned the impending split on the *Tonight* show, he drew a wistful sigh from the audience that seemed to say, "Gee, not on top of everything else." *New York Post* columnist Dick Young went as far as to suggest that Ali reunite with his second wife Khalilah. "It would be nice if she and Ali somehow found each other again," he wrote. "She was the best for him and could be still."

Although Lonnie Williams had been born and raised a Catholic, since she had moved to LA to help look after Ali she had converted to Islam. On November 19, 1986, Lonnie and Ali married in a small, private service in their hometown of Louisville, Kentucky. They moved into Ali's 88-acre farm in Berrien Springs, and Lonnie—a bright woman with a master's degree in business administration—tried to re-establish her husband as a seminal figure. Money was still a worry. In 1986 Ali and his lawyers filed an unsuccessful $50 million lawsuit against the US government for denying him conscientious objector status. Also, the sale of a powdered milk called "Primo" to third world countries failed, and the Muhammad Ali shoe polish was taken off the shelves after a rival company complained that the image of Ali on the tin resembled its own logo.

Failures were not exclusive to the boardroom either. In June 1988 Ali met a Dr. Rajko Medenica who believed that Ali's physical condition was not related to punches to the head, but pesticides in his blood. Lonnie supported the idea and Ali began a series of treatments in Medenica's South Carolina clinic. For several years Ali would undergo "plasmapheresis." He would sit for up to six hours while blood was removed, filtered through a machine to eliminate toxins and then returned to his body. This treatment was supposed to have done wonders for Marshal Tito in Yugoslavia, but there was no evidence that the treatment did Ali any good. Ali despised hospitals and sitting for hours with a needle in his arm must have been torture, even for a man of Ali's placid temperament. News of his friend and muse Bundini Brown's death in 1988 must have added to the anguish. Dante once wrote, "There is no greater sorrow than to recall in our misery the time when we were happy." As Ali lay there, tubes snaking out of his body, the memory of those championship days spent with his pal Bundini must have seemed tragically distant.

Another uncomfortable reminder of the past came in 1989 when the Internal Revenue Service began investigating Ali with regards to his 1978 tax returns. The investigation concerned millions of dollars that Ali gave away to friends. Ali's attorney, Richard Hirschberg, told

RIGHT: Ali in Africa, the most familiar face in the world. Dick Schaap, broadcaster and journalist: "If the Queen of England, the President of the United States, the Pope and Muhammad Ali walked down Fifth Avenue, a lot of people would say, 'Who are those three people with Muhammad Ali?'"

OPPOSITE: Ali meets Mother Teresa in India in 1990.

USA Today: "A lot of the people whom he gave the money to claim it was gifts. And we don't necessarily see it the way they do. Some of those people expected Ali to pay the gift tax for them. We didn't see it that way." The investigations came to nothing, but they were another indication of how poorly some of Ali's affairs had been orchestrated under his manager Herbert Muhammad.

Ali had great affection for the son of Elijah Muhammad, but many observers saw the hold Herbert had over Ali as unhealthy. Ali was one of the few remaining icons of the 1960s and arguably the greatest fighter who ever lived, yet by the end of the 1980s he had been reduced to a sad and tragic figure.

Cassius Clay Senior died in February 1990, which was the worst possible start to a decade that Ali and Lonnie approached with much hope. Ali had had a rather ambiguous relationship with his father for some years. His father liked a drink and, like his son, he couldn't resist women. He'd been separated from Ali's mother, Odessa, for several years. Clay Sr.'s major bone of contention was with his son's affiliation with the Muslims. Cassius Sr. was always of the opinion that the Nation of Islam was stealing his boy's money. Over the years they argued violently about this and the matter was never fully resolved. Nevertheless, his father's death was a terrible blow to Ali.

As usual, Ali rolled with the punches and tried to carry on as best he could. He began taking speech therapy in Berrien Springs and he continued to travel around the globe. He met Nelson Mandela after his release in February 1990, and it was hard to say who was the more thrilled. Mandela, who had boxed as a young man, adored Ali. Ali shook Mandela's hand warmly and they talked briefly. They were to meet again on several occasions. During a trip to India in the

same year, Ali was also introduced to Mother Teresa by his friend Omer Ahmed. Ahmed was worried how the two would get on, coming as they did from such different worlds, but he needn't have. Ali won Mother Teresa over with his magic tricks and his easy charm. He made a green handkerchief disappear and tried to levitate, much to her amusement. She then took him to a hospital where Ali spent some time trying to cheer up sick children.

Ali's humanitarian trips became more frequent. In November 1990 Ali made a much-publicized trip to Iraq and met with Saddam Hussein. Ali was concerned about the possible war between Iraq and the West and he wanted to do what he could to prevent it. Of course, Ali had no chance of preventing the conflict and in that sense the trip was rather futile. But Ali had been sincere and during the ten days he had spent in Iraq, 15 US hostages had been released. The trip showed to the world that Ali was not as sick as many thought and that he was still as spirited as ever.

The beginning of the re-emergence of Ali as a late 20th century icon undoubtedly came with the publication of Thomas Hauser's biography—*Muhammad Ali: His Life and Times*—in 1991. Hauser interviewed nearly 200 friends, associates and opponents of Ali, and in the five-year period it took him to complete his work he became close to Ali and Lonnie. With his "access all areas" pass, Hauser was able to gain first-hand acounts which accurately described Ali's medical condition and his relationship with the Nation of Islam better than anyone before or since. Unlike the earlier "autobiography" *The Greatest*, it was compiled and edited without having to be placed before the censorious eyes of Herbert Muhammad.

The book was a triumph and Ali and Lonnie accompanied Hauser on a signing tour. Herbert Muhammad, however, was enraged by it. He saw its publication and the growing influence of Lonnie as a threat to his hold over Ali. He was right, and it wasn't before time. Herbert was chronically out of tune. A case in point was the Muhammad Ali cologne which Herbert was plugging just as the book was released. How could a sick man front an aftershave? Herbert seemed to be unaware that Ali was no longer the virile stud he was in the 1970s. The cologne went down the toilet and, after a cynical attempt to wrestle Ali away from the book-signing tour, Herbert followed.

Ferdie Pacheco remembers how Herbert, in his desperate attempt to hold on to his managerial reigns, seriously jeopardized Ali's well-being: "Ali was going to England to publicize the Hauser book and immediately before he gets there he receives a phone call from Herbert who says he needs Ali for a day or two. Some sheikh will pay $1 million if he produces Ali. He wanted him to stay for Ramadan. Of course they held Hauser as the enemy because he had taken Ali away and written this best selling book, so Ali wasn't going [on the book tour]. So Ali goes with Herbert and he's supposed to stay for a couple of days. Do you know how long he stayed? Five weeks. He didn't have enough medication and they didn't let him call his wife and kids, Hauser, or the publishers. He disappeared. And when he gets back he was in terrible shape. That is why Lonnie denied Herbert any access to Ali. That was the final straw."

Ali's willingness to jump whenever Herbert hollered has been interpreted in different ways. Some think the idea that Herbert had some kind of hold over Ali was rubbish. Ali was his own man. "Nobody told Ali what to do," Angelo Dundee always said. But others suggest Herbert was the only man Ali listened to. "There was only one man who could have told Ali not to fight and that was Herbert Muhammad," Ali's friend Gene Dibble told Tom Hauser.

Ali liked Herbert, that was a fact. They had many shared experiences and they had made a lot of money together. Maybe it was just plain respect and loyalty to the son of his former mentor and spiritual advisor, Elijah Muhammad, or maybe it was Ali's good nature, his childlike desire to please everybody, or possibly just gross stupidity…only Ali

knows why he jeopardized his health to stay with Herbert on that trip. But one thing was for sure: it would be the last time Herbert spent any time with Ali. When Ali returned home, Lonnie sought legal advice on how to sever all ties with Herbert.

The split with Herbert was a bold and necessary move to give Lonnie the freedom to put Ali's affairs in order. A new company was set up called G.O.A.T—Greatest of All Times Inc.—and all of Ali's new businesses were relocated to an office at their home in Berrien Springs. And the offers rolled in. "Muhammad could never say no," said Ed Kelly, who had been a friend of Ali's for over 25 years. "Some people think that he travels around too much and that he should spend more time at home, but he loves to be around people. He thrives off it. If it wasn't for Lonnie he would always be travelling. The biggest problem for Muhammad is Muhammad."

When he wasn't travelling, Ali's daily routine was to rise at 5am for the first of his five daily prayer sessions and then spend most of the day signing photographs and Muslim pamphlets and answering letters. In 1992, Ali and Lonnie adopted a boy called Assad and Ali made sure he spent some of the day with his son. He had always regretted not having spent as much time with his other eight children as he had wished.

If Thomas Hauser's book had reminded a new generation of just how great Ali was, then the Atlanta Olympics in 1996 confirmed it. It had been a well-kept secret. Only the privileged few were privy to the fact that Ali would light the Olympic flame. In the city where Ali had returned to defeat Jerry Quarry after his three-and-a-half-year exile from the ring, Ali was about to make a comeback of epic proportions. "He was so proud," recalls his second wife, Khalilah. "He rang me up and told me and he was so excited. He said, 'I'm gonna be in the Olympics, gonna be in the Olympics.' I said, 'What you gonna do, run?' He laughed and said, 'I'm going to light the flame.'" "Lighting the Atlanta flame? Nobody wanted him to do that," said Ferdie Pacheco. "They were saying 'what if he drops it? He can't do it.'" It was a guy at NBC who responded and said: 'I think he can do it.'"

Suddenly Ali appeared, high up on the podium, and the 83,000 spectators packed into the Olympic stadium, and an estimated worldwide audience of three billion, held its breath. Ali stood holding the lighted torch in his trembling hand, his face stiffened by the mask of his illness. He raised his arm as he had in victory many times in his career, and he lit the 170ft fuse which set the flame to the giant Olympic cauldron. "I was crying and shaking," said Ali's friend John Ramsay. "I was singing out loud, 'You deserve that!' It felt like America was finally saying, 'Hey, listen, we've got a hero here and he's alive and willing and he wants to see you.'" Ali confided what was going through his mind as he lit the flame to his close friend Howard Bingham in an interview in Reader's Digest in 2002. "It showed that people in the past didn't hold it against me because here I am rejecting the Vietnam War, joining the Islamic religion, and then, of all people, raising the flag. They were thinking of me to light the Olympic flame, so that was a good thing."

It was an iconic image to rival the black power salute of Tommi Smith and John Carlos in the 1968 Olympics. Both, in their own way, represented pride and determination. But the symbolism was complex; it represented many things to different people. For some, Ali's image told the world that here was a man who had been persecuted and had forgiven. To others it gave a cheering illusion of some kind of racial

harmony in America. To those less cynical, however, Ali represented the triumph of the human spirit. Up there on the podium, for a moment, he gave hope to many people who suffered from illness and racism and poverty. It was, for millions, an unforgettable event.

A tidal wave of adoration followed and offers poured in. The release the following year of the excellent documentary about the Zaire fight *When We Were Kings* sent Ali's career off into the stratosphere once again. The inspiring documentary, which had taken over 20 years to make, won an Oscar and Ali joined the director, Leon Gast, on stage to a standing ovation.

And the applause continued until the end of the century and beyond. The wheels of the Ali industry were in motion once again, churning out enough kitsch and memorabilia—sold in auction and on the Internet—to fill Madison Square Garden. It seemed everybody wanted a piece of the silent and dignified ex-champion. At worst he was simply a giant money-spinner. But to the overwhelming majority, he was a much-needed hero amongst the morass of mediocrity. Ali's simple humanity was a perfect antidote to the growing cynicism in Western cultures.

As the century reached its end Ali needn't have bothered changing out of his tuxedo. The awards continued to tumble in. He was voted athlete of the century by the BBC, *Sports Illustrated*, and by everyone else with an award to hand out. There were endorsement deals worth up to $10 million a year and even rumors of a Nobel Peace prize for his humanitarian efforts. And, of course, there was the Muhammad Ali Center—a conference center and museum designed to inspire the young and old alike, overlooking the banks of the Ohio River where Ali used to roam as a youngster. Ali and Lonnie needed $80 million

to build the center. They planned to open it by the end of 2003. By 2002 they had over half of the money. Board members included Billy Crystal and Robin Williams. Even the United States Secretary of State, Colin Powell, had pledged his support. It seemed that few doubted that Ali's incredible determination—the determination that had seen him unbroken through the years of exile, that had helped him weather the Foreman avalanche, that had pulled him off the stool in that near-death moment in Manila, that had bailed him out of his Parkinson's sentence—would see it to completion.

Ali stood up and Don King listened. "Just need two good heavyweights, get in shape. Two or three top big guys. Ten rounds apiece. Then I'm ready. Sixty! Nobody ever won the title at sixty! Sixty! Ain't nobody ever won the title at sixty, right?" Don King agreed that Ali would be the first. "I'm so happy I've seen you. My heart is rejoicing. You're so good," he said. Ali seemed happy. "Sixty! Sixty!" he repeated. "I want you to be smooth again. Get yourself in shape and recapture the glory of yesteryear," said King.

King got up to leave and Ali walked with him to the door. It had been a long day. Before King left, Ali leaned over and gave him a peck on the cheek and whispered something in his ear. Lonnie didn't hear. Nobody else heard. It was just between Ali and Don. "He's still as devilish as hell!" said Don. "Still as devilish as hell." Lonnie said he was ready for a sleep and Don King watched him as he headed for the bedroom whispering "Sixty. Sixty," to himself.

Muhammad Ali's Fight Record

Amateur 100-5 Won; Olympic Gold Medal at 1960 Olympics

Professional TB 61; KO 37; WD 19; LD 4; KO by 1

KEY: **TB:** Total bouts **TKO:** Technical knockout **KO:** Knockout **WD:** Won by decision **LD:** Lose by decision **KO by…**Knocked out

Amateur Record

1956
Novice Title – Louisville
10.16.56   Luther Quisenbury: WD 3

1957
Chicago Golden Gloves Quarter-finals
2.26.57   Kent Green: KO by…2

1958
Chicago Golden Gloves Finals
3.5.58   Tony Madigan: LD 3

1959
Chicago Golden Gloves Finals
3.25.59   Tony Madigan: WD 3
        (Wins Intercity Golden Gloves)
National AAU Light-Heavyweight Championship
4.26.59   Johnny Powell: WD 3
Pan Am Games Quarter-final
3.9.59   Amos Johnson: L 3

1960
Chicago Golden Gloves
2.29.60   Wins as heavyweight
Intercity Golden Gloves, Heavyweight
3.21.60   Gary Jawish, New York: KO 3 (1:46)
National AUU Light-Heavyweight Championship
4.9.60   Jeff Davis, Toledo, OH: KO 2

May 18-20 Olympic Trials – Wins as Heavyweight
5.20.60   Allen Hudson, San Franscisco: KO

Olympics
9.1.60   Yves Becaus, Belgium: TKO 2
9.1.60   Gennady Schatkov, USSR: WD
9.5.60   Tony Madigan, Australia: WD
9.5.60   Zbigniew Pietrzykowski, Poland: WD

10.29.60 **Tunney Hunsaker**
Louisville WD 6

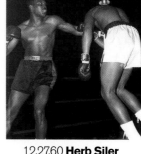

12.27.60 **Herb Siler**
Miami Beach TKO 4

1.17.61 **Tony Esperti**
Miami Beach TKO 3

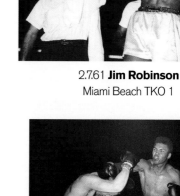

2.7.61 **Jim Robinson**
Miami Beach TKO 1

2.21.61 **Donnie Fleeman**
Miami Beach TKO 7

4.19.61 **Lamar Clark**
Louisville KO 2

6.26.61 Duke Sabedong
Las Vegas WD 10

7.22.61 Alonzo Johnson
Louisville WD 10

10.7.61 Alex Miteff
Louisville TKO 6

11.29.61 Willie Besmanoff
Louisville TKO 7

2.10.62 Sonny Banks
New York TKO 4

2.28.62 Don Warner
Miami Beach TKO 4

4.23.62 George Logan
Los Angeles TKO 4

5.19.62 Billy Daniels
New York TKO 7

7.20.62 Alejandro Lavorante
Los Angeles KO 5

11.15.62 Archie Moore
Los Angeles KO 4

1.24.63 Charlie Powell
Pittsburgh KO 3

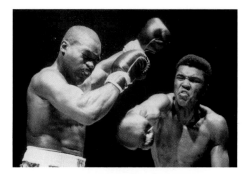

3.13.63 Doug Jones
New York WD 10

6.18.63 **Henry Cooper**
London TKO 5

2.25.64 **Sonny Liston**
Miami Beach TKO 7
Won World Heavyweight Championship

5.25.65 **Sonny Liston**
Lewiston, Maine KO 1

11.22.65 **Floyd Patterson**
Las Vegas TKO 12

3.29.66 **George Chuvalo**
Toronto WD 15

5.21.66 **Henry Cooper**
London TKO 6

8.6.66 **Brian London**
London KO 3

9.10.66 **Karl Mildenberger**
Frankfurt TKO 12

11.12.66 **Cleveland Williams**
Houston TKO 3

2.6.67 **Ernie Terrell**
Houston WD 15

3.22.67 **Zora Folley**
New York KO 7

28.4.1967 Refuses induction into the US Army and is stripped of world title by WBA and most state commissions the next day.
8.5.1967 Ali is indicted for draft classification by Federal Grand Jury.
20.6.1967 A Jury for the US District Court in Houston returns a verdict of guilty against Ali of draft evasion. He is fined $10,000 and sentenced to five years by Judge Joe Ingraham. Ali remains free pending appeals but is barred from the ring.
3.2.70 Announces retirement.

10.26.70 **Jerry Quarry**
Atlanta TKO 3

12.7.70 **Oscar Bonavena**
New York TKO 15

3.8.71 **Joe Frazier**
New York LD 15
For World Heavyweight Championship

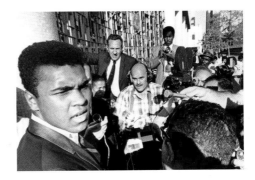

6.28.1971 US Supreme Court reverses
Ali's 1967 draft evasion conviction

7.26.71 **Jimmy Ellis**
Houston TKO 12

11.17.71 **Buster Mathis**
Houston WD 12

12.26.71 **Jurgen Blin**
Zurich KO 7
Won vacant NABF Heavyweight Championship

4.1.72 **Mac Foster**
Tokyo WD 15

5.1.72 **George Chuvalo**
Vancouver WD12

6.27.72 **Jerry Quarry**
Las Vegas TKO 7

7.19.72 **Al (Blue) Lewis**
Dublin TKO 11

9.20.72 **Floyd Patterson**
New York TKO 7

11.21.72 **Bob Foster**
Stateline TKO 8

2.14.73 **Joe Bugner**
Las Vegas WD 12

3.31.73 **Ken Norton**
San Diego LD 12
Lost NABF Heavyweight Championship

9.10.73 **Ken Norton**
Inglewood, CA WD 12
Regained NABF Heavyweight Championship

10.20.73 **Rudi Lubbers**
Jakarta, Ind. WD 12

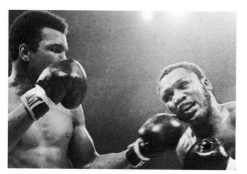

1.28.74 **Joe Frazier**
New York WD 12

10.30.74 **George Foreman**
Kinshasa Zaire KO 8
Regained World Heavyweight Championship

3.24.75 **Chuck Wepner**
Cleveland TKO 15

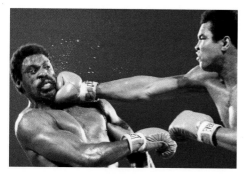

5.16.75 **Ron Lyle**
Las Vegas TKO 11

6.30.75 **Joe Bugner**
Kuala Lumper WD 15

10.1.75 **Joe Frazier**
Manila, Philippines TKO 14

2.20.76 **Jean-Pierre Coopman**
San Juan KO 5

4.30.76 **Jimmy Young**
Landover, MD WD 15

5.24.76 **Richard Dunn**
Munich TKO 5

9.28.76 **Ken Norton**
New York WD 15

5.16.77 **Alfredo Evangelista**
Landover WD 15

9.29.77 **Earnie Shavers**
New York WD 15

2.14.78 **Leon Spinks**
Las Vegas LD 15

9.15.78 **Leon Spinks**
New Orleans WD 15
Regained World Heavyweight Championship

6.27.79 Announces retirement

10.2.80 **Larry Holmes**
Las Vegas TKO 11

12.11.81 **Trevor Berbick**
Nassau LD 10

12.12.81 Retires from professional boxing

Bibliography

The following publications were used in the preparation of this book:

Muhammad Ali, His Life And Times, Thomas Hauser (Pan)

Muhammad Ali, Through The Eyes Of The World, Mark Collings (Sanctuary Publishing)

More Than A Hero, Hana Ali (Pocket Books)

Ali, Rex Lardner (Tempo Books)

Ali, Fighter, Poet, Prophet, Bockris-Wylie (Freeway Press)

The Autobiography of Malcolm X, with the assistance of Alex Haley (Penguin Books)

The Assassination of Malcolm X, George Breitman, Herman Porter (Pathfinder Press)

The Cassius Clay Story, George Sullivan (Fleet Publishing)

Come Out Smokin', Phil Pepe (Coward, McCann & Geoghegan)

Conflict In The Congo, Thomas Kanza (Penguin Books)

The Death And Life Of Malcolm X, Peter Goldman (Harper & Row)

Great Moments In Sport: Heavyweight Boxing, Gilbert Odd (Pelham Books)

Henry Cooper, An Autobiography, Henry Cooper (Coronet Books/Hodder Paperbacks)

In This Corner! Peter Heller (Dell)

Loser And Still Champion, Budd Schulberg (New English Library)

Sting Like A Bee, José Torres (Coronet Books/Hodder Paperbacks)

Soul On Ice, Eldridge Cleaver (Panther)

Ghosts Of Manila, Mark Kram (Harper Collins)

King Of The World, David Remnick (Picador)

Africa Magazine

Boxing Illustrated

Boxing International

Boxing Pictorial

Crawdaddy

Daily Mirror

Daily Telegraph Magazine

Ebony Magazine

Esquire Magazine

Louisville Courier-Journal

Louisville Courier-Journal & Times Magazine

Louisville Times

Newsweek

News Of The World

New Times

Observer

Penthouse Magazine

Playboy Magazine

The Ring Magazine

Readers Digest

Rolling Stone

Saturday Evening Post

Sepia

Sports Illustrated

Sportsworld Magazine

Sunday Citizen Magazine

Sunday Times Magazine

Time Magazine

Time Out Magazine

World Boxing Magazine

Photograph Credits

The publishers would like to thank the following for their kind permission to reproduce their photographs:

© Neil Leifer: Pages 16, 97, 101, 127, 137, 147, 151, 153, 155, 163, 169, 174, 175, 177, 193, 194, 195, 203, 209, 225, 243, 247, 251, 271, 282, 283

© Peter Angelo-Simon 1974/2002: Pages 20, 24-25, 157, 165, 178-179. 186-187, 189

© 2001 Sonia Katchian: Pages 12, 121, 211, 213, 214-215, 216, 222, 223, 259, 261, 265, Cover

© John Cairns: Pages 272, 273

© Omer Ahmed: Page 275

© Andy Hall/Katz Pictures Limited: Page 269

© Mark Bowes: Page 277

© Anton Perich: Page 160

Courtesy The Hank Kaplan Boxing Archive: Pages 14, 60, 128 (bottom), 138 (top), 204, 250 (top), 252 (top), 254 (top), 258 (top), 280, Endpapers

© Raymond Moore: Page 7

Esquire: Page 161

© Allsports: Back cover

© Associated Press: Pages 58, 65, 158, 172, 180, 199, 240-241, 244, 248-249. 254 (bottom), 255, 262, 264 (top), 281, 283, 284, 285

© Christie's Images: Pages 178 (top left), 190 (top), 192, 218, 238 (top), 242, Endpapers

© Bettmann/CORBIS: Pages 36, 40, 45, 63, 64, 66, 68, 69, 70, 70, 71, 72-73. 74, 76, 77, 84 (bottom), 85, 89, 90, 92, 93, 98, 100, 103, 104-105, 106, 108, 109, 112, 113, 115, 116, 118, 122, 128, 129, 133, 138, 139, 140-141, 143, 145, 146, 148(left top & bottom), 152, 156, 159, 162, 166, 168(top), 170, 171, 173, 183, 184-185, 190, 191, 196, 197, 198, 200-201, 205, 206-207, 212, 221, 231(right top & bottom), 233, 235, 238, 239, 245, 252, 253, 256, 260, 268, 281, 282, 283, 284, 285

© Michael Brennan/CORBIS: Pages 21, 257, 258

© Lynn Goldsmith/CORBIS: Page 234

© Hulton-Deutsch Collection/CORBIS: Page 83

© Empics/Sport and General: Pages 80, 142, 144 (top), 148 (top right), 250, 270, 282, 284

© The Courier-Journal: Pages 29, 30, 32, 33, 34, 35, 39, 41, 43, 44, 48, 49, 50-51, 53, 56-57, 59, 62, 99, 280, 281,

Getty Images: Pages 42, 107, 111, 149, 182, 282

Brian Hamill/Getty Images: Pages 218-219, 286-287

Harry Benson/Getty Images; Page 78

© *Muhammad Speaks*: Page 114

Photo 2000: Pages 2, 18, 164, 210, 217, 220, 226, 228, 229, 231 (left top & bottom), 232

© Popperfoto: Page 79

© PA Photos: Pages 264 (bottom). 276

Rex: Page 31

The Ring Courtesy London Publishing Company: Page 220

Sports Illustrated © Neil Leifer, James Drake, Tony Triolo, Hannah Scharfman, H. Lane Stewart: Pages 266, 267

© Sporting Images: Page 37

© Sportsfile: Page 283

© The Andy Warhol Foundation for the Visual Arts, Inc./ARS.NY and DACS, London 2002: Page 22

Topham Picturepoint: Pages 67, 82, 96, 102, 120, 124, 132, 134-135, 150, 167, 246, 282, 284,

Timepix/Rex: Pages 19, 52, 54, 55, 70 (bottom left & right), 81, 84 (top), 88, 91, 117, 130, 136, 144 (bottom), 148 (bottom right), 181, 237, 263, 274, 282

Courtesy Victor Bockris: Pages 17, 23

Picture Acknowledgement
Every reasonable effort has been made to acknowledge correctly and contact the source and/copyright holder of each picture, but should there be any unintentional errors or omissions, the publisher will be pleased to insert the appropriate acknowledgement in any subsequent printing of this publication.

Besides the many people previously mentioned in the text who kindly granted their time for interviews, we would like to thank the following persons for their assistance:

Susan Ready, Marie-France Demolis, David Jenkins, Harry Carpenter, Dick Pountain, Marion Hills, Bill Cardoza, Jann Van Den Berg, Lucy Lasky, the staff at the *Louisville Courier-Journal*, Thomas Hauser, Julie Carter, Jim Anderson, David Charlsen, Rev. Durden, Andrew Fisher, Peter Gibbs, Burt Sugar, Jeff Brovey, Mark Collings, Hank Kaplan, Omer Ahmed, John Cairn, Angelo Dundee, Dan Cuoco and Jeanie Kahnke at the Muhammad Ali Centre, Louisville.